OUR KINDRED CREATURES

OUR KINDRED CREATURES

How Americans Came to Feel the Way They Do About Animals

Bill Wasik
and
Monica Murphy

Alfred A. Knopf   New York 2024

Library of Congress Cataloging-in-Publication Data

Names: Wasik, Bill, author. | Murphy, Monica, 1974– author.
Title: Our kindred creatures : how Americans came to feel the way
they do about animals / Bill Wasik and Monica Murphy.
Description: First edition. | New York : Alfred A. Knopf, 2024. |
Includes bibliographical references and index. |
Identifiers: LCCN 2023003995 (print) | LCCN 2023003996 (ebook) |
ISBN 9780525659068 (hardcover) | ISBN 9780525659075 (ebook)
Subjects: LCSH: Animal rights—United States—History—19th century. |
Animal welfare—United States—History—19th century. |
Animals—United States—Moral and ethical aspects.
Classification: LCC HV4764 .W37 2024 (print) |
LCC HV4764 (ebook) | DDC 179/.3—dc23/eng/20231018
LC record available at https://lccn.loc.gov/2023003995
LC ebook record available at https://lccn.loc.gov/2023003996

For America's veterinarians—past, present, and future

CONTENTS

OUR KINDRED CREATURES

The passenger pigeon, which once traveled in huge
flocks across much of the continent.

A NEW TYPE OF
GOODNESS

They often were heard before they were seen—and theirs was the sound of American abundance.

Alexander Wilson, an early ornithologist, heard them while on a trip down the Ohio River: a "loud rushing roar," which at first he took to be a "tornado, about to overwhelm" the spot where he stood. In his novel *The Chainbearer*, James Fenimore Cooper compared it to "the trampling of thousands of horses on a beaten road." John James Audubon likened their distinctive din to "a hard gale at sea, passing through the rigging of a close-reefed vessel." After a guided trip to a Wisconsin roost in 1871, one rattled hunter wrote of his experience:

> The sound was condensed terror. Imagine a thousand threshing machines running under full headway, accompanied by as many steamboats groaning off steam, along with an equal quota of R.R. trains passing through covered bridges—imagine these massed into a single flock, and you possibly have a faint conception of the terrific roar.

The source of these staggering sounds was the passenger pigeon, which traveled in flocks so numerous and dense that they blotted out the sun for hours at a time as they passed overhead. When the birds converged upon a stretch of forest to roost or nest, several inches of excrement quickly accumulated beneath the straining, burdened trees. Under the weight of so many bunched-up, blue-copper bodies, mature limbs snapped off and crashed to the ground, whereupon distressed survivors shrieked and flapped back into the canopy to settle anew onto even more crowded branches, repeating the cycle. Audubon described a typical wooded roosting site as "a scene of uproar and confusion."

Their tendency to assemble into multitudes of millions (or possibly, according to some awestruck witnesses, billions) made the passenger pigeon an amazement to North America's European settlers and their descendants. Density made the pigeons easy to hunt, and their profusion made hunters even more rapacious in the harvest. Whenever the pigeons alighted en masse, excited locals arrived with rifles, to fire into the flock; with long poles, to poke the pigeons from their perches; with axes, for chopping down trees full of nests. Mark Twain, in a memoir, recalled clubs being the weapons of choice when he was a boy. For weeks, the local people feasted on nothing but pigeons: stewed with salt pork, roasted with gravy, stuffed with parsley and braised in wine, baked inside of a sweet potato, piled into a pie. What they didn't or couldn't eat right away, they preserved or fed to their hogs.

Trappers devised a spring-pole apparatus for capturing live birds. Packs of pigeons were lured by one or more tethered decoy "stool pigeons" to a rectangle of ground spread generously with grain or salt. When the trap-bed was flush with fowl, the trapper triggered the device, flinging a net over the scrum; a single throw of the net could trap several hundred birds at once.

Once captured, the birds would usually be killed on the scene, their necks snapped with a pair of pincers, and then salted and barreled for shipment around the country by rail. But quite a few of them would be shipped alive to sportsmen's clubs, to be used in "trap shoots"—events often drawing large crowds of spectators, in which hunters would compete to see how many birds they could kill. Often these shootoffs would end with mortally wounded birds littering the field, after other injured victims had flown or staggered off to an even more drawn-out misery.

By 1879, a group of Americans had come to believe that the suffering of the humble, seemingly inexhaustible passenger pigeon was due for reconsideration. Among them was George Thorndike Angell, president of one of the nation's most prominent animal-advocacy groups, the Massachusetts Society for the Prevention of Cruelty to Animals. He himself had spent little time on the pigeon-shooting issue during his early years as an activist, but the brutality of the tournaments had clearly begun to weigh on him. In his group's publication, he challenged readers on their hypocrisy:

> A man will sit up all night and watch a favorite horse suffering from a bruise or sprain; a woman will cry herself to sleep over injuries, by a prowling cat, to a pet canary; and yet they are never haunted by wounded pigeons with broken legs or maimed wings, left to die of starvation, helpless and fluttering.

He had no doubt, he wrote, that "gentlemen who shoot pigeons, and ladies who delight in looking on, believe it to be a harmless amusement which hurts nobody." But he cautioned that God saw it differently, noting that the wounded pigeons from these shooting tournaments were "left uncounted and forgotten save by Him who notes the fall of every sparrow."

That spring, Angell put forward a bill modeled on one that had passed in Michigan, with language that barred the keeping or using of any birds "for the purpose of a target, or to be shot at, either for amusement or as a test of skill in marksmanship." He attended a meeting of four hundred Boston-area clergy and convinced them to sign a petition against the practice, submitting their holy endorsements as a counterweight to all the outraged shooters who had begun lobbying legislators against the bill. In the end, the measure passed the Massachusetts state senate by a margin of two to one, and was signed into law in early April 1879. Soon thereafter, Angell secured what he believed to be the world's first conviction for a pigeon shoot: Six "young gentlemen" had to pay around $60 in fines.

It was a victory that Angell would celebrate for the rest of his life, but today one cannot see it as anything other than bittersweet. The disappearance of trap shoots from American cities came far too late for the passenger pigeon. By the 1890s, it no longer alighted to roost by the thousands, let alone the millions; and soon after the turn of the twentieth century, when a young man in Indiana shot the last known wild specimen, the passenger pigeon—that beautiful symbol of boundless American excess—was officially harvested to extinction.

.   .   .

On an evening in that same spring of 1879, nearly 1,500 people gathered in Tremont Temple, an auditorium in the heart of Boston, to celebrate the eleventh anniversary of the Massachusetts SPCA's founding. At half past seven, after some religious preambles—a unison reading from Scripture ("ask now the beasts and they will teach thee, and the fowls of the air, and they shall tell thee"), an opening prayer, and a hymn—George Angell stepped to the podium.

His theme was the movement against cruelty to animals and its accomplishments, which to him seemed nothing less than miraculous. In 1866, when his fellow pioneer for the cause, Henry Bergh, had founded the nation's first animal-protection society in New York, many states had no laws against the maltreatment of animals, and those on the books were woefully unenforced. The notion of animals and their welfare as a cause was absent, undiscussed, unconsidered in America. As Angell pointed out from the podium, when his Massachusetts group celebrated its first anniversary, in 1869, it still was one of just three in the country—the third, in Philadelphia, having been started up through the resolute energies of Caroline Earle White, the other major figure in America's founding generation of animal activists.

A mere decade later, Angell noted, there were now ninety-three animal-protection groups in the country, located in a majority of states in the union. Many of these societies, following the lead set by Bergh's group in New York—which Bergh had presumptuously named the American Society for the Prevention of Cruelty to Animals (ASPCA), despite its having jurisdiction only within the state—had pressured legislatures to pass anti-cruelty laws that the organizations had written, which gave them enforcement powers to arrest alleged wrongdoers and haul them before courts. The Massachusetts SPCA now had three full-time agents patrolling the streets of Boston, and a network of 465 other law-enforcement allies around the state, which had resulted, Angell crowed, in more than 21,000 investigations and 2,000 prosecutions over the group's short history; in the state of New York, which had nearly three times the population (and a leader, in Bergh, with an even greater zeal for punishment), total prosecutions since the ASPCA's founding had topped 7,500.

Alongside the laws had come new norms: There was now a sense that interactions between humans and their animals should be, and indeed must be, subject to moral scrutiny. Yes, an impatient driver flogging his horse could now face a fine or jail time, but perhaps more important was the fact that he also faced public opprobrium, the chance of being called out in the street by an outraged passerby. Dogfighting contests, where men of all classes could once be found placing bets, had become socially unacceptable, and then were essentially squelched by law enforcement in cities with SPCAs. Even food animals destined for slaughter were now seen in a new light: Influenced by a report from Angell in 1872, the U.S. Congress had passed a law requiring cattle cars on railroads to be regularly unloaded so the livestock could eat, drink, and rest.

The activists had proved themselves willing to discomfit some powerful people. All around the country, SPCAs sparred with the wealthy owners of horse-drawn streetcar lines—including, in New York, the Vanderbilts, the nation's richest family—whenever the teams struggled to pull overflowing cars, as often happened at rush hour or in inclement weather. In Philadelphia, Caroline White had become focused on the issue of "vivisection," then the term for scientific research on live animals, and was taking on the nascent medical establishment as a consequence. In late March 1879, two weeks after Angell's address at Tremont Temple, Henry Bergh could be found touring the slaughterhouses of midtown Manhattan, decrying one as a "hell of horrors" for the manner in which it hoisted cattle up with chains around the back legs, cutting them to the bone.

Rapid shifts in moral consciousness are often referred to as "awakenings," and it was hard not to feel as though America was collectively waking up to animal suffering. That same spring, in April 1879, *Scribner's* magazine published a lavish hagiography of Bergh, declaring in its opening words, "It may almost be said

of Henry Bergh that he has invented a new type of goodness."
That verb "invented" was a canard, as the author well knew; as
was noted elsewhere in the piece, Bergh had patterned the ASPCA
directly on the Royal SPCA in London, which had been in existence
for fully four decades prior. The phrase "a new type of goodness"
was an exaggeration for the same reason—to say nothing of the
fact that a reverence for animals and revulsion toward their suffering had flourished among a significant number of people, albeit
furtively and unevenly, for all of human history.

And yet "a new type of goodness" seemed perfectly to describe
the *feeling* that surrounded the animal-welfare cause in the spring
of 1879: for its fervent supporters, for its annoyed resisters, for all
those unsure or stuck in the middle. It was as if, in the span of little
more than a decade, animals had gone from being seen as objects,
mere things that humans were justified in treating however they
might like, to becoming creatures whose joys and sufferings had to
be taken into consideration. Eighteen seventy-nine would hardly
rank as the best year to be an animal in America, but it was, perhaps, the moment when it was most possible to believe—at least
for those in earshot of Angell's stirring address, or for the countless thousands around the country who thrilled to the rise of the
cause—that a national awakening to the suffering of animals had
fully and finally arrived.

.   .   .

Listening to his oration that night, audience members might have
guessed, if they didn't know already, that Angell was the son of a
Baptist preacher—a lineage that perhaps helped explain how he
had become the animal-welfare movement's premier evangelist in
America.

As it happened, his father, also named George Angell, had
been a dissolute and sinful young man until the age of twenty-one,
when a cruel sort of miracle befell him: a catastrophic illness of
unknown nature, rendering him so lifeless that a physician went
so far as to pronounce him dead. It was only after his parents had
begun to make arrangements for his burial that the young man
unaccountably, providentially, revived. Under the influence of his

first wife, the granddaughter of a Baptist preacher, he became a minister and established a church in Southbridge, Massachusetts, a town that had barely been incorporated. After his wife and two small children died, he remarried, to a young woman named Rebekah Thorndike; in 1823 she gave birth to a son, who would barely know the man whose name he inherited—three years later, the Reverend George Angell was dead, this time for real.

Throughout his life, George Thorndike Angell would be haunted by his father's two deaths. The false first demise terrified him that he might someday experience the same mysterious condition himself; upon reaching adulthood, and for decades thereafter, he carried a piece of paper on his person stating that under no circumstances should he be buried until his body had begun to visibly decay. And in 1864, at forty-one, the same age at which his father had perished for good, he drew up a will—one that contained an unusual provision. "It has long been my opinion," he wrote,

> that there is much wrong in the treatment of domestic animals; that they are too often overworked, overpunished, and, particularly in winter and in times of scarcity, underfed. All these I think great wrongs, particularly the last; and it is my earnest wish to do something towards awakening public sentiment on this subject; the more so, because these animals have no power of complaint, or adequate human protection, against those who are disposed to do them injury. I do therefore direct that all the remainder of my property not herein before disposed of shall, within two years after the decease of my mother and myself, or the survivor, be expended by my trustees in circulating in common schools, Sabbath schools, or other schools, or otherwise, in such manner as my trustees shall deem best, such books, tracts, or pamphlets as in their judgment will tend most to impress upon the minds of youth their duty towards those domestic animals which God may make dependent upon them.

That was in the midst of the Civil War, and Angell, like most establishment Bostonians, was a bitter opponent of slavery; by then he had become a successful lawyer, and for many years he had

practiced in partnership with Samuel E. Sewall, a prominent abolitionist who defended many of the formerly enslaved arriving in
Boston via the Underground Railroad. So it was noteworthy that
Angell, at that particular moment, found his conscience tugged by
this other kind of suffering—one that, once he began to look, was
evident all around him, right in his own community. Passing by a
cattle market, he saw young calves tied in a jumble, piled up like so
much firewood, and he couldn't shake the image. In streets filled
with working horses, he began to ponder the fates of those that
had grown too old to work any longer: sold at a pittance for rendering, or even left out in the bitter cold to die. But at that time,
though the earliest SPCAs had started up in Great Britain and
Europe, there was not yet a movement for animals in America.

It was no accident that the birth of that movement was delayed
until the war's end, when the campaign against slavery had finally
prevailed. Many of its activists, buoyed by the victory, had thrown
their energies into other causes that they came to see as analo-
gously just, including women's rights and workers' rights as well
as the animal-welfare crusade. In 1879, standing at that podium
in Tremont Temple, George Angell would have been speaking for

many of his audience members when
he described this whole complex of
issues as inextricably linked, the march
forward in all of them taking place in
lockstep and ordained by God. "If any
man believes the millennium a myth,"
he intoned, "and the time of peace on
earth and good will to men—foretold
by prophets and heard by shepherds, as
we are told, on the plains of Judea—will
never come, let him look at the events
of the past fifty years. The suppression
of the slave trade. The abolition of slavery. The growth of free government. The

George Angell, 1874.

elevation of labor. The coming-up of
woman toward equal rights with man. And now, the higher protection given to dumb beasts than was granted to colored men less
than twenty years ago."

To this he added, rapturously: "What may we not expect in the next twenty years?"

.   .   .

His notion—that progress on all these issues would only continue, to the century's turn and beyond—was, as we know today, far too optimistic. Even as he spoke, Congress had already abandoned Reconstruction in the South, clearing the way for a Jim Crow regime that would deny the most fundamental rights to the formerly enslaved and their descendants. Soon enough, the totalitarianisms of the mid-twentieth century would put the lie to Angell's belief in the ineluctable "growth of free government," just as American capitalism would eventually do the same, for decades if not permanently, to the "elevation of labor." None of what George Angell saw as divinely ordained inevitabilities were actually inevitable; they all had to be fought for, then, now, and forever.

As for his own cause, the animal cause, the century's end would bring to a close a defining period—a transformative thirty-year era beginning in 1866, with the founding of the first animal-welfare society—and this is the story that we have endeavored to tell in these pages. It is a story of activism and activists, of the men and women like Angell, Bergh, and White who propelled the anti-cruelty cause forward. But it's also a story of the rapidly changing America they lived in, three decades of cultural and economic transformation that created, among so many other things, the attitudes that contemporary Americans hold about the non-human creatures around us: the love for our pets, the reverence for (certain) wildlife species, the distant ignorance of the food animals that now live and die at great remove from us. If you want to understand *why* we believe what we believe about animals, why we feel the complicated feelings we have for them, you need to understand the thirty years in which those sentiments first coalesced.

As such, this story is also about many other figures from that era, Americans who spent those same three decades revaluing the nation's animals in other ways, sometimes in concert with the activists but often in tension with them. This period would see the early rise of veterinary medicine in America, thanks in no small part to the efforts of an idealistic, entrepreneurial Frenchman named Alexandre Liautard. They also would see the early growth of America's conservation movement, as it began to dawn on nature lovers like George Bird Grinnell and Harriet Hemenway that some of the nation's wild animal species were, like the passenger pigeon, on the verge of total disappearance. During roughly the same time period, the rise of scientific medicine would raise the question of research on animals, aka vivisection, a practice that anti-cruelty activists would decry but that eminent doctors like John Call Dalton and William W. Keen argued was necessary to alleviate human suffering. And meanwhile, P. T. Barnum—in the process of creating the industry of mass entertainment—was figuring out how to captivate audiences with the *individuality* of animals, telling (i.e., inventing) the stories of his exotic acquisitions and asking paying customers to meet them with reverence and awe.

All of these changes were happening against a backdrop of astonishing growth—in America's population, in its industrializing economy. Historians sometimes lean on the phrase "Gilded Age" as a catchall for this period, which might make readers think first and foremost about its wealthiest profiteers, but countless millions of Americans saw their jobs and lives transformed during this era by the rise of large corporations. Arising along with corporate capitalism was, perhaps, the most dispiriting mode of thinking about animals, one that reconceived them as yet another industrial input, a disposable source of meat, milk, eggs, hides, and more, to be raised and killed at unimaginable scale with no compunction. In Chicago, Philip D. Armour and other meat barons spent these three decades inventing, and then refining, the systems to do just that. That is: The "new type of goodness" would arise simultaneously with some new forms of institutionalized cruelty.

There is another, equally important reason to care about this story today. Animals aside, our own period in American history is proving itself to be a time of whiplashing moral shifts, when what once seemed like impossibilities—widespread acceptance of gay rights, for example, and of nonconforming gender identities—have become reality, even as what seemed like settled norms around issues of reproductive freedom, or even beliefs in racial equality, have become threatened, upended, clawed back. In trying to understand how such moral change happens, Americans today can look at the late-nineteenth-century revolution in attitudes toward animals as an illuminating case study: of what a vertiginous shift in norms can look like from the inside, and also of how tenuous and incomplete any such shift can be.

Unlike human victims of injustice, animals suffer but cannot speak of it, and neither can their families speak up on their behalf. For that reason, any movement on behalf of animals must hinge on a collective leap of imagination, on the power of narrative. Far from being a rational product of Enlightenment thought, the movement was really the child of Romanticism, that underappreciated revolution in human consciousness that placed the subjective experiences of the individual—its raptures but also its sufferings—at the center of the moral and aesthetic universe. Having made such a leap on behalf of humans, it became natural to make it on behalf of other consciousnesses as well; this helps explain how the ultimate Romantic, Lord Byron, came to write such an indelible epitaph for his Labrador, Boatswain, and for the whole canine species "whose honest heart is still his Master's own / who labours, fights, lives, breathes for him alone." As the animal-welfare movement grew, this radical empathy, couched in anthropomorphic prose and woven into narratives, would be one of the engines that propelled it.

For the first decade of the movement, building the institutions to police and punish cruelty would be its overriding goal. But over the two decades that followed, George Angell would lead what essentially became a movement of his own, an evangelical crusade focused precisely on the act of imagining animals into the circle of care. He dreamed of an army of kindness, and he set about making it real, enlisting the nation's children as his foot soldiers. He dreamed of creating a new literature of animal appreciation, and he succeeded beyond all expectation, launching one of the nineteenth century's best-selling novels and helping thereby to create a whole new genre of animal storytelling. And he believed, more fervently than any of his fellow activists, in the interconnection of human obligations, that resistance to war, racism, plutocracy, and animal cruelty were duties that walked hand in hand.

In a sense, all the transformations of America's animals during these three tumultuous decades were acts of reimagination, channeling new urges to tell new kinds of stories about them—as surrogate children, as bosom friends, as exotic visitors, as natural resources, as valuable tools of industry, as raw material for medicine or food. It was hardly a coincidence that this also was a time when animals were all around, living cheek by jowl with human populations in a rapidly urbanizing nation, as well as one in which the nation's wild animal populations were beginning to plummet. Today, of course, that feels like a lost world, and a different kind of imagination is required to bring it into view. Read on, and you will get to meet our present-day approximation of a nineteenth-century American bestiary: the domestic animals in the nation's teeming cities, the livestock bred for fast growth and slaughter, the once-ubiquitous wildlife species now dwindling, the exotic creatures exhibited for rapt crowds.

As humans, we can never entirely know what it was like to be any of these animals, but the story of the crusade to ease their suffering in the Gilded Age—an inspiring, incomplete, important moment in the history of American social change—is ultimately a story about the attempt to bridge that unbridgeable divide. By imagining what we can never experience, we allow ourselves to reckon with the moral obligations we have to all the creatures around us.

Part One

BEACHHEADS

(1866–1876)

Prized as a menu item in American cities, sea
turtles became lucrative targets for hunters.

Chapter 1

KINDLING KINDNESS

Imagine their agony, if you can: a hundred or so green sea turtles, lying on their backs in the hold of a schooner, sailing slowly north from Florida in May 1866. From their nesting place on the Indian River, the saltwater lagoon that stretches along the state's Atlantic coast, these turtles had spent decades ranging across huge swaths of ocean, gorging on seagrass and algae and growing to hundreds of pounds in size. To turtle hunters in southern Florida, just one of these gentle giants meant serious money. Standard practice was to steal upon a female laying her eggs on the shore and wrest her onto her back, a job for one man if the specimen was smaller, two men if full-sized. Captives were often stored and fed in a shallow pool while waiting to be sold off for export.

These unlucky hundred turtles, once sold, had been carted onto the schooner, the *Active,* for a three-week journey up the coast, with Captain Nehemiah H. Calhoun at the helm. Incapable of righting themselves, the sea turtles pitched helplessly atop their inverted dorsal shells. To further immobilize them, holes had been pierced through their fins and carapaces with cords run through them, binding the supine beasts together.

Green sea turtles assume a tranquil, passive demeanor when upside down, making them easy cargo to ship. But their acquiescence belies the miseries manifesting within their shells. Evolution has equipped the marine turtle for a life afloat. Since making the risky nighttime dash seaward as a hatchling decades earlier, the *Chelonia mydas* female has been constantly in the ocean—

excepting only the hours, every couple of years, during which she hauls her heavy body up onto the beach to make a nest above the tideline. She is built for swimming: limbs modified into muscular flippers to propel her across oceans, a flattened top to minimize drag as she navigates the currents, and a large lung capacity, filling the space beneath her shell, to enable long dives.

On their backs, in the darkness below the ship's deck, the weight of the turtles' organs would have put pressure on their lungs, so their breathing became deliberate and deep, as though they were diving beneath many fathoms of seawater. Although turtles are able to go many months without food, they require water to maintain normal organ function. The *Active*'s crew might have thrown buckets of water on the turtles occasionally during the voyage, but that is no real substitute for immersion in the salty sea. These turtles—their bodies desiccating, their wounds festering, their air fetid—were being kept in conditions that, over the weeks of their journey, were steadily killing them.

So it was a race against time for the *Active* to sell off its cargo, because the purchasers of green sea turtles in the mid-nineteenth century were eager to do the killing themselves. This was the heyday of turtle soup, a dish so prized that restaurants would sometimes take out newspaper ads, or maintain special outdoor signage, declaring the hour at which the day's batch would be ready for sale. Dispatch of the live animal was generally performed in the style recorded by *Cassell's Dictionary of Cookery:* "Cut off the head, hang it up by the hind fins, and let it drain all night."

The *Active*'s destination was the Fulton Market in Manhattan, where it arrived late in the month, docking at nearby Pier 22 on the East River. Like its sister establishment, Washington Market, on the Hudson side of the island, Fulton offered the mid-nineteenth-century New Yorker fruits, vegetables, clothing, newspapers, coffee, tea, and much more, serving hordes of customers out of a motley agglomeration of permanent structures, makeshift stalls, and ships lying in berth at the piers. But the main attraction at Fulton Market, overwhelming all the senses but especially the olfactory one, was the fish. Two hundred fishing boats sold some fifty tons of catch through the market daily. While the *Active* lay in dock, as Captain Calhoun attempted to sell off his cargo, all around it along the riverside would have been boats and stalls peddling oysters—Fulton Market moved a significant percentage of the roughly 25,000 slurped up by city residents each day—cod, halibut, herring, mackerel, flounder, eel, bass, and just about anything else edible that a boat could drag out of the water within a five-hundred-mile radius.

On the afternoon of Wednesday, May 30, when a tall man with a military mien and a prodigious mustache led a party on board the *Active,* the skipper no doubt assumed that this was merely another prospective customer, dreaming of turtle soup. But in fact this man had come on a mission that most of his fellow citizens of 1866 could scarcely understand. A wealthy child of old New York, Henry Bergh had returned to his home city less than a year before, at the age of fifty-two, with a startling new set of moral precepts and an evangelical fervor for their spread. He had chartered an organization, the American Society for the Prevention of Cruelty to Animals (ASPCA), which the legislature of New York State had authorized to enforce a new anti-cruelty law that he himself had written. In the weeks since then, Bergh had personally carried out the arrests, sometimes singlehandedly, of various workingmen for their cruel treatment of animals: drivers beating their horses, butchers callously transporting livestock.

Now, as he and his men stepped aboard the *Active* to drag off Captain Calhoun and his crew, he was demanding moral and legal consideration for a creature that most Americans of the era, if they thought of the matter at all, imagined to be barely more deserving of kindness than a cockroach, if not a cabbage. In the process, he was carrying out a deliberate provocation against not merely the city's sea captains and live-animal sellers but against any New Yorker who believed that the revolution against cruelty to animals would end in a comfortable place. The exploits of the past month had made him famous. The prosecution of Captain Nehemiah H. Calhoun, soon to be known to all New York as the "Turtle Case," would make Henry Bergh infamous. And during the two decades to follow, his fame and his infamy, his victories and his overreaches, would change the way Americans thought about the suffering of the living creatures all around them.

.   .   .

When Bergh began his campaign, the ideas underlying it were already circulating widely in England and Europe. But how did they arise?

For centuries, the inheritors of a Western culture based in the Judeo-Christian tradition—the founding texts of which offer few prescriptions against cruelty to animals, even as they make ringing statements of human "dominion" over the natural world—could travel through their daily lives without giving much thought to how domestic animals in their overwhelmingly agrarian societies were treated. Few Europeans truly believed, as the French philosopher René Descartes theorized in the early seventeenth century, that animals should be classed as soulless machines—that, in the summation of one of Descartes's disciples, Nicolas Malebranche, animals "eat without pleasure, cry without pain, grow without knowing it; they desire nothing, fear nothing, know nothing." And yet animals' inability to *testify* to their desires, fears, and knowledge made it possible for many to put the question of their suffering entirely out of mind, given their seemingly preordained place in the natural order as mere possessions to be worked and consumed.

To rebel against that suffering, or indeed to see it as worthy of consideration, was—and remains—first and foremost an act of imagination. So perhaps it's not surprising that resistance to animal suffering began flourishing first in literary minds, before its full flower as a social movement. Shakespeare, in *Measure for Measure* (c. 1605), spared a thought for "the poor beetle that we tread upon," imagining that it "in corporal sufferance finds a pang as great / as when a giant dies." Molière wrote a character in *The Miser* (1668) who declares "such a tender feeling for my horses that when I see them suffer, it seems to be happening to me." Jonathan Swift, in *Gulliver's Travels* (1726), devoted his final fantasia to the land of the Houyhnhnms, horses that rule over their local humans, but express horror to Gulliver when he describes the maltreatment of their kind taking place in England. Some who made this imaginative leap began to practice vegetarianism—among them Jean-Jacques Rousseau, who by the 1750s was adhering to (and advocating for) a non-meat diet on the grounds of morality as well as health.

One might date the true birth of the movement to 1776, when Humphry Primatt, a retired Anglican vicar living outside London in the town of Kingston-on-Thames, published what could be considered its founding text, *A Dissertation on the Duty of Mercy and Sin of Cruelty to Brute Animals*. In the introduction to this volume, the Reverend Primatt laid out what he intended to prove: just as "the Love and Mercy of God are all over his works," he wrote,

> our Love and Mercy are not to be confined within the circle of our own friends, acquaintance, and neighbours; nor limited to the more enlarged sphere of human nature, to creatures of our own rank, shape, and capacity; but are to be extended to every object of the Love and Mercy of GOD *the universal parent*.

Converging in Primatt's book were a number of crucial forces that would shape the character of the international movement to follow. First, he devoted his *entire* 326-page volume to the subject of animals, marshaling the biblical evidence for a human obligation to their care. As the first known book-length argument against cruelty to animals, *Duty of Mercy* symbolized and indeed enacted what would be a crucial leap for so many supporters of the movement—the moment when they became willing to move animals from the margins of their consciousness to the center of it.

The second key dimension of Primatt's book was its devout character, and the Romantic theology it embodied. We tend to think of Romanticism as a literary movement, but the earliest and in many ways most transformative emergence of the Romantic sensibility was in the pulpit, where the oftentimes vengeful or callous Creator of earlier centuries became supplanted by a deity of love above all—"Love is the great Hinge upon which universal Nature turns," Primatt begins his first chapter—who saw the consciousness and suffering of individuals as worthy of his divine consideration. This, increasingly, was the God preached around England and elsewhere in Europe, and soon enough in America, too: a celestial Carer who throbbed with feeling for the unfortunate and smiled upon those who took it on themselves to alleviate suffering. It was this religious climate that prompted the English theologian John Wesley, not long before his death in 1791, to remark that "benevolence and compassion toward all forms of human woe have increased in a manner not known before, from the earliest ages of the world." And it was this religious climate that would give succor to all the humanitarian movements of the nineteenth century, the cause of animals being just one among them.

A third aspect of Primatt's book, more subtle but nevertheless crucial to the movement to come, was the manner in which he synthesized his religious commitments with the evolving scientific understanding of animals. Central to the Reverend Primatt's vision of "universal Nature" is the notion that animals are "no less sensible of pain than a Man," because they possess "similar nerves and organs of sensation"—reflecting a new awareness (ironically, one informed in part by decades of often agonizing experimentation on live animals) that the physiology of humans was analogous to that of other creatures, in ways both large and small. It would still be a century before Charles Darwin and others took that observation to its logical, deeply irreligious conclusion, but in the meantime, the implications for Primatt and future animal advocates were profound. God, having so famously made mankind in his own image, had also seen fit to design animals in a comparable manner, endowing them with a capacity for suffering that must be just as keen, given the similarities in their divine construction. If "all forms of human woe," in Wesley's phrase, had become impossible to ignore, then the non-human woes of these suffering creatures must also command human attention.

And finally, there was Primatt's deft linking of animal cruelty to the evil of slavery and the cause of abolition, which in so many ways became the fount of moral energy into which all other nineteenth-century humanitarian causes in Britain and America, including the one on behalf of animals, would tap. "It has pleased GOD the Father of all men, to cover some men with white skins, and others with black skins; but as there is neither merit nor demerit in complexion, the *white* man, notwithstanding the barbarity of custom and prejudice, can have no right, by virtue of his *colour*, to enslave and tyrannize over a *black* man," Primatt wrote. "For the same reason," he went on, "a man can have no natural right to abuse and

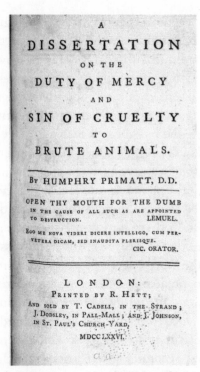

A

DISSERTATION

ON THE

DUTY OF MERCY

AND

SIN OF CRUELTY

TO

BRUTE ANIMALS.

By HUMPHRY PRIMATT, D.D.

OPEN THY MOUTH FOR THE DUMB
IN THE CAUSE OF ALL SUCH AS ARE APPOINTED
TO DESTRUCTION.   LEMUEL.

EGO ME NOVA VIDERI DICERE INTELLIGO, CUM PER-
VETERA DICAM, SED INAUDITA PLERISQUE.
CIC. ORATOR.

LONDON:
PRINTED BY R. HETT;
AND SOLD BY T. CADELL, IN THE STRAND;
J. DODSLEY, IN PALL-MALL; AND J. JOHNSON,
IN ST. PAUL'S CHURCH-YARD.
MDCCLXXVI.

Title page of *A Dissertation on the Duty of Mercy and Sin of Cruelty to Brute Animals* by Humphry Primatt, 1776.

torment a beast, merely because a beast has not the mental powers of a man. For, such as the man is, he is but as GOD made him; and the very same is true of the beast."

It was just this sort of moral logic that provoked William Wilberforce—who championed the abolitionist cause for decades in Parliament, beginning in the 1780s, soon after his conversion to Evangelicalism—to take up the cause of cruelty to animals as well. In the year 1800, Wilberforce and his devout allies in Parliament unsuccessfully backed a bill to ban the practice of "bull baiting," a savage old rural tradition in which a bull was tethered in a village square and set upon by dogs. Primatt's arguments were invoked nearly word for word by Sir Thomas Erskine when, in 1809, he rose to drum up support in the House of Lords for his own, much broader bill—ultimately unsuccessful as well—to prevent "malicious and wanton" cruelty to animals. "I am to ask your Lordships," he said, "in the name of that God who gave to Man his dominion over the lower world, to acknowledge and recognize that dominion to be *a moral trust*." Erskine's chief proof was the same as Primatt had noted three decades earlier, i.e., the similarities with which humans and animals were endowed by their Creator: "Almost every sense bestowed upon Man is equally bestowed upon them—Seeing—Hearing—Feeling—Thinking—the sense of pain and pleasure—the passions of love and anger—sensibility to kindness, and pangs from unkindness and neglect are inseparable characteristics of *their* natures as much as of *our own*."

These growing sentiments would become formalized in 1822, when Britain passed its first animal-welfare law: the "Cruel Treatment of Cattle Act," otherwise known as Martin's Act, in honor of its sponsor, the dogged Irish MP Richard Martin. In June 1824, at the urging of the Reverend Arthur Broome—another minister who had taken to preaching on behalf of animals—a group of notable animal lovers, including Martin, Wilberforce, and a number of clergymen, met to found the world's very first Society for the Prevention of Cruelty to Animals. The group struggled in its early years: Its first secretary did a brief stint in debtor's prison over its financial woes, and his successor wound up leaving in 1832 to found his own splinter group. But by 1840, when Queen Victoria extended her sponsorship to the organization, allowing it to become the *Royal* Society for the Prevention of Cruelty to Animals (RSPCA), it had set a template for animal-welfare organizations that would extend for the rest of the century.

Inspired by London's example, Stuttgart had already launched Germany's first humane organization, and by the time Paris's organization started up in 1852, scores more had emerged across Germany, Austria, and Switzerland. In the summer of 1860, they held an international congress in Dresden—more than forty delegates from societies all across Europe attended—and then another, less than a year later, in Paris, where Napoleon III declared his support for their cause.

By then, a revolutionary new scientific idea had captivated Britain and America. The publication, in 1859, of *On the Origin of Species* reordered popular thinking about humanity's position relative to other living things. Charles Darwin's key observation, that the struggle within and between species for natural resources and the opportunity to reproduce rewards those best suited to their environment, applied equally to humans and non-human animals, implying an order to the biological world defined less by dominion and more by interdependence.

Long before Darwin, scientists had understood humans and animals to have much in common. A century earlier, in his widely adopted system of taxonomy, Carl Linnaeus had classified *Homo sapiens* with other primates in the mammalian class of vertebrate animals. Since then, comparative anatomists and physiologists, cell biologists and biochemists had cataloged numerous similarities in structure and function between human and non-human organisms, both extant and extinct. Animals and humans shared a living likeness that was far from superficial, including retinal pigments, patellar reflexes, appendicular skeletal structure, and secretion of stomach acid. Although Darwin's *Origin* didn't explicitly address the primate parentage of humankind, it intimated that what connected man and animals was more than a mere resemblance; it was a common heritage.

.　　.　　.

It took an unlikely messenger to bring the movement across the Atlantic. During Henry Bergh's life and for decades afterward, the nature of his friendship with friendless beasts was a peculiar and much-debated subject. Despite the campaigns that he would later wage against slaughterhouses in the city, he never embraced vegetarianism. He appears never to have kept a pet, nor did he evince much particular fondness for those kept by others.* (The actress Clara Morris recounted a visit from Bergh during which one of her beloved dogs, "a three-pounder in weight," jumped onto the sofa next to him and "laid a small, inquiring paw upon his knee." At once, Morris recalled, "the man's whole body shrank away, and unmistakable repulsion showed in every feature.")

---

* He did have a "carriage-dog," a Dalmatian that ran beside his carriage for protection, a common sight in the nineteenth-century city.

He had been born in 1813, the younger son of Christian Bergh, one of New York's preeminent shipbuilders. The family empire had begun in 1799 and had grown to encompass a prodigious ship- yard on the East River, not far from where the Williamsburg Bridge now makes landfall, on the protrusion called Corlears Hook—an area whose many brothels in that era (one estimate in the 1830s, when young Henry might perhaps have been of an age to frequent them, was eighty-seven) are believed by some historians to have bequeathed to us the word "hooker." The captain of one Bergh- built craft, the *Antarctic,* was so pleased with its performance on a South Sea expedition that he named three Micronesian islands for Christian's elder son, Edwin, senior to Henry by eleven years.

Around 1843, the year Christian died, the business was sold off and Henry and Edwin inherited a multimillion-dollar fortune. This gave Henry the freedom to travel abroad, and he and his wife, Catherine Matilda, largely abandoned New York for a life of lei- sure in Europe. It was on a visit to Seville, Spain, in April 1848 that Bergh received what he later would describe as a great awaken- ing to the cause of animal suffering, one of two he described over and over again. One torrid afternoon, he and Matilda (as his wife was known) were sitting amid 12,000 people at the Maestranza, the stately eighteenth-century stadium that was and remains the grandest temple of Spanish bullfighting. The *corrida de toros* had by then become a national obsession, as well as a staple for curious tourists like the Berghs, a crucial box to check in order to feel that one had truly savored Iberia.

With each successive performance by the toreros, Bergh became increasingly repelled. Then as now, the human bullfighters almost always survived the performance, but during the first stage of the fight, when mounted picadors attack with lances, bulls would fre- quently disembowel horses. (Since the 1930s, the horses have worn padded armor called *petos,* making equine death an uncommon sight in the bullring today.) During the two days of bullfighting that Bergh attended, the ghastly death toll ran to forty-seven horses and sixteen bulls.

Bergh's travel journal from the period records his dismay: "[N]ever before has a similar degree of disgust been experienced by us, or such hearty contempt for a people calling themselves civilized + at the same time Christians." He was impressed by the dexterity of the star matador, the legendary José Redondo, known far and wide as "El Chiclanero," after the region near Cádiz from which he hailed. "At the instant that the bull bounds toward him," Bergh wrote two weeks later, in a long letter to the *New York Evening Mirror*, Redondo "adroitly winds himself into it with the tact and composure that an Andalucian puts on his capa"—that is, his cape—"before he sallies out to serenade his mistress." But the elaborate savagery of the outcome provoked a disturbance in Bergh. "The cause of humanity would doubtless be better served," Bergh acidly proclaimed in the *Mirror*, "were all the actors in these demoralizing exhibitions slain"—including the local politicians, he added, "who so wantonly desecrate their high positions" by appearing at the events.

"Can any one doubt," Bergh added, "that a people depending upon pastimes of so cruel a character, must eventually become degraded?" It was a notion Bergh would return to again and again over the course of his life, one that he would eventually call *cruelism*—the idea that witnessing cruelty to animals had a coarsening influence on human minds, particularly those of the young, priming them for further acceptance of cruelty against man and beast alike. Later in life, he would recall with particular disgust a group sitting near him at the Maestranza, a family of Spanish nobles who had brought their adolescent daughters along. "Whenever the bull tore out the bowels of the wretched horse," he remembered, "these girls laughed and applauded as if in a theater."

When it came to the theater, Bergh knew whereof he spoke. An aspiring poet and playwright, he went on to spend much of his peripatetic thirties and forties—as he and Matilda sojourned back and forth between Europe and America—trying to get his work published or performed. A manager of Booth's Theater in New York recalled how relentlessly Bergh plied him with his various attempts at light comedy. "There was positively no merit in them," he said, "and I wondered at his persistence. He was totally devoid of humor." A rare success came in 1858, when a Philadelphia theater put on one of Bergh's plays, entitled *The Empire City!, or New*

York Physically, Intellectually and Liquor-ally Considered—but the effort never made it to a stage in the city that inspired it.

Bergh won the most attention for a comedic poem about marital mores of the day, *Married Off*, published in 1860, but most of that attention was scathing—a fact that prompted Bergh's publisher to teach him a lesson he remembered his entire life. "Mr. Bergh," the animal-welfare activist later recalled the publisher telling him,

> I have been in the publishing business more than half my life, and have some knowledge of the business. It is certainly pleasant to have one's book spoken of in terms of approbation; it is the next best thing to have it well blown up. The most fatal thing that can happen is for the press to say nothing about it.

Bergh set aside his literary aspirations in 1863 to accept a post in St. Petersburg, Russia, as a diplomat in the Lincoln administration—and it was there that he experienced his second great awakening to the animal cause. He was out one day in the carriage of his boss, Cassius M. Clay, the anti-slavery Kentuckian who was then the chief minister to Russia, when Bergh witnessed a local droshky, or coachman, brutally whipping his horse. Bergh bade his own driver to stop, and he stepped out of the carriage in order to upbraid the man. His uniform, resplendent with gold lace, had an instantaneous effect, he noted, as the workingman fell to his knees in abject apology.

If his experience at the bullfight had been an epiphany about his own feeling for animals, this second epiphany was somewhat less pure: an awakening to the power of his stature, both physically (his six-foot build) and socially. He began making a practice of cruising St. Petersburg's side streets, in search of more droshkies to harangue. The would-be dramatist had discovered the role of a lifetime; and, as he learned from his experience as a published author, he would not let stubborn audiences or bad reviews dissuade him. Through his extensive travels in Europe, he was more than aware of the movement to organize societies for the passage and enforcement of anti-cruelty laws, and he realized that in St. Petersburg he had already become an SPCA unto himself. "Encouraged by my success," he later recalled to a Philadelphia paper, "I made up my mind that when I came home I would prosecute those who persecuted poor dumb brutes."

Bergh left his post in Russia not long after Lincoln's assassination. On his way home, he visited with the leadership of the Royal SPCA, in London. The group was fortunate, after its tumultuous first few decades, to have found a steady hand in the figure of John Colam, who took over the secretary job in 1861 and would remain in it for decades. By then, the society's emphasis on prosecution had markedly increased—it employed five regular inspectors, and was convicting hundreds of offenders per year (the figure in 1861 was 554)—and this shift, no doubt, was music to Bergh's ears; for all his heartfelt words over the years about the power of kindness, he would always regard law enforcement, not education or sermons, as the leading edge of his own revolution against cruelty to animals.

Though it was as yet untouched by the animal-welfare movement, the America that Bergh returned to in the summer of 1865 had transformed in important ways during his decades in Europe. The Romantic turn that began sweeping through English pulpits in the last decades of the eighteenth century was now sweeping through the United States—a trajectory seen dramatically in the person of Henry Ward Beecher, who by the 1860s had become the best-known religious figure in America. Born in 1813, the same year as Bergh, Beecher imbibed the stern Calvinism of his own preacher father, and as a young minister in Indianapolis he made his reputation warning young men against the dangers of alcohol, gambling, and other vices. But in the years after he moved to Brooklyn, in 1847, to assume the pulpit at Plymouth Church on Henry Street, he began an evolution toward an optimistic, soaring liberalism; by 1860, he could be found preaching a sermon on "The Love of God" that closely echoed Humphry Primatt in its conception of divine love and what it commanded. "What is God's perfection?" Beecher asked, and then answered:

> It is boundless benevolence. It is the perfection of a being who sends all providential blessings upon men, whether they are good or bad, deserving or undeserving. We must be perfect *as* he is. There is to be a comprehensive beneficence in us.

And it was this vision of compulsory beneficence that had pulled Beecher toward the anti-slavery cause—writing strident columns throughout the 1850s and editing an anti-slavery publication, *The Independent*, in the early years of the Civil War.

Such was the fertile ground that awaited Henry Bergh on his return to America: a nation that, in ways large and small, was primed to join a moral revolution against animal suffering. One could perceive it in the writings of Beecher's sister, Harriet Beecher Stowe—whose blockbuster anti-slavery novel, *Uncle Tom's Cabin*, overwhelmed American imaginations with its depictions of physical suffering—and even more directly in the work of Lydia Maria Child, another anti-slavery novelist who, by 1865, had written on a few occasions about the cause of cruelty to animals. That year, in an essay meant for the education of the formerly enslaved, Child exhorted kindness to animals in direct analogy to her readers' own anguish under the whip: "The best way to cure the disheartened and obstinate laborer is to give him just wages and kind treatment," she wrote, "and the best way to deal with the discouraged and stubborn horse is to give him light loads and humane usage." For Stowe, Child, and so many other anti-slavery activists, the end of the Civil War would mark a new era, in which their moral energies were freed to be channeled into other causes, and their imaginations, trained for decades on ghoulish narratives of cruelty to enslaved people, would turn to the misery of other beings.

One could see it in a nascent movement for vegetarianism, which itself sat at the intersection of a host of other "reform" movements, particularly temperance and women's suffrage. In 1853, a vegetarian banquet in New York drew three hundred diners, who enjoyed a bill of fare that included "moulded farina," "wheat meal cakes," "stewed cream squash," and "Graham bread"—made from the flour invented by Sylvester Graham, the eccentric vegetarian minister and health visionary who had recently died after a course of opium enemas. Attendees at the banquet included the eminent newspaper publisher Horace Greeley, who served as the master of ceremonies, as well as the feminists Susan B. Anthony and Lucy Stone, who were in town for the Whole World's Temperance Convention; given that alcohol, too, was unwelcome at the banquet, *The New York Times'* mocking account noted that "the spirit was, of course, all in the talking." Vegetarians of that era were mostly focused on human health, but their short-lived publication, *The American Vegetarian and Health Journal,* included many essays urging kindness to animals.

And one could even read about it in the newspapers. Bergh's journal from 1862 included another obvious source of inspiration, a pasted copy of a *Times* essay that clearly prefigured so many of the preoccupations that the ASPCA would take up in its early years: the "teamster who goads with whip and curse his overloaded beast"; the livestock "piled in living agony one upon the other, and dragged half smothered in butcher carts to be dumped into the slaughter-pen, and there dismembered into joints and cuts, to be served up for our delectation into smoking chafing dishes." Three issues of *Frank Leslie's Illustrated Newspaper* in 1865 offered a series of pointed scenes about the scourge of animal cruelty in New York; one of them showed several men pummeling a horse with clubs and whips while a policeman looked on. An item in the *Leslie's* series even asked, rhetorically, "Shall we ever have among us a Society for the Prevention of Cruelty to Animals?"

Henry Bergh would see to it that they did, though the forces arrayed against him were formidable. Some were comparable to those faced by the RSPCA in London, or its fellow societies in the other Old World cities of Europe: for instance, the chaos of nineteenth-century urbanization, and the coarseness of attitudes toward laboring animals prevalent among workingmen. There were unscrupulous streetcar companies to litigate against, dog-fighting rings to be broken up, exotic animal exhibits and horse races to monitor, little boys to educate in the habits of kindness.

But in the United States of the late nineteenth century, those challenges of everyday city life were being compounded by an astonishing growth unlike any society's in human history. In 1865, the United States was a nation of roughly thirty-five million people, hardly more than the population of the United Kingdom (approximately twenty-eight million). By the end of the century, while the UK's population grew by roughly a third, America's population would double, creating seventy million bodies to move from place to place, seventy million mouths to feed with meat and milk. That growth would power the creation of the biggest economy on earth, one where industrial magnates could amass untold fortunes by creating businesses of enormous scale and complexity, including those selling animals and animal products. In London, as in the streets of St. Petersburg, Henry Bergh had learned a playbook for fighting and prosecuting the cruelty of individuals. What his movement would confront, over the decades to come, was the difficulty of fighting the cruelty of systems.

In America's mid-nineteenth-century cities, animals
were pervasively seen, heard, and smelled.

Chapter 2

ANIMAL NEW YORK

The urban dairy horse of the mid-nineteenth century worked alone, save the milkman, with shafts buckled into either side of her leather harness, reins connecting the bit in her mouth to the interior of the boxy, single-springed milk wagon where her human co-worker sat amid clattering milk cans. She plodded the same route every day, stopping at fixed points while the milkman scurried to and from customers' homes, dropping off butter and eggs, ladling milk and cream into waiting vessels. Frequently, the horse would memorize her route, right down to the duration of each stop. After the last delivery, without prompting, she would wheel about and head for home while the milkman tallied his accounts or snoozed inside the rattling wagon. If the milkman were detained at a doorway, drank himself silly, or even died on the route, the horse would likely proceed along her practiced path, returning the wagon to the dairy loading dock at precisely the usual hour.

Millennia of selective breeding made this possible—transforming *Equus caballus* from a swift herbivore, whose small herds roamed prehistoric Eurasian grasslands, into the dutiful dairy horse drudging through downtown New York City. Several species characteristics made the equine amenable to its eventual role in human society: size, strength, simple dietary needs, and sociability. *E. caballus* is sufficiently larger and stronger than the average *Homo sapiens* that its labor multiplies the man's, but not so huge and powerful that it cannot be, to some extent, physically controlled by a determined person. The equine can subsist on relatively inexpensive grasses and grains, foodstuffs that lend themselves to transport and storage, ensuring a stable year-round supply. And, perhaps most important, the horse forms tight social bonds—with other horses and, since domestication, across species. Horses respect hierarchical relationships, and look to their leaders, horse and human, for goading and guidance.

Domestication made the horse into man's most valuable servant: source of meat and milk, laborer behind the plow, warrior under saddle, and, in the nineteenth-century city, reliable transporter of dairy products, dry goods, coal, and commuters. And yet, the residue of its origins as a prey species lingers: The horse's mobile ears and widely spaced eyes constantly scan all directions for danger. Perception of even a slight disturbance in the landscape served the ancestral wild horse as an early warning system, protecting him from predators, but this same keen sensitivity could be a liability for the urban workhorse. Treading a nineteenth-century New York street, a horse might be spooked by, among other things, a nightshirt flapping on a clothesline, a frenzied fight between two cats, the clang of a church bell, a snort from a steam shovel, a gunshot, a slamming door, a squalling child, a sudden gust of wind, a whistle, a pigeon taking flight, a page of newsprint blowing by. In response, a startled steed might rear, buck, kick, or lunge, teeth bared, in a show of fearful aggression—but, more often, the anxious animal would take evasive action: shying sideways or backwards away from the threat, or bolting forward, sometimes at a blind gallop sustained for several city blocks.

Contemporary newspapers frequently contained accounts of horses that had snapped—resulting in severed hands, thrown riders, trampled pedestrians, overturned carriages, kicked cartmen, and collisions involving every possible combination of animal, vehicle, and movable or fixed object. On February 9, 1866, page 4 of *The Sun* noted a series of runaway horse incidents in south Brooklyn occurring two days prior. First, at the corner of Hamilton Avenue and Smith Street, near the open landfills and shanties of the swampy Red Hook peninsula, an undertaker's horse abruptly startled, galloping south for nearly a mile before coming to an uneasy rest at 24th Street and Third Avenue. The young driver of the hearse, B. T. Sawyer, was significantly injured, and the vehicle a total loss (no mention of its cargo). A short time afterward, a horse attached to a grocery wagon took fright while turning onto Third Avenue two blocks away, at 22nd Street, throwing its passengers—two married couples—violently to the pavement. After a long chase, Officer Nolan of the 48th Precinct succeeded in capturing the frothing animal, still attached to the intact wagon. The policeman attempted to drive the horse to the station house, but it panicked a second time, dumping Nolan onto the street and obliging another officer to chase down and catch the rattled creature. This second spree prompted a team of two horses belonging to Arnold Lott of New Utrecht to bolt from where they had been left untied alongside Third Avenue, galloping away until they were apprehended by passersby.

Even on its best behavior, the nineteenth-century horse contributed to a stampede of daily traffic on city streets. It's a common present-day misconception that the Industrial Revolution, having reached American shores in the early part of the nineteenth century, immediately swept all beasts of burden off the road, replacing them with machines. Paradoxically, the opposite was true: For the better part of a hundred years, the industrializing American city brought more working animals onto its avenues.

As the metropolis spread outward from the southern tip of Manhattan, and filled with purposeful human beings—Americans leaving farms for trades or factory work and foreign immigrants attracted by New World opportunities—foot travel increasingly became inadequate for moving New Yorkers between the places where they lived, worked, and took recreation. Private horse-drawn carriages kept the wealthy safe from muck and molestation as they made the journey from their uptown residences to downtown offices, shops, and amusements. The growing middle class could afford to hire a single-horse hackney cab, at least some of the time, for their in-town trips. The stagecoach, pulled by a succession of sturdy four-horse teams, conveyed several ticketed passengers at a time between downtown New York and further-flung locations, according to a set schedule. Intracity mass transit began in the 1830s, with the invention of the horse-drawn omnibus, which catered to the city's working classes, who had to put up with tight bench seating, stifling air, fleas, perverts, and pickpockets. The hazards of the omnibus weren't limited to its interior: Competing with one another for passenger fares, the heavy vehicles lurched from one side of the street to the other in an unpredictable zigzag, creating perils for pedestrians and other drivers alike.

By 1866, tracks had been laid throughout the city, and railway streetcars had become ubiquitous on New York thoroughfares. The reduced friction of the rails relative to rough city streets decreased the horsepower necessary to pull a passenger-stuffed car from a muscular team of four down to a sturdy harnessed pair or even a single animal—the strength and stamina of each horse was put to maximal use by railway companies. The capital involved with embedding and maintaining miles of urban rails had encouraged corporate consolidation of transit, and big railway companies endeavored to make the most of their investments through economy of scale. A horse-pulled streetcar designed to carry fifty paying riders comfortably often became uncomfortably (but quite profitably) loaded down with twice that many—as a poem in *Harper's Weekly* memorably described it, "Thirty seated, forty standing / A dozen more on either landing. . . . / Packed together, unwashed bodies / Bathed in fumes of whiskey toddies."

Alongside these passenger vehicles lumbered horse-drawn freight carts and wagons of all sizes and shapes, hauling dry goods and groceries, building materials, whiskey barrels, refuse, furniture, fire engines, stacks of newspapers, casks of whale oil, and many, many tons of coal. Even as coal-fired steam engines had begun to power trains, boats, and factories, it was horses and other hoofstock that moved the stuff—ponies pulled the coal out of the mountainous ground; mule-powered winches loaded it onto trains and barges (as cargo and fuel); horses, hitched to delivery wagons, dropped off domestic orders. Without equine help, America's coal could fuel nothing but the imagination.

Restrained by harnesses and headcollars, hampered by heavy loads, the horses of New York and other industrial-age cities only occasionally were the ones inflicting injury. Far more often they were on the receiving end. Those tasked with driving the animals were often poor men, not infrequently Irish or African American, recently arrived from a rural setting; whether drivers of single horses or teamsters taking the reins of two or more, their meager livelihoods depended on the timely completion of their routes. And so, while there was ample evidence of human-horse cooperation—like that between the mild-mannered milkman and his dairy dray—there was also conflict, cruelty, and neglect.

.   .   .

The *Sun* reader—glancing one column over from the paper's brief account, on that February 9, of Brooklyn's recent equine escapades—might have spotted an item acknowledging a special meeting of the American Geographical and Statistical Society, held the previous evening. The society's featured speaker was Henry Bergh, and the crowd who gathered to hear him was a distinguished one, including such notables as the mayor, John T. Hoffman, and the department-store magnate A. T. Stewart. Despite a lashing winter storm and a host of competing entertainments (L.B. Lent's New York Circus at the Hippotheatron on 14th Street, Italian opera at the Brooklyn Academy of Music, Mr. Edwin Booth playing Cardinal Richelieu at the Winter Garden theater), this eminent group had assembled at Manhattan's Clinton Hall—a Greek-style venue, formerly home to the Astor Opera House, that stood on Lafayette Street between Astor Place and East Eighth Street—to hear Bergh deliver a landmark lecture on the subject of cruelty to animals.

Bergh began by acknowledging that abuse of the "mute servants of mankind" stretched back almost to Creation—when animals were, according to his progressive Protestant thinking, committed to man's care. He proceeded to lay out a version of Western history that linked man's cruelty toward members of his own species with the abuse of the animals he lived among. As Bergh saw it, the blunt brutality of early, primitive man toward early, primitive beasts led to the organized spectacles of human slaughter in the classical Roman Colosseum, and the sadistic evils of the medieval Inquisition laid the gory groundwork for the barbarity of the modern bullring that had so scandalized him in Seville.

To establish the need for change in the here and now, Bergh went on to catalog what he considered to be contemporary depravities: everything from epicurean excesses like foie gras to vicious experiments practiced by European vivisectionists. He took issue

with modern blood sports—including hunting, ratting (the killing of rats, especially competitively, either by humans or other
animals such as dogs or ferrets), and cockfighting—which, given
their widespread popularity, might have been pastimes of not a
few of the gentlemen present in the audience at Clinton Hall. He
decried the transporters of calves and sheep bound for slaughter—
and the conduct of the slaughterhouses themselves. Every member
of the audience, Bergh knew, would have personally witnessed at
least one pervasive form of cruelty to animals: the mistreatment
of horses. At length, he denounced the everyday callousness of the
city's coachmen, streetcar operators, and horse racers.

After this recitation of human degeneracy and its deplorable
effects on helpless living things, Bergh proposed his genteel remedy.
The American Society for the Prevention of Cruelty to Animals
would attempt to persuade by means of a broad educational effort,
he explained, but when education failed to effect the necessary
changes, the society would see to the enforcement and prosecution of cruel misconduct. According to Bergh, fines garnered from
abusers would provide much of the funding for the entire humane
effort, as was the case in Britain.

Bergh concluded his remarks by calling on the better natures of
the gentlemen present: "This is a matter purely of conscience. It
has no perplexing side issues. Politics have no more to do with it
than astronomy or the use of globes. No, it is a moral question in
all its aspects." By the end of the evening, the Geographical Society
had passed a resolution backing Bergh in the creation of his new
organization. Bergh departed Clinton Hall with numerous commitments of support for the charter he would seek from the state
legislature, adding to his growing list of powerful signatories—city
fathers like Peter Cooper; Hamilton Fish, the former governor and
U.S. senator (and soon to be secretary of state); the newspaperman Horace Greeley; the Harper brothers of publishing fame; and
scores more.

Within several weeks, with the help of State Senator Charles Fol-
ger, Bergh had shepherded a charter of incorporation through the
New York legislature in Albany, recognizing the ASPCA as an
instrument of the public's interest in animal welfare and granting
the organization the authority to enforce animal-protection laws

throughout the state. The broad language of the document anticipated the passage of subsequent legislation to more broadly define
and more harshly penalize cruelty to animals than what was stipu-
lated in the existing, weak anti-cruelty statute dating back to 1829.
Streetcar and slaughterhouse interests pushed for a narrower
organizational purview less likely to endanger their profitable
enterprises, but they proved no match for Bergh's mobilizing energy
among New York City's political and social elite.

Nine days later, on April 19, 1866, New York legislators passed
"An Act Better to Prevent Cruelty to Animals" ensuring that
"Every person who shall, by his act or neglect, maliciously kill,
maim, wound, injure, torture or cruelly
beat any horse, mule, ox, cattle, sheep
or other animal belonging to himself
or another, shall upon conviction, be
adjudged guilty of a misdemeanor."
The maximum penalty for such an act
was up to a year in jail, a $250 fine, or
both. In practice, common violations
such as beating, cruel confinement,
abandonment or forcing an injured animal to work brought fines ranging from
$10 to $25 (more than a week's wages
for a driver), with only an occasional
sentence of one or two days in jail.

Portrait of Henry
Bergh, circa 1870.

The legislature established multiple
mechanisms for enforcement of the new
animal protections. First, the ASPCA charter obliged the police to
cooperate with the group, and to carry out arrests on its behalf.
Second, the new state law empowered citizens who had witnessed
an act of animal abuse to make reports directly to a magistrate,
who might then issue a summons to the accused or a warrant for
his arrest. But, for the most part, it was officers and agents of the
ASPCA who patrolled the streets, confronting inhumane actors
and identifying them to the police.

No one embraced this task more enthusiastically—or
theatrically—than Bergh himself. The very night of his return from
Albany, where he had personally supervised the bill's passage, he

armed himself with paper copies of the law and the ASPCA charter and stepped confidently, in gentleman's dress, from his Fifth
Avenue brownstone into Manhattan's frenetic, filthy streets. He
intended to use his new powers to personally prevail against cruelty
to animals, abuser by abuser, before as many witnesses as possible.

He began by approaching a driver, who was in the midst of flogging his feeble horse. With a haughty cry—"Stop! . . . You can't do
that anymore!"—Bergh advised the man that he was in violation of
the state's new humane law.

"Can't beat my own horse?" the driver replied. "Go to hell—
you're mad!"

So much for Bergh's first attempt at law enforcement. He had
expected a more ingratiating response, like that of the droshky
driver in St. Petersburg. The New York driver's bull-headed reaction struck him as distinctly American, and he quickly adjusted his
methods: The mere threat of prosecution would not be enough, he
concluded, to stop the raised arm of a rough Yankee.

His second attempt, made the subsequent afternoon with the
assistance of New York City police, produced a more satisfying
result—the arrest of a Brooklyn butcher, charged with cruelly
transporting a wagonload of recumbent calves, bound and stacked
like cordwood. The head of one hung helplessly in proximity to a
sharp stick, so that its eye was in danger of being gored out with
every bump of the turning wheels, as Bergh sprinted in pursuit
of the vehicle. The driver was brought before a magistrate, who
ordered the payment of a $10 fine. Picking up momentum, Bergh
supervised the arrest of three more men the next day for inhumane
transport of calves. Each received a day in jail along with payment
of a similar sum.

Over the weeks that followed, more and more New Yorkers
had the opportunity to witness firsthand a colorful confrontation
between a towering, top-hatted gentleman and a working-class
animal abuser. Bergh quickly came to relish these performances,
often following an arrest with a spontaneous curbside speech
for the gathered crowd: "Now, gentlemen, consider that you are
American citizens, living in a republic. You make your own laws;
no despot makes them for you. I appeal to your sense of justice and
your patriotism. Oughtn't you to respect what you yourselves have

made?" He would then walk listeners through the origins and the ideals of the animal-welfare movement. In this way, Bergh sought to turn each intervention into an opportunity for evangelism. It also generated colorful copy for newspaper reporters on the city beat, and increasingly they began to follow him about town, which in turn provided Bergh with even more encouragement.

Bergh never had to look far for new cruelties to confront. Urbanization and industrialization had already begun to disrupt the direct relationships that had traditionally existed between human beings and the rest of the living world, but the fracture was still far from complete. The abundant presence of animals—hoofstock, poultry, pets, strays, and wildlife—meant there were many opportunities for New Yorkers to treat animals poorly.

Not all beasts of burden Bergh encountered were equine. Oxen, commonly worked in the country, would occasionally haul heavy cargo into the city. Lightweight wagons, carts, and carriages could be pulled by goats. Some of the poorest residents of the slums, who survived by salvaging rags, glass, and paper from refuse for recycling, depended on dogs to pull their meager carts. Besides pulling wheeled conveyances, some animals—particularly dogs and sheep, along with horses—worked on treadmills, powering washing machines, butter churns, grindstones, and cider presses.

Even as the expanding metropolis was displacing farms outward from the urban core, food animals were still very much part of the city's milieu. Free-roaming pigs, despite having been officially outlawed below Manhattan's 86th Street in 1860, continued to root around in downtown gutters for food scraps and refuse. Here and there, dairy cows and goats lowed from residential lots and tenement courtyards. Hens clucked and raised small clouds of dust, scratching at the ground beneath the larger livestock and anywhere else they might find a few crumbs.

Before refrigeration, animals were necessarily slaughtered close to where they would be consumed. Herds of food animals raised elsewhere could still be seen transiting New York's streets and avenues, being driven from a railway terminus or steamship pier to a marketplace or slaughterhouse. Stressed-out cattle, swine, and sheep jostled shoulder to shoulder, nose to tail, filling the thoroughfares and temporarily halting all wheeled and foot traffic as they were hustled along. Smaller animals intended for New Yorkers' dinner plates were carted rather than marched to their final destination: calves, lambs, and cages stuffed with fowl were loaded onto horse-drawn vehicles.

The pitiful bellows of animals at the slaughter yards and knackeries (rendering operations) were audible throughout surrounding city blocks. Awash in blood and ingesta and piled with bones, hides, and heaps of offal, these places were also attractive to scavenging critters: Rodents and birds, but also cats and dogs, alone and in packs, made off with whatever they could.

Strays were ubiquitous. Even those dogs and cats considered to be pets tended to live effectively at large, their associations with particular households or stores being rather loose. In the century before litter boxes and effective flea treatments came into use, cats and dogs would usually only be allowed indoors part-time, if at all. Neutering of pet species was rare before the twentieth century, and a surplus of dogs and cats roamed the streets, ready with the slightest provocation to attack one another over territory, access to a mate, or a bit of sustenance. The ruckus of fighting dogs erupted frequently amid New York's daytime bustle, while the violent shrieking of cats ruled the night, after human and other animal sounds had stilled. One late-nineteenth-century New York neighborhood was so plagued by the midnight howling of rowdy felines that the *Times* described their plight under the headline: "DWELLERS IN FIRST WARD, BROOKLYN, ALMOST IN DESPAIR. CAN'T SLEEP NIGHTS OR LEAD CHRISTIAN LIVES—NOISIEST CATS ON EARTH, AND LOTS OF THEM."

In 1866, the same year that New York State enacted its anticruelty law, the city established its newest dog pound, a simple shed on the East River at the end of 25th Street. Until 4 p.m. every day, the pound functioned as a fine place to acquire a dog at a very reasonable price. During those same hours, it took in whatever stray dogs had been found running loose throughout the city, and the owners of lost dogs could retrieve them for a fee. The pound paid fifty cents for each dog collected, which created a perverse incentive for neighborhood boys to "find" dogs in homes and yards. *The New York Times,* in its report on the new pound's opening, noted the tale of a man who "redeemed a favorite Newfoundland puppy eleven times in the course of five weeks, and only kept him at last by compromising with the dog-thief, and paying him a dollar a week during the season." Every afternoon, as 4 p.m. neared, it was not unusual to see a parade of anxious owners making their way to the end of 25th Street, running on foot or rushing out of horse-drawn carriages, hoping to find their pet and ransom it. Because at the stroke of 4 p.m., it would be too late: The day's unclaimed dogs were killed by drowning in a giant metal box, measuring ten feet long, six feet wide, and eight feet tall, used to dispatch some sixty to eighty dogs at a time.

Animals were not only constantly heard and seen throughout the city, but also very pervasively smelled. Excrement was everywhere, left behind in the streets by animals on the move, shoveled out of stables into enormous piles, and carted through the streets to be re-piled elsewhere. Street cleaning, not yet a civic function, was done piecemeal by laborers hired by wealthier neighborhood associations. On the poorer streets animal wastes accumulated heavily, especially after free-roaming pigs were banned—their indiscriminate appetites had helped keep city streets clean. Carcasses, particularly of larger animals, were often abandoned where they fell, and sometimes were left to rot until they had reached a state where they might more easily be broken up for transport. The stench of animal slaughter and processing operations drew complaints from neighbors for many blocks around, but were nonetheless a fact of urban life.

Inconveniences and dangers to humans caused by the animals in their midst abounded, and this contributed to rampant abuses. So did the precarious circumstances of many of the humans tasked with working directly alongside animals—for whom an animal's uncooperativeness or poor performance might cause a ruinous reduction in pay. Four-legged workers who disobeyed orders, failed to move fast enough, or faltered in the fulfillment of their tasks were frequently subjected to rough treatment.

.   .   .

In addition to systemic causes of cruelty, there were more incidental, wanton acts of brutality. Someone might kick a dog that crossed his path, throw rocks at a pigeon, intentionally spook a horse, or set a cat's tail alight. Not infrequently, these big and small barbarities were committed by children, who were themselves often running around loose without benefit of more wholesome occupation.

Some adults, too, made an entertainment out of violence against animals. Blood sports straddled class divides in New York City and elsewhere. Sport hunting remained primarily the purview of the wealthy, but rich and poor alike frequented boxing matches and cockfights, though not always the same ones. And it was not uncommon for top-hatted society swells to be caught slumming alongside lower-class enthusiasts at the ringside of dogfights, ratting contests, and "bear baits," in which chained bears were pitted against one or more dogs. Several seedy downtown venues specialized in this sort of event when Bergh began his patrols. One in particular would become the focus of his humane enforcement efforts.

Christopher Keybourn, better known as Kit Burns, opened Sportsmen's Hall in 1863, a few blocks south of the Five Points slum where he had come of age as a member of the Dead Rabbits, a notorious Irish immigrant gang that battled the nativist Bowery Boys for

"Dog Fight at Kit Burn's [sic]," from James D. McCabe,
The Secrets of the Great City, 1868.

control of the Lower East Side. The saloon's location at 273 Water Street made it convenient to sailors on shore leave, as well as to the various cheats, toughs, crooks, and con men who preyed on them. Neighboring businesses specialized in hard drinking, dancing, drugs, prostitution, or a filthy class of lodging. While Sportsmen's Hall was noted to accommodate "every variety of vice" within its narrow three-story edifice, its specialty was blood sport.

Customers entered a gas-lit bar, where house-made whiskey was abundantly poured. Some lingered here, surrounded by pictures of prizefighters and hunting scenes, enjoying the convivial company of the stout, square-jawed proprietor. "To hear Kit talk, when mellowed by his favorite beverage to an oratorical mood," observed a correspondent from the *New-York Daily Tribune,* "is equal to any treat that ever comes off in his bar-room."

The heart and soul of the establishment was at the rear of the building, accessed from the barroom by a narrow, curving hallway designed to thwart surprise police raids. There, at the center of a low amphitheater, surrounded by spectator boxes and rough wooden bleachers, sat an oval pit tightly enclosed by zinc-clad panels. Within this ring, animals fought for their lives in brutal contests that provided spectacle and wagering opportunities to hordes of raucous spectators. "The room will hold 250 decent people and 400 indecent ones," noted the *Tribune,* "as indecency can always be packed closer than decency."

"Rat baiting" served as Sportsmen's Hall's principal entertainment. Burns kept a weasel, able to chase and kill rats on instinct alone, for exhibition purposes. Audiences far preferred to place bets on his several eager young terriers, who had been trained to the task and performed it with maximum precision and alacrity. The *New-York Tribune* reporter, treated to a demonstration, described it thus: "The rat attempted to run around the pit; but the dog, with the velocity of an arrow, sprang upon it; we heard one click of his teeth" and instantly the wiry little black-and-tan canine was looking for his next mark, not pausing even briefly to see whether the first rat was dead. "A dog that has been trained to kill 100 rats in a given period of time has no leisure to *look* after his victims," marveled the journalist. " 'He must know by the *feel,*' as Kit said, 'when he bites 'em, that he's done the business for 'em.' "

"In the dialect of the rat-pit, a rat-killing is called an '*Interesting Event*,'" explained the *Tribune* reporter, describing an evening's amusement at Sportsmen's Hall. "The 'killing' is sometimes a match between two dogs, to see which of them can kill a certain number of rats in the shortest time; sometimes it is a sweepstakes, including several dogs, the one killing his rats soonest being the winner, and sometimes it is a 'time match,' that is, a bet is made that a certain dog will kill a given number of rats within a specified time."

The rats released in each heat numbered from five to one thousand—spectators were expected to pay more to see a greater multitude of them murdered. A competitively trained terrier might dispatch as many as one hundred in under forty-five minutes. A few champions, such as "Jack," whose lovingly taxidermied remains decorated Kit's barroom, reportedly did so in less than ten. A night's program thereby necessitated a lot of living rats, for which Burns relied upon a young man, said to have both a "'gift' and a 'mission'" for apprehending them at nearby wharves and slaughter yards. Burns was mysterious about the precise method used to capture them alive. "Lots of folks have tried to find it out, but 't'ain't no use."

"The performance," contemporary observer James Dabney McCabe wrote, after attending a packed rat-baiting contest at Sportsmen's Hall, "is greeted with shouts, oaths, and other frantic demonstrations of delight. Some of the men will catch up the dog in their arms, and press it to their bosom in a frenzy of joy, or kiss it as if it were a human being, unmindful or careless of the fact that all this while the animal is smeared with the blood of its victims. The scene is disgusting beyond description."

A less regular occurrence than rat-baiting, dogfighting was a marquee event at Sportsmen's Hall. The *Tribune* reporter called it the "'royal game' of the dog-pit," but McCabe was less admiring in his description:

Two huge bull-dogs, whose keepers can hardly restrain them, are placed in the pit, and the keeper or backer of each dog crouches in his place, one on the right hand, the other on the left, and the dogs in the middle. At a given signal, the animals are released and the next moment, the combat begins. It is simply sickening. Most of our readers have witnessed a dog fight in the streets. Let them imagine the animals surrounded by a crowd of brutal wretches whose conduct stamps them as beneath the struggling beasts, and they will have a fair idea of the scene at Kit Burns's.

A scheduled fight between two dogs was the culmination of years of training, planning, and a negotiation of terms. Each dog would undergo conditioning on a spinning tabletop surrounded by rival dogs, furiously barking and inciting him to lunge and gallop full speed for hours at a time, until he was a lean mass of muscle. His grit and ferocity would be practiced on a series of unfortunate bait dogs, until his killer technique and timing were perfect. Then his owner would enter a formal written agreement with the owner of another fighter, fixing a date, location, purse, and ground rules for battle—typically including a maximum weight for the matched dogs, the selection of a referee and umpires, the expected conduct of the handlers, the penalty for withdrawal, and the procedure for pre-fight bathing and "tasting" of the animals.

"Tasting" was carried out before and sometimes after a fight, to ensure no pernicious substances were applied to the dogs that might interfere with the biting action of a rival. After bathing (by two men, one representing each separate dog's interests) in hot water, soda, and Castile soap, the dog would be licked and gently bitten all over by its opponent's owner. If anything numbing, caustic, or otherwise harmful had been applied, the owner would lose his entrance fee, according to the standard agreement. The same happened if a dog's weight, within an hour of the match, exceeded the set maximum, since, according to Kit, "[a] difference of a pound, or even a half a pound in weight, would give a dog a great advantage."

The dogs were regularly forced to battle to the bloody death with one another, but in other areas of life they were sometimes treated with great consideration by their owners. At Sportsmen's Hall, the *Tribune* reporter observed, "The choicest dogs are kept in what might be called canine boudoirs up stairs, where they are surrounded with all the comforts of a home and supplied with all the delicacies of the season in which the canine palate delights. They are fed on the most nourishing viands—Kit says his famous dog Belcher has much better food than he eats himself."

As proof of their twisted bond, Kit Burns displayed the stuffed remains of another favored fighting dog, "Hunky," in the Sportsmen's Hall barroom, alongside those of the little ratting terrier, Jack. "The *cognos centi* of Water St. will tell you, with bated breath, that Hunky 'went out game,' first killing his dog, and then dying himself," reported the *Tribune*.

.   .   .

As his society's first year stretched on, Bergh began to experiment with the limits of his authority. In addition to prosecuting cases involving the inhumane transport of calves and the beating—with whips, sticks, cart-rungs, and paving stones—of horses and mules, the ASPCA's agents prosecuted drivers of lame or injured horses, a man who shot a goat, abandoners of horses, men who plucked the feathers from living chickens, and men who dragged or strangulated horses.

There was also the sensational prosecution of Captain Nehemiah H. Calhoun for his cruel conveyance of sea turtles. Bergh served as the prosecution's primary witness, and as recorded by a reporter for the *World,* his opening deposition was forceful and stern. It began with the question of the cords passed through the turtles' fins to immobilize them. "The fin of the turtle consists of flesh, skin and bone," he declared. "The perforation of the skin of a turtle is cruelty; every moment the turtles remained in that condition was attended with pain." As to the matter of their prostrate state, he thundered, "Nature never designed that turtles should be placed on their backs."

For Calhoun's defense, his counsel had scared up a physician named Henry Guernsey. "The composition of the fin of a turtle is similar to that of the hoof of a horse, and is destitute of all power of feeling," the doctor opined, not at all accurately. He added: "The nervous organization of a turtle is of the lowest order." On cross-examination, he became even more dismissive, venturing that "I don't believe that boring a hole through a turtle's leg would inflict more pain than the bite of a mosquito on you or I." As for the obvious fact that the turtles were on the verge of death, Dr. Guernsey blithely said, "Dying is not so painful as toothache," a remark that convulsed the crowded courtroom with laughter.

The outcome of the case, it became clear from the start, would hinge on a question of classification: Did New York's new law against animal cruelty apply to the humble turtle? E. J. Anderson, the counsel for the defense, declared that turtles were not "animals," but instead mere fish, channeling a confusion that bedeviled both the English language and the popular imagination during the mid-nineteenth century. When the legal circus reconvened for a verdict on the following Saturday, June 2, the judge announced that he accepted the defense's argument. A turtle was a fish; Captain Calhoun would walk free.

Nowhere on the docket during the ASPCA's first several months was a case involving dogs. In November of that year, an article appeared in *The New York Herald* demanding the society take notice of the cruelties regularly being practiced at Sportsmen's Hall. "The horse is not the only animal which is made to suffer. They should have the authors of these amusements brought up at our police courts, where no magistrate will dare to let them go unpunished. Where are the police? Where is the Society for the Prevention of Cruelty to Animals?"

Bergh's initial attempts to prosecute dogfighting as animal cruelty were undermined by a lack of support among police and courtroom authorities. Sympathy for the dogfighters and their spectators ran strong among those at all levels of law enforcement, who tended to view the bloody pastime as a hearty, if not quite wholesome, masculine diversion. Long-standing loyalties between the Dead Rabbits gang and the Tammany political machine also made movement against Kit Burns a questionable career move for any servant of the city.

After considerable agitation by Henry Bergh, eight arrests were made at Sportsmen's Hall on December 1, when police interrupted the start of a highly anticipated battle between a dog kept by Burns and another belonging to one William Riordan. Captain Thorne of the 4th Precinct brought the men before Justice Joseph Dowling at the Tombs, charging them with disorderly conduct and disturbing the public peace—for which all but Burns and Riordan were summarily reprimanded and discharged without penalty. The two principals had already been approved for bail pending trial when Bergh appeared in the courtroom, requesting to be allowed to prosecute the defendants for cruelty to animals. The judge denied his petition on the grounds that the police hadn't brought the animal cruelty charge against the men at the outset of the proceeding. According to *The New York Times,* Justice Dowling "suggested, however, that dog fights had frequently occurred at 'Sportsmen's Hall,' and would no doubt again occur, when Mr. Bergh could take whatever action in the premises he might see fit."

. . .

As 1866 drew to a close, it was clear that the city did not quite know what to do with the moral revolution that Henry Bergh was attempting to enact in its streets. In the newspapers, one could see a whole range of reactions—sympathy, admiration, bewilderment, ridicule, and sometimes all of those at once.

The *New-York Tribune,* run by the liberal gadfly Horace Greeley, himself a vegetarian and a founding member of the ASPCA, provided the most consistent endorsement. After the passage of the Animal Cruelty Act, it declared, "Provisions so eminently proper, and so fully warranted by hitherto uncorrected abuses, cannot fail to have the approval of all right-thinking people." The *New-York Atlas,* too, took a broadly sympathetic line: "Every reflecting man of ordinary sensibility will hesitate to cause wanton pain to any creature that possesses feeling, however low it may be on the scale of organic life." The *Times* offered somewhat more conditional support: After Bergh accomplished his first arrest, the paper asked, earnestly, "Who will next imitate this example, and thereby testify to these torturers of brute creation, that their long carnival of cruelty is drawing to a close?" Its support for the cause found its limits in the turtle case. "We urged the formation of this Society, we welcomed its advent, we have sustained nearly all it has done, and we now only fear the effect of public ridicule upon its mistakes."

Many papers, however, did not wait for Bergh to make mistakes before skewering his society's efforts. His most relentless journalistic antagonist over the following decade would be *The World,* under editor Manton Marble, best known during the Civil War for his Confederate sympathies and willingness to publish any unsubstantiated rumor, half truth, or hoax that might damage Lincoln or the Union cause; in 1864, the paper was charged with fraud after its staffers forged a pamphlet in which Republicans supposedly endorsed miscegenation as government policy. Now, with the postwar humane energy of many abolitionists flowing into animal welfare, *The World* weighed in with precisely the sort of jeering and derision that the *Times* had predicted: After the "ineffectual effort to mitigate the tortures of turtles," the paper noted in one story in the wake of the Calhoun case, "Bergh is now melted in the contemplation of the calamities of cattle, over the woes of which he has already shed brine enough to float him."

The most ambitious (and disgusting) act of ridicule came from the *Daily Herald,* which—under the leadership of its founder, James Gordon Bennett Sr.—had developed a reputation for salacious, scandalous, and sometimes poorly substantiated stories, a toxic brew that had won it, by 1866, the highest circulation of any newspaper in America. On May 13, 1866, the paper published a satirical piece entitled "Prevention of Cruelty to Animals—Great Mass Meeting at Union Square," which imagined the city's animals demanding civil rights in the language of Reconstruction-era African American activists and reformers. Eventually, the writer made the point explicit: "The animals, like the abolitionists, are not contented with better treatment than they have ever received before. . . . The negroes, who were groaning under the lash a year or two ago, are now aspiring to seats in Congress, instead of thanking Providence for the boon of freedom. So the animals are no sooner relieved from cruelty than they at once desire to be our masters."

If the editors of the various New York newspapers frequently made light of the ASPCA's mission and methods, the educated readership tended toward a sincere sympathy. And glimmers could already be seen of the approaching future in which women became the engine of the movement for animals around the world. In the very earliest days of Bergh's crusade, he saw a letter to *The Sun* that he clipped and treasured, in which a Brooklyn woman expressed such delight at reading about Bergh's Clinton Hall address that she "cannot resist the inclination to shake hands with you across the East River, by means of pen and ink." She added: "Can we women do anything in the matter? Command us, if we can."

By the time of the society's first annual meeting, its list of two hundred or so members and donors was dotted with women— Mrs. E. C. Collins, Miss Ellen Dolan, Elizabeth Hicks, Mrs. J. F. Kedenburg, Mrs. John B. Murray, and so on; one of them, Antoinette Otto, was almost certainly the famed nineteenth-century opera singer of that name. More interesting still was Cora A. Syme, a philanthropist and labor advocate whose name can also be found in a range of donor lists from the period. In 1866, she was a member of the American Association for the Promotion of Social Science, and she was a donor to a women's rights convention in New York in 1867, her name listed just after Susan B. Anthony's. In these linked donations of a forgotten figure, one can catch a glimpse of the broader spirit that was bringing so many women of the late nineteenth century to a broad array of humanitarian causes— first as quiet supporters, but eventually, over time, as leaders and visionaries.

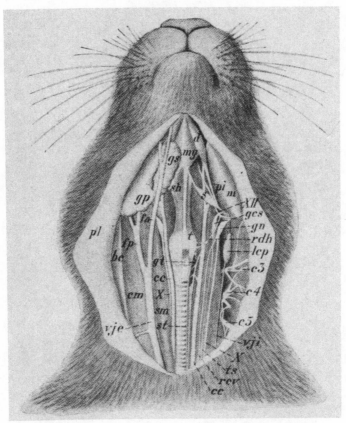

Medical schools used live rabbits—and many other
animals—in painful demonstrations.

Chapter 3

UNDER THE KNIFE

Twelve sets of cranial nerves wire the human head, and medicine has long numbered them by the order, front to back, in which they emerge from the brain stem. The first pair of cranial nerves carries smell, the second sight, the eighth sound; the third, fourth, and sixth control the motion of the eyes. By the mid-1860s, all of this had been known for decades if not centuries, the fruits of medical research dating back to the Roman physician Galen. But untangling the functions of two particular cranial nerves—the fifth and the seventh—posed a riddle that had only somewhat recently been solved. And that solution, to doctors in the budding medical specialty of physiology, had become a symbol of the era's phenomenal progress: of mankind's newfound, and now seemingly boundless, capacity to decode the deepest mysteries of its own anatomy.

This is why medical schools of the era would often supply their doctors-to-be with a demonstration of this finding. The fifth cranial nerve, the professor of physiology would explain, controls the biting and chewing movements of the jaw, but also carries sensation to the entire face; the seventh governs the motion of the upper face, producing facial expression (smiles, scowls, sneers, in humans), while also helping to convey the sense of taste from the mouth. But in facial tissue, the two sets of nerves can be difficult to distinguish, creating dangerous confusion for physicians. For example, in treating a malady that medicine today knows as trigeminal neuralgia—also known by its French moniker, *tic douloureux*—doctors of the era would sometimes sever the wrong nerve, resulting in facial paralysis with no lessening of pain.*

Having explained that much to his students, the professor would produce the subject of the day's demonstration: a rabbit. As the medical students looked on, the professor would anesthetize the animal with ether and then sever a branch of the fifth nerve. Afterward, students could observe the nerve's peculiar functions via their absence: Other than immobility in the jaw on that side, the rabbit could still move its facial muscles normally, and yet much of the region was now entirely devoid of sensation. Often the demonstration would climax with the experimenter poking the rabbit's cornea, in order to show that the eye could feel no pain at all.

The whole display was ultimately fatal to the rabbit, and it added nothing new to the scientific record. Nor was it especially relevant to the young doctors in training for whose benefit it had been staged. In the mid-1860s, there were perhaps seventy medical schools in America, which together graduated well under two thousand doctors per year. Typically an undergraduate education was not required to matriculate. One graduate from later in the century estimated that, of his class of 135 at a medical school in Chicago, only seven had arrived with a college degree in hand; he mirthfully reminisced that "the refined, well-educated, neatly dressed, well-to-do student" in young adulthood found himself learning alongside some "rougher specimen who, after twenty to thirty [years] as a teacher, druggist, traveling salesman or western farmer, had given up his former occupation because he thought he could make more money." The vast majority of graduates would immediately set out their shingle as general practitioners, confronting the full range of human medical needs: catarrh, consumption, cholera, childbirth. Vanishingly few of them would ever need to locate the fifth pair of cranial nerves in a human, let alone a rabbit.

But to New York's physiological researchers—most notably John Call Dalton, of the College of Physicians and Surgeons, and Austin Flint Jr., of Bellevue, the two founding fathers of American physiology—exposing students to these demonstrations was a matter of principle. In 1854, Dalton had been the first American

---

* Today, trigeminal neuralgia can generally be treated with anticonvulsant drugs.

to publish the results of experiments on live animals, and he continued to do so regularly in the pages of what then was the nation's premier medical journal, the *American Journal of the Medical Sciences;* Flint, a decade younger, would follow suit beginning in 1862. Their interest in animal research derived in no small part from the fact that they, like a growing number of American physicians, had spent time in Europe as part of their medical training, absorbing the more scientific attitudes (including the routine use of animal experimentation) that were fast transforming the discipline. The days in which a salesman or farmer could trade up to the credential of doctor would not persist for long, Dalton and Flint knew. Increasingly, to be a doctor was to be a "man of science," a phrase that captured the *professionalization* of science, the sense that science was a realm of knowledge to whose mastery a human intellect must be given over for an entire lifetime.

A lifelong bachelor, Dalton seemed to live only for his work, keeping residence (as a colleague later remembered) "in a tiny suite of rooms, eating quietly at his club, unstirred by the venal ambitions of the roaring world of greedy trade around him in New York." He was a lover of medical literature but also literature full stop, a man as likely to be found with his nose in the *Arabian Nights* as in a medical journal. He was a skilled rider of horses, and as a physician in the Civil War—for which he volunteered immediately after Fort Sumter, joining New York's Seventh Regiment in its rush to secure Washington, D.C., though his time in the field was later cut short by illness—he was reputed for his self-possession under fire. None of the stereotypes of the animal abuser, no cynicism or callousness or sadism, could find any expression in his personality or his biography.

In 1866, after Henry Bergh stepped to that podium in Clinton Hall and included the medical establishment among the perpetrators of cruelty to animals, right alongside drunken coach drivers and dogfight profiteers, John Call Dalton saw the challenge it presented to himself and to the future of medicine more keenly than any other American. To the various roles he had already taken on in his field—physician, professor, researcher, administrator—he very quickly felt obliged to add another: the nation's chief explainer and defender of research on live animals, aka "vivisection."

·   ·   ·

"Of all the horrible pangs inflicted on animal creation, those done in the name of anatomical science are at once the most fearful and revolting, and the most plausibly defended," Bergh had said during his address at Clinton Hall. That last, rueful clause was no doubt informed by the frustration of his colleagues in London, where the fight against research on living animals had been taken up for decades with little success. Not long after the RSPCA's founding, the French physiologist François Magendie had come across the Channel to visit the anatomy school on Great Windmill Street, in Soho, where he carried out a series of controversial demonstrations. Richard Martin, the Irish parliamentarian who had pushed through the nation's historic Cruel Treatment of Cattle Act two years earlier, began recounting one of them while on the stump: an operation on the nervous system of a greyhound, which Magendie then refused to put out of its misery. ("Gentlemen, as the animal cost me so much I must make it the subject of another operation," Martin claimed the Frenchman said. "If my servants take care of the animal to-night, and keep it alive, I shall be able to perform further operations on the other side of the jaw to-morrow.") In the years that followed, scores of English doctors lent their signatures to anti-vivisection petitions, and the RSPCA co-founder Lewis Gompertz, who had left to found his own group, the Animals' Friend Society, offered a cash reward to anyone who could offer evidence leading to the conviction of medical experimenters who "cut up Dumb Animals Alive." But Parliament's anti-cruelty law specifically exempted medical research from its strictures, and by the middle of the century anti-vivisection activism had essentially gone nowhere.

The RSPCA and other advocates for animals continued to include "the vivisectionists" on their lists of habitual offenders, and when Henry Bergh arrived in New York he made sure to do the same. Yet the language of his own anti-cruelty law, let alone the codes of nineteenth-century New York society, would not allow him to haul off doctors from the city's medical laboratories with the same alacrity that he was bringing to the arrest of working-men in the streets. So Bergh began his war against the vivisectors through stealth, sending two ASPCA agents to Bellevue, the city's premier hospital and medical school, to see what they could dig up.

The Bellevue physiology lab was presided over by Flint, the only figure who could rival Dalton's claim to the title of America's pre-eminent physiologist. Like Dalton, Flint was an obsessive reader of the medical literature, and also an enthusiastic animal researcher, who had begun to publish his own experiments on live animals in the early 1860s. He shared Dalton's belief that the demonstration of results on animal specimens was a crucial part of medical education.

Bergh was vague about how his ASPCA agents had gained admittance to the Bellevue physiology department—whether they paid to enroll, or merely slipped into lectures—but he was quick to pass along what they witnessed. One etherized dog had its spleen removed and then was awoken, in Bergh's ominous phrasing, to be "kept alive so long as it could survive the dreadful mutilation." (In reality, dogs, like humans, can survive quite well without their spleens, an important medical fact that this nineteenth-century research might have played some part in shoring up.) In another demonstration performed with no anesthesia at all, a "creature" had its "brain" excised while alive and then its head sewn up; almost certainly Bergh was describing a demonstration innovated by Dalton, who would remove part of the cerebellum of a pigeon in order to show that it could sometimes recover motor functions lost in the immediate aftermath of the excision.

Armed with these and other incidents, Bergh returned to Albany in an attempt to amend the anti-cruelty law, proposing language that would make it the world's first law to regulate medical research on animals. In the ASPCA's first year of operation, he had perceived a number of limitations in the original law and hoped to remedy them too.

The medical establishment quickly rallied against the proposed anti-vivisection amendment, through the eminent personage of John Call Dalton. That December, at a meeting of the New York Academy of Medicine, Dalton delivered a speech with the title "Vivisection: What It Is, and What It Has Accomplished."

"As the subject of vivisection has been recently brought to the public notice in a way calculated to excite especial interest in its merits and demerits," he began, "I have thought it appropriate to make it the topic of a brief address, and to examine the question of its propriety and usefulness, as a means of improvement in the medical art." The oration that followed was anything but brief, with the published version (which appeared two months later) running to nearly 20,000 words. The address presented an impressive, nearly encyclopedic case that animal suffering at human hands was necessary, and had been for centuries, in order for human medicine to move forward. Perhaps most effectively of all, it invoked—through its rhetoric as much as through the facts it marshaled—the emerging moral code of nineteenth-century science. New Yorkers in 1866 may have been primed to understand the immorality of needless animal suffering, but the fight between Bergh and Dalton asked them to answer a more difficult question: What about when animals are asked to suffer in the name of progress?

.   .   .

As Dalton's address made plain, there is no doubt that a great deal of what physiologists knew by 1866—and were still learning, day by day, around the world—derived from animal experiments, many of them painful. How much of that knowledge could have been discovered a different way, especially with the help of today's imaging technologies, is a different question; animal-welfare advocates from Bergh's day onward have put forward ingenious counterfactuals to argue that animal research has been unnecessary for us to enjoy the caliber of health care we do today. In the actual event, however, modern medicine has been built on the suffering and killing of countless innocent animals from the ancient world to our own.

As early as 450 BCE, the Greek physician Alcmaeon of Croton deduced which nerve was the optic nerve by severing it in a living animal and confirming that the creature could no longer see. By 200 BCE, physicians in Alexandria had used vivisection to differentiate between sensory and motor nerves. Not long thereafter, Galen used operations on living animals to illuminate the mechanics of the heart and lungs; he partially severed the spinal cords of other animals to see which parts of their bodies became paralyzed. He

even carried out vivisection on animal brains, attempting to determine which regions were responsible for the movement of various
parts of the body. In his classic book *On Anatomical Procedures*,
he told students to carry out such experiments "without pity or
compassion."

Following a medieval period when animal experimentation fell
out of favor in Europe—in part, ironically enough, because Christian notions about divine creation sowed doubt about how similar
animal and human physiologies really were—the seventeenth century saw experimentation pick up again with vigor. In the 1620s,
Italian physicians were unlocking the secrets of the lymphatic
system through experiments on dogs, while at roughly the same
time, the English scientist William Harvey was doing the same for
the circulation of blood. "In the time of Harvey, two hundred and
forty years ago," Dalton reminded his audience at the New York
Academy of Medicine, "it was believed that blood in the veins
moved from the heart outward toward the extremities," rather than
recoursing toward the heart. Harvey, through a series of vivisections (mostly on rabbits), proved the contrary, and far more than
that.

After Harvey, mystery after mystery fell to the probing knives
of the vivisectionists, as Dalton's address cataloged. There was
respiration—from Robert Boyle, in 1670, who "experimented on
kittens, birds, frogs, snakes, and insects . . . and showed that in
all these animals the presence of atmospheric air is necessary to
the maintenance of life," to Antoine Lavoisier, who in the 1770s
used experiments on sparrows to unlock the composition of air
and the role of oxygen as the key element therein. There was the
role of the periosteum—the outer membrane of bones—in bone
growth, which was established by experiments on birds, pigs, and
later dogs during the late eighteenth and early nineteenth centuries. There was the then-novel practice of blood transfusion, which
James Blundell showed could revive a victim of blood loss, based
on thirty-three experiments on dogs in the late 1810s; in his address,
Dalton pointedly devotes a page to describing in detail the fourteen
then-documented cases of humans saved by transfusion.

And, of course, there was the nervous system, the subject of so
much experimentation in Dalton's day. His address offered lengthy

encomia both to Charles Bell, for his triumph in elucidating the fifth and seventh cranial nerves, and to Magendie, that bugbear of animal lovers on both sides of the Atlantic, who performed a similar trick on the nerves of the spine. Dalton quoted the path-breaking report on this latter experiment at great length, which involved operating on eight puppies: exploring their spinal nerves, severing some at the root, watching the effects over the course of several days.

Why, in an address designed not merely to enlighten his fellow physicians but to win a political debate against the opponents of vivisection, would Dalton give over so much of his address to such an account? The answer, though he might not have put it in these terms, was that assuming an impassive pose toward animal experimentation—not just carrying it out, but doing so routinely, and describing the results for posterity in clinical prose—was central to his own, equally emergent moral faction. In the new ethical code of nineteenth-century science, the ends of laboratory research, even if they amounted to infinitesimal increases in human knowledge, seemed to justify nearly any means when it came to animal pain or death. In many respects the central message that Dalton conveyed to his fellow physicians at the New York Academy of Medicine, just as in his animal demonstrations to young doctors in training, was less his reasoned defense of vivisection than his pose in describing it: the sangfroid and abstraction of the true man of science.

.   .   .

New York's two apostles of physiology had similar biographies, which illustrated the changing nature of nineteenth-century medicine. Both were born in Massachusetts and named for their doctor fathers: Dalton, born in 1825 as one of eight children to a family physician in Chelmsford; Flint, in 1836, as the only child of a more academically inclined doctor in Northampton. Even as late as the 1830s, American medicine was hardly more grounded in science than it had been a hundred years prior; doctors trained at elite universities practiced alongside "bonesetters" (i.e., self-trained orthopedists) as well as adherents to "botanic" medicine, a cultlike

John Call Dalton Austin Flint Jr.

school of proto-naturopathy then sweeping the nation. In 1835, Jacob Bigelow of Harvard famously delivered an address acknowledging that much conventional medical treatment of the era did more harm than good, calling it "the unbiased opinion of most medical men of sound judgment and long experience" that "the amount of death and disaster in the world would be less, if all disease were left to itself."

But the seeds of modern medicine were quietly germinating. In the late 1830s, soon after his son's birth, the elder Flint became one of a different breed of American doctor, the kind that his own son and John Call Dalton would both become as well: one whose career was devoted almost completely to medical research and instruction. In this, they were adopting the self-consciously scientific attitude to medicine that was being pioneered in Europe, and so, for Americans who wanted to take part in that burgeoning school of thought, a stint across the pond became de rigueur. Thus did both Dalton and the younger Flint find their way, during their respective medical training, to the teaching hospital of the Collège de France, known as the Hôtel-Dieu, where they each came under the sway of Claude Bernard, a protégé of François Magendie who would become perhaps the most influential physiologist of the late nineteenth century.

It was at the Hôtel-Dieu, under Magendie and then Bernard, that animal research had become routinized—as part of what the historian Anita Guerrini notes was the first "continuous tradition of systematic experimental research, in which one experiment led to another." It helped that greater Paris was also the epicenter of the nascent field of veterinary medicine, which provided researchers in human medicine with some new intelligence about animal physiology and how it did (and didn't) mirror that of human subjects. Magendie's own research career had begun at Alfort, the most sophisticated of France's veterinary schools, where he developed a practice of constant hands-on exploration in which dead humans and live animals yielded up their mysteries.

By the time he handed over his lab to Bernard, his longtime assistant, in 1854, Magendie had mapped a great deal of the nervous system and divined the functions of various nerves. Bernard went on to illuminate the workings of the pancreas, the underlying pathology of diabetes, and the metabolism of sugar in the liver. "In twenty years," one of his students later noted, "Claude Bernard found more dominating facts, not only than the few French physiologists working beside him, but than all the physiologists in the world."

No record survives of Dalton's course of study with Bernard, but Flint's handwritten notebook from his days at the Hôtel-Dieu can be found in the medical archive of New York University, which inherited Bellevue's archives some years ago. The majority of the thick volume details what he learned from months of instructional rounds with hospital patients, but in the back are Flint's notes on Bernard's physiological lectures, given at the Sorbonne. "M. Bernard appears to be about 40," Flint writes. "He is tall, thin, very black hair and eyes; a fine forehead, and his expression is both pleasing and intellectual. He speaks fluently, and his style, like that of all the teachers here, is strictly didactic and simple."

That "style," as Dalton would exhibit amid the great debates over vivisection, was one of Bernard's great bequests to his pupils. Flint's notes make plain the commanding yet casual manner in which Bernard pulled animals into his physiological demonstrations, somewhat as another teacher might grab for a piece of chalk. In one lecture on the nervous system, Flint writes, Bernard "illustrated his subject by several experiments which were conducted with great neatness and entire success." He enumerated two of these experiments in detail:

1. To illustrate the effect of electricity in inciting contractions of the muscles after death. The current was made to pass through the body of a dead leech. Motions resembling those proper to the living animal were produced. . . .

2. To demonstrate that a current of electricity, passed through a portion of a muscular nerve, excites muscular contractions, without the current being transmitted to the muscular fibres, he killed a frog, separated one of the hind legs from the remainder of the body, and isolated an inch or two of the nerve leading to the separated limb. He then transmitted a current through a segment of the isolated portion of the nerve, and muscular contractions were produced.

A parade of rabbits, pigeons, dogs, and still more frogs followed. It was clear that these specimens were seen in Bernard's laboratory simply as scientific reagents, to be probed and prodded and killed to whatever extent necessary to yield up more knowledge—much as the horse had become an industrial input in late-nineteenth-century cities, to be bred and used and broken at unprecedented speed and scale.

"The physiologist is no ordinary man," Bernard would later write. "He is a scholar, a man who is seized and entirely absorbed by a scientific idea. He does not hear the pain-wrung cries of the creatures. He is blind to the blood that flows. He has nothing before his eyes but his idea, and organisms that are hiding secrets from him which he has means to discover." This attitude, too, he passed along to his American acolytes. One of Dalton's colleagues recalled a story he often told, about how during his stint at the Hôtel-Dieu he once casually remarked to Bernard, on some subject or other, "I think it must be so." Bernard, in Dalton's telling, quickly retorted, "*Think!* Why think, when you can experiment?"—as if the scalpel were an extension of the brain.

·   ·   ·

To those who decried him as an enemy of science, Henry Bergh responded that he did not intend to shut down experimentation entirely. Instead, he pointed out, his objection was entirely to experiments performed on animals without anesthesia. And for all the intemperance of his public remarks, he had attempted to open a genuine dialogue with the city's physicians on the subject. In September 1866, he sent a letter to Edward Delafield, then the president of the College of Physicians and Surgeons, asking "whether the practice of that branch of surgery known as vivisection could not be wholly dispensed with, or so modified, without detriment to science, as to exempt from suffering, by the employment of anæsthetics, the animals operated upon."

But ultimately, in the first skirmish in a bitter war between scientific researchers and animal-welfare activists in America that would last for decades, Henry Bergh and his allies came away with nothing. When the legislature finally took up Bergh's amended bill in the spring of 1867, the vivisectionists would remain above the grip of the law: "Nothing in this act contained," the state senate had added, to Bergh's great consternation, "shall be construed or interfere with any properly conducted scientific experiments or investigations, which experiments shall be performed only under the authority of the Faculty of some regularly incorporated medical college or University of the State of New York."

Even so, Dalton was not entirely satisfied. He himself had written the rider up to the word "investigations," only to have the caveat about colleges and universities added over his objection—he believed that independent medical researchers, even those not associated with any institution, should be free to vivisect with impunity. Like his mentor Claude Bernard, he saw the practice of continual experimentation, including that on animals, to be the right and indeed the duty of the medical scientist.

For all the clinical detachment that defined the vivisectors, perhaps the quality in them most difficult to confront is the *rapture* they sometimes reported falling into during the act of experimentation. Bernard's famous "red notebook," in which he jotted down his research notes between 1850 and 1860, intersperses his clinical findings and anatomical diagrams with high-flown remarks about the "consciousness of God" and the relationship between "science and art, reason and emotion." In an encomium to Dalton after his death, one of his protégés, S. Weir Mitchell, describes the experience of first seeing a beating heart in an anesthetized animal. "The swift certainty of the successive motions of this bounding thing," Mitchell wrote, "filled me at once with a fresh conception of the delicacy and wonder of the vital mechanism amidst which I had been moving, so to speak, with but the slightest realization of its marvel and mystery." Surveying the cut-open animal—its mechanisms testifying both to the glories of Creation and to the power of human intellect in perceiving, for the first time, its inner workings—these men were accessing what seemed like a new and rarefied emotional state, some sublime destination at the intersection of morality, science, and aesthetics.

In June 1867, soon after Dalton's triumph in Albany, he featured prominently in a *New York Herald* article about the city's most eminent doctors. "He illustrates his lectures on the living animal by vivisection," the article noted,

> demonstrating his lessons to the senses, giving to scientific truth the vital reality of fact. It is impossible to overestimate the value of such lessons. Many of the facts of physiology are of such a nature that a single glimpse, one minute's evidence of the senses, is worth years of abstruse study. It is better to see the heart move in the chest than to read a thousand descriptions of its movements. Knowledge gained thus at the expense of a dozen dogs may be the means of saving many human lives. This is one of the humanities of our age.

Over the decades to come, the truth of that judgment would become a matter of bitter disagreement. It was a debate that would pit animal interests against human ones, present-day sacrifices against future advances, demonstrable pain against hypothetical gain. And it would draw a line, even more vividly than the fight between Dalton and Bergh did, between the emerging morality of science and that of the humane reformer.

At his American Museum, P. T. Barnum honed the art
of selling animals as edifying entertainment.

Chapter 4

THE LIVING CURIOSITIES

As the vast glaciers of the last ice age retreated toward the poles some hundred centuries ago, most of the small, playful white whales that had foraged at the southern edge of the glacial mass migrated northward to the Arctic seas. Several thousand stayed behind, having found a bit of stable habitat at the mouth of what would eventually be called the St. Lawrence River, a deep channel of cold, fresh water flowing northeast from the Great Lakes basin to the Gulf of St. Lawrence off the Labrador coast. Here, the mixing of massive liquid volumes causes an upwelling of micronutrients, supporting a diverse food chain. The St. Lawrence beluga whale, cut off from the rest of its species, thrived here for millennia near the apex of the ecological web. During summers, female belugas and their young ascended the tidal river while a mostly male population of adults swam near its mouth. In the winter, both groups retreated to the loose-pack ice regions of the lower estuary and gulf.

Singing, squeaking, squealing, chirping, clicking, whistling, whirring, and mooing to one another, beluga whales form a noisy society. Their varied vocalizations resound through air and water, as well as the hulls of ships, inspiring the old sailors to call them "sea canaries." Beluga pods range in size from a few individuals to a few dozen, and their social affiliations are loose, often transient. Together, sometimes in perfect synchronization, their white bodies slip through the water forward, backward, surfacing, spouting, and diving—sometimes deeper than twenty meters below the surface—in pursuit of a variety of prey: big fish, like salmon and cod, but also sandworms, shellfish, squid, octopuses, and schools of little fish. When the whales are not chasing meals, they often chase one another, in what scientists describe as social locomotor play. Belugas are among the species that researchers have observed playing with toys in the wild, including found objects, exhaled bubbles, and living things found in their waters.

Orcas were the principal predators of beluga whales in the St. Lawrence River until humans migrated to its shores. Then, for at least several thousand years, indigenous people hunted the beluga from open-top canoes, driving them into the shallows and dispatching them with spears. When French explorer Jacques Cartier made his second exploratory voyage up the St. Lawrence in 1535, he noted the presence of both the Iroquois hunters and the snow-white whales, describing the latter as delicious. Basque sailors joined the beluga hunt in the 1600s, building fixed weir nets on the mudflats near the river's mouth; when the tides went out, the whales would get trapped in the meshings and become easy prey for the hunters. French colonists followed, and, after receiving a white-whale fishing concession from French administrators, many found the commercial harvest of whales for their oil and skins to be a lucrative occupation. The introduction of harpoons and guns in the nineteenth century accelerated the slaughter, and, thereafter, the local whale population suffered a steep decline.

Even when the species was still common on the St. Lawrence River, the beluga whale was an extreme oddity to the landlubbing New Yorker, several hundred miles to the south. The creature's slippery, deep-sea strangeness, its perfect pallor, its size, its thrilling association with ancient tales, its incongruity in the industrial dry-land cityscape ensured that, should one ever splash within city limits, the populace would be helpless to look away from the spectacle. Is it any wonder, then, that the idea of bringing a beluga whale to the heart of the metropolis, to be feasted upon by the public gaze, became an animating ambition of museum owner and impresario Phineas Taylor Barnum? As he would later recall in his autobiography:

In 1861, I learned that some fishermen at the mouth of the St. Lawrence had succeeded in capturing a living white whale, and I was also informed that a whale of this kind, if placed in a box lined with sea-weed and partially filled with salt water, could be transported by land to a considerable distance, and be kept alive. It was simply necessary that an attendant, supplied with a barrel of salt water and a sponge should keep the mouth and blow-hole of the whale constantly moist. It seemed incredible that a living whale could be "expressed" by railroad on a five-days' journey, and although I knew nothing of the white whale or its habits, since I had never seen one, I determined to experiment in that direction. Landsman that I was, I believed that I was quite as competent as a St. Lawrence fisherman to superintend the capture and transport of a live white whale.

And so the beleaguered St. Lawrence beluga had a new enemy: the American showman, who would stop at nothing to have the charismatic cetacean on display in his museum. As with his other animal attractions, Barnum seemed to relish the challenges of capturing and conveying the whales to New York—elaborately griping to reporters about the hardships and expenses he suffered in the effort, reinforcing the rarity and value of the animals to a breathless public eager for new amusements.

After preparing an eighteen-by-forty-foot tank made of brick and cement in the basement of his American Museum—for "the reception of the marine monsters"—Barnum himself undertook the trip to French Canada, where he contracted local fishermen to assist in the capture of at least two beluga whales. They constructed a large V-shaped weir, or "kraal," made with wooden stakes, and waited several days for two whales to enter the trap together during high tide. When a beluga pair finally wandered into the stockade, fishing boats blocked their retreat with splashing and yells until the tide went out, so that, in Barnum's description, "the frightened whales would find themselves nearly 'high and dry,' or with too little water to enable them to swim, and their capture would be the next thing in order." The fishermen secured heavy ropes around the whales' tailfins and dragged the helpless creatures out of the water and into separate seaweed-lined wooden crates. The crates were then loaded onto a sloop and sailed upriver to Quebec City, where they were loaded onto the special railcar Barnum had hired for the long trip back to New York. The showman had already provided a thrilling account of the whale hunt to newspapers in Quebec and Montreal, and telegraphed communities along the train route announcing the impending arrival of the crated whales. "The result of these arrangements may be imagined: at every station crowds of people came to the cars to see the whales which were traveling by land to Barnum's Museum," Barnum crowed, "and I thus secured a tremendous advertisement, seven hundred miles long, for the American Museum." Upon the belugas' arrival at their destination, a writer for the *New-York Tribune* gushed, a "real live whale is as great a curiosity as a live lord or prince, being much more difficult to catch, and far more wonderful in its appearance and habits."

Barnum's advance publicity effort ensured that by the time the whales sloshed into their ice-cooled tank, in the dank basement of the American Museum, thousands of New Yorkers crowded the entrance, impatient to lay eyes on the great "white whales." They would have to hurry: These two belugas would not be at the museum long. "I did not know how to feed or take care of the monsters, and, moreover, they were in fresh water, and this, with the bad air in the basement, may have hastened their death, which occurred a few days after their arrival, but not before thousands of people had seen them," wrote Barnum, with evident overall satisfaction, in one of his autobiographies.

Barnum being Barnum, he "resolved to try again." Weeks later, he had installed a new tank made of slate and thick glass plates, twenty-four feet square, on the museum's more commodious second floor. Fresh water from city taps was replaced with murky brackish water from the mouth of the East River; Barnum had situated a steam-powered pumping apparatus at the harbor's edge and laid a network of iron pipes under city streets (with the purchased permission of a Manhattan alderman) to ensure that his next two Labrador whales bobbed before visitors in a circulating supply of untreated harbor water. Alas, these whales quickly died as well— "their sudden and immense popularity was too much for them," Barnum later quipped. If museum visitors were troubled by the serial cetacean fatalities, it did not deter them from paying their twenty-five-cent admission fees and lingering in the second-floor

BARNUM'S AMERICAN MUSEUM.

Christmas and New Year Holiday Bill.

The Manager has been determined to make these Holidays the most attractive and bewitching of any of their predecessors, and trusts that the following combination of Novelties, Curiosities, and Dramatic Entertainments, will prove this determination successful.

THE GREAT
LIVING WHALE

From the Coast of Labrador is alone a wonder worthy the attention of every educated and scientific person, as well as the merely curious. He is seen at all hours swimming about his large tank in all his native grace and grandeur.

THE LIVING
HIPPOPOTAMUS

From the River Nile in Egypt, the great Behemoth of the Scriptures, see Job, chap. 40, is the first and only one of these colossal animals ever brought to America, and the greatest wonder of the world.

SIGNOR PIETRO D'OLIVERA'S
200 EDUCATED WHITE RATS

Perform a great variety of amusing and interesting tricks ; Children especially find this exhibition replete with interest.

The Aquarial Garden,

Occupying one of the large Halls of the Museum, is of itself an Exhibition worth more than the cost of Admission to the entire Museum. Its numerous crystal ponds of River and Ocean water, abounding with Living Fish from nearly every River and Sea, are alive with interest to all classes. One tank has 8 LARGE SPECKLED BROOK TROUT, the largest and finest ever seen together; another has 12 BEAUTIFUL SEA HORSES, the most interesting tiny inhabitants of the great deep, the heads and necks of which resemble, in their graceful curves, those of the horse. No visitor should fail seeing them. Indeed, every tank in the entire collection is replete with interest.

THE LIVING HAPPY FAMILY
In the upper Saloon, is always surrounded with a crowd of smiling faces.

THE LIVING MONSTER SNAKES are more wonderful than pleasing, yet always surrounded by crowds of interested spectators.

THE LIVING LEARNED SEAL is regarded universally, as a *"Beautiful Creature !"* and his sparkling eyes are the admiration, if not the envy, of many of his fair admirers. These, and many more curiosities, are all to be seen at all hours, while EVERY AFTERNOON AND EVENING during the entire Holiday Season there will be

SUPERB DRAMATIC PERFORMANCES,

and on CHRISTMAS AND NEW YEAR DAYS these Performances will be given nearly EVERY HOUR, Day and Evening, that every visitor shall be enabled to see one such performance, as well as all the Curiosities.

☞ To add still further to the interest of THIS GREAT FESTIVE SEASON, the Manager has expended over Seven Thousand Dollars in the preparation of a New Holiday Piece, never before seen in America, entitled,

THE BOWER OF BEAUTY,
OR, THE
HOME OF THE FAIRIES
In the Enchanted Forest, in which occurs a
GORGEOUS MECHANICAL SCENE
By Randall, of London, in which appear
40 BEAUTIFUL YOUNG LADIES,
NYMPHS OF THE AIR.

This scene will be one of dazzling splendor, the most magnificent thing of its kind ever gotten up in this country, and will alone repay fourfold the cost of admission to the entire Museum. It will be produced every Afternoon and Evening during the entire Holiday season, and at each performance on Christmas and New Year days.

Admission to all only 25 cts. Children under 10 years, 15 cts.

Wynkoop, Hallenbeck & Thomas, Book and Job Printers, 113 Fulton St., N. Y.

Barnum's American Museum handbill, 1864.

galleries to behold their short-term antics. And so, Barnum continued to exhibit whales on the second floor of his museum, one
pair after another, in cheerful, morbid succession. "NOW IS THE
TIME to see these wonders," declared a newspaper advertisement
announcing the most recent arrivals in 1865, "as THEIR LIVES
ARE UNCERTAIN."

It is disconcerting to see that phrase there, in stark capital letters, and to imagine how little it seemed to have troubled the moral
sense of the man who paid to have it printed—to say nothing of
the countless men, women, and children drawn to the museum in
droves by this grim sales pitch. Perhaps the most charitable way
to imagine it is that the possibility of seeing a whale in New York
City stimulated a curiosity so implacable—the irresistible pull, in
an era before it was easy to visit zoos or aquaria or travel long
distances, of seeing creatures that had been brought so far, with a
physiology so enormous and strange—that the moral sense could
not be engaged. But that supposition makes it all the more remarkable that, by the following year, the arrival of the animal-welfare
idea would render such flagrant disregard for animal suffering and
death in a New York newspaper advertisement nearly inconceivable: arguably illegal, but perhaps more important, unfashionable.

The moral awakening would arrive too late to help any of the
animals in Barnum's five-story museum. On July 13, 1865, not
long after noon, a fire ignited in the basement of the building, at
Broadway and Anne Street, where a wood-fed steam engine powered the museum's ventilation fans and aquarium pumps. It spread
quickly, as flammable objects including taxidermied birds, old oil
paintings, wax likenesses of historical figures (including a recently
added figure of Jefferson Davis dressed in women's petticoats), and
three Egyptian mummies fueled the conflagration. Within minutes,
visitors descending the main staircase from the third-floor lecture hall observed smoke billowing around the mighty feet of the
stuffed elephant near the whale tank. Fortunately, the morning's
performance—which, that summer, might have featured a glass-
blowing demonstration, a one-legged dancer, or an unusually cor-
pulent woman—had just let out, and most of the morning's four
hundred or so visitors were already in the process of exiting the

building. Museum staff, including various persons on display as living "curiosities," made a frantic evacuation, grabbing personal effects and portable exhibited items as they fled.

Samuel Hurd, Barnum's manager on-site, after seeing the last customers out the door, directed the remaining staff to ready the museum's great water pumps and hoses to inundate the galleries, and rushed to the office to move important documents, bonds, and rolls of cash from Barnum's desk to a fireproof safe. Police arrived in a brave attempt to secure Barnum's treasures from looting, but not a few of his "one million objects" nonetheless made their way from the building into oblivion. Pandemonium reigned outside; arriving volunteer fire brigades had to fight their way through unruly crowds toward the spreading inferno. Thirty thousand New Yorkers gathered at the convergence of Broadway, Park Row, Vesey, and Ann Streets, blocking traffic and crowding the steps of St. Paul's chapel and the southwestern tip of City Hall Park. Pickpockets crept profitably among the throngs riveted by the destructive blaze.

Firefighters raised ladders, scrambled up the sides of the building, and crashed through windows onto the museum's upper floors. For less than half an hour, before the "laddies" were forced to retreat, they swung their axes and shouted at one another through their trumpets as they tried in vain to slow the conflagration. Desperation mounted quickly, so who knows how much hesitation those battling the blaze on the second floor experienced before they smashed their axes against the thick glass panels of the steaming whale exhibit. They hoped the cascading mass of murky water would douse the burning floors of the grand saloon, extinguishing the flames, and so they sacrificed the helpless inhabitants of the tank: The next day's *New York Times* reported that "the leviathan natives of Labrador, when last seen, were floundering in mortal agony." This last-ditch maneuver by the firefighters proved to be insufficient, however, and the museum was lost.

Amazingly, no human lives were claimed in the fire, but plenty of animals died in company with the whales. Only one animal escaped from Barnum's American Museum with its life: Ned, "the Learned Seal." Among those lost to the hungry flames were aquaria filled with exotic fish, alligators, and an electric eel, as well as monkeys,

rodents, dogs, cats, tropical birds, a porcupine, a large collection
of snakes, and a solitary kangaroo. "Almost in the twinkling of an
eye, the dirty, ill-shaped structure, filled with specimens so full of
suggestion and of merit, passed from our gaze," the *Times* intoned,
mourning the loss of an institution that "opened to us the secrets
of the earth, and revealed to us the mysteries of the past," as well
as one that "afforded men of learning and of science opportunities
for investigation and research."

When the Ann Street side of the building eventually collapsed,
amidst the blackened wreckage that spilled from the edifice onto the
sidewalk were the enormous bodies of the two Labrador whales.
Barnum, who traveled from Connecticut the next day to view the
smoking remains of his museum, catalogued them, with a sniff of
disgust, among his prodigious material losses. What was left of the
once-magnificent whales lingered there beside the street for days,
rotting, stinking, and drawing vermin, offering one last curiosity
for New Yorkers to gawk at, for free.

.   .   .

The small, staid town of Bethel—known in the early nineteenth
century mainly for the efficient productivity of its hat-, shoe-,
and comb-making factories and the fervor of its Congregational-
ist church—may seem like an unlikely birthplace for the man who
would become the king of American showmen, but Phineas Taylor
Barnum ("P.T." in public life, but "Taylor" or "Tale" to his friends)
identified strongly as a Connecticut Yankee, and embodied the values of industry, cleverness, and sharp humor prized by the New
Englanders he grew up with. At age eighteen, having already tried
his hand at farmwork, cattle-driving, shop-clerking, operating a
cash lottery, and keeping a tavern in Brooklyn, among other occupations, Barnum used his entire accumulated savings of $120 to
open a small fruit and confectionery store out of one half of his
grandfather's carriage house in his hometown. Soon enough, he
expanded his little shop into a dry-goods emporium, scaled up his
lottery operation, married, established a newspaper (largely as a
propaganda organ to battle state legislative efforts to limit lotter-

ies), served jail time for libel, became a father, and moved with his family to New York.

Barnum's initial entertainment gambit was deeply ignoble, but nonetheless successful: he exhibited an enslaved African American woman, aged and disabled, claiming she was the 161-year-old nursemaid of George Washington. The turning point came in 1841, when he acquired Scudder's American Museum, a somewhat dreary collection of moth-eaten taxidermy, seashells, wax figures (including one ostensibly rendered headless by the authentic French guillotine standing beside it), panoramic oil paintings, and the like, and revolutionized the institution from the inside out. Advertising, in the form of illustrated posters and handbills, flooded the city. Barnum cultivated relationships with New York newspapermen running daily and weekly papers to ensure that alongside paid notices of current attractions offered by the museum there were fawning public-interest articles and glowing editorial reviews. The museum edifice was festooned with banners announcing the exhibitions inside, while an off-key orchestra played persistently from a balcony overlooking Broadway, and barkers prevailed on passersby to come inside.

For those who crossed the threshold, Barnum provided an elaborate bounty of entertainments. He acquired artifact after artifact and crammed them in among Scudder's specimens. He put on display a working steam engine made of glass, a weaving loom powered by a dog, a replica of Niagara Falls ("with real water!"), wonderful automatons, "educated fleas," and complicated knitting machines. Barnum displayed genuine ceramics from Pompeii and Native American ceremonial objects, alongside the trunk of a tree under which Jesus's disciples were dubiously claimed to have rested and the club that supposedly killed Captain Cook. He renovated the lecture room, which had previously hosted dry discourses on scientific topics, and presented onstage entertainments including musical performers, magicians, a full-scale dramatization of *Uncle Tom's Cabin*, puppet shows, exclusive appearances by human beings who were unusually large, small, hairy, tattooed, pigmented, fat, thin, or conjoined—but always a central attraction were the *Real! Live! Animals!*

His early animal exhibits relied heavily on his so-called "humbug,"
a practice he elevated from mere deception to artful enticement:
"'Humbug' consists in putting on glittering appearances—outside
show—novel expedients, by which to suddenly arrest public attention, and attract the public eye and ear," Barnum explained in a
manual he wrote on the subject. The year after he took over the
museum, Barnum drew wide notice for a creative taxidermy display dubbed "The Feegee Mermaid," consisting of the desiccated
upper body of a female primate stitched carefully onto the stiff-
ened lower body of a fish. Barnum first billed the hideous item
as a genuine biological specimen, but later as an object of deep
controversy, ultimately claiming that his paying public relished the
pleasure of scrutinizing the carcass and formulating an independent opinion about the mermaid's authenticity. Barnum relied on
similar tactics to attract a crowd to a "Grand Buffalo Hunt," which
turned out to be nothing more than a few unkempt, undernour-
ished bison penned on the New Jersey side of the Hudson, and
the exhibition, at the museum, of a "woolly horse," which was a
fuzzier version of a regular horse, ostensibly (but not actually) representing a new "complex" species discovered by John C. Frémont
during his famous Rocky Mountain expedition. When Frémont's
father-in-law, a U.S. senator, sued Barnum for fraudulent use of
Frémont's name, museum tickets continued to sell briskly to those
who wanted to observe the object of outrage for themselves.

After a triumphant tour of Europe with the charismatic two-
foot-tall child star General Tom Thumb, Barnum was able to
acquire genuine animal marvels for his museum back home. From
the Royal Surrey Zoological Garden in London, Barnum purchased
a female orangutan for $3,000. Upon her 1846 arrival in New York,
"M'lle Jane" was heralded as the "only living Orang Outang in
either England or America," and the *Tribune* pronounced her "a
curiosity worthy [of] all lovers of natural history." Although it
would be more than ten years before Charles Darwin and Alfred
Russel Wallace would propose the evolutionary mechanism of natural selection, Americans were already buzzing with the idea of
evolution through transmutation of species as described in an
anonymously published 1844 bestseller, *Vestiges of the Natural
History of Creation*. Barnum boldly promoted his orangutan as

the apparent "Grand Connecting Link between the two great families, the Human and Brute Creation." "No Orang Outang ever brought to this country has ever excited such general interest as this chimpanzee," declared a reporter for *The Evening Post,* confusingly, about the ape.

By the 1850s, Barnum's successes had allowed him to diversify his interests. He acquired additional museums in New York, Philadelphia, and Baltimore, and, in 1851, launched the "Asiatic Caravan, Museum, and Menagerie," a traveling extravaganza featuring Tom Thumb, an Egyptian mummy, the ten elephants Barnum's agents had hijacked from their herd in Ceylon, six "beautiful lions! fresh from their native forests," and a variety of other charismatic creatures displayed under a big-top tent. Several of these would periodically appear on exhibit at the American Museum during the 1850s, including a mature male Indian rhinoceros ("the unicorn of the Holy Writ"), a pair of giraffes (the "cameloleopards" Colossus and Cleopatra), and a twenty-three-foot boa constrictor ("the prince of serpents"). In 1860, Barnum sponsored an East Coast tour for the "Grizzly Adams California Menagerie and Traveling Show," a collection of native California wildlife that Adams claimed to have captured personally: bears, wolves, mountain lions, buffalo, elk, and a sea lion named Old Neptune. In 1865, the untimely demise of Barnum's first pair of beluga whales left a prodigious vacancy in his unhealthy basement aquarium, and so he quickly installed another living wonder without precedent: an enormous hippopotamus, apparently the first of its species to be exhibited alive in North America.

P. T. Barnum, circa 1861.

Among the ill-fated amphibious mammals exhibited by Barnum, it was Ned who best embodied the plucky persistence of the impresario himself. Ned was sometimes known as "the learned seal," and sometimes as "the educated seal," but in either case his schooling took place before he arrived in the unhappy confines of the American Museum. He and another harbor seal, Fanny, were acquired as pups by James Ambrose Cutting of Boston, who, after a successful career as a photographer and inventor, invested his wealth into the creation of a grand public aquarium, the first of its kind. At its opening in 1859, a handbill announced the Aquarial Gardens to be "the latest novelty in the world of popular science . . . an extraordinary addition to the circle of fascinating, yet interesting and exceedingly instructive amusements." Glass aquaria held "corallines and polyps, water-soldiers and hermit-crabs, sea cucumbers and starfish, water-beetles and sea mice," but Ned and Fanny quickly became the star attraction. Cutting trained them himself, as described in the souvenir booklet, *The Domestic History of the Learned Seals, "Ned" and "Fanny,"* using exclusively positive, reward-based methods. He found them to be apt pupils, intelligent and willing, with excellent memories. Fanny learned to perform vignettes of physical comedy, such as pretending to be asleep, snoring loudly, and then startling awake, while Ned performed more complex sequences like taking a bath on command, obsequiously bowing to the crowd, shouldering a rifle(!), and grinding a hand organ. This last was apparently his favorite, as he reportedly would pick up the instrument and energetically play it whenever he found the apparatus lying about, day or night.

The Domestic History of the Learned Seals portrays Ned's early life as intensely humane, and the closing paragraph of the booklet expresses unusual optimism about his and Fanny's future.

[W]e are well assured, after months of daily observance of this "interesting couple," that their domesticity and intelligence are beyond those of any animal we have seen below the rank of man in the scale of animate creation, and their affection is equal to either their docility or their intelligence. The visitor to the Gardens will have observed how their bright eyes beam with joy at the sound of Mr. Cutting's step or voice. This pleasure is manifested even more strongly when he is alone with them, then when he greets them in the presence of visitors. We can assure the reader that the expression of delight that illuminates the "bright black eyes" of "Ned" and "Fanny" as Mr.

Cutting approaches them *is no part of their performance*. It is a genuine expression of joy, springing from an intercourse, the giving and receiving of instruction, that has been marred by no unpleasant episode.

Sadly, the ambitious expansion of the Aquarial Gardens led to its insolvency. Buried in debt, Cutting and his partner sold the enterprise to P. T. Barnum in early 1862. Remodeled and reimagined as Barnum's Aquarial Gardens, the attraction reopened in June of that year with a miscellany of new exhibits and a diverse bill of entertainments for the months that followed: demonstrations of laughing gas, serpent wrestling, a baby show, and, of course, General Tom Thumb. Ned and Fanny continued to perform their old gags under new management for a time, but eventually Ned was relocated, without Fanny, to the American Museum in New York.

On July 13, 1865, the day of the disastrous fire, Ned was in his second-floor enclosure when the flames began to move through the museum. According to the memoirist Thomas Floyd-Jones, Ned was saved from the conflagration by one Clifford Pearson, a Brooklyn firefighter. "He took it under his arm, and going down Fulton Street to the market, put it in Alfred Dorlon's fishtrough." One can picture Pearson in his heroic moment, bustling about the burning second floor of Barnum's American Museum, buttoned into his firefighter uniform, as he locks eyes with Ned, who returns his gaze with open intelligence and trust. Perhaps Pearson, in deciding Ned was owed a rescue, saw in those "bright black eyes" what Cutter had seen years earlier.

.   .   .

And what did the paying customers see when they gazed upon the creatures in Barnum's museum? What kept them coming back to gawk? As lurid as his exhibitions may sound today, exotic animals—in marked contrast to the everyday bestiary outside, which, in the clamor of their footfalls, the stench of their excrement, the occasional danger they posed to life and limb, embodied all that was mean and unsalubrious about urban life—had come to represent a kind of refinement, even enlightenment. The living and dead specimens that burned with Barnum's museum in 1865 might have been curated with less scientific rigor than the collection destroyed the following year, when a fire at a medical college on 14th Street consumed the New York Lyceum of Natural History's extensive repository of reptile and fish specimens, but the appeal to the general public was not dissimilar. The subject was seen as so edifying, and as such an urgent subject of public interest, that the American Museum of Natural History was founded just a few years later; meanwhile, an ad hoc proto-zoo was just then growing up in Central Park, with wealthy city residents donating hundreds of live animals to feed the public fascination.

One can chalk up this fascination in part to the same human desire for novelty, for seeing what one has never seen before, that would propel Barnum's whole career, but there was something deeper too—a burgeoning sense that the animal kingdom and its taxonomy could help unlock the deepest secrets of the natural world. Throughout the 1860s, brochures for the traveling menagerie run by Isaac Van Amburgh, the legendary lion tamer, would begin with an homage to this noble new field of knowledge: "There is no study that is more important to the youth of a rising generation, or to adult age, than that of Natural History. It teaches man his superiority over the brute creation, and creates in his bosom a knowledge of the wisdom and goodness, and omnipresence of a supreme and All-wise Creator."

An appreciation of exotic animals redounded not just to the glory of God and the service of science but to the power of nineteenth-century industry and imperialism; it was impossible to disentangle the romance of animal exhibitions from the colonial exploits that had helped bring the specimens across oceans. In England, where Barnum acquired so many of his attractions, the exotic animal trade was intimately bound up with empire; by the 1830s the London Zoo had begun making a habit of exhibiting native animal keepers from Africa and Asia alongside the animals themselves, the humans becoming as much of a spectacle as the creatures. (The imperial connection extended to the acquisition of research, of course, not just specimens—the HMS *Beagle,* it must not be forgotten, was a sloop of the Royal Navy and its fateful tour of South America an imperial surveying trip, conducted with one scientist and ten guns onboard.) When Barnum wanted elephants in 1850, he dispatched two of his agents to Sri Lanka, which was then the British territory of Ceylon; with the colonial governor's blessing, they enlisted a platoon of natives to ply their elephant-rustling skills, which involved using shouts and gunfire to pen in an unwitting herd and then attaching ropes to their legs. Of the nine specimens that Barnum's agents succeeded in absconding with, one died on the 12,000-mile journey, and its body was thrown overboard just past the Cape of Good Hope.

Barnum's exhibitions played to all these fascinations, and yet his obsessive imagination added another kind of appeal. Where the natural historian yearned to turn each creature into a perfect representative of its species, Barnum the showman pushed to make each of his as special as possible—he could not stop himself from imbuing his animals with what can only be described as *personality*. Hence all those "learned" seals and "educated" fleas. Hence those whimsical animal names, like that of Cleopatra the giraffe, which created a whole imaginative construct through which to project a character onto her—when Barnum took her to Brooklyn for an engagement, the *Tribune* described her exit in this regal language (likely suggested to the paper, if not literally penned, by Barnum): "The distinguished African, being too delicately constituted to endure the chill air of this northern clime, was wrapped up with the greatest care, and conducted by her keepers from the Museum into a carriage provided for her especial accommodation."

Perhaps the most remarkable illustration of this tendency was an exhibit called "The Happy Family," which Barnum kept up in some form over most of his long career in animal exhibition. This consisted of a single large cage in which scores of different animals— the version that burned up in 1865 had more than sixty—lived together in what Barnum claimed was perfect harmony, "contentedly playing and frolicking together, without injury or discord," despite some of the animals being natural predators of the others. From the perspective of natural history, it was a farce, and as humane animal husbandry, it was an abomination: Newspapers loved to describe, in lurid detail, the not-infrequent incidents in which one member of the supposedly happy household would eviscerate another. But Barnum, who cared a great deal about husbandry *and* loved to claim (at least when it served his purposes) the mantle of science, couldn't keep himself from creating and recreating this same purportedly magical tableau, in which the laws of nature had somehow been suspended.

For reasons that were not entirely coincidental, Henry Bergh began his defense of animals at precisely the time that the worlds of science and spectacle in America were definitively parting ways. During the first half of the century, a figure like Scudder or Barnum could apply the word "museum" to his uneasy mélange of live and dead animals (and humans), with placards offering a blend of true natural-historical facts, dubious pseudoscience, and outright hokum, and somehow come out the other side with not just profitability but a strange sort of respectability intact.

But by the end of the 1850s, American science had come into its own, both in the nation's institutions of higher learning and also in the public esteem—thanks to the emergence of popular public lecturers like the Swiss-born scientist Louis Agassiz. During his early career in Europe, Agassiz had built a reputation as a meticulous cataloger of extant and extinct freshwater fishes, after which he set out to prove and popularize the theory that a series of glacial ice ages defined the earth's geological past. Upon immigrating to the United States and joining the faculty at Harvard College, he became America's most famous and well-respected scientist.*

This coalescing scientific community began to seize the mantle of the "museum" for itself, most notably with Agassiz's founding of a natural history museum at Harvard in 1852, and then the founding in Washington, D.C., of the United States National Museum, now known as the Smithsonian Institution, in 1857. If Americans wanted to look to natural history to learn their "superiority over the brute creation," they would not do so for much longer at institutions like Barnum's American Museum. In fact, just months after

---

* This despite the fact that, even amid Darwin's discoveries, Agassiz's scientific worldview remained a fundamentally creationist one, including a truly noxious view on human racial origins.

his first, rancorous battle with Henry Bergh, Barnum would never own a "museum" again.

. . .

The summer after the fire, Barnum rented a new space on Broadway near Spring Street, on the site of what once had been the Chinese Museum. Soon thereafter, Isaac Van Amburgh died suddenly in Philadelphia, and Barnum did not hesitate to snap up the animal collection of his former competitor. By December 1866, what had begun as Barnum's New American Museum now sported the ungainly moniker of Barnum & Van Amburgh's Museum and Menagerie Combination; an advertisement from the first of that month promised visitors "the ENTIRE VAN AMBURGH COLLECTION of living WILD ANIMALS, consisting of Elephants, Double Humped Bactrian Camel, Royal Bengal Tiger, White Himalaya Mountain Bear, Silver-Striped Hyena, Lions, Tigers, Leopards, Bears, Wolves, Sacred Cattle, Tapir, Panthers, Zebra, Ibex, Performing Mules [by two weeks later, they will have become "Wonderfully Educated Mules"], Ostrich, Deer, Pelicans, Monkeys, etc., and over 200 Australian birds."

A few lines down, there appeared this promise: "The Animals will be fed in presence of visitors at 12 o'clock, noon." And here is where Barnum's troubles with Henry Bergh began.

While laying down the groundwork for his animal-welfare campaign, Bergh had not ranked animal exhibitions highly, if at all, in his tallies of the worst offenders. But the killing of animals for entertainment sat invariably at the very top. Newspaper accounts of his inaugural address at Clinton Hall lingered on his account of those fateful bullfights that he and Catherine had witnessed in Spain, and his description of the delighted family sitting next to them, including the lovely daughters who, rather than "shudder and avert their eyes from the horrid butchery," instead seemed entirely seized by "joy and admiration" for the torero and his murderous exploits in the ring. This was the essence of cruelism, as Bergh defined it: animal suffering that eroded the moral character of the humans who witnessed it.

Therefore, when accounts of the public feedings at Barnum's

new museum began to trickle back to him, in particular, about the museum's boa constrictor, which was being fed live rabbits as museum-goers looked on, he did not much care whether this was proper snake husbandry or not. This, to Bergh, was blood sport. After personally visiting the museum to protest the practice, with no good result, he fired off a letter to Barnum on December 11. "It may be urged that these reptiles will not eat dead food—in reply to this I have to say, then let them starve." But, he added, "I am satisfied that this assertion is false in theory and practice, for no living creature will allow itself to perish of hunger, with food before it."

Bergh closed his letter with a warning: "On the next occurrence of this cruel exhibition, this Society will take legal measures to punish the perpetrators of it."

Barnum was traveling out west when this threatening missive arrived, but his managers took it extremely seriously. On December 29, the museum's snake tamer and his assistant packed up the boa in a trunk and removed it to Jersey City, along with two boxes full of suitable live prey. There they remained for two days in a rented hotel room, safely outside the ASPCA's jurisdiction, as the snake devoured five rabbits, two chickens, three pigeons, and four guinea pigs. (It was only upon checking out, according to a story in the Commercial Advertiser, which reported on the sojourn the following week, that the museum staffers revealed to the hotel's proprietor the contents of their trunk.)

On the scientific merits, Barnum had the better part of the argument, especially as regards Bergh's claim that "no living creature will allow itself to perish of hunger, with food before it." Snakes invariably eat whole, intact prey: mammals, birds, fish, invertebrates, other reptiles, and sometimes eggs, but they, particularly the larger-bodied species like the boa constrictor, eat infrequently, and are capable of surviving many months without a mouthful. When exposed to the wrong environmental temperature or humidity, or provided with inadequate space or inappropriate substrate, a snake might decline to accept any offered food, even after a prolonged fast. And, while it is now understood that captive snakes can, and should, be trained to receive dead animals in place of live ones—thereby making them less vulnerable to injuries inflicted by aggressive, frightened, or hungry prey—the wild-caught serpents in Barnum's museum would almost certainly not have been taught to accept pre-killed critters.

Barnum took great pride in his living specimens, especially the rare and temperamental ones. Indeed, as noted above, he publicized not only the expense and difficulty of their acquisition but also the elaborate efforts he made to provide for their ongoing survival needs in captivity—needs he took pains to understand as thoroughly as possible by consulting expert opinion, hiring experienced native keepers, or, as in the case of the unlucky whales, through repeated experiment. How many gallons of water changed daily, how many pounds of oats (or bottles of ale), how much energy required to heat the enclosure: these details, once determined, found their way into advertising copy and newspaper write-ups describing Barnum's ever-improving soaring, roaring, splashing, slithering collection of animal wonders.

On Barnum's return, he saw a way to make hay out of the situation, as he so often did. After enlisting the expert opinion of Louis Agassiz—"I do not know of any way to induce snakes to eat their food otherwise than in their natural manner, that is alive," Agassiz confirmed—Barnum wrote back to Bergh on March 4, threatening to publish Bergh's threat, along with Agassiz's reply, unless the crusader was willing to publicly withdraw his objections to the museum's practice of feeding snakes "in accordance with the laws of nature."

This, in turn, touched off a further exchange of even more intemperate letters between the two men. Bergh, on March 7, dismissed Barnum's plan to publish their correspondence as yet another bit of PR trickery from the infamous master of "humbug." He predicted that doing so, far from rallying the public to Barnum's cause, would "cause parents and other guardians of the morals of the rising generation to discontinue conducting them to a mis-called museum, where the amusement chiefly consists in contemplating the prolonged torture of innocent, unresisting, dumb creatures." Barnum's reply, on March 11, was an almost stream-of-consciousness rant that attacked Bergh in the bitterest possible terms: "dictatorial air," "low breeding," "a surplus of self-conceit," "the brain of a man mounted upon stilts." Bergh's dismissal of Barnum's museum, in particular, was too much for Barnum's pride to bear:

> When private enterprise has invested half a million of dollars, and incurs a yearly disbursement of $300,000 in which to place before the public a full representation of every department of natural history for a mere nominal sum—an enterprise never before attempted in any city in the world without governmental aid—it simply is disgraceful for you to assert that the "amusement chiefly consists in contemplating the prolonged torture of innocent and unresisting dumb creatures." How weak must a person feel his position to be when he attempts to fortify it by such thoughtless and absurd statements, and how little does he appreciate the true dignity of his office when he thus descends to miserable pettyfogging and the unjust imputation of bad motives to those who take quite as humane and much more rational view of the subject than himself.

Barnum, now in his mid-fifties, was one of America's most famous men. He had recently been elected to the Connecticut state legislature and was just then preparing a run (ultimately unsuccessful) for the U.S. Congress. He had Agassiz, the most famous scientist in America, endorsing his point of view on the underlying subject of debate. But what Barnum perceived, correctly, in Bergh's tone was the coalescing moral code of a new, reformist urban elite that took a dim view of his form of popular entertainment.

Almost exactly a year after this last exchange, another fire would make literal what elite opinion had judged: P. T. Barnum's "museum" days were over. The blaze began early on Tuesday, March 3, 1868, on a bitterly cold night with the city buried in snow. Just after 12:30 a.m., flames appeared in a third-floor window. As fire spread through the structure, a ghastly moan from the first-floor menagerie started up. "Lion, tiger, hyena, leopard, camel, zebra and screaming baboon, frightened at the unusual phenomenon, joined voices in a terrible concert," a reporter for the *Herald* wrote, "the crescendoes and diminuendoes of which were enough to set centipedes of ague running with hundred-footed scramble along one's spinal column—every one in its own individual manner venting its mortal agony of fear upon the stricken night air."

When the firefighters finally arrived after navigating the snow-clogged streets, they found the nearby hydrants frozen solid, so it took them still more time to get water flowing to their hoses. By then, it was too late. Scores of animals died; just twenty-two survived, including two camels, five llamas, a zebra, and three moose. Entirely lost was the heart of the Van Amburgh menagerie, the six large trained cats that had toured the country for years. "These animals half the children in the land have seen," noted a *Times* story, "and the remembrance of their feats forms the great event in the memory of them all." A photograph from the following day captures a remarkable memento mori: the carcass of Barnum's last museum, encased in cascades of ice.

Our Dumb Animals

"WE SPEAK FOR THOSE WHO CANNOT SPEAK FOR THEMSELVES."

"I would not enter on my list of friends,
Though graced with polished manners and fine sense,
Yet wanting sensibility, the man
Who needlessly sets foot upon a worm."

Vol. 1.   *BOSTON, JUNE 2, 1868.*   **No. 1.**

Our Dumb Animals.

PUBLISHED MONTHLY
BY THE

Massachusetts Society for the Prevention of Cruelty to Animals,

AT THE SOCIETY'S ROOMS,

46 Washington Street . . . . Boston.

TERMS.— $1.00, in advance.

Postage in the city, FREE. To all parts of the United States, outside of Boston, TWELVE CENTS PER ANNUM for each package of four ounces, payable in advance, at the office where received.

Articles for the paper may be sent to the President. Subscriptions, to the Secretary or Agent.

GEORGE T. ANGELL . . . . *President.*
CEPHAS BRIGHAM . . . . *Secretary.*
J. W. DENNY . . . . *Agent.*
AMOS A. LAWRENCE . . . . *Treasurer.*

Publishing Committee.

GEORGE T. ANGELL,   WILLIAM GRAY
RUSSELL STURGIS, JR.

ALFRED MUDGE & SON, PRINTERS, 34 SCHOOL ST., BOSTON.

OUR WORK.

We issue of this the first number of our paper 200,000 copies for gratuitous distribution, which we think will enable us to put one copy into almost every family in the State. Hereafter we shall issue on the first Tuesday of each month, an edition sufficiently large, to supply all the members of the Society, all subscribers for the paper, and as large a number for gratuitous distribution, as we think the finances of the Society will warrant. If hard work and untiring perseverance will accomplish it, we mean to have before the end of the current year, members and patrons of our Society in every city and town of the Commonwealth, and a very large monthly circulation of this paper not only in the State, but through the country. Our Society already numbers over fifteen hundred members and patrons. It has received gifts from all classes, from many so poor as to occupy but a single uncarpeted room in the cheapest tenements of this city. We have on our Board of Officers, Roman Catholics and Protestants, Democrats and Republicans, License men and Prohibitory men. We have no politics,

no theology, are working only for one purpose, that our citizens may become more merciful, our animals hereafter be better cared for and protected. And to that end we propose to gather all information that can be obtained, either at home or abroad relating to the well-being of animals, stories for the children, and matter worth thinking of by older people.

Those whom we are compelled to prosecute, those who drive horses to death, or starve them all, who wilfully, and maliciously torture dumb animals, may expect to find their names and deeds faithfully recorded for the public inspection. *We shall strive to prevent rather than punish.* But every form of cruelty that now disgraces this Commonwealth, whether on the part of high or low, rich or poor, we shall not hesitate to attack. Many interesting questions will be coming up: such as why there should be no place in Boston, off its Common and Public garden where a thirsty animal can get water, — why there should be inspectors of meats in European Cities, and none here, — why the citizens of this State should be fed so largely on the diseased meats of tortured animals, questions of paving, and horse cars and steam car transportation, all questions relating to the keeping of animals and their health, as well as that of those who consume their meats or milk. There are over a hundred Societies of a kindred nature scattered over Europe, some of whose publications we have already received, and with whom we shall soon be in correspondence. Every subscription to this paper, will add so much to its circulation, so much to an earnest effort to increase the wealth, the health, and the humanity of the State. All wishing to subscribe are requested to send their names to the Secretary or Agent at the office of the Society, 46 Washington Street, Boston.

The Massachusetts Society for the Prevention of Cruelty to Animals.

A short Sketch of its History and Work thus far, by the Secretary pro tem.

An Act to incorporate the Society having been obtained by Messrs. Angell, Howe, and Gray, a meeting was called by them and held at the offices of Mr. Angell, at three o'clock on Tuesday, March 31st, 1868. Somewhat more than forty persons were present. Mr. Angell gave the reasons which induced

him to take the initiative in the formation of the Society, stating that for many years he had felt deeply the cruelties practised upon animals, and that the fatal over-driving of the superb mare "Empress" had broken his silence and forced out a call, the response to which was instant and large. He spoke of many common abuses of animals, and expressed his belief that the time had now come when they were to cease. The act of incorporation was accepted, and a Constitution, proposed by Mr. Angell, was adopted. A list was then opened for the signatures of those desiring to become members of the Society, and was signed by most of those present, nearly three persons. A Board of Directors was then chosen, who *immediately* held their first meeting and entered upon their work.

Two months have not yet elapsed, and that which was so auspiciously begun has gone on without hindrance to the following most successful results. Letters of sympathy and offers of aid have poured in from all sides. One hundred of the most prominent men in the State, including His Excellency the Governor and Lieut. Governor, have accepted the position of Vice-President of the Society. His Honor the Mayor also has not only become our Vice-President, but, with the ready consent of the Committee on the Police, under the advice of the City Solicitor, he detailed policemen to aid the Society, thus giving them knowledge of its work and making them its friends, and so stamped it with the sanction of the City Government. We have thus been enabled to distribute without cost more than thirty thousand circulars, and to put them into every house in this city.

Here already the society is thoroughly well known. The members and patrons number more than fifteen hundred, while funds enough for the opening of its work have been received. To carry on the work, we need, as may be seen by an article in another column, all that our friends may be disposed to give. Our Legislature, without hesitation or opposition has given the society a law to work under, stronger than that of any other State. And now, with two men whom we believe to be thoroughly fit for it, we enter upon our work in well appointed and centrally situated rooms, confident that the success of the society is now a foregone conclusion, and that by the end of this year, it will have become as thoroughly and generally known throughout the State, as it is now known throughout this city.

The prestige of the Society has already enabled us, before the passage of our law, by moral power alone, to interfere successfully in every case of cruelty reported; in one instance obliging a man who kept his horses in a stable where they could scarcely stand (five feet and three inches was the height), to alter it so as to give them space to stand and move. In another case, one who had always carried calves

Chapter 5

TO PHILADELPHIA
AND BOSTON

In its earliest days, the ASPCA made its headquarters in two tiny rooms, the attic of a building at the corner of Broadway and Fourth Street. The shabbiness of the office quickly came to symbolize Bergh's single-minded devotion to animal welfare over any extraneous comfort. An oft-told anecdote recounts John Hoffman, the governor of New York State, visiting the offices, which had been outfitted with what Bergh called "the very plainest kind of kitchen furniture," and offering to pay for a new carpet. "No, thank you, governor," Bergh is said to have replied. "But send me the money, and I will put it to better use for the animals."

Among the parade of visitors to those attic rooms in the first years of the ASPCA were animal lovers from other cities, who came to inquire about how to start similar societies, as Bergh himself had done in London before his return home. One such pilgrim, a thirty-three-year-old Philadelphian named Caroline Earle White, appeared in September 1866, stopping through the city after summering in the Adirondacks. The well-educated daughter of an abolitionist Quaker family, White had dabbled in causes but never struck out on her own. Reading about Bergh's crusade in New York had galvanized her. Bergh laid out for her the playbook that he himself had used—a sort of cheat sheet for establishing organizations and passing legislation in the oligarchic politics of nineteenth-century American cities.

The campaign would have to begin with a petition, he explained. She would have to gather signatures of support from as many eminent local figures as possible. Then, as the list of signatures grew, some noble souls would have to sign on as the officers of the new society. Bergh could supply the language for the petition, and he could even supply the language for the law—but only locals could whip up the support and the leadership, which Bergh believed (with some justification) would need to come from the city's elite.

White returned to Philadelphia filled with ideas, but it was not until after New Year's that she wrote to update Bergh on her progress: She had attracted the interest of some signatories, but no leadership was forthcoming. "[A]ll the gentlemen to whom I have appealed say the same thing," she wrote. "They all seem to approve highly of the plan and say they will become members, also that they will attend if possible the meeting which is to be called to organize the Society, but they are too much taken up either with business or with charitable and benevolent pursuits to be able to give much time to this." It was only after Bergh and the society's secretary, William Waddell, suggested that White meet with two other sympathetic Philadelphians they had corresponded with—M. Richards Muckle, a prominent military veteran and journalist, and S. Morris Waln, a local shipping magnate—that the list of signatories began to grow, and Waln agreed to become the new society's president.

Later in 1867, another woman came to visit Bergh in those shabby attic offices: Emily Warren Appleton, of Boston. She was Boston royalty, enthroned in a grand townhouse at 76 Beacon Street, across from Boston Common. After Bergh had written her petition for her, he instructed her to procure the names of local grandees. She started with her own family: her cousin David Sears Jr., an aging philanthropist who had been painted by Gilbert Stuart; her husband, William Appleton, son of a former U.S. senator and eminent banker of that same name; Jonathan Mason, her stepmother's younger brother, himself the namesake of a senator father, also painted by Stuart; and on and on. The governor, John A. Andrew, happily lent his signature and support, and the list grew past a hundred distinguished names.

In the end, White and Appleton would each prevail in establishing their local societies, though neither of them, in keeping with the rigid gender notions of the day, would assume leadership roles, instead installing their husbands in their place. "If I were a man," White wrote Bergh during the petition campaign, with a barely submerged bitterness, "I am quite sure that I should follow your example but as it has pleased Almighty God to create me a woman, I must be satisfied with a more limited sphere of labor, and do the little good I can with my tongue." Notions about women's proper role in activism would change significantly over the following decades, but Appleton's leadership would functionally end with the establishment of the Massachusetts Society for the Prevention of Cruelty to Animals. White, who was fifteen years her junior, would go on to found two new organizations of her own, the Women's SPCA of Pennsylvania and the American Anti-Vivisection Society, establishing her as a rival for Bergh and George Angell as the most important American animal-welfare leader of the nineteenth century.

The two societies that White and Appleton helped launch would each go on to supply one of the defining innovations of the movement's early era. In Philadelphia, it was the animal shelter, which replaced the casual brutality of city pounds with a humane (if bare-bones) approach to capturing and housing strays. In Boston, it was a new type of moral propaganda, in the form of a monthly publication—*Our Dumb Animals*—that mixed fiction and nonfiction, polemic and poetry, aimed toward a family readership. It is hardly an accident that both these innovations emerged from societies co-founded by women, in that both represented a move from the then highly masculine zones of politics and law enforcement into realms then seen as feminine: the quasi-domestic sphere of the animal "home," and the pedagogical sphere of moral education. By providing an avenue for women to engage with the societies, as volunteers in their shelters and correspondents for their publications, these innovations helped draw more women into the movement as its crucial foot soldiers, if not yet its generals.

· · ·

It is impossible to understand Caroline Earle White's remarkable fifty-year career in animal-welfare activism without understanding the political and religious upheaval in which she was raised, as a Philadelphia Quaker in the decades leading up to the Civil War.

Her mother, Mary Hussey, was a cousin of Lucretia Mott, the fiery Philadelphia orator and Quaker minister who for decades toured the nation to denounce slavery and extol women's rights. In 1840, when Caroline was seven, her father, Thomas Earle—an eminent local lawyer who also dabbled in newspaper publishing—stepped briefly onto the national stage as the vice-presidential candidate of the abolitionist Liberty Party, with James G. Birney at the top of the ticket. The pair would garner only 0.3 percent of the popular vote. Abolitionist groups routinely met in the Earle home when Caroline was a child, and on at least one occasion, she gave up her Christmas money as a donation to the anti-slavery cause.

During Caroline's childhood, the march of industrialization had brought even more manufacturing to Philadelphia than to New York, allowing for a concomitant explosion in wealth—an accounting in 1845 found that the number of million-dollar fortunes in Philadelphia (ten) had grown to twice that in New York (five), with Philadelphia also having the most hundred-thousand-dollar fortunes by a margin of 234 to 212. But the city's rise to prominence in iron and steel production, as well as the manufacturing of locomotives and ships, also meant an escalating ordeal for the city's working animals. For White, the most heartbreaking sight was the "burden cars" that carried coal and other freight along the city's streetcar lines. "It would make your heart bleed, I am sure, my dear Sir, if you knew the treatment that the poor mules receive here," she wrote to Bergh, adding: "For years I have never been able to cross Broad St. without an inward shudder, and I have many times gone several squares out of my way to avoid crossing where a train of coal cars was about being started."

Caroline Earle White, undated photograph.

White never left behind an account of her political awakening, but her childhood amid abolitionism must have played a role. After the Civil War, the fate of the nation's formerly enslaved people clearly weighed on her: A newspaper ad from November 1866 shows her as the secretary of the local branch of the American Freedmen's Union Commission, which had formed to perform charity work among freed African Americans in the South.

And one imagines that she learned from watching the rise of Lucretia Mott just how influential a woman activist could be—but also how women struggled to make their way in the male-dominated activist groups of the time. In 1833, the year of Caroline's birth, Mott and her husband, James, were instrumental in the founding of the American Anti-Slavery Society (AASS); Lucretia was one of just a handful of women present at the creation, and the only one to join in the public debates, helping to draft the language of its Declaration of Sentiments ("We may be personally defeated, but our principles never," is a line credited to her). But there was never any question of her being allowed to serve as a leader in that group. And so that same week, she and women allies formed the Philadelphia Female Anti-Slavery Society (PFASS), perhaps the most eminent of the women's abolition groups that together provided so many of the ground troops of the anti-slavery movement in the coming decades. And by 1840, when her cousin's husband was mounting a desultory campaign for vice president, Mott was in London as a delegate at the World's Anti-Slavery Convention.

In 1848, when Caroline was fifteen, Mott and her husband visited her sister in Auburn, New York, leading to one of the most important events in the history of American social movements. At a party in nearby Waterloo, at the home of fellow Quakers Jane and Richard Hunt, Mott got to talking with Elizabeth Cady Stanton, whom Mott had met years earlier in London at the World's Anti-Slavery Convention. The two decided to host a meeting on women's rights, to be held one town over in Stanton's hometown, Seneca Falls. Mott wound up delivering multiple speeches at the two-day convention that July, the texts of which have sadly been lost to history, but the *Seneca Falls Courier* delivered this report about the evening session on the first day: "The chief speaker was Lucretia Mott, of Philadelphia. This lady is so well known as a pleasing and eloquent orator, that a description of her manner would be a work of supererogation. Her discourse on that evening, whatever may be thought of its doctrine, was eminently beautiful

and instructive. Her theme was the Progress of Reforms. In illus-
trating her subject, she described the gradual advancement of the
causes of Temperance, Anti-Slavery, Peace, &c., briefly, but in a
neat and impressive style."

For Mott and many other Quaker activists, all these causes
(women's rights, anti-slavery, and temperance—often itself seen as
a women's issue, due to the domestic violence that drunken men
inflicted on women and children) were linked to one another but
also to a revolution in spiritual thinking: a belief that the individual consciousness, not merely deserving of divine attention and
care, could have direct access to divine guidance, to the "higher law
inwardly revealed," as Mott put it. She once wrote in a letter that
"no text of Scripture however plain can shake thy belief in a truth
which thou perceives by intuition, and make thee believe a thing
which is contrary to thy innate sense of right and wrong." These
views found perhaps their most dramatic expression a year after
the Seneca Falls gathering, in a famous speech at her home meet-
inghouse on Cherry Street in Philadelphia, in September 1849. "It
is time that Christians were judged more by their likeness to Christ
than their notions of Christ," Mott declared, and her subsequent
remarks made clear that this likeness was not simply a matter of
following Christ's moral example. She believed that Christ's divine
mission was hardly unique. "His spirit is now going up and down
among men seeking their good, and endeavoring to promote the
benign and holy principles of peace, justice, and love," she said.
"They are the anointed of God, the inspired preachers and writers
and believers of the present time."

Such were the ideas in the air as Caroline Earle grew into adolescence. At a moment when education for young women remained a
controversial choice, she studied Latin and showed a general knack
for languages that remained with her—as an adult, she was fluent
in French, Italian, and German, and also conversant in Spanish.
Astronomy, too, was a passion, and later in life she would turn her
hand to fiction, publishing novels and short stories.

Caroline's own spiritual journey would take her to a surprising
destination, though in a crucial sense it remained in keeping with
the timbre of her time and place. At seventeen, she met Richard
P. White, an Irish immigrant five years her elder who was newly

arrived in the city. Two years later, they announced their intention to wed. This created no small amount of friction with his staunch Catholic mother, who sent Caroline some books about Catholicism, which she declined to read.

Not long thereafter, though, with her new husband in ill health, she took a journey across the Atlantic that would wind up altering her spiritual course. On the advice of his doctor, the couple visited her husband's family in Londonderry, on the River Foyle in what is now Northern Ireland. There she experienced a deep encounter with the Catholic faith, through the personage of one Mr. O'Brien, a young friend of her mother-in-law who had recently interrupted his Jesuit training due to his own health issues. As she would later put down in a written account of her conversion, Caroline was extremely taken with his intellectual disposition, his "impression, without making any display, of moral goodness and religious devotion." The young man wanted to guarantee each person's salvation, it was clear, in the same humane spirit that abolitionists wanted to free each enslaved person from the lash.

Back home in Philadelphia, her questioning continued; the intellectual independence she had acquired from her Quaker upbringing was now pulling her toward a less individualistic spiritual view. What nagged at her in particular was whether God, in his infinite wisdom, would leave it to each soul to arbitrate the truth of these matters on her own, with no divinely ordained helpers in doing so. Her famous cousin Lucretia continued to crisscross the country preaching about following one's inner voice, about the "higher law inwardly revealed." Yet the cruelest enslavers no doubt had inner voices preaching the truth of their abhorrent conclusions, and with biblical support (albeit dubious) for their position, specifically Genesis 9:18–27—the infamous "Curse of Ham," in which God seems to condemn Noah's son Ham and all his descendants to servitude, enabling a widespread notion in slaveholding communities that dark-skinned African people were of this lineage—and Ephesians 6:5–7, which famously begins, "Servants, be obedient to them that are your masters."

White found it entirely vexing that "two men, equally learned, intelligent and devout could take the Bible and with regard to certain debated points come to entirely opposite conclusions." And this realization, ultimately, is what led her to the necessity of conversion. "It seemed to me," she later wrote, "that Almighty God would never allow His children in so important a matter as religion to wander in the dark without a clear explanation of His doctrine and the laws by which He intended that we should govern our conduct."

Having been raised at the leading edge of a Protestant tradition that over centuries, from Martin Luther up to the Hicksite Quaker strain of her family, had slowly rejected the authority of priests in favor of an individual, mystical relationship with God, White was now ready to pledge herself to the Christian denomination that most embodied a commitment to the priesthood as God's designated interlocutors on earth. At the age of twenty-three, two years after her marriage and her trip to Ireland, she accepted Catholic baptism and became a lifelong and steadfast member of St. Patrick's Church, just off Rittenhouse Square.

This tension she explored during her conversion, between individual conscience and godly authority as dueling sources of moral insight, would rear its head often during her many years of activism on behalf of animals. As Bergh had already discovered, asking a coach driver to search his "innate sense of right and wrong" (in Lucretia Mott's formulation) would not necessarily stop him from flogging his horse; Bergh believed that only the force of law could do so, and that only a legally ordained retreat from "cruelism" could stop the next generation of children from treating animals as roughly as their parents had. And yet the authorities, as White would increasingly learn, were themselves prone to seeing animals as things or inconveniences instead of consciousnesses worthy of consideration.

One has to read her acerbic remark to Bergh a decade later, in 1867—"as it has pleased Almighty God to create me a woman, I must be satisfied with a more limited sphere of labor"—through the lens of this lifelong struggle. Her sphere of labor would soon increase, and her deference to authority would wane. But S. Morris Waln, not she, would become the society's president. Her husband, Richard, who by then had become a lawyer, would put his training to work in drafting the society's charter, and he would also become its treasurer. In April 1868, Pennsylvania's SPCA was incorporated, making it the second state in America to have an institution for the protection of animals.

.   .   .

By then, Massachusetts was on its way to being the third—spurred on by a spectacular act of cruelty. It had happened on a Saturday morning in February 1868, when the residents of Boston had been invited to witness a novelty: a sleighing horse race. Each horse, "known to be possessed of remarkable powers of endurance," as a story in a local paper put it, would pull 400-pound sledges thirty-eight miles from Boston to Worcester, for a purse of $1,000 (nearly $20,000 in today's money).

At the time, organized horse racing in America was in its infancy. That very year would see the launch of the American Stud Book, which essentially marked the beginning of Thoroughbred breeding in the country. The number of official tracks could be counted on one hand; the whole enterprise of racing was so disorganized and sporadic that a compendium a few decades later would list the day's race as one of just thirteen notable horse races undertaken in all of America during the entire 1860s.

The race was to begin at the Charles River Hotel, in Boston's Brighton neighborhood, near what today is the eastern foot of the Arsenal Street bridge. A crowd of racing fans had already gathered by the time the two competitors were led to the starting line, soon after 10:30 a.m. On one side was Empire State, who had accomplished the same distance (in the opposite direction) the previous summer, pulling two men in a buggy at a pace of nearly eleven miles per hour. On the other side was Ivanhoe, the local Boston favorite, owned by one Mr. Foster; the horse had already proved its endurance by keeping up a fifteen-mile-per-hour pace around a track, pulling two men in a sturdy wagon.

But neither animal had been subjected to a competitive race like this. At 10:46, the two horses set off, heavy burdens in tow. Despite the season, snow cover was light in the initial stretch of road, so that the five-mile trip to Waltham meant pulling the sledges over bare, rutted earth. From the beginning, Empire State established a commanding lead, and he and his driver arrived at Northborough, more than two-thirds of the way home, by 12:37 p.m. There, his minders attempted to feed him—gruel, wine, water, and hay—but the horse refused, and seemingly "possessed" (as observers later described it) he trotted off again at an even faster pace. Ivanhoe, meanwhile, struggled mightily with his load; after his driver brought him into Northborough and learned how far behind they had fallen, he pulled the horse from the race. Empire State pressed on, arriving at the race's end in Worcester at just ten minutes after 1 p.m., having traversed the distance at a remarkable pace of 15²⁄₇ miles an hour.

For both horses, the race would prove to be a fatal affair. The winner, ironically, was the first to fall. No newspaper ever offered a clear accounting of how it happened, but veterinary medicine of today can hazard a likely explanation. During his two-and-a-half-hour ordeal, Empire State's unprecedented exertions had drawn blood flow to his muscles and dangerously away from his gastrointestinal tract, upending the peristalsis that keeps horses' delicate digestive systems working. This can lead to a condition whose name is still dreaded among horse owners and vets: colic. Sometimes, in colic, the gut stops moving entirely; at other times, as in the case of Empire State, there is a disorganized motion that moves food through too quickly. Both versions of the condition are miserable—an unending, sleepless agony—and even today some of its victims don't survive. By midnight on the very day of his victory, Empire State was dead.

For Ivanhoe, the consequences would come weeks later. He, too, might have been felled by colic, but based on the chronology, the more likely explanation is another grim consequence of overworking a horse: kidney failure. Overexertion of the muscles can cause muscle cells to die, and the by-products of that cell death—specifically, myoglobin—have a toxic effect on the kidneys. Whatever the cause, the losing horse died in a Boston stable early that April, having never recovered from the ordeal of that Saturday afternoon race.

.   .   .

One Bostonian who read about the spectacle with disgust was George Thorndike Angell. Despite his stirring words about animals in his will, drawn up in 1864, that was two years before the

ASPCA's founding, and the notion of animal advocacy as a *calling*, as something to devote one's time and money to—let alone one's whole life—would have seemed an alien concept in Angell's world.

As an avid reader of his local newspapers, he might have seen the occasional item counseling kind treatment of animals (one such squib from January 1864, in the *Massachusetts Ploughman*, sat sandwiched between an item warning dairy producers to keep their cows fat and profitable, and another titled "Farmers' Wives—Why Insane") or retelling some particularly gruesome instance of cruelty in the streets, but nothing about anyone who was doing anything about it. Only an exhaustive reader of Massachusetts newspapers could have had cause to know that across the Atlantic, in London and Paris, organizations had been launched to take up the cause of animal suffering—only someone who laid eyes on, say, a tiny item in the *Evening Transcript*, August 1852, about London setting up watering troughs for dogs in its streets, or a small mention in the *New England Farmer*, November 1860, of a home for stray dogs being instituted there.

But after 1866, coverage of Bergh and the ASPCA was extensive, and the tragic horse race of February 1868 finally convinced Angell to devote himself to the growing cause. He fired off a letter to the *Boston Daily Advertiser:*

> In your paper of this morning, I see that the race on Saturday terminated in the death of the winning horse. . . . It seems to me that it is high time for somebody to take hold of this matter in earnest, and see if we can not do something in Boston, as others have in New York, to stop this cruelty to animals. And I wish further to say through your columns, that I, for one, am ready to contribute both time and money; and if there is any society or person in Boston, with whom I can unite, or who will unite with me, in this matter, I shall be glad personally or by letter to be informed.
> Geo. T. Angell,
> 46 Washington Street.

The Henry Bergh of Boston had suddenly declared himself. Within twenty-four hours, Emily Appleton and a parade of other animal lovers had come to visit him, and still more sent letters. A few days later, Angell published an appeal in multiple newspapers asking for donations, and he drew up an act of incorporation that he presented to the speaker of the state house of representatives. On March 31, a crowd of more than forty people packed into his law offices at 46 Washington Street to officially organize the Massachusetts Society for the Prevention of Cruelty to Animals. A few days later, on April 3, the society held its first public meeting, at which Angell pointed out the inadequacies of the state's existing anti-cruelty law and laid out the new law he would soon be proposing: fines of up to $250, or prison for up to a year, for "overdriving, overloading, torturing, tormenting, depriving of necessary sustenance or mutilating any ox, horse or other animal," as well as new rules for the humane killing of old horses.

From there, April was a flurry of activity for Angell: testifying to the legislature for his new law, wheedling more donations from wealthy Bostonians, setting up the Massachusetts SPCA's offices. (He rented a space in the same building as his law practice and had the two offices connected with a speaking tube.) "It was already pretty clear to my mind," he would write later, "that I was entering upon a life-work."

.   .   .

On May 20, 1868, Angell called a special meeting of the Massachusetts SPCA's board of directors and informed them of his boldest idea. He wanted to launch a newspaper, one that the society could try to put in every single household in the commonwealth of Massachusetts. His directors were slightly shocked at the estimated cost, but they gave their assent, and by June 2 the first number of *Our Dumb Animals* had been printed.

From the very first issue, it represented a remarkable vision and wager. The society printed 200,000 copies; it distributed 30,000 in Boston and then worked with members of the legislature and nearly 700 postmasters to get the rest out into every single town. It reprinted the state's new anti-cruelty statute—thereby removing from the future defense of any animal abuser in the dock the argument that

he was ignorant of the law—as well as
a series of passionate mission statements from Angell. It excerpted relevant
newspaper articles, letters penned to the
society, guides for proper animal care.
It ran two-paragraph items on both the
"Jewish mode of killing animals" and
the "English method of killing calves,"
holding each up as an exemplar against
the more savage modes of dispatch practiced by the typical American butcher.

George Angell, 1870.

And yet even in the earliest issues
were glimmers of the more expansive publication that *Our Dumb
Animals* would soon become. One poem, an original penned by the
Reverend George F. Worthington of Baltimore, spoke directly to
children and cautioned them to treat animals with kindness:

> *The gentle cow, and gentler sheep,*
> *Browsing the tender sod*
> *Do these not come, like all good gifts,*
> *From our dear Maker, God?*

Another poem, "Little Bell," detailed the adventures of a blackbird
as he flies along a country road, calling out greetings to humans
and animals alike. From a publication called "Four-Footed Favor-
ites" was excerpted a short story about Flora, a young filly, and the
kind family who purchase her. Even the nonfiction essays tended to
come framed in the kind of simple, direct address featured in moralized fiction of the era, like this short piece about the "check rein,"
a painful apparatus for horses that was then stylish:

> Look at your horse's mouth, my friend, and see how he suf-
> fers, and how hot and fretty he is.
>   Don't you see that his mouth is hurt and stretched by the
> bit, with that tight check rein; and that the more he pulls, the
> more he is punished? If you were working would you like to
> have your head buckled up in that manner?

In many of *Our Dumb Animals'* offerings, the vast majority of which were unsigned, a reader can discern the voice of George Angell himself, who threw himself into the periodical as his primary outlet and passion. Henry Bergh had a knack for dudgeon and an impulse for attention-getting, but Angell was something more—a gifted rhetorician who channeled both the slashing moralism of a newspaperman and the celestial fire of a preacher. Tucked into the second page of one early issue was an item entitled simply "Who Eats It?," which managed to serve simultaneously as an advertisement for Angell's paper but also as a summation of his society's chief causes at the time:

> If thousands of cattle, sheep and swine are brought over our railroads without food, drink or rest, and by reason of this transportation their flesh, fevered and diseased, becomes unfit for food, as we have shown in the past numbers of our paper,—who eats it?
>
> If the cattle that furnish the milk for our tables are deprived of proper food, air, sunshine, exercise, companionship, shelter and protection from the weather, until their milk, like the milk of a sick nurse, becomes poisonous,—who drinks it? If your horse, my friend, by overloading, overworking or overdriving, drags or runs his life out in ten years, when he would otherwise have lived twenty,—who profits by it?
>
> If you permit your boys to kill useful birds and plunder their nests until your orchards are overrun and your fruit destroyed by insects,—whose loss is it? And so on through the whole catalogue of animal cruelties. No fact is more certain than this: that God has established laws for the protection of animals as well as men, and you cannot violate those laws without incurring the penalty.

Perhaps the most prescient innovation during the first year of *Our Dumb Animals* was a serialized story, beginning in September 1868, entitled "The Story of a Good and Faithful Horse." At that time, fiction narrated from the first-person perspective of an animal was rare; it would still be nearly a decade before a middle-aged invalid in England would publish the most famous first-person animal tale in history, *Black Beauty*. The author of "The Story of a Good and Faithful Horse" saw the concept as gimmicky enough that he or she felt compelled to add a subhead: TOLD BY HIM-SELF TO A DEAR HUMAN FRIEND WHO UNDERSTOOD THE LANGUAGE OF HORSES.

"My earliest recollections are of a rich and fragrant pasture in Massachusetts," the equine narrator begins, "where I played by my mother's side, drinking her warm milk, and learning by degrees to nibble the sweet grass." It is in this mode, rich with adjectives designed to underscore his depth of consciousness, that the horse goes on to recount the events of his life: his mother's loving min-istrations, as she looks after him and protects him from bullying children (using her body as a shield whenever "a boy more ignorant or more rough and cruel than the rest" would throw stones at him), or his interactions with birds ("I came to know where many nests were, and I must confess would sometimes mischievously look in upon and scare the wee, callow, chirping things").

But very quickly his life is beshadowed by miseries, at the hands of thoughtless humans. "[O]ne day in May," he recounts, "some men came who said my tail was too long and must be docked, and so they tied me up and brought a great knife, something like a pair of huge scissors and cut through flesh and bone and all, and as if this pain was not enough, they brought a red hot iron and seared the bleeding stump and put me in such agony as I cannot describe." By his second year, the working world having disabused him of all innocence, he lays out a litany of maltreatment in a voice curiously similar to that of George Angell:

I saw poor, hard-worked and half-starved horses that were exerting all their strength in the service of cruel masters, often fearfully beaten. I saw fine, high-spirited animals urged with whip and spur to a speed beyond their capacity. I heard loud yells of triumph or horrid curses and imprecations from drivers of fast horses. I saw horses that had been injured by bad management in their youth, and others that had become, by cruel treatment, sulky and obstinate, dreadfully beaten— kicked, and even maimed, when they refused to draw heavy loads—and I began to dread the future.

Our Dumb Animals would publish for more than eighty years. If the whole animal-welfare impulse had been born of imagination, Angell and the Massachusetts society were the first to understand how fiction could be combined with the rising methods of mass production and distribution to teach a new set of moral principles to millions. Even if a reader might fail to entirely suspend her disbelief, to contemplate the question of animals' thoughts at all is to confront the plain truth that they experience joy and suffering, that they have interests that diverge from our wishes and whims. Through fiction, all the dumb animals around us can be made to speak, thanks to some dear human friends who understand their language.

·   ·   ·

Caroline Earle White witnessed many acts of animal cruelty on the streets of Philadelphia, but she was particularly appalled at the manner in which the city captured and housed stray dogs. Armed with what were essentially lassos, the city's dogcatchers threw them over the necks of target dogs from great distances, then swiftly pulled the lassos tight and dragged their victims to the "dog-wagon" waiting nearby. The dogs were then taken to a miserable building with a dirt floor, where they were kept for forty-eight hours with no food or water. If no one came to claim them, they were killed in a manner even more barbaric than the infamous drowning tank along the East River in Manhattan: the dogs were suspended by chains and beaten to death.

So when White formed the Women's Branch of the Pennsylvania SPCA—which met for the first time on April 14, 1869, at the home of PSPCA president S. Morris Waln—it didn't take long for her to settle on lost animals as a subject of her group's ministrations. In June of that year, the group approved a motion to create "a refuge for lost and homeless dogs, where they could be kept until homes could be found for them, or they be otherwise disposed of." They wrote to George Angell, then traveling in Europe, and asked for him to report on two humane shelters already operating on that side of the Atlantic, the Dog Hospital in Paris and the Home for Lost Dogs in the Battersea neighborhood of London.

That latter institution, founded in 1860, had become the source of some curiosity among American correspondents. An account in *Harper's Weekly* noted acidly, "It seems a mockery of Christian charity that when the streets of London are full of starving people, when almost every paper, in this inclement season, contains a sad story of death by suffering and privation, there should be an extensive asylum in that city for the reception and protection of destitute dogs!" But the accompanying woodcut was loving and sensitive, showing a rough pen with wooden walls in which all manner of dogs expectantly await rescue. Angell wrote back to White and her Women's Branch colleagues that at the Battersea home, dogs "are kept several days to be reclaimed by owners: afterward if not claimed, [they] are given to such persons as wish for them and will undertake to properly care for them. If no one offers to take them, after a length of time, varying according to their apparent value, they are mercifully killed."

And so this question of merciful killing—assumed to be a necessity, given the finite space and resources of the proposed shelter—became a priority of White and the Women's Branch, long before any other animal-welfare organization in America seemed to take it seriously. Even in advance of Angell's letter, the women had created a "committee on inquiring into the least painful mode of killing," and set themselves assiduously to the task of considering as many such modes as might be available. For their first euthanasia chamber, they settled on "carbonic acid gas," aka carbon dioxide.*

The dogs they planned so carefully to kill would largely be healthy strays, to keep them off the streets. From the vantage of today, when animal advocates in the developed world have become deeply uneasy with this practice, it can be hard to understand why Caroline Earle White—who, then and over the coming decades, would show herself to be more radical and far-seeing than America's other animal-welfare leaders—would commit herself so enthusiastically to perfecting it. Partly, no doubt, it was a matter of sheer numbers: Absent a widespread spay-and-neuter campaign (which

---

* In 1874, after considering some other alternatives—including charcoal fumes and chloroform—the shelter switched to "carbonous oxide gas," aka carbon monoxide, which still is seen as superior to CO_2 as a euthanasia drug.

would not become a common population-management tool until the 1970s), dogs proliferated too quickly in the city's back alleys to be absorbed by large-hearted families. Then there was the ever-present threat of rabies, fears of which would often lead to brutal culls of street dogs in nineteenth-century cities. White would also have been well aware of the other fates such dogs might face: tortured by mobs of boys, their bones and spines cracked under wagon wheels, bellies distended from hunger and parasites.

The Women's Branch members did not employ the term "euthanasia," but it would soon be in the air as a descriptor for what they sought. After centuries of use to describe the peaceful "good death" that human beings could hope and pray to experience, the word was repurposed in 1870 by Samuel Williams, a British businessman, for a published piece in which he advocated that physicians be granted the legal right to humanely hasten death through the use of anesthetics. While his piece was roundly decried (in its journal, the American Medical Association accused him of asking the physician to "don the robes of an executioner"), his moral logic came to seem inescapable to a small but increasing number of people. Wasn't it true, they reasoned, that death was preferable to some forms of suffering? And in a cosmos in which humans, as Lucretia Mott so stridently argued, should not merely pray for justice but follow their own moral instincts to carry it out, why could they not redefine the "good death" as one brought about at the hands of their fellow man?

As that movement grew over the hundred years that followed, animal advocates—who, even as they came increasingly to value dogs and cats as members of the family, continually refined their practices of humane killing—were always ahead of them. The first bill attempting to legalize euthanasia for humans, in 1906, would be put forward in Ohio by Anna Hall, a Cincinnati physician whose mother had died painfully of cancer. "When a dumb animal is hopelessly crippled or ill, we are permitted to end its sufferings," she said. "Why not be as considerate with human beings?" The very word "euthanasia," which animal advocates resisted using for decades, soon became a word applied more to pets than to people, and, indeed, it would be left to the veterinarian's office to provide the most vivid illustration of just how peaceful and cathartic a "good death" could be.

. . .

In many ways, Caroline White's public emergence as an animal-welfare leader can be dated to April 6, 1870, at an event held to mark the first anniversary of the Women's Branch. The site was the lecture room of the Mercantile Library, an institution that had been recently installed in an imposing structure on 10th Street between Chestnut and Market. The city's mayor, Daniel Fox, was there to lend his support, and Henry Bergh had made the journey from New York. Perhaps most important, the city's newspapers, which had hitherto regarded the Women's Branch with comedic condescension, had sent reporters to cover the proceedings. Some in the audience questioned the propriety of White's leadership, a fact referenced archly by Bergh, who remarked, "It has been said that your president ought not to read her own report, because it might appear to partake of anti-feminine attributes."

But White did read her own report, speaking first and at length. At this point, the Women's Branch had close to four hundred members, nearly as many as the men's society, and the city—to the great surprise of Waln—had given them authority over the city's pound and animal-control measures. Almost immediately the women had begun to prepare a permanent move of the pound, away from the infamous building that had so disgusted White and to a new structure, a "Temporary Shelter for Lost Animals" four miles north of the city center. The Women's Branch also had somehow acquired the power to inspect the city's working horses for signs of cruelty or neglect. "Our agent began, in the first place, to work chiefly by moral suasion, a method which we should always prefer," White said. But, she added darkly, "There are some so brutal that they can only be acted upon through fear," and she laid out the details of the twenty-three arrests that had been made during the first five months of the program. The group recently had hired a second agent, she said, and soon hoped to hire more, "for we do not consider that the city could be properly attended to with less than five or six."

Taking a page from the Massachusetts society, White announced the society's plans for literary outreach to children: five thousand copies of a children's book called *Early Lessons in Kindness,* and a thousand little slips that reproduced "The Horse's Petition" (a parable about an old horse who rings a bell) as well as Dryden's famous couplet, "Take not away the life you cannot give / For all things have an equal right to live."

But the bulk of her remarks were devoted to the coming shelter, the announcement of which had triggered a wave of mocking press coverage. "No sooner was our plan made public," she noted, "than we were made the recipients of a vast number of attacks from several of the daily journals of this city"—most of which now had reporters there in the audience. "It was stated that we proposed to erect a hospital for dogs; that we were about to employ a corps of nurses to attend to them; that we had petitioned Councils for $25,000 with which to build this hospital or asylum; that our esteemed friend, Mr. Bergh, the excellent president of the New York society, had originated the idea, and induced us to adopt it, and a number of other absurd statements, which it is not worth while to repeat." In actuality, White went on, her group was merely constructing a "pound conducted upon a humane system," and the sum involved was $2,500, no more and no less than what the city was already spending on the catching and care of stray dogs.

The women's emphasis on housing strays struck many as an overly sentimental, stereotypically feminine way of thinking, in contrast to Bergh's emphasis on prosecution—months earlier, reporting on White's plans, the *New-York Tribune* had groused that women "no sooner get hold of a theory or principle than they be-frill and be-ruffle it, precisely as they would a dress." To the contrary, though, the Philadelphia shelter (much like *Our Dumb Animals,* with its forays into fictional moralism) did not be-frill Bergh's theories so much as deepen their philosophical commitments. To believe that animals can suffer, and that that suffering is worthy of moral consideration, is to understand that not just depraved assaults on them but their everyday treatment must become a matter of urgent human attention.

When the shelter opened in the summer of 1871, it made news around the country. The yard had been constructed just to White and her colleagues' specifications, allowing for the separation of dogs into discrete groups: large dogs from small, males from females. Lattices of grapevine shaded the yards; water was made available to all dogs at all times, and all were fed a healthy diet of horsemeat, cornmeal, and crisped pork skin, even those destined for culling.

And then there was the completed euthanasia chamber, which in many ways stood out as the shelter's most remarkable attribute, and might well stand today as its most enduring (and double-edged) legacy. It was an airtight box with a glass lid, so that observers could see how little the animals suffered. A seventy-gallon tank, attached, used a mix of water, carbonate of lime, and sulfuric acid to generate the carbon dioxide. The *Philadelphia Inquirer,* in its report from the shelter's opening day, described the elegance with which the chamber did its work:

> The best of it was that the animals had no previous expectation of their death, and had no time to exclaim in their forcible manner against leaving the world. They were, in the presence of a grave assemblage of spectators, placed in the inclosure, made air-tight, or nearly so, and then shut up to await their fate.

"There was not really much to be seen about it," the *Inquirer* correspondent went on. "The animals in each case quivered for a moment, slowly sank to the ground, and in a few moments expired, as if sleeping away."

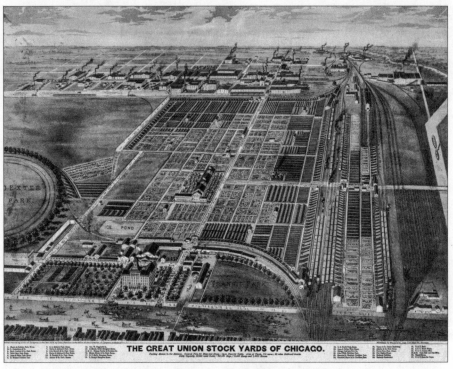

THE GREAT UNION STOCK YARDS OF CHICAGO.

The Union Stock Yards, which helped put Chicago
at the center of the nation's meat industry.

Chapter 6

MEATROPOLIS

On a square mile of Illinois prairie, not far from the western shore
of Lake Michigan, a strange sort of city was rising. Its construction
had happened over a matter of months, consuming fifteen million
feet of lumber, planked by as many as a thousand men at a time.
The resulting community boasted fifty linear miles of streets and
alleys—the largest dubbed Broadway, a wide thoroughfare stretching from a grand hotel on one side of the district to a gabled brick
bank building on the other—and comprised roughly five hundred dwellings in all, which during 1867, less than two years after
construction, would provide temporary housing to some 115,000
souls. Perhaps most important, nine different railroad companies
had laid track into the complex, eager to help its residents make
one-way journeys all across the nation.

This was the Union Stock Yards, and here the future of America's livestock industry was rapidly taking shape. An explosion of
railroads before the Civil War had already allowed midwestern
farmers to become cattle and pig exporters to the East Coast, but
the opportunity had become too big for this ad hoc network of
small producers to exploit. And so Chicago, looking to grab market share from Cincinnati and other rivals, had made a bold decision: to consolidate the city's entire livestock trade into one central
clearinghouse, located in the unincorporated town of Lake, six
miles due south of the city center.

Every aspect of the new yards was built for scale and efficiency.
An 1867 account in *The Atlantic Monthly* described how elegantly

the process ran. "A cattle train stops along a street of pens; the side of each car is removed; a gently declining bridge wooes the living freight down into a clean, planked enclosure, where on one side is a long trough, which the turn of a faucet fills with water"—fruits of a complex-wide system that stood as a particular source of pride for the yards, six miles of pipe fed by tanks containing some 220,000 gallons in all. Once the seller had found a buyer at the exchange building and agreed to a price per pound, the animals would be driven back toward the rail yards through a special weighing pen, capable of sizing up thirty cattle per minute. That task completed, the buyer and seller would return to the exchange building, "where the money is paid, all the cattle business being done for cash; after which they conclude the affair by dining together at the hotel, or at an excellent restaurant in the Exchange itself."

And thus, *The Atlantic*'s correspondent went on, "a repulsive and barbarizing business is lifted out of the mire, and rendered clean, easy, respectable, and pleasant."

Pleasant, above all, had clearly been a priority for the developers from the start. At this mammoth and dusty new stockyard, built on the prairie near an agglomeration of rail yards, they had incongruously constructed a first-class hotel, called the Hough House, with fine mosaic floors in the grand lobby and a billiard room in the basement. Even before its completion the hotel was being marketed to potential guests as "the most enjoyable retreat in the country," offering from its verandas and balconies "a more intensely romantic scene than is afforded at any of the fashionable resorts of the East." (Some of the visiting cattlemen would feel the romantic pull a little too strongly, and the hotel eventually was forced to implement a "no women above stairs" rule—wives of guests being a carefully policed exception—in order to squelch prostitution.) Six stories tall with a mansard roof and a cupola on top, the structure towered high over any other building within miles, such that a cattleman driving southward out of Chicago would almost immediately witness the Hough House shimmering up on the horizon, a white-brick oasis of civility.

Indeed, as the amount of livestock and money flowing through the yards each year grew and grew, the sense of the Union Stock Yards as a city unto itself, a bustling competitor to the more conventional metropole six miles away, grew up in equal proportion. During the summer of 1867, the yards' owners opened a horse-racing track at Dexter Park, just south of the hotel; a few years later, this sporting park would cement a place in baseball history by hosting the first practice game of an outfit called the Chicago White Stockings, which eventually would become the Cubs. By 1869, the stockyards had its own newspaper, the weekly *Sun,* printed in the attic of the Exchange Building. Within a decade of the yards' founding, it was estimated that roughly one in five of the city's workers depended on it for their livelihoods. And it had become a tourist attraction, too, with the *Chicago Tribune* remarking that visitors to the city had begun to see missing the stockyards as an oversight comparable to "visiting Egypt, and not the pyramids; Rome, and not the Coliseum; Pisa, and not the Leaning-Tower."

To the cause of animal welfare, the Union Stock Yards—and the other livestock-related trades that would soon consolidate nearby—represented a challenge to the basic moral calculation upon which it had been founded. Henry Bergh's theory of "cruelism," which to some degree was shared by all his fellow reformers in America and abroad, imagined humans interacting in their daily lives with the animals whose fates they controlled. The barbaric whipping of a horse or callous handling of a calf in the streets was believed not just to incur suffering in a sentient being; it was thought also to normalize cruelty among a whole neighborhood of human passersby who might witness the deed. And these two ill effects, animal agony and human moral rot, seemed intrinsically bound up together. So many of the prosecutions being undertaken by Bergh and the other SPCAs were targeted at just such malefactors in city streets, butchers and cattle transporters among them.

The stockyards, by contrast, showed just how radically the railroads could dilate the distance between the practices of an industry and the consciences of its consumers, who might now reside hundreds or even thousands of miles away. As cattle trudged by the score off of trains, and then back through weighing pens onto different trains, no customer need be present to witness whatever cruel treatment they did or did not experience. The stockyards were a metropolis in which, by and large, the only humans walking its streets were those with an abiding financial interest in the brisk sale of its animal inhabitants. The six miles of physical separation from Chicago symbolized a more profound separation of livestock from human society than had ever been known before, with food animals shunted off into a shadow realm where the rhythms of the natural world no longer applied. Thanks to rail travel's ability to cut easily through snow, a once-seasonal industry could now take place year-round, and meanwhile a state-of-the-art lighting system in the yards made it "quite as possible to transact business at midnight as at high noon."

That sense of isolation from traditional human community was profound in the yards' earliest days, an experience not soon forgotten. One early visitor noted that from the hotel's south veranda, eighty-four feet in length, the prairie "rolls away southward in one unbroken sea of land. Not a single object appears to mar the exquisite beauty of the scene, until it is lost in the horizon, or in a hazy mist of gathering smoke and clouds." It was a view "worthy of the pencil of the landscapist," he went on; "the newspaper drops from the hand as the eyes wander over the broad expanse of level land—the aboriginal prairie of Illinois."

.   .   .

It was George Angell, among the animal reformers of America, who would most keenly grasp the depredations of the Union Stock Yards and the unique challenge it posed to his cause. But during his first two strenuous years in the movement, the Illinois prairie was the furthest place from his mind. Not long after he launched *Our Dumb Animals,* his beloved mother had died in Vermont—the sentence *"No man ever had a better mother"* would later appear, italics his, on page 2 of his memoirs—just as he was throwing himself into the task of recruiting humane enforcement agents in towns around the state, as well as prosecuting the society's first case, a man who had overloaded a horse. (The man was acquitted, prompting Angell to pen a lengthy broadside against the decision in a Boston newspaper: "Must an animal be worked until he breaks a blood-vessel or drops dead, before the law takes cognizance?")

And so it went, through the end of the year. "My time was fully occupied, not only week-days but Sundays," he later recalled; "my nights were any thing but restful, for when I retired it was with candle, paper, and pencil in a chair at my side," to jot down thoughts that came in the night. Angell's health began to falter under the burden, and so he "decided, under advice of my physician, that rest and travel on the other side of the ocean would be judicious." By then, the Massachusetts SPCA had brought on a new secretary, a man named Frank B. Fay who had previously served as mayor in the town of Chelsea. In early 1869, Fay was perhaps surprised to find his new boss essentially placing the entire organization on his shoulders.

For more than a year, Angell traveled through Europe, his progress tracked through a series of long letters dutifully reprinted in *Our Dumb Animals*—the great theme of which, accurately or not, being the greater enlightenment that Europeans displayed toward the creatures in their midst. He began in Ireland in mid-April ("In Cork, I found a hospital for the cure of sick horses and dogs, with a *Turkish bath for animals*"), went on to Scotland ("I have not seen in Glasgow a single case of apparent overloading such as I see in Boston almost every day"), and then to London, birthplace and spiritual home of the movement ("I have been three weeks in London, visiting its great races, horse-shows, dog-shows, riding almost every day through its streets and jams of carriages, and I have not to my remembrance heard one profane word, or seen one unkind act to either animal or man"—a sentence that no doubt raised an eyebrow among Londoners who chanced to read it).

At the Battersea shelter in London and then, by July, in Paris, he carried out his reconnaissance work for Caroline White and her colleagues in Philadelphia. Soon it was on to Geneva, and then Zurich, where an "International Humane Congress" of animal-welfare organizations was being convened in August. September found him in Germany, where he was somewhat less impressed with the quality of mercy on display (at a Cologne slaughterhouse, he watched in horror as two calves were "dragged in, struggling, slipping on the bloody floor, thrown upon and bound to trestles, and their throats cut"). By October, though, he had found a more humane spirit in Amsterdam, where he noted in particular a sign at the local zoo: Anyone "teasing the animals" would be fined five guilders. For months after that, he essentially settled down in Paris, striking out for occasional trips to Italy and elsewhere and publishing letters in *Our Dumb Animals* that were hardly distinguishable from those any American tourist might send home.

In the summer of 1870, he returned to Boston, where an encounter with an old friend sent him packing again. He had been back just a few weeks when he ran into John C. Dore, a schoolmate of his from Dartmouth. Like Angell, Dore took a job as a teacher after college; over time, he became a principal, before being offered the job of Chicago's superintendent of schools. After just a couple of years in the young western city Dore smelled opportunity, and left education to become a businessman and politician, even dabbling in the cattle industry. But he had become convinced of the rightness of his old friend Angell's cause, and as a member of the Illinois state senate he had already secured the passage of an anti-cruelty law, despite the fact that no organization yet existed to enforce it.

Dore urged Angell to come help him start one. So Angell headed west, arriving in Chicago on October 1, 1870. As he would recall, it seemed as though cruelty pervaded the whole place: "Men were too busy making money," he wrote, "to think of any thing else." Old horses, when they were no longer suitable for work, were often left to starve or freeze to death in the brutal winter. One story, passed along to him by a reporter from a local newspaper, horrified him in particular. After a cow had wandered across a railroad track and got knocked down by an engine, its legs wound up crushed by subsequent trains, and it lay there in agony for more than twenty-four hours before anyone had the decency to kill it. "While she was lying there lowing plaintively, and every now and then trying to rise," Angell remembered, "a crowd of persons was at different times around her, some laughing at her, and some poking her with sticks." But he quickly learned that the more glaring locus of cruelty in Illinois was the new metropolis rising six miles to the south: "The cruelties at the stock yard," the reporter told him, "are enough to sicken any humane man."

So one morning he threw on an old hat and coat and traveled out to see for himself. The sight that met his eyes, as he loitered around the rail spurs, was quite different from the one sketched out by *The Atlantic* three years earlier. No "gently declining bridge" was there to "woo" animals off trains, as the *Atlantic*'s correspondent had reported. Instead, Angell saw hogs being prodded to leap from the top floors of two-story livestock cars, in "an almost perpendicular descent to the platform." In loading and unloading cattle, men would use hickory switches made of saplings six feet long, with inch-long spikes embedded in the ends. Angell saw some animals get stabbed with the spike up to forty times. He protested to a workingman nearby that some cattle were getting gouged in the eye.

"*They* don't care," the man scoffed.

Significantly, Angell also became aware on his visit of just how much cruelty was inherent in the process of transportation itself. With each arriving train, he noted that after the living animals had been prodded off and driven toward the pens, a few dead ones would have to be extracted from each car. One former Texas drover told him that the same was true of the Mississippi River steamboats that were bringing cattle north to St. Louis and Cairo, Illinois—that forty or fifty animals could die on one trip.

With more digging, still more outrages surfaced. Far from the scene of easy comity sketched by *The Atlantic*—buyers and sellers raising a glass of claret to another mutually beneficial deal—the livestock transactions involved some Boschian gamesmanship behind the scenes. Prospective buyers, Angell was told, would routinely enter the pens of cattle in the morning and beat them with whips and clubs, a practice said to provoke defecation, in order to make them weigh less at auction; sellers, meanwhile, would sometimes starve cattle before feeding them, or feed salt to hogs in order to provoke them to drink prodigiously, both meant to nudge their weights temporarily upward.

By early November, Angell had rented a back office in downtown Chicago, at the Connecticut Mutual Life Insurance Company building on Washington Street, and begun the work of setting up a new society by way of the standard playbook: compiling a list of local grandees and trying to get a handful of them to sign on as leaders. By November 22, he had published the names of his hundred prominent backers, and others would soon be added. A local banker and newspaper publisher, J. Young Scammon, agreed to serve as chairman, and E. Payson Porter, an official in the then-new telegraph industry, became the organization's secretary. (Just two years before, Porter had played a key role in the adoption of the QWERTY typewriter, when he bought them for his telegraph operators to transcribe messages for customers.)

All that was left was to commemorate the new society with a public meeting. Angell booked Farwell Hall, the city's grandest auditorium, and hired an organist, negotiating his fee down from $40 to $20. Guests arrived to find more than three thousand copies of the latest issue of *Our Dumb Animals,* sent by the Massachusetts SPCA at its boss's behest. In Angell's address to the assembled crowd, he apologized for his limited rhetorical gifts, and then began to speak about the breadth of the movement that had now come to Chicago, a movement that he had seen in full flower in Europe at the International Humane Congress. He recounted all he had seen and heard about the cruelties of Chicago stockyards, and he brandished, with high drama, one of the spiked six-foot goads he had seen being used on cattle during the unloading process. He read out some of the letters he had received from local citizens, bearing witness to the cruel treatment of animals throughout the city. A shiver ran through the crowd when he said that animals too sick to be sold at the stockyard exchange were often butchered for local consumption, meaning that Chicago, meat purveyor to the nation, was endangering its own health with the industry's dregs.

But now, Angell announced, a remedy was at hand, in the form of the Illinois Humane Society. Drawing on his experiences in Boston, he rattled off all the ways that even a small society could immediately begin to end cruelty to animals in Chicago. And he underscored a point that for him had become an article of faith: that humane treatment of animals would ultimately be good for the meat industry, which was becoming so central to the Chicago economy. A more humane railroad-car design, he noted, could stop cattle from shedding so many pounds during their arduous journeys from Chicago to the East Coast—a gain sufficient, he believed, to pay for the associated costs. Cruelty was not merely a transgression against all that was holy or moral; it ultimately, he believed deep in his bones, was bad for business.

.   .   .

By the spring of 1871, when Angell returned to Boston after six months setting up the Chicago society, he and the other movement leaders of America could look around and see a phenomenal success in the making. Just five years in, SPCAs had formed in eight of the nation's ten most populous cities: New York (#1) and Brooklyn (#3) were both covered by Henry Bergh's original group, founded in spring 1866; Philadelphia (#2), Boston (#7), and San Francisco (#10) all formalized their societies in 1868, with Baltimore (#6) doing likewise in 1869; and now, in 1870, St. Louis (#4) and Chicago (#5) had followed suit. (The holdouts among the top ten were Cincinnati and New Orleans, which would form societies in 1873 and 1885, respectively.) As in New York, these were not toothless advocacy groups but organizations granted law-enforcement powers by their state legislatures, on the basis of anti-cruelty statutes that, in most cases, their founders had been instrumental in getting passed. Nearly every single day, Americans were being taken to court and threatened with fines or even prison for acts that, six years earlier, would not have been prosecuted or even openly condemned anywhere in the country.

Indeed, were it not for the problem represented by the Union Stock Yards—in essence, the ascendant problem of industrial capitalism, and its ability to concentrate both wealth and suffering at an astonishing, unaccountable scale—one might look at the power then being wielded by humane agents in American cities and see a welcome check against the rising oligarchs of the Gilded Age.

In the brutal winter months of early 1871, for example, Bergh mounted an uncompromising campaign against New York's horse-drawn streetcar lines, which were chronically overloaded even in the best of weather. Of the twelve lines that crisscrossed the city, seven ran essentially north–south along avenues, in a manner that resembles some present-day subways and buses, while others took routes that seem fanciful today: one formed a circular route from downtown to Central Park, and another zigzagged from West 42nd Street to Grand Street, and still another, the Bleecker Street Line, cut from West 14th Street down to Fulton Ferry. The lines were owned by a welter of different companies of varying size and profitability, but no one could deny that streetcars had become a big business: the Fourth Avenue line was owned by Cornelius Vanderbilt, the nation's richest man.

For years, Bergh had remonstrated with the heads of the various lines to put teams of four horses, not two, on fully packed cars, but with mixed success. That February 14, as the evening rush hour began amid a driving snowstorm, Bergh was chagrined to see that the Third Avenue line was running with just two-horse teams, and by 6 p.m. he was so incensed that he forced one of its cars downtown to stop and hitch to a post, effectively shutting down the entire line. When the owner attempted to reroute some of its cars along Fourth Avenue, Bergh shut that line down too. Only at 7 p.m., when he saw that the Third Avenue company had bowed to his edict and added extra horses to their cars, did he consent for both lines to resume their service and allow thousands of customers to make their way downtown.

A few days later, Bergh went even further in his crusade. During another morning of cold, slick weather, he discovered that crowded horsecars on the Bleecker line were laboring with just a pair of horses, even on what then were somewhat steep inclines downtown, and so yet again he hitched an offending car and shut down the line. By 11 a.m., with fifty cars backed up along the track and no end in sight, the president of the Bleecker Street Line, John T. Conover, hopped on the detained car himself and tried to drive off with it. In response, Bergh and his agents arrested Conover, hauling him before a judge who himself trundled out to the intersection in order to make a ruling. The roads, he declared, were clear enough for two-horse teams, so Conover was free to go.

Even in defeat, the symbolism was remarkable: Bergh had arrested the president of a New York streetcar company and brought him before a judge, forcing him to account for the treatment of animals on his line. The symbolism seemed more striking when, the following week, the ASPCA made a comparable stir in New York newspapers by hauling in John Jennings and Michael Daisey, two downtown ruffians who had put on a rat-killing exhibition in the dog pit at Sportsmen's Hall. The message could not have been clearer: Abuse animals and you will face prosecution, be you a Five Points thug or a railway president.

But that message had its limits. Despite Bergh's plutocratic parentage and despite his reliance on city eminences for every bit of the authority he wielded, he did not hesitate to take the fight to the wealthy whenever he thought it appropriate. The trouble was that in letter and spirit, New York's anti-cruelty law condoned the prosecution of the man who directly harmed an animal but less so the man whose orders made it inevitable, let alone whichever man or men profited most from the deed. Had John T. Conover not showed up to climb aboard the underpowered horsecar himself, he likely would have suffered only the receipt of a stern letter or two from Henry Bergh, not an arrest and hearing before a judge among the murderers and rapists at the Tombs.

Stern letters, at any rate, were the extent of Bergh's approach to Cornelius Vanderbilt, in response to some incidents that same year. The first focused on the treatment of horses at Vanderbilt's depot on 42nd Street. "Twice each week I have occasion to pass there," Bergh wrote. "It is of daily occurrence to see two poor horses beaten until they finally succeed in starting two heavily-loaded passenger-cars, which, when under way, frequently crush one or both animals, whose feet get caught in the numberless rails which intersect one another at that place. . . . I now appeal to your humanity and commanding influence to put a stop to these disgraceful outrages, and visit in person the scene thereof."

A few months later, Bergh penned another missive to "the Commodore," attempting to convince Vanderbilt that the domestic horse as a species deserved some cosmic credit for his unprecedented fortune. "At the mines," he wrote, "at the plow, in the wilderness, in the rocky excavation, on mountaintop, and in the earth-pierced tunnel, this patient and devoted friend has ever been found by the side of men. And here, too, upon the hard and slippery streets of our Metropolis, is heard his steady tramp by day and night, giving wealth and ease to all who seek his services." After chastening Vanderbilt for the treatment of horse teams he witnessed on the Fourth Avenue line, he concluded: "I have enjoyed your acquaintance since my boyhood, and I indulge the belief that you will attribute no other purpose to me than that which I profess and for which I have made and am making many personal sacrifices in my efforts to alleviate the miseries of those humble creatures confided by heaven to the care and compassion of mankind."

Beyond such florid appeals to the Commodore's decency—a quality for which Vanderbilt was hardly known—these letters were notable for their literal shortsightedness about animal suffering within his vast empire, of which horse-drawn streetcar lines were a small and increasingly quaint portion. As Angell had witnessed in Illinois, untold numbers of cows and pigs were now crisscrossing the country at any given moment, many of them on rail lines owned by Vanderbilt, suffering for hours or days on end in deplorable conditions. But Bergh, even as he imagined all the credit due to working animals in a hypothetical accounting of Vanderbilt's rise, remained obsessed with the suffering he could see with his own eyes, in his daily perambulations.

And he remained obsessed, above all, with the moral transaction between individual human beings and the animals they physically interacted with. In a pamphlet he distributed to the city's butchers that year, Bergh made clear that he understood the forces that were bringing livestock into the city, but he placed a particular moral burden on the men who took on the final step of slaughtering them. Knowing that many if not most New York butchers were Jewish, he tried to make common cause with them on religious grounds— "you acknowledge, and try to serve that great God whom Jew and Gentile must alike adore"—before appealing to them on the part of all the livestock that "come to you exhausted with long travel in close cars, faint with hunger and parched with thirst." He went on: "Already bruised and wounded by the trampling hoofs and sharp horns of their fellow captives, by the heavy cudgels of drovers, and the teeth of worrying dogs, they lift their weak, imploring eyes to you in dumb entreaty for a little food, drink and shelter, a little kindly treatment, a brief respite from terror, pain and anguish, before their harmless lives shall end."

.   .   .

This focus on individual treatment and appeal to individual consciences was, as we've seen, the movement's founding impulse, springing forth directly from its Romantic origins. It might even have been suited to addressing cruelty to animals in the urban economy of Bergh's childhood, when, as the son of New York's most prominent shipbuilder, he "enjoyed the acquaintance" of its most prominent ship buyer, Cornelius Vanderbilt. In that Manhattan, farms still dominated uptown, and the vast majority of livestock butchered in the city had been raised a short cart ride or boat trip away, if not a long walk. All the businesses involved were smaller, more human-scale; a medium- to large-sized breeder, or dairy, or butcher shop might make its owner a wealthy man, but he still would likely be actively engaged with his daily operations and thereby accountable, on a personal and visceral level, for the treatment of animals on-site.

By the 1870s, though, a new kind of animal economy was taking shape. The great disappearance of animals (and their excrement) from city streets was still decades away, but the reorganizing influence of the railroads began to operate on every industry, including those that handled animals, multiplying scale and stretching out geographic reach. Meat animals were coming from farther away, in larger numbers, which required more butchers with operations set up to slaughter them quickly and efficiently, with more and more employees. Soon enough, the conditions were in place for an owner to know as little about the killing of each cow as Cornelius Vanderbilt did about the loads borne by each horse team on Fourth Avenue. Horses, meanwhile, were the engine that moved all this freshly slaughtered meat around town, along with so many other goods—the animals required in such numbers that they became a scaled-up industrial good of their own, bred and shipped greater distances and warehoused in increasingly gargantuan stables.

Because of his experiences in Chicago, George Angell perhaps saw this more clearly than Bergh did. The decade of age and gulf in social class that separated the two men no doubt made a difference too, offering Angell a degree of modernity that the elder man could not quite achieve, and a greater facility (as seen in his writing for *Our Dumb Animals,* e.g., "Who eats it? . . . Who profits by it?") for systematic thinking about capitalism.

At around the time Angell returned to Boston, a shocking incident in the nearby suburb of Brighton lodged the livestock issue even more prominently in his mind. In April 1871, a butcher named George E. Temple dropped dead of a mysterious illness, and at the inquest it came out that he had fallen ill a few days prior after butchering meat from a dead ox—one that had perished aboard a freight car on the Boston and Albany Railroad. Neighbors and associates described a smell so strong in his shop that they couldn't bear to set foot inside. The dead man's son testified that when the creature had been opened, parts of it were black and putrid, but on orders from their boss they went ahead and prepared cuts of meat from the less-decomposed half of the animal. The medical examiner speculated that Temple had wiped his face with a towel during the butchering process, allowing an infection (anthrax, perhaps) to pass from the diseased ox to a sore on his face. By the time Temple died, the meat had already been sold off at Faneuil Hall in Boston.

The incident touched off a broader investigation by a state committee, which interviewed scores of men in the local meat trade and released a report that September. Investigators described a system in which local animal dealers sold livestock on consignment, making it profitable to ignore health problems with the animals they sold. And the state of animals arriving in Boston was a miserable one, as ninety to a hundred calves and two hundred hogs or sheep were packed into each car for days, standing in their own excrement, with little access to food or water. As a result, the committee wrote, many animals died and still more emerged from their journeys "panting, fevered and unfit to kill."

Angell was galvanized by the thirty-three-page report—a fact made clear in his personal copy of it, which now resides in the library at the Massachusetts Institute of Technology. Across from the title page, in his distinctive hand, he has sketched in an outline for what he was beginning to see as the new linchpin of humane education about livestock: an argument that meat from cruelly treated animals posed a threat to human health. It was an idea best articulated in a quote—which Angell summarized, seemingly from memory, in his makeshift outline—from Augustus Hamlin, a top medical official in the Union army during the Civil War. "The flesh of mammalia undergoes a great change in its nutritive qualities by reason of fasting, disturbance of sleep, and long continued suffering," Hamlin had written, "resulting in its not only becoming worthless, but deleterious." Angell's scribbled outline gathered a few other supporting details, which he would go on to cite for years in future writings and speeches: a stray remark from Louis Agassiz about "the dangers arising from the ill treatment of beef cattle before slaughtering them," and an incident in New York in which hogs died after being fed blood and entrails from animals sickened in transit.

In our day, one wants to imagine that cruelly raised and slaughtered meat will be dangerous to eat, and the inverse notion is perhaps even more appealing—that meat from humanely treated animals ought to be more nutritious and delectable. (Niman Ranch, one of America's most popular purveyors of humane meat products, announces on its website that "our farmers' and ranchers' passion for their craft, dedication to their animals and respect for the land can truly be tasted in our finished product.") In fact, the notion has some truth to it: Maltreated animals will be flooded with cortisol and other stress mediators, which can negatively affect the quality of their meat, and there is some evidence (albeit nonconclusive) that stress might also modestly increase the likelihood of bacterial infections in livestock that can lead to foodborne illness in people. But by putting forward consumer safety and satisfaction as a justification for oversight, Angell and other reformers would help give rise to a regulatory regime in which animal suffering itself was neglected, even invisible, so long as meat remained saleable and outbreaks rare.

The notion of a link between cruelty and health also flowed into a larger faith of Angell's, which he had preached from the podium at Farwell Hall in Chicago: that humane treatment would ultimately be good for the livestock business. In early 1872, Angell published what would become his greatest contribution to the debate over American livestock handling, a lean essay called "Cattle Transportation in the United States." After summarizing all the various horrors that the Massachusetts committee and other investigators had turned up—as well as some of the fruits of his own research in Illinois—he laid out two proposals for how to remedy the problem. The first was a bill that had already passed the U.S. House of Representatives, forcing railroad personnel to unload livestock periodically for food, water, and rest; Angell's essay, printed and distributed widely by the Massachusetts SPCA, would prove instrumental in pushing the bill through the Senate and across the desk of President Ulysses S. Grant.

It was his second proposal, already on the near horizon, to which Angell devoted the bulk of his essay, seeing it as a win-win for everyone concerned: adoption of an improved cattle-carrying car, the innovation he spoke of at Farwell Hall, which an inventor named John W. Street had begun to test out in the Midwest. These cars essentially functioned as movable stables, with partitions between each animal and systems in place for feeding and watering on the go. While this design accommodated significantly fewer cattle per car, it allowed journeys to proceed without stops for feeding and unloading, saving three days of transit and delivering the livestock in notably better shape. "It is for the interest of shippers and con-signees, as well as railway companies to have these cars adopted," Angell wrote in his essay, "because the saving of animals that now die on the passage, and of the large shrinkage on those that get through alive, and of the damage to their hides, saying nothing of interest and insurance, will much more than cover the increased costs of transportation." He offered some back-of-the-envelope calculations to support this claim: Given that experts had found a rail trip from Chicago to Boston to result in "shrinkage" (the euphe-mistic industry term for body weight lost in passage) of at least 10 percent in cattle, this meant that 29.4 million pounds of saleable beef were being sacrificed each year on that route alone.

"It seems to me then entirely clear," Angell wrote, "that the cattle transportation of this country *must be changed;* and that the sooner the change is brought about the better it will be for the interests of all concerned."

.   .   .

Soon enough, those more humane rail cars would indeed be used to ship animals around the country. But it was a third possibility, only gestured at in passing in Angell's essay, that would complete the transformation of the livestock economy in the late nineteenth century.

Out on the Illinois prairie, abutting the Union Stock Yards, a different sort of animal metropolis was rising. Its foundations were laid in the summer of 1868, when the yards put a portion of its land on the market and billed it as "The Packers' Addition." That meant meatpacking—the process of butchering meat for shipment, rather than shipping live animals for butchering. In that era, the meatpacking industry was hamstrung by the quality of the product it could offer: The cuts of beef and pork generally had to be pickled (a typical brine involved molasses, rock salt, and saltpeter), yielding a form of meat that, while edible, barely resembled its freshly slaughtered counterpart. Even so, with the economics of rail transit, the competitive advantage of packed meat had already become formidable. Instead of shipping an entire animal, a seller paid only to send the meat, a tremendous cost savings that could be passed along to customers.

Most of the city's packing operations had until then clustered along the south branch of the Chicago River, stretching inland from 18th Street, but the advantages offered by proximity to the stockyards were notable. Beyond cheaper land, the Packers' Addition offered immediate access to animals and rail yards, as well as freedom from the city regulation that prohibited the movement of animals through the streets during workday hours. Of the many packing entrepreneurs who moved their businesses south, the most important from a historical perspective was Philip D. Armour, who relocated there in 1872, buying twenty-one acres that eventually would become the seat of an astonishing empire.

Philip D. Armour in 1853, age twenty-three.

It was a very strange and very American journey that brought Phil Armour to fame and fortune as a packed-meat magnate. A middle child among eight on a farm in Stockbridge, New York, he was kicked out of a religious school in nearby Cazenovia for taking a girl on a moonlight ride in a horse and buggy. At nineteen, he joined the gold rush, and quickly saw that there was money to be made in selling water to miners, who needed it to sift for gold. So he and a partner dug irrigation trenches from the Sacramento River and then sold access for a hefty price, eventually hiring round-the-clock guards to make sure that no one took water without paying. After the boom went bust, Armour found himself in Milwaukee, where he set up a meatpacking concern with a partner—just in time for the Civil War to provoke an enormous demand for barreled meat, necessary to feed the prodigious armies in the field. The firm made a killing when Armour, foreseeing the end of the war, performed a "short-selling" operation, contracting to supply future barrels at the wartime price of $40 apiece and then delivering them after the price had plummeted to $18. That gambit alone netted his firm at least a million dollars, and earned him a lifelong reputation as a cutthroat financial thinker.

He invested his own share in Chicago, where two of his brothers had already started a provision firm. In 1867, the three brothers started a packing concern along the South Branch, and a few years later they had become the sixth-largest pork firm in the city, processing some 65,000 hogs in a single winter. By then another innovation had come along to make meatpacking, at least of pork, even more efficient and profitable. This was the so-called slaughtering machine, which a Chicago inventor by the name of Windsor Leland had brought to nearby butchers.

Slaughtering hogs until then had been a difficult and time-consuming process, in large part because of the labor involved in moving the just-killed pig around; the carcasses also needed to be dipped entirely in near-boiling water in order to soften the bristles on their skin, which would then need to be scraped off before proper butchering could begin. Leland's "machine" was in reality more of a (dis)assembly line, which automated the moving of the massive creatures. A reporter for the Chicago Republican watched the machine in action in the packinghouse of one of the machine's earliest adopters, in 1866. "Everything in and about the establishment is conducted with perfect precision, order, and system," he noted, "and, as much as it is possible, with neatness." One man placed an iron clamp around a hind foot of each live pig, which was immediately hoisted up to dangle from an elevated rail, along which it moved as each step of the operation was performed: A second man "with a dextrous flourish of the weapon severs the windpipe and main arteries," and then another plunged the dying animal into the scalding bath, and then on to the scraping and the gutting, all handled in a span of two to three minutes.

This automated method, packinghouses soon found, came with an important and unexpected benefit—the quick bleeding through gravity resulted in better meat. It did also have one unexpected drawback: The sudden hoisting of a pig by its hind leg led to a prodigious squeal from the victim, heightening the din in these already noisy slaughterhouses to a nearly unbearable cacophony.

But six miles from Chicago, out on the aboriginal Illinois prairie, no one was there to hear it—no one, at least, who was not being paid to work through it. Soon, new technology would only increase the packers' market share, as automated scraping helped butcher hogs faster and steam-pressure autoclaves allowed for better-tasting canned meat. By 1874, Armour & Company would introduce their own innovation: a storeroom surrounded by an icehouse, creating what is believed to have been the first refrigerated room in an American packinghouse, which would allow what long had been a seasonal business to carry on even in the heat of summer.

The rise of the Packers' Addition, later to be rechristened "Packingtown," completed the vexing transformation of the livestock economy into one where animal suffering was routinized and multiplied on an astonishing scale, even as that suffering became hidden from the everyday lives of most citizens. And Armour & Company, within a matter of decades, would become one of the nation's largest and most sophisticated corporations, one that would transform industrialized animal slaughter into a startlingly bureaucratic affair. In so doing, it would expose the greatest weakness of America's founding generation of animal activists, and of the organizations that they founded. All the factors that had made the Union Stock Yards difficult to police for cruelty—its size, its isolated location, the financial incentives that its workers had to look the other way—would apply even more so to a closed system of slaughterhouses from which no animals emerged alive.

When horses fell ill, they could be transported via the ASPCA's
horse ambulance to another innovation: the veterinary hospital.

Chapter 7

THE HORSE DOCTORS

All of a sudden, the horses were coughing. It began in September 1872, near Markham, Ontario, but within days it was observed in the city of Toronto, fifteen miles south. It would start as a dry cough: harsh, nonproductive, and loud, erupting seemingly at once from all the horses in a stable. Ears back, neck stretched forward and down, forelimbs extended, haunches up—the entire equine apparatus was thrown into the effort of each noisy paroxysm.

After a few days, it grew worse. The hacking horses began to bring forth yellow sputum with each painful expulsion, and they were sneezing, too, stringy mucus streaming from their clogged nostrils and reddened, lusterless eyes. Worried stablehands called it "the snot." The lymph nodes of the throat were enlarged and tender to the touch; high fevers gripped the horses' whole bodies with sweating, shivering, and malaise. The illness would not prove to be particularly deadly; only a few out of a hundred sick horses would expire. But they were depressed, weak, uninterested in food, and—most critically to their owners and drivers—unable to work.

Even as Toronto succumbed to the disease, Lord Frederick Dufferin, Canada's debonair new governor general, who was then on a tour of the recently independent dominion, decided to go ahead with a planned reception in Niagara Falls, Ontario, some eighty miles to the southeast. The glamor of the occasion induced an American gentleman to drive his team of four horses across the border to attend. Soon after his return, one of the horses developed a cough. A day or two later, his entire stable was stricken. By October 11, the disease was coursing rapidly through his city of Buffalo, New York. And by Monday, October 21, it had raced across the state, as reported in the *Rochester Democrat:* "The Canadian horse disease first showed itself here to any extent on Friday last. It soon attacked nearly every animal in the livery and horse car stables, and yesterday we were assured that over five hundred animals were suffering from it." *The New York Times* estimated that more than half of the horses in Rochester were, by that date, incapacitated. This number included "every horse in O'Brien's Circus," which itself had recently returned from Canada. By this time, reports of widespread disease were coming in from Montreal and Ottawa; Albany and Boston, too, had begun seeing cases.

When the Great Epizootic (as it was soon to be called, employing a scientific term that has long been the animal version of "epidemic") swept into New York City, it would affect nearly every equine in the metropolis, moving in a rapid wave from one end of the city to the other, stable by stable, putting horse after horse after horse off the job. Some drivers, with uncompromising employers or their own business fortunes at stake, forced their ailing horses to work despite their debilitation. Sick horses falling down in their traces, too ill to bear their burdens or even stay on their feet, were observed throughout the metropolis. This prompted the ASPCA to send its state-of-the-art horse ambulance—a conveyance built soon after its founding, the first vehicle ever designed and deployed specifically for the transport of ill and injured horses. (The equine ambulance made its rounds for two years before Bellevue put the first ambulance for humans into service.) The vehicle was a boxy affair, similar in its basic design to the trailers one sees hauling horses over highways today, but with a seat for a driver at its fore, and large wheels at the rear to smooth the ailing animal's passage over rough stone pavements. The most severely affected horses, or those housed in conditions that the ASPCA deemed inadequate for their recovery, were delivered directly to another innovation: the veterinary hospital.

Although not quite yet a fixture of the New York City streetscape, facilities devoted to the outpatient and inpatient care of infirm horses and other animals were becoming more common in the years leading up to the epizootic. Many were humble enterprises overseen by amateurs, charlatans, or horseshoers, but more and more practices led by formally trained "veterinary surgeons" (as they were then called, in the European style) were opening for business in the city, applying recognizably modern medical and surgical techniques to non-human patients. The foremost among these was the hospital attached to the New York College of Veterinary Surgeons, America's first durable institution dedicated to the education of veterinarians. In 1872, the college was growing quickly in size and reputation under the leadership of an accomplished and opinionated French veterinary surgeon named Alexandre Liautard.

.   .   .

Alexandre François Augustin Liautard devoted his professional life to establishing the scientific discipline of veterinary medicine in the United States. When the epizootic arrived in 1872, his campaign to professionalize American veterinary practice was well underway, and he had already achieved great personal success in New York despite being an immigrant of undistinguished origins; Liautard was born at home on February 15, 1835, in a modest apartment adjacent to his father's locksmith shop on Rue Neuve-Saint-Augustin in Paris's prosperous second arrondissement.

Alexandre's father, Jean-François Liautard, had arrived in Paris several years earlier from an Occitan-speaking town in the south of France to practice his craft. He was part of a large wave of European immigration and urbanization that would double the city's population during the first half of the nineteenth century. Jean-François married Alexandre's mother, a nineteen-year-old native Parisian named Charlotte Gabrielle Héloïse Vives, in 1827, and in the coming years, income from the locksmith shop and a contracting business allowed the family to flourish. Alexandre and his two sisters grew up enjoying the comforts of middle-class life and the stimulation of a vibrant metropolis. Even after losing his mother at the age of six, Alexandre was allowed to pursue the full extent of educational opportunities available to his class. While many sons of nineteenth-century artisans were apprenticed from a young age, Alexandre was permitted to attend high school, alongside scions of wealthier families.

His father's influence was evident in the choices Alexandre would make later in life—to emigrate far from home, to marry into a different culture, to build a successful business based on the application of his carefully honed professional skills. The particular course of Alexandre's studies, meanwhile, followed an example set by another family member, his maternal uncle, Étienne Gabriel Vives, a veterinarian in the French military. Vives served in an artillery unit under King Louis Philippe from 1843 until the Revolution of 1848, then served in Louis-Napoléon Bonaparte's Imperial Guard until retiring in 1860. During these turbulent years, France experienced wave upon wave of domestic volatility, while fighting alongside Britain in the Crimean War and aggressively expanding its overseas empire. France's formidable and very active army was horse-powered, which meant its ground transportation, supply lines, and communication relied on the efforts of military veterinarians to keep valuable animals on their feet. It was reported that the Imperial Guard went to war with one physician per one thousand men but four veterinarians per one thousand horses. Uncle Étienne would have performed physically grueling work in his role with the cavalry, and faced difficult living conditions during wartime, but he also must have cut a fine figure in his Lancer's jacket, making an impression on his eager young nephew. Alexandre perhaps envisioned a heroic future for himself when, in 1851, at the age of sixteen, he enrolled at the prestigious National Veterinary School of Alfort, located in the southeastern outskirts of Paris.

By the time the young Liautard put on the school uniform—a high-collared blue coat with gilded copper buttons—and walked through the high stone arches framing the Alfort college gates, the school was well established as a world-class scientific institution, offering its students a combination of laboratory and didactic training along with opportunities to observe clinical practice and participate in original research. Since its founding almost a century earlier by the nobleman Claude Bourgelat, the school had amassed a prodigious collection of anatomic and pathologic specimens for instructing pupils in the material manifestations of health and disease. Students were expected to apply themselves seriously to their studies, and discipline was rigidly enforced. Subjects covered in the four-year curriculum included anatomy, physiology, pathology, microbiology, parasitology, surgery, and animal husbandry. The on-site hospital and clinics saw many hundreds of cases annually, including horses, dogs, ruminants, and donkeys (in that order of frequency). Liautard succeeded academically but apparently struggled under the severe authority exercised by the faculty over the students.

As he neared the completion of his fourth and final year of his veterinary education, his progress was disrupted by the death of his father and his abrupt expulsion from the college, five days afterward, "for a very grave disciplinary infraction." Details of the incident are lost, but in 1856, several months after completing the bulk of his coursework at Alfort, Liautard accepted a degree from the National Veterinary School of Toulouse. He nonetheless would forever consider himself a product of the Alfort school, and throughout his life would frequently cite the institution for its robust program of experiential training and its propagation of a professional ethos. It would be the model for the veterinary educational system he would help establish in the United States.

At the time that Liautard arrived in his adopted country, animal health and healing remained a mostly amateur affair, usually carried out by the owners themselves or their subordinates. The application of basic first aid and nursing care to the creatures who lived among people had surely been taking place almost since these treatments were devised for human use, and these ancient arts remained common practice

Alexandre Liautard, circa 1865.

in North America in the early 1800s. A gentleman might dress a wound on his hunting hound's tail, or his groom apply a poultice to his carriage horse's sore hoof; a farmer might hydrate a newborn calf through a diarrheal illness, or a young child and his mother might improvise a bandage for the broken wing of a songbird mauled by their cat.

Agricultural journals circulating in nineteenth-century America disseminated specific knowledge and practices that sometimes improved upon commonsense care for healthy and sick animals, but often did not. In 1832, the editor of *American Turf Register* suggested this remedy for "lockjaw," caused by tetanus infection: "A cure of this affection, hitherto supposed impracticable, has been performed in a horse, by simply using the muriate of soda, or common table salt, with severe bleeding. The Horse took about five pounds and a half." *The Cultivator* published in 1838 a "Substitute for Spaying" in hogs, which involved the insertion into the reproductive tract of a goose quill loaded with rifle shot. Several years later, *The American Agriculturalist* printed correspondence from a reader who reported having lost all of his cats and dogs over a number of years to convulsive fits. After receiving advice that bleeding would remedy the situation, he wrote, "I am now trying it . . . by cutting off a piece of the tail each time they have a fit . . . economizing the tail as much as possible, that it may get a fair trial. . . . Some other cure would be preferable, as a bobtailed cat is rather an unsightly object. Still, better even a bobtailed cat than none." In 1845, *Michigan Farmer* contained advice for an "infallible" treatment of calf diarrhea, used by one correspondent for thirty years without failure. The method required putting half a pint of good cider into a bottle, then adding an equal quantity of blood from a vein in the calf's neck: "Shake it well together quickly and before it has time to coagulate, put it down the calf's throat."

In the U.S. during the nineteenth century, numerous book-length animal health manuals provided laymen with a comprehensive resource for do-it-yourself diagnosis and treatment of veterinary illness, finding broad readership through bookshops, mail-order sellers, and public libraries. Among the most popular of these were works by British veterinary surgeon William Youatt, whose volumes on individual domestic species (particularly *The Horse*, but also *The Sheep, Cattle,* and *The Dog*) circulated widely in the United States beginning in the 1830s, first as pirated editions of British books, then as authorized American versions. In 1850, another British veterinary surgeon, Edward Mayhew, came out with a competing equine volume entitled *The Illustrated Horse Doctor: Being an Accurate and Detailed Account of the Various Diseases to which the Equine Race are Subjected, Together with the Latest Mode of Treatment, and All the Requisite Prescriptions Written in Plain English*. This work went into multiple editions, as did his *Dogs: Their Management: Being a New Plan of Treating the Animal, Based Upon a Consideration of His Natural Temperament*. Youatt's and Mayhew's advice included commonsense measures such as avoidance of overfeeding and improving sanitation as well as the administration of (frequently inefficacious, sometimes dangerous) "medicines," the implementation of minor surgical procedures (including wart removal and suturing wounds), and "heroic" interventions (related to those popular in human medicine): bleeding, purges, blistering, and branding.

Concerned horse owners didn't have to go it alone. Anyone could call themselves a "horse doctor," and many untrained entrepreneurs did. Also, since antiquity, experts in hoof care, called farriers, had been providing technical expertise specifically in the shoeing and soundness of horses. Shoes have been devised for horses since ancient Egyptian and Persian civilizations began tying woven grass sandals to horses' hooves. Romans fashioned iron and leather "hipposandals" for their steeds, and horseshoes made of forged bronze or iron have been in use since at least the Middle Ages. Farriers trim horse hooves to restore symmetry, then apply fitted shoes—including correctives, if needed, for hoof defects and injuries—with the goal of promoting soundness and resilience of the equine locomotor apparatus. The role of the farrier expanded over the centuries to include surgical services like bloodletting, abscess-draining, and castration as well as certain medical therapies like the administration of laxatives. Occasionally, nineteenth-century farriery went beyond footwear and folk medicine and attempted to harness the supernatural to treat veterinary ailments. A remedy for bleeding publicized by farrier John Grim in a Winchester, Virginia, newspaper instructed readers to "take one piece of wood and make three little wedges of the same. Make them a little bloody from the wound, and stick them in a crack of a log on the sunrise side of a house or barn, two or three inches apart, and strike each wedge three strokes with a hammer or stone."

It was not uncommon for farriers to be consulted about animals other than horses, but specialists in different domestic species emerged to offer their own particular services. Cow-leeches, or cow-doctors, treated cattle. Dog-leeches treated dogs. Physicians often could be persuaded to look in on a sick animal between human patients, if they didn't find it too debasing to do so. Homeopaths and druggists saw an opportunity to expand their markets and devised a vast pharmacopeia of remedies and patent medicines for animals, sold directly to the consumer. "Good for man and beast" was a slogan of those who would peddle an endless variety of tonics, oils, and tinctures to overcredulous animal owners inclined toward DIY veterinary medicine. One, Merchant's Celebrated Gargling Oil, purported in an 1849 advertisement to be effective against "spavin, sweeney, ringbone, wind galls, poll evil, callous, wounds, bruises, sprains, fistula, lameness, foundered feet, grease, mange, rheumatism, bites of animals, external poisons, nervous affections, frost bites, corns, burns, chillblains, chapped hands, caked breasts, etc."

Not until the 1850s, the decade during which young Alexandre Liautard immigrated to the United States, were any serious attempts made to create institutions of veterinary education in North America. Three veterinary colleges opened their doors during those years, in Philadelphia, Boston, and New York City, but none of them would produce more than a handful of graduates—of somewhat doubtful competence—or last longer than fifteen years.

By 1860, Liautard was in practice at 205 Lexington Avenue in New York City. The United States Census that year counted some thirty-one million souls spread across forty-three states and organized territories—including 392 self-professed veterinarians. That number was likely made up of a mixture of European-trained vets like Liautard, new graduates of the three incipient American veterinary colleges, physicians who had pivoted to horses, and various untrained quasi-professionals. Together, they represented a substantial increase in the profession from the forty-six members counted ten years prior (the first time veterinarians appeared in United States Census results) but nonetheless demonstrated a dearth of veterinary expertise in a society that depended so utterly on animals.

Along with building his private practice, Liautard spent his early years in America perfecting his English, attending (human) medical school (at the time, a not uncommon way for serious veterinarians to establish themselves as the professional peers of physicians), growing a fashionable set of side-whiskers, and courting Emily Joséphine Stouvenel, an American-born daughter of immigrants from the Lorraine region of France. After not many years in New York, Liautard had created a great demand for his services, attracting enough paying veterinary clients to ensure his household's financial security while he pursued an expanding variety of professional interests.

His most durable creation was hatched on June 7, 1863, when he and two other New York practitioners placed a small notice in *The New York Times:*

> To Veterinary Surgeons. There will be a meeting of Veterinary Surgeons at the Astor House on the 9th of June, at 2 o'clock P.M. All interested in the advancement of veterinary science are invited to attend.

Forty veterinarians assembled two days later in a commodious hotel living room provided by an "admirer of the profession." The men hailed from all over the northeastern United States. Robert Jennings of Philadelphia and A. S. Copeman of Utica, New York, exhibited pathologic specimens, while Robert McClure of Philadelphia gave an address on "The Origin and Importance of Veterinary Education and Science." But most of the conversation that took place during the two days of the congress centered on the establishment of a national veterinary society, the United States Veterinary Medical Association, "to contribute to the diffusion of true science and particularly the knowledge of Veterinary Medicine and Surgery." A few decades later, the group would be renamed the American Veterinary Medical Association (AVMA), which lives on to this day.

Soon thereafter, Liautard made another ambitious step toward formalizing the profession when he offered up his practice on Lexington Avenue to house a veterinary school, the New York College of Veterinary Surgeons, which had been founded several years earlier but quickly closed due to lack of enrollment. At the reopening ceremony, held November 6, 1865, Professor Copeman addressed the incoming students, describing in enthusiastic detail the robust course of study ahead: Anatomy, Physiology, Materia Medica and Therapeutics, Surgery, and his own dear subject, Theory and Practice. He admonished the inaugural class to vigorously attend to their duties: "Recollect you have not come to this institution for pleasure, but for gaining a knowledge of a difficult profession. Be zealous and unremitting. . . . Stick to your lectures, your dissections, your hospital practice 'with a will,' and the thing is done." Liautard was not just the college's host but also its registrar and professor of anatomy. By 1870, he had succeeded the college's original founder, the Irish-American physician John Busteed, as its president, and the population of students was steadily growing. Liautard had taken over direction of the college hospital; amassed a substantial collection of anatomic and pathologic specimens, of which he was justifiably proud; and assumed a second professorship, of surgery. He had also become one of two veterinary surgeons who served the ASPCA in an official capacity: testifying against alleged perpetrators of cruelty, inspecting various animal facilities, and directly caring for the animal victims of abuse.

.   .   .

When the epizootic swept through in the fall of 1872, Liautard and other veterinary surgeons were forced to work night and day to tend to the city's horses, not just at their practices but all around the metropolis. Wealthy horse owners could afford a house call from a qualified veterinary surgeon; so, too, could the large stables of the transit, stage, and livery companies that didn't already employ one on-site. An illustration from the ASPCA's annual report shows how one large railroad company dealt with the scope of the illness—setting up a field hospital of sorts in an open-air pavilion adjacent to the stables, where horses are scattered at some distance from one another atop a deep straw bed. Workers bustle amongst the ill animals, hand-feeding roughage and layering on blankets to nurse them through their fevers. Sturdy overhead slings, suspended from the rafters, cradle several of the horses' midsections, saving them the burden of standing on their weakened legs.

Out in the streets, meanwhile, a strange quiet reigned: the clip-clopping hooves of thousands of saddle and cart horses were stilled, as were the rattling wheels of delivery wagons, carriages, omnibuses, and rail cars that the horses normally pulled. Men picked up wheelbarrows and put on harnesses to haul, with human brawn, whatever they were able. Claiming exorbitant prices of up to twelve dollars a day, farmers and entrepreneurs from the surrounding region supplied fresh horses, which would themselves quickly succumb to the contagion, and teams of oxen, which were impervious to the illness but lumbered too slowly and intractably along city streets to be a good substitute for urban equines. Steamboats ferried commuters uptown and down-, between Harlem and the Financial District, carrying double the usual number of passengers.

Horse-drawn fire engines were stuck in their station houses while buildings blazed. Ambulances were unable to transport the prostrate to hospitals, and patients at home waited in vain for visits from carriage-borne physicians. Even the city's locomotive and industrial steam engines were quieted, since there were no horses hauling the coal that powered their furnaces. Undelivered milk went sour, ice melted, produce withered, meat spoiled. Construction projects wound down as supplies dwindled. Mail service was suspended. Carters could not pick up the garbage, which accumulated in stinking piles along the curbs. Hearses and horse-powered ferries fell out of commission, interrupting travel plans for the living and the dead.

Some policemen found themselves at loose ends: On October 29, describing the previous afternoon, a reporter for *The Sun* wrote, "The absence of the horses from the streets was more noticeable than on any previous day, and the good-looking policemen who were wont to escort the ladies across perilous Broadway found their occupation gone." Elsewhere in the city, new duties were being created for idle officers of the law. "On car 85 of the Third Avenue line, going uptown at 3 pm, was a lady carrying a child, who wished to get off," it was reported in *The Sun*. "Being an up grade the driver was afraid to stop, and the lady dared not jump. Finally a policeman took the child, another gentleman lifted the lady from the platform, and the debarkation was thus completed." The reason for her precarious situation was that the streetcar drivers, fearful that their team would be unable to get moving again, resisted halting full streetcars to pick up or drop off passengers. Disembarking passengers were obliged to jump from the height of the moving car onto cobbled pavements—a particularly challenging maneuver for ladies, given the restrictive bodices and bustled skirts of the day.

Complaints about the treatment of transit horses poured in to the ASPCA offices. The Third and Fourth Avenue lines, among the last in the city to shut down amid the epizootic, had drastically curtailed service, resulting in vast numbers of passengers crowded into a fraction of the usual number of cars. Overloaded cars placed insurmountable burdens on the weakened horse teams, leading to frequent breakdowns. Car companies resorted to stationing fresh horses at short intervals along the road, to replace downed horses or those that could no longer draw their load.

On the evening of October 30, Henry Bergh stood with his supporters outside of Cooper Union, at the convergence of the Third and Fourth Avenue streetcar lines—over which a few horse-drawn rail cars continued to roll, despite the weakened condition of the animals pulling them along. Writers for newspapers as far away as Sacramento provided descriptions of the scene:

> He displayed his professional shield, and in the name of the august Society for the Prevention of Cruelty to Animals ordered the brutes to stop driving the gasping beasts. There was of course a rumpus, but Bergh, being reinforced by the police, carried the day. The horses were untacked, the passengers were "spilt," as some of them professionally expressed it, and the drivers and conductors were reduced to the condition in which Othello found himself on at least one memorable occasion. This caused a general standstill in city travel.

Consternation about the horse flu's chaotic effects was matched by some confusion as to its nature. What variety of affliction was this—a distemper, a diphtheria, or some other sort of scourge?

One clue lay in the pattern of its spread—the fact that other northeastern cities were brought to a halt almost simultaneously with New York. The epizootic transmitted along regional rail lines, Erie Canal towpaths, and other intercity commercial routes, and then radiated out to smaller towns and rural environments. As the virus traveled down the Eastern Seaboard and then across the continent, it wreaked different sorts of havoc in the communities it visited. Philadelphia was obliged to release recently convicted prisoners when they could not be transported to Moyamensing prison by wagon. Washington, D.C., reported nearly deserted streets on November 5, the day Americans voted to re-elect Ulysses S. Grant to the presidency. That winter, New Orleans postponed its horse-racing schedule. In the West, battles between the Apache Indians and the U.S. Cavalry were carried out on foot for want of mounts. A humorist noted in the *Daily Alta California* that April, "I think I had begun to feel a little slighted by the epizootic—it was so long in coming, but it is here at last, and California is not behind the times."

Alexandre Liautard and his colleagues quickly agreed that the disease was a contagious influenza, of what they called the "catarrhal" form. Influenza viruses have bedeviled man and domestic animals throughout history. Because influenza viruses are prone to surface antigen alterations that allow them to change virulence, increase infectiousness, or jump species, an influenza iteration may manifest as a massive outbreak. Modern virologists have theorized that the 1872 equine epizootic might have been a highly pathogenic avian flu spillover event—that is, an avian flu that developed the ability to attack horses. This hypothesis is supported by the historical observation that, during the months that the equine epizootic (*hippozootic*) was circulating in North America, newspapers across the continent were simultaneously reporting a rapidly spreading avian epizootic (*ornicephalzymosis*). Contemporaries noted the coincidence, even if they couldn't explain it according to the science of the day: The experimental investigations of European microbiologists Louis Pasteur and Robert Koch, which would eventually provide evidence for a bacteriological "germ theory" of disease, were still in the process of being carried out, and even once their findings were published, the American medical community would take years to fully accept and apply them.*

---

* At the time of the Great Epizootic, physicians and veterinarians often subscribed to a confusing and apparently self-contradictory array of views con-

When it came to treatment, the epizootic presented yet another opportunity for educated veterinary surgeons to distinguish themselves from those who brought their untrained opinions to bear on questions of equine health and healing. The so-called "veterinarians"—horse doctors, farriers, patent-medicine purveyors, and others—had rushed forward with a contradictory mess of solutions. According to a story in *The New York Herald,* "Nearly every doctor has his own peculiar method of treating the disease, and aconite, tar water, solution of tar, alcohol, and belladonna are all administered." A *New York Times* writer observed, "Of the modes of treatment, homeopathy appears to be in the most general favor, and to be used more successfully." Wealthy newspaper magnate and trotting-horse breeder Robert Bonner asserted, in multiple outlets, the efficacy of an oral remedy containing a toxic brew of tartar emetic (used to kill intestinal parasites) and niter (an ingredient in gunpowder). A letter from Union army general Benjamin Roberts printed in *The New York Times* advised readers to apply turpentine to the skin overlying the afflicted horse's throat and rub vigorously until blisters formed. Letters published elsewhere suggested a variety of alternative therapies, including washing the throat with alcohol, applying essential oils (peppermint or balsam copaiba) to the tongue, or supplementing the animal's feed ration with large quantities of ginger or salt. Drivers smothered their horses in blankets or devised neck-scarves made of carpet, cloth, or rags. Even the most basic question of convalescence was somehow made controversial. A *New York Herald* reporter wrote that "[t]here is a diversity of opinion as to whether rest is good for

---

cerning the propagation of diseases. The scientific debate over spontaneous generation had brought to light evidence that some diseases of the flesh are associated with the presence of microbial elements, but mid-nineteenth-century investigations focused on fungal organisms, rather than bacteria or viruses, because these were more discernible under the relatively affordable light microscopes prevalent at the time. Reporting on the epizootic several days after its arrival in the city, a *New York Times* story suggests this view: "Practically, the case stands thus. Epidemics in man and animals are in great proportion dependent on vegetables or spores, which are taken into the body, multiply with inconceivable rapidity, and wear it out as crops wear out a soil, as the oidium, one of these vegetable growths, exhausts and ruins the grape."

the horse or not, as some of the large horse owners insist that the horses afflicted with the disease kept on constant work are doing better than those resting in the hospital."

By contrast, the educated veterinary surgeons offered advice that was more or less in accordance with today's standard of care for equine influenza, at least for uncomplicated cases. "The treatment of influenza," wrote Liautard,

> must be in accordance with the symptoms. During the simple catarrhal form of the disease the diet should consist of dry or boiled oats, rye, mashes, or corn meal gruels, roots and fruits. These articles should be varied and given in small quantities. The temperature should be regulated by blanketing, bandaging of the extremities, and general or local friction. Good disinfection should be secured, and disinfectants used in moderation.
>
> In the majority of cases, the hygienic measures above mentioned, together with rest, will prove entirely sufficient to effect a cure. Rest is of the utmost importance. Without it the animal will scarcely escape some of the sequelae of the disease.

But Liautard went on to describe a variety of questionable treatments for the more severely affected horse: mustard applications, steam from marshmallow leaf-tea, belladonna, antimony, soap laxatives, "stimulants" like ammonia or camphor, drenches of ale or brandy—none of which are superior to those recommended by the quacks Liautard loathed.

Nonetheless, by highlighting the healing power of rest, Liautard and his colleagues powerfully reinforced the messaging of the animal-welfare community, which had been decrying the evils of overwork since long before the epizootic. "Experience has taught me that rest is of paramount importance, for all those animals whose labors were suspended as soon as they were sick escaped complications and resumed work in a few days. On the other hand, a large mortality occurred among railroad and stage horses. Many of these animals, being kept constantly at work, were attacked by serious complications," Liautard wrote. The efforts by animal advocates—through public education, shaming, and the threat of arrest—to prevent owners and drivers from overworking their sick or injured horses helped veterinarians to save more of their equine patients.

.   .   .

The epizootic swept into Boston just as George T. Angell was preparing for his wedding, at the age of forty-nine, to a widow named Eliza Martin. Two days later, a historic fire tore through the city, beginning in the basement of a downtown dry-goods store on the evening of November 9. While some of Boston's horses were recovering by then, the fire department had few healthy ones to rely on, which meant that most of its water trucks had to be pulled to the scene by hand—losing precious moments in which the fire was able to cross Summer Street and surge north. Observers would debate for years whether healthy horses might have prevented the catastrophe that ensued: some 776 buildings burned, with a total estimated economic loss of $73.5 million, or $1.5 billion in today's money. In the days following the disaster, a false rumor began to spread among Bostonians that the Massachusetts SPCA had forbidden the firefighters to use their horses, leading to threats of lynching against Angell and the society's other officers—a grave enough prospect that the society felt compelled to issue a sternly worded denial.

Despite the devastation, Angell saw the horse flu as a tremendous boon for the Massachusetts SPCA. "To societies like ours," *Our Dumb Animals* opined in the first week of November, just before the fire, "we look upon this public calamity as a missionary agent. Every man, woman, and child in the community has been affected by it; it has made people think about animals, and feel for them." A month later, in the fire's aftermath, the paper struck a similar note: The flu, it wrote, "has passed, and left its record, not only upon horses, but upon men. Nothing but a war or pestilence could have more engaged the public attention, affected more the public interests, occupied more space in newspapers, or more time in people's conversation."

Humane education had always been, and remained, Angell's true passion, and it was the area where he continued to forge a new and strange sort of consciousness in his readers about the animals in their midst. This came out most clearly in the nominally factual stories that *Our Dumb Animals* curated for its readers, generally pulled from other publications, tales in which animals were found to display an improbable and at times miraculous intelligence. The mule in Louisville that kicked its driver as punishment for whipping it. The dog in Wilmington that ran to warn his mistress when she had forgotten to turn off the gas in the nursery one night. The mother cat that, having witnessed her kittens drowned by her owner, retrieved a neighbor cat to come help her dig up the bodies. The Newfoundland dog that helped a girl navigate a deep snowfall by making a path for her. The family of geese that, having been stolen and imprisoned in a barn, were rescued after the gander escaped and led his owners to the scene.

The truth or falsity of these tales was left up to the reader's imagination, but by presenting them in issue after issue, Angell encouraged a sense that some deep well of *enchantment* existed in the minds of our animal friends, and in the animal-human bond itself, an enchantment that lurked just below the grasp of present understanding. And here and there, in these tales, one began to see a place for the new cultural figure of the veterinary surgeon—as a symbol of expert caring, somewhat akin to the kindly country doctor who had begun to rear his head in Victorian literature.

Consider, for example, the remarkable story of the actress Leo Hudson, who performed equestrian feats on stages across America with her horse, Black Bess. During a matinee in St. Louis on May 11, 1873, both horse and rider fell from a high ramp nearly fourteen feet to the stage. In an issue that autumn, *Our Dumb Animals* excerpted a newspaper account that described what happened next with astonishing pathos:

As soon as the accident occurred, Miss Hudson summoned a veterinary surgeon; and every effort was made to save the life of the pony, but in vain. Miss Hudson, bruised and lacerated as she was by her severe fall, never left her pet until it was dead, but sat holding its head in her arms, talking to it and soothing its sufferings as she might have done for a human being she loved. When it died, she became almost frantic with grief. Her own injuries had seriously shocked her nerves; but she held out for more than twelve hours by the side of her dying pony, utterly refusing to leave it even for the sake of the rest and care she herself needed almost as imperatively as did her poor dumb patient. When the pony died she was utterly exhausted with the shock of her injuries and loss of her sleep; and this, with her passionate grief, brought on an attack of brain fever, of which she soon after died.

In reality, almost everything in this dual death scene was exaggerated: As more rigorous news accounts had noted, Hudson actually outlived her pony by weeks, not hours, even recovering enough to take in a circus performance, before dying on June 2. As for Black Bess, far from expiring with her head cradled in her owner's arms, she had been killed by the veterinary surgeon with a bullet to the brain, as was customary and humane. Yet these distortions by a fantasizing reporter were, in a sense, more telling than truth. To properly sentimentalize the tale, it was necessary not only to have Hudson die of grief, unable to survive for even a day without her beloved animal friend; it was desirable to keep the veterinarian there looking on, a kindly, passive figure whose role was merely to confirm that no happier outcome was possible—not, as in reality, employing his agency to end suffering in a way that no human doctor could or can.

Even as Angell's publication was helping to create the template for this kind of sentimental animal storytelling, his own interest in the nascent field of veterinary medicine tended to focus around this question of humane euthanasia, which already had become a critical duty for the educated veterinary surgeon. During Angell's years in Europe, he had noticed that the best slaughterhouses tended to have veterinary surgeons present, ensuring that the killing of livestock was carried out in as humane a fashion as possible. As he used the pages of *Our Dumb Animals* to argue for a similar provision in the United States, he also looked to the eminent veterinary surgeon D. D. Slade to codify the scientific understanding on the subject more broadly. In April 1874, Slade, a longtime MSPCA board member who had originally trained as a human doctor before turning his attention to animals and studying briefly at Alfort, contributed a long species-by-species guide to euthanasia, which reiterated the importance of fast killing with bullets or blows to the head and provided illustrations that specified where to strike. And in the wake of Slade's essay, the MSPCA began providing hammers and hoods to police stations in and around Boston, along with instructions for how to use them.

·   ·   ·

That same year in New York, following a dispute within the New York College of Veterinary Surgeons' board of trustees, Alexandre Liautard resigned. On leaving, he took with him not just his extensive museum collection but also the whole instructional faculty and the entire student body, and he promptly installed all of them in a new school, which he called the American Veterinary College. He purchased a building at 141 West 54th Street to house the college's laboratories, classrooms, and clinical facilities. Liautard would himself live, practice, and teach at that address through the end of the century.

The hundreds of veterinarians who trained directly under Dr. Liautard—"Frenchy" to his students, but never to his face— would remember their professor as "very fatherly with his students, stern, and yet intimate, without allowing familiarity. Severe and friendly, strict to all and demanding of each the exact performance of his duties, he was very much liked and yet feared more or less by all." Liautard's influence on veterinary education extended beyond the institutions he helped establish and maintain. Throughout his career, at meetings and in the pages of veterinary journals, Liautard participated in the lively debate among leading members of the profession about what veterinary medical education should consist of, in terms of admissions criteria, subjects taught, years of study, and requirements for graduation. As veterinary schools multiplied, first as private ventures in America's booming horse-powered cities, and later at publicly funded land-grant universities, they followed the basic scheme proposed by Liautard—which is to say, the Alfort model. Later, Liautard pushed American veterinarians to set a new educational standard, surpassing those of European countries—to require a national examination for veterinary graduates, administered by an elected board of examiners, before they would be recognized as qualified veterinarians. He declared that this innovation would finally ensure "the prevention of quackery, or at least the prevention of its increase beyond its present extent."

To Liautard's ongoing dismay, charlatanism remained a persistent problem in New York and across America, as unqualified practitioners continued to compete for clients against a growing number of educated veterinary surgeons. One grocer's reminiscence from this period describes the signage fronting a series of Brooklyn establishments: "Professor Ricord, Veterinarian. A graduate of the school of experience. All curable diseases of the horse skillfully treated. Consultation Free," read one on State Street. "Office of Professor Baker, the Common Sense Horse Doctor," trumpeted another on Flatbush Avenue.

For this and other reasons, the interests of professional veterinarians and animal-welfare advocates would remain favorably aligned throughout the era. Historian Ann Norton Greene has noted that while the economic value of horses provided a financial incentive for their owners to invest in veterinary care, American veterinary surgeons discovered that "emphasizing the affective value of horses proved to be a way to promote the utility of veterinary medicine and enhance veterinary status." The public perception that relief of animal suffering was a worthy end in itself, and the positioning of the veterinary surgeon as one professionally bound to provide the animal with relief, reframed the relationship between the veterinarian, animal patient, and owner, elevating the status of the educated veterinarian. The veterinarian's opinion about whether an animal was in pain or distress began to outweigh that of its handlers. ASPCA prosecutions often hinged on the expert testimony of the veterinarian. Eventually, the provision of veterinary care came to be thought of as an essential humane duty owed by an owner to his or her animal.

A few years after the new college's founding, Henry Bergh spoke at its opening exercises. He pointedly lectured the incoming veterinary students about the particular vulnerabilities of their principal species of patient, and on the humane duties owed especially to this animal since the epizootic had revealed its social and economic value:

> It is a fact as strange as it is abhorrent to every sentiment of justice and gratitude, that of all the lower animals, the one which is most useful, profitable, and indispensable to mankind, is the most abused, and that is the horse!
>
> It is more particularly towards that noble creature that your scientific and humane practice is directed; and the wisdom which dictates that earnest and exceptional solicitude, has a ready explanation in that great popular panic, which a few years ago manifested itself, when this country was threatened with the loss of labor of that unequalled servant.
>
> In order to protect him from harm, and to repair injury by the least painful methods, you penetrate the mysterious economy of nature, and interrogate the sources of life and motion. To accomplish this laudable purpose, and to prevent waste and agony resulting from the ignorance and insensibility of impiricism, the experienced gentleman, Dr. Liautard, to whose untiring perseverance this College mainly owes its existence, has placed it within your power, gentlemen, to obtain the necessary skill.

Bergh continued, optimistically, with what must have been music to Liautard's ears: "The 'Horse Doctor' has disappeared, to be replaced by the veterinary surgeon, who takes rank by the side of the human practitioner. And I fail to discover, gentlemen, any essential differences between the principles and purposes which underlie the human and animal medical sciences."

Systematic hunting of bison for their skins made the
animals' fate the subject of a national debate.

Chapter 8

EVERY BUFFALO DEAD

During the Pleistocene epoch, from two and one-half million to twelve thousand years ago, glaciers sucked up so much of the planet's water that the ocean level dropped away from established coastlines. Thus was exposed a six-hundred-mile-wide swath of seabed between Siberia and Alaska, which gradually became home to a succession of lichens, mosses, grasses, shrubs, and trees. Generation by generation, animals traversed this temporary corridor between continents. The opportunity for ecological exchange across this vast stretch of tundra seems fleeting to Anthropocene humans looking back across the eons, but to the animals who tramped the Bering steppe it must have felt anything but. They lived, struggled, reproduced, and died, redrawing their range, century by century, with meandering footfalls in search of conditions favoring their survival and that of their kin.

Horses, camels, and caribou wound west across this so-called land bridge to Asia, while moose and mammoths trudged east to America along with heavy bovids classified as *Bison,* and their predators: wolves, lions, brown bears, and humans (who may have been joining members of their species already arrived by boat). These ancestral bison multiplied and diversified into at least two distinct species, the larger of which eventually died out under conditions of climate change and human predation, leaving faster, nimbler *Bison bison* to populate the continent—at which it succeeded on an astonishing scale. The original combined range of *Bison bison*'s two subspecies covered most of North America, from the Alaskan north slope down to the Gulf of Mexico coastline and from west of the Cascade mountain range to east of the Chesapeake Bay. Across the grasslands of the Great Plains, where *Bison bison* subspecies *bison* particularly thrived, tens of millions of animals grazed the wide-open landscape so thickly in places that they seemed to blanket the earth with their hulking, huffing forms.

The immense stature of the mature bison, up to six feet at the shoulder and two thousand pounds for males, and up to five feet and a thousand pounds for females, is achieved despite a relative paucity of nutrients in the grasses they forage. Deficiencies in quality are made up for in quantity, and like other bovids, bison rely on foregut fermentation to convert biologically inert cellulose into the rich raw materials of life. As enormous as they are, wild bison have an outsize effect on their environment: As they graze the prairie, their selective browsing stimulates new plant growth and provides a check on aggressive herbage. The rubbing of their hairy bodies and horns against woody vegetation reduces the encroachment of trees on open grasslands. Wallowing behaviors, in which bison roll in disturbed soil to cool themselves and to discourage ectoparasites, further benefit plant heterogeneity by creating damp depressions where alternate species can thrive. Bison footprints aerate, and bison droppings and dead bodies enrich, the underlying earth. Rather than depleting prairie vegetation with their prodigious appetites, herds of bison create conditions of ecological health and resilience on North American plains.

Within the herd, made up of females and their calves, juvenile males, and sometimes a handful of older bulls—bachelor males travel separately in small bands—an annual cycle of birthing, mating, and migrating marks their collective life on the range. Neonates, arriving in the first weeks of spring, struggle onto their spindly legs and begin nursing within minutes of being born. Before an hour has passed, they are ready to run with the group. If mother and baby are separated, they will reunite through recognition of one another's breathy grunts and familiar odors, picking one another out from a swirling sea of similar brown bodies. Several weeks after the females have calved, herds converge into great gatherings of many hundred head, now joined by the bachelor bulls, to engage in the grand pageant of the summer rut. Amorous males posture and battle for opportunities to mate the females, who cycle in and out of estrus until successfully bred. By the end of the rutting season, more than 90 percent of adult females are pregnant once again. Herds separate and spread out, increasing their daily traveling distance as they head southward, where they will spend the harshest winter months before making their way north again.

Historically, the maneuvering, massing, and migrating of millions of bison enabled a variety of other animals to make a successful home where they roamed. Elk, deer, pronghorn antelope, bighorn sheep, ground-nesting birds, pollinating insects, and prairie dogs all benefited from the effects of huge bison herds on native vegetation. Amphibians and others made use of rainwater puddling in bison wallows. The abundance of prey animals supported a variety of predators: Cougars, bobcats, black bears, grizzlies, wolves, coyotes, foxes, ferrets, snakes, and skinks all patrolled the plains productively, as did human hunters from the late Pleistocene epoch (at least 11,000 years ago) onward. The bison were not only the most visible but arguably the most critical members of this teeming ecosystem, which persisted until the nineteenth century turned it on its (buffalo) head.

Bison numbers had begun their decline even before then. During the 1700s, white settlers (and their diseases) displaced the Blackfoot, Cheyenne, Comanche, Crow, western Sioux, and other indigenous groups from their productive farmlands in the Missouri River basin out onto the open prairies. Adapting to the use of horses and a fully nomadic lifestyle, many of the Plains tribes vastly intensified their hunting of bison—upon which they came to depend utterly: for food, fuel, clothing, shelter, tools, and tradable goods. The direct effects of harvest conspired with environmental degradation, drought, and disease to substantially decrease bison herds by the early decades of the nineteenth century.

Soon the bison slaughter accelerated, thanks to a huge expansion in trade between the western territories and the eastern markets made possible by the chuffing incursions of steamboats, then railroads, into the North American frontier. Demand for particular buffalo products—salted tongues for eating, and furry skins for fashioning into fleecy robes—drove the killing of millions more animals. Instead of sharing communally in the spoils of summer hunts, thriftily making use of every bison bit, Indians increasingly traded the results of their kills with whites for manufactured goods: steel arrowheads and knives; riding equipment and rifles; clothing, blankets, sugar, wheat flour, and whisky. Fleshy carcasses stripped of saleable commodities littered the prairie in the wake of profligate hunts, fattening families of scavenging carnivores or simply rotting right where they fell.

Trains also brought eager eastern sport hunters out onto the western range. Guided expeditions on horseback (often outfitted and accompanied by army personnel) shot gratuitously into bison herds, leaving hundreds of head to litter the prairie as carrion. Sometimes passengers would even shoot at bison from their rattling railcar windows. Newspapers printed stories of high-profile personages blustering their way through buffalo bloodbaths staged by professionals in order to give them a taste of the chase.

According to the environmental historian Andrew C. Isenberg, who has written the definitive account of the bison's destruction, such recreational hunters were not the primary culprit in the species' plummeting population numbers. Rather, it was a new breed of professional white hunter who, in the 1870s, began slaughtering bison full-time for profit. Improvements in tanning technology had made it possible to process large amounts of leather for carriage fittings, upholstered furniture, and the drive belts that powered factory machines. Bison skin possessed a soft, supple elasticity that made it superior for industrial uses. To answer the new demand, innumerable small teams made up of a campsite manager, a marksman, and two to four skinners dispersed across the prairie in pursuit of scattered bands of bison.

Standing at a distance downwind, the shooter systematically killed his quarry, one by one, usually with a single bullet to the lower chest, trying hard not to spook the animals still grazing nearby. He would continue firing his high-powered rifle until a day's work for the skinners lay dead on the ground. Despite efforts at efficiency, the methods of the market hunt, especially during its early years, engendered tremendous waste. Missed kill shots, skinning mistakes, and spoilage prevented the hides of an estimated four out of five dead bison from making it to market. Collectively, commercial hunters produced unprecedented carnage. The already diminished herds that had formerly dominated the plains now faced total annihilation—threatening impoverishment of both the Indians and the ecosystem.

.   .   .

On January 25, 1872, a letter from a high-ranking officer at Fort Hays, Kansas, describing the devastating effects of sport and hide hunting on local bison populations, reached the New York desk of Henry Bergh. "The buffalo is a noble and harmless animal, timid, and as easily taken as a cow," Major General W. B. Hazen informed the president of the ASPCA. "I would most respectfully and earnestly request that you use such proper influences as may be at your disposal to bring this subject before Congress, with the intention of having such steps taken as will prevent this wicked and wanton waste both of the lives of God's creatures and the valuable food they furnish."

Wasting no time, Bergh forwarded Hazen's letter to *The New York Times,* where it appeared the next morning under the headline "Wanton Butchery." Over the weeks that followed, newspapers across the country reprinted the general's grim assessment, often alongside sympathetic editorial remarks. Hazen's letter prompted at least one other officer on the western frontier, Lieutenant Colonel A. G. Brackett of the U.S. Cavalry, to write to Bergh in condemnation of the slaughter. "The wholesale butchery of buffaloes upon the plains is as needless as it is cruel," he wrote from Nebraska's Omaha barracks. "It is time that something should be done for their protection, and I trust you will make an effort to have Congress interfere in their behalf."

General Hazen and Colonel Brackett, both distinguished veterans of the Union army, observed the bison slaughter from western military posts where the federal government had amassed troops to enforce its brutal policies against the Indian groups that continued to roam the plains in pursuit of vanishing herds. In order to secure access to valuable natural resources, especially mineral wealth and grazing land for cattle, the United States sought to confine the Plains tribes to less-valuable tracts of land set aside as reservations. The same native nations that had been dislocated from their farming settlements during the previous century were thus to be forced back into agriculture or exploitative industrial occupations.

To some U.S. leaders, then, the bison could not disappear fast enough. Many attributed the Union's Civil War victory to its willingness to wage war against the entire Southern economy, and predicted that success in subjugating the Indians would depend upon the same hard approach. "Kill every buffalo you can," Lieutenant Colonel Richard Dodge encouraged a sport hunter visiting Nebraska in 1867. "Every buffalo dead is an Indian gone." In his 1872 annual report to Congress, Interior Secretary Columbus Delano put it more soberly: "The rapid disappearance of game from the former hunting-grounds must operate largely in favor of our efforts to confine the Indians to smaller areas, and compel them to abandon their nomadic customs and establish themselves in permanent homes. So long as the game existed in abundance, there was little disposition manifested to abandon the chase."

General Hazen didn't agree. "The theory that the buffalo should be killed to deprive the Indian of food is a fallacy," he insisted in his letter to the ASPCA, "as these people are becoming harmless under a rule of justice." Other military observers went further, proposing that allowing the bison slaughter to continue would provoke, rather than subdue, the native population. *Our Dumb Animals* printed a letter from Edward Wynkoop, a longtime federal agent in Indian country who had resigned his post in protest over the burning of a Cheyenne village, eloquently making the same point. Wynkoop described the bison slaughter as "one of the greatest grievances the Indians have" and "their strongest incentive to declare war," and he related a story about an interaction he once had with a Cheyenne chief after some of his men had killed an ox belonging to a white family: "Your people make a big talk, and sometimes make war, if an Indian kills a white man's ox, to keep his wife and children from starving; what do you think my people ought to say, and do, when they themselves see their cattle killed by your race, when they are not hungry."

The idea that slaughtering the Indians' food source might be not only militarily counterproductive but also immoral received some attention, too, in the wake of Hazen's letter. *The Baltimore Sun* editorialized that "Mr. Bergh should use his influence in behalf of the poor Indians as well as the poor buffalo, who in a short time will have ceased to exist, like the noble beasts who have challenged Gen. Hazen's sympathies, unless their white neighbors pay more respect to their property and persons."

.　　.　　.

That sense of twin disappearance, of bison and Indians, haunted some white Americans. In the summer of 1872, one of them, a twenty-two-year-old New Yorker named George Bird Grinnell, headed west determined to witness, and take part in, an Indian buffalo hunt.

It was not Grinnell's first trip out west. Two years prior, as a Yale student, he had joined an expedition led by a professor of paleontology there, Othniel C. Marsh, to dig up ancient animal bones for study, sending back thirty-six crates of fossils that demonstrated the existence of scores of extinct species. The whole five-month odyssey had enchanted Grinnell, the son of a wealthy banker, particularly the time he spent with fur trappers in the region. "Their mode of life appealed strongly to a young man fond of the open," he would later write, "and while I was with them I could not imagine, nor can I imagine now, a more attractive—a happier—life than theirs."

And so, even as he reluctantly returned to New York and to a job in his father's business trading stocks, he dreamed of mounting another western sojourn. He had heard many travelers speak with awe about Indian bison-hunting practices, where hundreds of men on horseback would make a "surround" of a thousand-strong herd, gathering enough meat in the process to sustain their community through an entire winter. That July, Grinnell and a friend hired a guide to help them join up with the Pawnee, who had left their reservation lands in Nebraska to make a major hunt in Kansas. When they finally caught up with the tribe, what they found was essentially a traveling city of four thousand men, women, and children, disassembling and reassembling their lodges day by day and moving along the prairie in search of their quarry.

Fortuitously for Grinnell, they did not find it until the day after he and his party caught up, allowing the young men to join some

George Bird Grinnell

eight hundred Pawnee hunters on horseback as they made a ten-mile sprint to the herd's location. Only at a half-mile's distance did the bison perceive the danger they were in and begin to lumber off toward the opposite bluffs. Grinnell watched with fascination as the fastest Pawnee hunters raced past the herd and circled around the front, attempting to turn the fleeing animals back toward the plain. While not entirely successful, this effort did throw the herd into confusion, and the Indians—mostly armed with bows and arrows—proceeded to make quick work of their slaughter.

In Grinnell's account of the hunt, written the following year and published in a new magazine called *Forest and Stream,* which eventually he himself would own and edit, he made two pointed observations about the ethics of the Pawnee hunt. One was about the way in which certain leaders, whom he called the "Pawnee Police," patrolled the leading edge of the chase, in order to make sure that no individual hunter could take too much game at the expense of the collective. And the other was the admirably conservation-minded attitude that the tribe took toward killing, doing it for their and their families' sustenance, not merely for sport. "How different would have been the course of a party of white hunters had they the same opportunity," Grinnell wrote. "They would have killed as many animals, but would have left all but enough for one day's use to be devoured by the wolves or to rot upon the prairie."

Over the coming decades, Grinnell would become one of the most important figures in American conservation, and he was not alone in finding an unusual sort of inspiration in Indians' attitude toward the natural world. As white Americans awoke to new ways of thinking about animals in the decades after the Civil War, many of them found occasion to reflect on how the continent had, in fact, already nurtured centuries-old cultural and spiritual traditions that took their obligations to animals more seriously than the Judeo-Christian tradition ever had. It is foolhardy, of course, to make generalizations about the hundreds of Indian nations that still lived over much of the continent in the mid-nineteenth century, but they all seemed to be united in a sense that humans were part of the natural world, not its divinely ordained masters, and therefore were obligated to use its bounty with care. To certain groups, this responsibility was one that transcended the human lifespan: Quite a few believed in reincarnation, and imagined that animals, not just people, went through the same cycles of death and rebirth.

Some white Americans, obsessed with identifying a Native equivalent of Heaven, bowdlerized those beliefs into the idea of a "happy hunting-ground" in which people and their animals would be united after death—a notion that particularly delighted animal-welfare advocates, many of whom had revised their own personal views of the Christian afterlife to imagine animals there. In November 1872, *Our Dumb Animals* printed a treacly poem that had been written by a doctor in honor of his deceased Newfoundland, and it included this stanza:

> *Oh! well may the Indian hunter*
> *Lie calm on his couch of skins*
> *When the pain of this world ceases,*
> *And the joy of the next begins!*
> *On the "Great Spirit's" prairies,*
> *Under the blue skies of yore,*
> *Will not his stud and watch-dog*
> *Answer his call once more?*

On matters of conservation, too, an awareness of Native stewardship practices over the land—in contrast to the rapacious tendencies of white frontiersmen—was also arising. This was bound up with a tendency (which the historian Shari Huhndorf has called "going native") to fetishize Indians, casting their vanishing way of life as a more innocent and authentically natural counterpoint to the speed and churn of East Coast modernity. One could see this most vividly in the rise of Indian-themed "fraternal" organizations, like the Improved Order of Red Men, or the rise in boys' camps and clubs with Indian names, both of which began during this period. As Huhndorf points out, any positive sentiment toward Indians was almost always bound up with an ironclad sense of their inferiority, as well as the inevitability of their disappearance. For example, members of a group called the Grand Order of the Iroquois trafficked not just in Indian-themed rituals but in genuine ethnological data on the Iroquois tribe, even as they also tended to believe, in the words of one member, that the "superiority both mental and physical of the Anglo-Saxon race" would render it "impossible" for Indians to continue to exist. As Grinnell himself would write much later, after ruefully describing the atrocities against tribes in Alaska during the Klondike gold rush: "[T]here is an inevitable conflict between civilization and savagery, and wherever the two touch each other, the weaker people must be destroyed."

As the conservation sensibility began to take root in the early 1870s, it became clear that what was to be conserved were the animals and the natural setting, not the indigenous way of life that had conserved both over the centuries. This position was illustrated vividly in one of 1872's most historic developments: the establishment of Yellowstone as the nation's first national park. At the moment when President Grant signed the mammoth park into existence that spring, hunting parties from multiple indigenous groups were camped within it, and Grant's pen stroke suddenly made it illegal for them to continue living off the land the way they and their ancestors had for generations. Over the years that followed, federal troops would use the force of arms to prevent them from returning.

.   .   .

By the 1870s, many Americans recognized that the continuation of the bison slaughter would bring about not just a reduction in their numbers but their complete elimination. Since the end of the previous century, when French naturalist Georges Cuvier determined, based upon a study of several fossils, that some creatures that had once flourished upon the earth had subsequently vanished from it, the idea of extinction had gradually gained wide acceptance. Cuvier's generation of scientists tended to see extinction as a prehistorical phenomenon—a cataclysm ending an old Creation before the initiation of a new one. According to this theory, if extinction still sometimes occurred, it did so as an accident of nature, falling outside of the Creator's plan. But with each passing decade humans observed more extinction occurring in real time, particularly as a local phenomenon, and often as a direct result of human activity. Nineteenth-century naturalists documented the great auk and the Charles Island tortoise going the way of the dodo and the Steller's sea cow. In North America, species that had once been common on the Eastern Seaboard were retreating westward in front of white settlement—the bison and the passenger pigeon among them.

The revolutionary work of Charles Darwin, even while affirming the animal-welfare idea that humans and the creatures around them were part of the same extended family, capable of comparable sufferings, also recast extinguishment of entire animal species as a natural consequence of interspecies competition. The discoveries of Othniel Marsh, Grinnell's professor at Yale—who by 1873, after five western expeditions in all, had brought his tally of documented extinct species up to more than two hundred—helped bolster the sense that extinction was not something to become overly sentimental about. That January, the *Topeka Commonwealth* delivered a report on the bison in Kansas, laying out the "terrible arithmetic of his destruction": 43,000 hides shipped from Dodge City in just three months, following the arrival of the railroad there in September 1872. This "magnificent butchery," the paper noted, "forecasts the speedy extinction of the prairie denizen," but added that the bison's dying out "is serving a great purpose in the social economy of the nation":

[B]y the time the last buffalo has disappeared from Kansas the raw frontier will be subdued to civilization, and be habitable and self-supporting. The buffalo will in this, or at the furthest, the next generation, take its place in the natural history books along with the dodo, as an interesting animal, no living specimen of which can be found in nature.

What few Americans seemed to understand, as of the early 1870s, was that the crisis among the continent's wildlife species stretched far beyond the bison, and that concerted human action would be necessary to prevent a whole host of disappearances. But the young scientist who would soon become the late nineteenth century's great prophet of extinction, Joel A. Allen, was beginning to formulate both thoughts.

A decade older than Grinnell, Allen began collecting animal specimens as a teenager on his family's farm in Springfield, Massachusetts, and eventually found his way to Harvard, where he studied under Louis Agassiz. At around the same time that Grinnell joined an expedition to collect bones for Marsh, Allen was collecting present-day animals for Agassiz and his Museum of Comparative Zoology. In the summer of 1871 and then again that winter, Allen embarked on bison hunting in Kansas, trying to bring back skeletons and skins of as many different kinds as possible: cows and bulls, full-grown and calves. He also hunted birds and smaller mammals; when he and his party returned east in January 1872, they shipped with them 200 mammal skins, 60 full skeletons, 240 additional skulls, 1,500 bird skins, and 100-plus whole birds preserved in alcohol.

He made an additional specimen-collecting trip to Yellowstone the following year, but after that, the remainder of Allen's long career as a zoologist and ornithologist was devoted to original research. He proved himself not merely a brilliant taxonomizer of specimens but also a remarkable reader of history, both natural and human. He noted accounts from seventeenth-century priests near Montreal, detailing how five-hundred-strong herds of elk and deer "seemed to follow them everywhere"; a record of one hunt in Mississippi, circa 1796, that killed a hundred bears; tallies of seventeenth- and eighteenth-century bounties paid out by townships in Massachusetts and Pennsylvania, rewarding those who killed wolves, panthers, lynxes, bears, skunks, squirrels, and more; trading statistics from the 1780s showing how hundreds of thousands of fur animals could be harvested in a single year. He dug up accounts from European explorers that described flocks of waterfowl "darkening the air," the noise of them resembling the "rumbling of distant thunder"; one explorer in 1584 encountered a gathering of cranes so large that their cries sounded "as if an armie of men had showted all together." He found passages in which Thomas Morton, the early New England colonist, described flocks of a thousand turkeys and a thousand geese at a time, and reported seeing "millions of turtle-doves"—that is, the now-doomed passenger pigeon—perched in a single grove of trees.

In 1876, a few years after his Kansas sojourn, Allen published *The American Bisons, Living and Extinct,* an ambitious two-part work consisting of 221 pages of text, an appendix, a colored map, and twelve meticulously labeled lithographic illustrations. Based on careful measurements of fossils in Agassiz's museum, Allen determined that some of the specimens previously thought to belong to separate extinct bison species actually belonged to a single diverse species. Although, in his final analysis, he mistook two contemporaneous species for two occurring along the same lineage leading to modern bison, his findings correctly simplified the existing understanding of bison prehistory in North America, showing it to exemplify the Darwinian idea of variation as the raw material of evolution by natural selection. The book went on to survey the natural history of *Bison bison,* describing at length its gradual retreat from the eastern United States; wherever possible, Allen took care to quantify the losses over defined periods of time, in order to demonstrate the slope of the diminishment. He made clear where he thought the species was headed. "These facts," he concluded, "are sufficient to show that the present decrease of the buffalo is extremely rapid, and indicate most clearly that the period of his extinction will soon be reached, unless some strong arm is interposed in his behalf."

Joel A. Allen

During the same year, Allen would publish a series of articles in which, almost a decade before other commentators, he sounded the alarm—the necessity of action to forestall the disappearance of countless species beyond the bison. He prophesied that "the close of the next half-century will witness a large increase in the list of the wholly extirpated species, and a great decrease in numbers of others that are now comparatively abundant." He called for the creation of game preserves, and for laws to forbid the killing of threatened species when their numbers dropped too low. He hoped that the nation's SPCAs would take up the mantle of bird protection, and that new societies would take on birds as their "express object," a wish that would find fulfillment before century's end in the Audubon movement.

Yet when it came to the bison, even Allen was pervaded with defeatism. He supported measures to stop them from dying out altogether—a ban on hunting cows and juveniles for hides, for example, and on hunting any bison at all during certain seasons of the year. "[I]t is greatly to our disgrace," he wrote, "that nothing has as yet been done to check the wholesale and almost useless murder of these defenseless beasts." But he perceived that the conditions under which these noble animals had dominated the American heartland could no longer obtain, not with the spread of white settlement, which brought a level of agriculture incompatible with their prodigious migrating herds. (He raised the idea that the nation might find at least a temporary preserve for bison in "the more worthless portions of the public domain" that were "useless for agricultural purposes.")

For all his nascent conservationism, Allen could not see beyond white America's self-sustaining belief in the inevitability of westward expansion—the sense that the Indian and bison, in their twinned, nomadic modes of existence, simply had to be sacrificed to the interest of white civilization. "Though both are noble in their way," he wrote, the bison and the Indians were both vanishing in order "to give place to a higher grade of life and a fuller development of the natural resources of the continent." Indeed, he praised the bison for all the ways that it had contributed to the settlers' cause: "After having formed for thousands of years the main subsistence of hundreds of thousands of the native inhabitants of this continent, his products have added greatly to the comfort of more civilized humanity, and rendered possible the exploration and development of our vast plains at a much less sacrifice of comfort and pecuniary means than could otherwise have been the case."

·   ·   ·

A similar defeatism, in the end, would doom the effort to create federal bison protections. In March 1874, Representative Green-bury Fort of Illinois stood before his House colleagues to recommend, on behalf of the Territories Committee, a bill "to prevent the useless slaughtering of buffaloes" within the unincorporated territories of the United States. The language of the bill, introduced as H.R. 921, prohibited anyone other than an Indian from killing or wounding a female bison for any purpose, or from killing or wounding a male bison except to harvest its meat, hide, or both. Fort's was not the first bill introduced for the protection of the bison, but it was the first to make it out of committee for general debate. New York Representative Samuel Cox indignantly opposed the exception made for indigenous Americans, believing the white settler to have an equal or greater claim over what he called "our public meat." Others echoed Interior Secretary Columbus Delano's position that the government would never succeed in "civilizing" the Indian nations so long as the buffalo roamed the range. But the real reason to reject the bill, according to Representative Omar Conger of Michigan, was its futility. "There is no law that Congress can pass," he claimed, "that will prevent the buffalo disappearing before the march of civilization."

Even those who viewed the animals' destruction as a necessary evil acknowledged a reverence for the species and the American wilderness it evoked. Congressmen on both sides of the debate denounced their indiscriminate killing with words like "wicked," "wanton," and "barbarism." Pro-protection delegate Richard McCormick of the Arizona Territory read excerpts from General Hazen's and Colonel Brackett's two-year-old letters to Henry Bergh, but he, like his opponents, judged the lawmakers' efforts to be in vain. "I do not believe that any bill will entirely accomplish the purpose for which this bill is presented," he admitted, "but I think we ought to make an enactment that will at least have a tendency in that direction." H.R. 921 passed the House with 132 votes in favor.

The bison bill came before the Senate on June 23. Again, the provision allowing Indians to hunt without restriction roiled the legislators, almost resulting in the procedural death of the bill without a vote. "Certainly this is a very important bill," protested Kansas Senator John James Ingalls. "Unless some measure of this kind is adopted the entire race of buffaloes will be exterminated in a very few years." Whether or not his colleagues believed his implicit sense that the bison might yet be saved, a vote was called, and the bison surprisingly won the day. The Senate forwarded H.R. 921 to the White House for presidential review and signature.

Had the president signed the legislation, the American bison might have persisted on the northern plains into the next century at least, allowing future generations an opportunity to permanently protect their habitat and migration routes, leading to durable conservation of the charismatic species. Instead, pessimism prevailed. President Grant allowed H.R. 921 to expire on his desk, unsigned.

THE FRIEND OF THE BRUTES.

Henry Bergh became the face of the movement's
accomplishments, as well as its perceived overreaches.

Chapter 9

SLIPPERY SLOPES

On February 11, 1875, *The World* introduced its readers to a term they likely had never seen before: *polypragmonous.* The word derived from Plutarch, the newspaper explained, and described a person "who cannot be happy unless he is either prying into other people's affairs or regulating other people's conduct." After supplying a few examples of such busybodies in history and literature, the paper opined that New York's current polypragmon par excellence was Henry Bergh, as evidenced by a bill then under consideration in Albany: one "proposing that his jurisdiction shall be stretched so far as to include not only the quadrupeds but all the bipeds of the city."

The bill in question was indeed a remarkable one, and its existence underscored just how fully Bergh's moral crusade had entrenched itself in nine years. In collaboration with Elbridge Gerry, the ASPCA's longtime legal counsel, and a wealthy Quaker philanthropist named John D. Wright, Bergh had brought a bill to Albany that would empower a new organization to prosecute cases of cruelty to *children.* Under the terms of the proposed legislation, the new Society for the Prevention of Cruelty to Children (SPCC) would have the power to arrest parents who abused their offspring, and even to remove the victims temporarily or permanently from their care.

Most of the city's newspapers were heartily supportive of the bill. The *World* was largely alone in its disdain at the thought of Bergh, that incorrigible polypragmon, being authorized "to break into the garrets of the poor and carry off their children upon the suspicion of a spanking." Not even the bill's supporters would deny that it was being put forward with the city's destitute children in mind, and Catholic clergy in the state had become alarmed at the implications, suspecting, with some justification, that poor Catholic immigrants could be disproportionately caught up in its machinery, and also fearing the bill's wording might result in Catholic children being given over to Protestant institutions. In the event the law should pass, one legislator warned, "poor parents, inexperienced in law and without means to engage counsel, are at the mercy of the society, who can shipwreck their domestic happiness and break up their homes."

The problem for these opponents was that the moral logic of the SPCC, once one had come to accept the existence of the SPCA, seemed close to inescapable. Moral norms really can evolve by way of analogy: An awakening to the injustice of one behavior is often achieved through a new understanding of how it's similar to another, manifestly unjust behavior. If a man should be imprisoned for beating his horse with an axe handle—to pick one example of a case that Bergh had recently prosecuted—why not the men who routinely beat their children bloody, a deed that was arguably illegal under existing New York law but seldom if ever prosecuted? And why should such parents be allowed to keep their children? Bergh's own critics had long invoked this precise argument in belittling his cause: How could he expend so much effort and money on animal suffering when so many humans also suffered?

Yet one could see how the moral logic might run in the opposite direction—and here is where the power of analogy always cuts both ways. The right of parents to raise their children as they saw fit seemed like a bedrock principle of American life. If Bergh's campaign against cruelty implied that this principle needed to be thrown out, then wasn't his whole campaign, including the part on behalf of animals, a tyrannical one? Think of the "monstrous offence against justice and Christianity" that Bergh had carried out only recently, the *World* reminded readers, "when he actually caused a poor laboring man, the father and sole support of a family of three children, to be sent to jail for three months in the depth of this cruel winter, for the atrocious crime of killing a cat."

The notion that a seemingly reasonable change is inadvisable because it might lead to some further, unacceptably extreme outcome is called a "slippery slope" argument. It's generally classed as a logical fallacy, given how easily this form of argumentation can be abused: A byzantine chain of analogy can invariably be constructed to link the most innocuous action with something wholly abhorrent. (One infamous defense of incest, usually attributed to the philosopher Sextus Empiricus, observes that it is perfectly normal to touch your mother's toe, and the rest differs only by degree.) And yet as norms evolve, that sense of involuntarily *sliding* toward some new change, as a natural moral consequence of a change that has come before, can feel very real for those caught up in it, whether or not they welcome the destination being slid toward.

America in the spring of 1875 was caught up in moral slippery slopes, much like the one surrounding the SPCC. A decade after the surrender at Appomattox cemented the end of slavery, the fervor that surrounded the abolitionist cause had spilled out into a whole host of other issues, but so had a fear that this wave of activist energy might go too far, or might already have done so. First and foremost, of course, was the struggle of the formerly enslaved themselves, whose attempt to gain the basic recognitions of citizenship was collapsing amid the brutal backlash to Reconstruction; the specter of social equality between the races would become the slippery slope that convinced white Americans to renege on the fundamental promises of the Constitution. Activism swirled, too, around the question of women's proper roles, which inspired some radicals to see gendered injustice in the basic structures of the family, like marriage and monogamy. Nor was it lost on the burgeoning postwar business community that many of their workers, mired in an economic depression since the Panic of 1873, had begun gathering inspiration from Europe's radical left, from the ideals that had birthed the short-lived Paris Commune. The accelerating changes of the postwar economy were creating new extremes—extreme wealth, extreme thoughts—even as a newspaper culture of extreme saturation, powered by the telegraph, could make the entire nation aware (and wary) of it all.

· · ·

Henry Bergh's campaign to protect children had begun on a spring day in 1874, when he was visited at the ASPCA offices by Etta Wheeler, a church volunteer in the tenements of Hell's Kitchen. Wheeler pleaded with Bergh to intervene in the case of a little girl being kept in barbarous conditions by her foster parents. It was not the first time that Bergh had been approached on behalf of a child, but this time he decided to act: Two days later, on April 9, the affair came before Judge Lawrence of the state supreme court. The little girl's name was Mary Ellen McCormack, and she was about to make history as the first prosecuted case of child abuse in the United States.

Mary Ellen was ten years of age at the time, though her definite birth year was only established later. In her stream-of-consciousness testimony before the court, she said, "I don't know how old I am; my mother and father are both dead; I have no recollection of a time when I did not live with the Connollys"—the abusive foster parents from whose ramshackle tenement on West 41st Street she had been rescued. It was a heartrending detail to hear, and the child made quite a visual impression as well, with the *Herald*'s correspondent remarking on her "rare and exquisite beauty," adding: "In every lineament of the face could be read suffering, and its infantile freshness was marred by marks of fresh cuts and bruises." The cause of those injuries, revealed in the child's statement, was shocking: "Mamma," she said, in reference to Mrs. Connolly,

> has been in the habit of whipping and beating me almost every day; she used to beat me with a twisted whip—a rawhide; the whip always left black and blue marks on my body; I have now on my head two black and blue marks which were made by mamma with the whip, and a cut on the left side of my forehead which was made by a pair of scissors in mamma's hand; she struck me with the scissors and cut me; I have no recollection of ever having been kissed, and have never been kissed by mamma.

Over the years, a myth would develop that Bergh used the state's animal-cruelty statute to prosecute the Connollys and free Mary Ellen, on the argument that children, after all, were members of the animal kingdom. This misunderstanding might well have begun with Jacob Riis, the famous reformer and photographer who was then a cub reporter on the crime beat. "The child is an animal," an 1892 book by Riis quotes Bergh as having said to Etta Wheeler when she first came to see him about the case; "if there is no justice for it as a human being, it shall at least have the rights of the stray cur in the street." But no contemporaneous account suggests this quote is genuine. The *Times* noted in its trial reporting that Bergh, who sat beside Mary Ellen in the courtroom, knew that the case "was not within the scope of the special act to prevent cruelty to animals" and "desired it to be clearly understood . . . that in no sense has he acted in his official capacity" as ASPCA president in pursuing justice for the girl.

Regardless, the case did represent a startling extension of Bergh's mission. The legal basis on which Gerry, the ASPCA's attorney, brought the case before a judge was the constitutional guarantee of habeas corpus—a novel use of the provision, and one that implied an abusive home could be seen as a form of unlawful imprisonment. (It no doubt helped his case that the Connollys were adoptive, rather than biological, parents, and also that the child had been *indentured* to the family at the time of her adoption, a colonial-era practice that had mostly died out but would continue to bind some children through the rest of the century.)

Equally startling was the fact that Bergh sent two of the ASPCA's agents to invade the Connollys' home and retrieve the girl—a fact made more, not less, noteworthy by his acknowledgment in court that her plight fell beyond his organization's authority. But this was the reality of justice in the 1870s, when it was not altogether uncommon for private organizations to do the work of law enforcement; since the Civil War, Pennsylvania, among other states, had laws allowing the employees of certain companies, railroads in particular, to assume police powers, and Allan Pinkerton was hard at work building the "detective" agency that would soon become nothing less than a private anti-labor army.

The historian Susan J. Pearson, who has closely studied the rise of anti-cruelty laws in the period, observes that because nineteenth-century police forces evolved out of an old "constable and watch" system, they tended to be oriented less toward fighting crime than to maintaining a more holistic sense of order in neighborhoods—as Pearson notes, the police "tended streetlamps, maintained sewers, removed obstructions from the roadways, fed and lodged the homeless, returned lost children to parents, inspected docks, carriages, and omnibuses, issued licenses for serving liquor, controlled building permits, and rang fire alarm bells." Moreover, American police forces of the era tended to be somewhat meager in number, and chronically unprofessional: Misconduct charges against New York police in 1874 ran to an estimated thirty a week, and that same year, an order requiring officers to consistently wear uniforms was rescinded due to resistance in the ranks.

This helps explain why much of the public—like the court, which did not waste time before deciding in Bergh and Gerry's favor—was little bothered at the thought of organizations like the SPCA commanding what were in essence private police forces. The law that the two men then lobbied for in Albany, which passed in April 1875, set up the SPCC with comparable powers; hence the *World*'s dark vision of Bergh stealing into families' homes and carting off their young ones. Unmentioned by the *World*, but important in the years and decades to come, was the fact that New York had also recently made public school attendance mandatory for all children ages eight to fourteen; soon enough teachers, as well as neighbors and bystanders like Etta Wheeler, would be flagging possible child-cruelty cases for investigation and prosecution.

More broadly, at a time when the government's reach into the lives of families remained extraordinarily small by today's standards—the Civil War–era attempt to impose the nation's first income tax, on only the top 3 percent of earners, had fizzled out—the arrival of these two New York laws, mandating compulsory education in 1874 and then empowering a child-welfare agency in 1875, suddenly gave the state a new and unprecedented reach into the most intimate domains of life. The slippery slope that the *World* worried about did eventually lead to the strong modern state of the Progressive era and beyond, and here at the beginning, no one embodied the first slips down that slope more than Henry Bergh.

The *World*'s uneasy sense of Bergh as a law unto himself was underscored in late February 1875 when he was caught up in another legal imbroglio. It revolved around the case of a Lower East Side dogfighting ring that his agents had broken up a couple of months prior and which had landed before a grand jury. In Bergh's opinion, it was an open-and-shut case (the malefactors had been apprehended with their hands literally covered in the blood of wounded dogs), but the grand jury declined to move forward with prosecution. Bergh then fired off an intemperate letter addressed directly to the jury's members, declaring that "a scandalous stain upon our civilization has been condoned."

When this came to the attention of the city court recorder, the powerful Tammany politician John K. Hackett, Bergh was hauled in for a series of brusque hearings on the charge of contempt of court. The issue was not just that Bergh had impugned the grand jury's decision and its motives, but that direct lobbying of the jury by any outside party was illegal. Ironically, when the contempt charge was dismissed, Hackett made clear that what persuaded him was the depth of Bergh's official powers: Bergh had presented him with paperwork demonstrating that, because of the ASPCA's law-enforcement authority, he personally was considered by the city to be both a deputy attorney general and an assistant district attorney.

Bergh's critics in the press had relished the chance to see the avenging angel of kindness laid low. His letter to the jurors was still another sign, alongside the SPCC controversy, that Bergh was itching to poke his nose into the private affairs of nearly everyone. The *Herald* compared him to Torquemada—the infamous overseer of the Spanish Inquisition—and sarcastically suggested that still more laws were in order to further his expanding crusade: for example, one criminalizing "the failure to sympathize with Mr. Bergh in his noble and philanthropic enterprises," and another specifying that "everything that Mr. Bergh does or proposes to do is right."

· · · ·

In 1876, Philadelphia would play host to the Centennial Exposition—the first-ever World's Fair in the United States, honoring the hundredth anniversary of the Declaration of Independence. In Fairmount Park, more than two hundred buildings were constructed to house the six-month exhibition, the largest of which boasted more than twenty-one acres of floor space, making it the biggest building constructed to date in the world. Four grand hotels, encompassing more than three thousand rooms, sprouted up to serve those expected to attend, along with what was in essence an entirely new neighborhood of the city on the outskirts of the park—restaurants, beer gardens, ice cream parlors, theaters—rising up on what until then had been an open field. The local business press was foreseeing that the horse-drawn railroad line serving the park would need to increase service to one car per minute, and "even at this rate it will be utterly impossible to prevent the overcrowding of cars, whatever the 'Society for the Prevention of Cruelty to Animals' may do or attempt to do to prevent it."

The local SPCA remained smaller and less focused on law enforcement than its New York cousin: In 1875, Philadelphia was about a quarter smaller than New York by population, but it had prosecuted just 152 cases of cruelty to animals that year, 80 percent fewer than Bergh's society did. Under the leadership of Caroline Earle White, the Women's Branch of the society continued to lead through its humane shelter, which had housed more than 3,100 dogs during the year, 578 of which had been redeemed by their owners (or adopters) for $2 apiece; the others had been killed through the shelter's painstakingly researched euthanasia chamber, except for six that had escaped.

In April 1876, White convened the Women's Branch to give her annual report, in which she laid out priorities for the year that were far more visionary than the workaday issues that consumed the Pennsylvania group as a whole. The first subject on her agenda, echoing George Angell, was cattle transportation—lending her group's support to the use of the new humane rail cars. The second subject, to which White devoted the bulk of her address, represented an important turning point for her group, and for her personally: The Women's Branch, she declared, was putting the fight against vivisection at the center of its mission.

This had long been a personal crusade for White, who had tangled with local medical researchers over the issue ever since the Women's Branch took over the city's animal-control operations. In one particularly dramatic episode, a group of local doctors—led by S. Weir Mitchell, John Call Dalton's protégé, who had taken up residence as the eminence of physiology at Philadelphia's own College of Physicians—had obtained a signed letter from the mayor authorizing them to help themselves to shelter animals at their leisure. White implored the mayor to withdraw this authorization, which he did. Mitchell appealed to the Pennsylvania SPCA's male leadership, but Morris Waln, then on the brink of death, backed White unconditionally. "I hope your branch will remain firm as a rock, and not yield an inch," he wrote her soon before he died.

White was inspired by the continuing rise of anti-vivisection activism in England, a movement that was now led overwhelmingly by women. She was especially drawn to the model set by Frances Power Cobbe, who the previous year had started up the first anti-vivisection organization in London and whose essay on the subject, "The Moral Aspects of Vivisection," had been widely reprinted as a pamphlet, including by the Pennsylvania Women's Branch. Cobbe was another uncategorizable nineteenth-century woman, born into an eminent and devoutly Catholic family in Dublin but emerging from it as a feminist freethinker and reformist gadfly. Her essay on vivisection was particularly noteworthy in how it probed the emerging morality of science, which presented its ends as the advancement of human well-being overall but seemed willing to sacrifice an untold number of innocent animals in the process: "I may remark that the mental constitution of a man must be somewhat exceptional," Cobbe drolly observed, "who is enthusiastically anxious to relieve the sufferings of unseen, and perhaps unborn, men and women, but who cares in comparison nothing at all for those agonies which are endured immediately under his eye."

This offended Cobbe's bedrock theory of "intuitive morality," which she had laid out years before in a treatise that sought to formalize the notion, implicit in so much preaching in the Romantic vein all the way up to Henry Ward Beecher, that moral truths can be perceived intuitively by the human mind. It was a premise that Caroline White might have recalled from the spiritual rhetoric of Lucretia Mott, her famous cousin. These figures, though based in disparate religious traditions, all believed that a gut-level revulsion to suffering, instilled by God, had been key to convincing individual souls of the evil of slavery, and that the existence of this ingrained moral sense is also what would bring about the future progress they hoped for: votes for women, an awakening to the evils of alcohol, and more. The idea that animal researchers could intellectualize their way past the suffering right in front of them seemed incompatible with this concept of moral intuition.

In her April address, White laid out at some length the coalescing—and somewhat contradictory—case against vivisection that Cobbe and her new group were advocating in England. Even if experiments on living animals were useful, this argument ran, they would be barbarous; but in point of fact, the argument went on, such experiments were *not* useful. This was an opinion that Cobbe and other anti-vivisectionists bolstered through a carefully curated set of questionable quotations: a secondhand reminiscence from an associate of William Harvey, for example, in which the seventeenth-century scientist supposedly said his anatomical observations on humans, not his experiments on rabbits, deserved the credit for his breakthroughs on circulation; a remark by Charles Bell denigrating animal research was often cited, despite the fact that his own great work on the cranial nerves relied heavily upon such research. Thus could Caroline White declare, in her report, that "the main weapon of the vivisectors has been wrested from their grasp; their stronghold has crumbled into atoms."

In the minds of White and so many reformers, underlying this exercise in selective science criticism seemed to be an impulse that moral truth and scientific truth *had* to coincide, just as the intuitive nature of moral truth *had* to compel an ever-increasing number of people to choose the side of right. "We are well aware," White said, "that the chief cause of the apathy here upon the subject is that the majority of people in the community are unaware of the horrid details of this cruel practice, or even that such an abuse exists in this land of progress and reform and in this enlightened nineteenth century." Awakened to the depravity of the vivisectionists, the public would turn decisively against them, White believed—a judgment echoed in Cobbe's pamphlet. "As the main work of civilization has been the vindication of the rights of the weak," Cobbe had written, "it is not too much, I think, to insist that the practice of vivisection . . . is a retrograde step in the progress of our race, a backwater in the onward flowing stream of justice and mercy, no less anomalous than it is deplorable and portentous."

That last word was itself portentous. It signified a danger Cobbe perceived keenly but White, perhaps, did not: that through this emerging mindset of the vivisectionists, the arc of moral progress *could* conceivably reverse; that their mentality, in its blithe, abstracted disregard for the suffering of the weak, might well give birth to a new, broader movement bent on using scientific principles to justify the dominance of the strong. This fear, of course, would prove to be well founded in the decades to come, with the rise of eugenics and other strains of scientific anti-humanism, achieving their apotheosis on the tables of Josef Mengele. Instead of "retrograde step," Cobbe could as easily have employed another, comparable metaphor: the first step down a slippery slope.

.   .   .

When the Centennial Exposition opened on May 10, 1876, it was a spectacle unlike any the nation had ever seen. An estimated crowd of 50,000 had massed outside the park before the gates even opened, and by the time President Grant delivered the opening address—rain clouds giving way to sunshine, reporters noted, at the moment he set off for the grounds—the throng had swelled to 250,000 or more. Grant's cabinet and the entire Supreme Court were arrayed around him, as were scores of foreign dignitaries, including the emperor of Brazil. The *Herald*'s correspondent noted Frederick Douglass in the crowd, though he had to fight through a police line to get in. Richard Wagner had composed an original march for the affair, commissioned by the city of Philadelphia (Wagner's primary inspiration for the piece, it is said, was the $5,000 fee), and this was duly performed. The final musical work of the program was the Hallelujah Chorus from Handel's *Messiah*, after which the exhibition was officially opened with a hullabaloo of noise: artillery fire, clanging bells, and steam whistles.

The hundredth anniversary of the nation's independence was also the tenth year of the animal-welfare revolution in America, a fact that all the movement's founders felt keenly. Bergh fired off a letter that very day to the editors of the *Herald,* with much to boast about. "Ten years ago," he wrote,

> there was not a single statute law in the country for the pro-
> tection of that vast portion of God's creation, which we call
> "the inferior animals." Cruelty to those mute beings, which
> serve us so faithfully and without whom civilization would be
> impossible, was regarded as below the consideration of States
> and individuals, and, strange to say, all the while that a theft
> of a ham or a pair of shoes by a needy criminal was viewed
> with stern severity, the demoralizing consequences of cruelty
> to a defenceless animal were almost completely ignored. Ten
> years ago such a reproach applied to us as a nation.

This revolution in kindness did not go unrepresented at the Centennial. In the Main Exhibition Building's east gallery, inside the exhibit of the Massachusetts Educational Department, George Angell had curated a host of inventions that stood to improve the lot of America's animals. There were models of the humane rail cars, with compartments for individual cattle and hogs, that had become Angell's preoccupation. There were new devices to ease the burdens of horses: a harness saddle with adjustable pads (invented by H. H. Hallett of Rockland, Massachusetts); a "duplex whiffle-tree" that used a rubber block to help spread out the force of pulls upon the reins (E. C. Gordon, Salem, New Hampshire); a rubber-covered bit (Alfred Hale & Co., Boston); and a wide array of new horseshoe models. There was even a "gyro-pigeon," invented by Jacob Glahn of Meriden, Connecticut—"made of thin metal, wing-shaped, with a paper parachute, and being thrown into the air by a spring," Angell noted in *Our Dumb Animals,* which "furnishes a suitable mark for the gunner, giving him the practice without the cruelty of torturing live birds."

Bergh had curated an exhibit too, in which he had chosen to emphasize cruelty instead of the prospects for its future alleviation. He had covered an entire wall with photographs of offenders and victims in cases prosecuted by the ASPCA, as well as a ghoulish collection of artifacts: wounded pigeons from shooting matches, a horse's tongue cut out by its owner, a taxidermied bulldog from a fighting ring in the Bronx, its head and body chewed to a pulp. Bergh pointedly included two skulls of dogs from the raid on the Lower East Side that had prompted his trouble with the grand jury. With each documented incident, the exhibit indicated how much prison time the society had secured for its offender.

The *World* denounced the whole enterprise as an "offense to good taste," asking, "In what way do the skulls of dead bull-dogs illustrate the development of American industry?" But Bergh, to his credit, did not see technology as the suffering animal's friend. The evidence was right on display in the exposition's Agricultural Hall, where those seeking visions of the future could admire— alongside newfangled farm equipment like steam threshers and a "self-loading excavator"—some of the butchering and meatpacking machines that were enabling the birth of industrialized cruelty on a truly unfathomable scale. Bergh's hall included a silk banner displaying the thirty-two states of the Union that by then had formed anti-cruelty societies and passed anti-cruelty laws, representing a remarkable ten-year shift in law, society, and morality. But the forces of the American economy were shifting, too, in ways that the animal-welfare movement only dimly understood. In the killing machines of Machinery Hall, one could see the first steps down a new slippery slope in animal cruelty, a slide that had only just begun.

Part Two

STANDOFFS

(1885–1896)

"The Alarm-Bell of Atri" was one of many inspirational
works that George Angell disseminated to the masses.

Chapter 10

A NEW ORDER OF
CHIVALRY

The beginning of 1885 found George T. Angell hunkered down in New Orleans at yet another World's Fair—this one called the World Cotton Centennial, in dubious recognition of a barbarous milestone, namely the hundredth anniversary of the international cotton trade. The six-month exposition proved to be an underwhelming affair, attracting considerably less news coverage than the one in Philadelphia had, and a paltry fraction of the crowds. That said, it was more electrifying in a literal sense: Attendees gawked at the nighttime brilliance of the enormous Main Building, a behemoth the size of three city blocks that had been lit by five thousand Edison lights, at a moment when few New Orleans buildings were electrified. Outdoors, Jenney arc lights brought a comparable level of illumination to the whole of Upper City Park. America's increasingly wired lifestyle made its effects known in other ways as well: President Chester Arthur officially opened the fair from the White House via telegraph.

Angell had come to make sure, once again, that the animal cause was represented amid the assembled grandeurs of man. His assigned office was in the exposition's second most gargantuan structure, the cavernous Government Building, and he had chosen to turn the space into an inspirational library. "My department is now in perfect order and attracts universal attention," Angell wrote to a hometown paper in January. "My office is about twenty-five feet by thirty, with no cover but the roof, some eighty feet above my head, and plenty of chairs for all to sit while reading, writing or talking." All around, the walls and surfaces were covered in didactic animal art, and the tables and shelves were piled with humane publications, tens of thousands of copies in all: editions of *Our Dumb Animals,* pamphlets from the Massachusetts SPCA and the Women's Branch of the Philadelphia society, various books and also an array of periodicals from England.

He was now in his sixties, with a bushy white beard, but his energy remained enormous and his faith in the cause unflagging. Henry Bergh's health was by now failing—in three years he would be dead—leaving Angell as the nation's most forceful advocate for the humane movement. As ever, he occupied the role in a very different fashion. While he did not stint on the prosecutorial side of the crusade (for example, pushing his ban on pigeon shooting through the Massachusetts legislature in 1879), Angell had always been more of a thinker than Bergh, more of a traveling preacher, more of an institution builder. During the late 1870s and early 1880s, he had personally helped start up or revive SPCAs or humane societies in Detroit; Milwaukee; Newport, Rhode Island; and Saratoga Springs, New York. He was the kind of public speaker who would propose, on the spot, that the audience vote to form a new society—in the fall of 1879, it was the Ladies' Moral and Humane Education Society of Minneapolis, the first and only group of its kind.

In 1881, Angell had set up shop in Washington, D.C., to restart the moribund local SPCA, believing that a healthy humane agency in the capital would be crucial to influencing Congress. Two years later, when the U.S. Department of Agriculture asked him to come to New Orleans for the exposition, offering him a place to tout kind treatment of animals alongside displays about crop pests and varieties of grasses and sugars, he jumped at the opportunity. He believed that the government was going to grant him $10,000 to assemble a grand exhibit, showcasing all the inventions and best practices for preventing cruelty: horse ambulances, better cattle cars, methods of euthanasia, and so on. Alas, the money was not forthcoming, and he was left to put together whatever materials he could get for free.

Still, Angell was an optimist. New Orleans remained the nation's largest city without an animal-protection group, and soon after his arrival he set to remedying that lack, helping to convene a meeting at the St. Charles Hotel in February 1885. Per the usual playbook, dozens of eminent New Orleanians were enlisted, but his greatest ally was Eliza "E.J." Nicholson, the thirty-five-year-old publisher of the New Orleans *Daily Picayune,* who had already given over a recurring column in the paper ("Nature's Dumb Nobility") to the cause.* Barely had the meeting taken place when Angell and his wife announced plans to travel onward, to Florida, in order to spread the gospel of kindness there.

In the meantime, as long as the Cotton Centennial ran, Angell presided over his library. "There are pictures of beautiful well fed horses and cows," a writer for the *Picayune* noted, "then of the poor, worn-out old slaves the cab-horses, hardly able to lift their feet, and pictures of the faithful devotion of man's greatest friend—his dog, and above these the illuminated text, '*Blessed are the merciful.*'" The most prominent piece of art, which stood some ten feet tall and hung twenty feet above the floor, was a painting of a weathered old horse with a rope in its mouth. This was an iconic reference to one of the defining animal-welfare tales of recent years: a parable about an elderly horse that, cruelly abandoned by its owner, uses its teeth to ring the bell in the town square, a bell that the local monarch had hung for citizens to ask for justice in the event of a wrong. In the story—which Henry Wadsworth Longfellow had turned into a poem called "The Alarm-Bell of Atri"—the monarch, moved by the horse's wordless plea, orders its owner to take care of it into its dotage. In Longfellow's rendering, the king declares that animals, who labor for us in silent obedience, deserve even more consideration for their pains than fellow humans do: "He who serves well and speaks not, merits more / Than they who clamor loudest at the door. / Therefore the law decrees that as this steed / Served you in youth, henceforth you shall take heed / To comfort his old age, and to provide / Shelter in stall, and food and field beside."

Looking around Angell's temple of kindness in New Orleans, one could see it as testament to a new phase that the movement

---

* Nicholson had inherited the paper from her late husband, Colonel Alva Morris Holbrook, a man four decades her senior whom she had married at twenty-three. This development had so enraged Holbrook's ex-wife that she marauded through the new couple's home with an ax and a gun, shooting twice at Eliza but failing to connect.

had entered by the mid-1880s—a more evangelical, but also more uncertain, turn. It was a phase when legal protection against cruel treatment had been achieved in most of the country, but activists could not feel satisfied, given how much cruelty they still saw in the streets. It was a phase when leaders of the movement found themselves opposed, particularly on issues like vivisection and the treatment of livestock, by hard-nosed men who dismissed sentimental soft-heartedness toward animals as an impediment to progress. It was a phase, not coincidentally, in which women were emerging more fully as the leaders of animal-welfare societies, after many years as their most energetic supporters.

What Angell wanted, what he believed was possible, was nothing less than a moral revolution in America, one carried along by human emotion in rebellion against suffering of all forms. "Some of our friends most deeply interested in animal-protection societies are frequently charged with being *sentimental*," he wrote in an October 1884 essay, as he was preparing to make the journey to New Orleans. He embraced the insult, for what was "sentiment," he wrote, if not "thought prompted by feeling"? He went on:

> To protect the weak, bind up the broken-hearted, defend the defenseless, raise the downtrodden, give liberty to the enslaved,—these are all sentiments.
>
> Women have died in hospitals, and men on battle-fields, and martyrs at the stake, and as the flames curled around them have sung hymns of praise, all for sentiment.

For nearly seventeen years now, around the animal cause, Angell had yearned for that surge of sentiment, had studied it, had tested methods of engineering it. In the decade that followed, his schemes for provoking sentiment in the American public would become ever more ambitious, even as the forces arrayed against sentimentalism became ever stronger.

.   .   .

The most ambitious of his campaigns, launched in 1882, was aimed at the nation's children. It was called Bands of Mercy—a network of social clubs, which adolescent leaders around the country were encouraged to start up and then exhort their friends and classmates to join. Members were required to take a solemn pledge: *I will try to be kind to all harmless living creatures, and try to protect them from cruel usage.* (Those who wanted to take their commitment to the next level were encouraged to strike the word "harmless.") At their regular meetings, the children would talk about the virtue of being kind to animals.

Like so many of America's best philanthropic ideas, it came from England. The inspiration began with a program that started in the late 1840s, called Bands of Hope; it was a pledge-based campaign around the issue of temperance, which asked young people to sign a statement that they would not drink alcohol. By the mid-1880s, a million and a half young people had signed the pledge, an astonishing figure in a nation where only an estimated eight million people were in the target age range. In 1873, Catherine Smithies, a London philanthropist, had the idea of applying the same concept to animal welfare, naming it Bands of Mercy; when she died a few years later, her campaign was taken over by the Royal SPCA.

It is not totally clear when Angell became aware of the English campaign, but he had spent years musing about his desire to create a "new order of chivalry" for American schoolchildren. By the time of his speech to the ladies of Minneapolis, his language had shifted to become "Legions of Honor," which would command their young charges not merely to abjure cruelty to animals but to "speak no falsehoods" and to "read no criminal or obscene publications." By 1882, when he met Thomas Timmins—an English minister who had started an especially successful Bands of Mercy group in his hometown of Portsmouth—who was on a visit to New England, Angell had no doubt become aware of the Bands of Mercy, but it was that encounter that prompted both men to throw themselves into establishing and spreading the idea in the United States.

Angell launched this new crusade in the pages of *Our Dumb Animals.* He barraged readers with advertisements promising that any "intelligent boy or girl fourteen years old can form a Band with no cost, and receive what we offer" (a free year's subscription to *Our Dumb Animals;* a pamphlet of Band of Mercy songs, not a few of them penned by Angell himself; twelve lessons on kindness;

eight humane leaflets; and an imitation gold badge for the young president). The British and American campaigns were roughly similar, certain national peculiarities notwithstanding—the RSPCA made sure, for example, that children knew the design of their Band of Mercy medals had been "executed under the personal direction of Her Majesty the Queen," who had ordered that a cat be added to the tableau of animals on the front in hopes that "these little feline companions may be honoured equally with other favourites." First and foremost was the pledge, which opened every Band of Mercy meeting, inviting each child to reflect on the commitment he or she had made, and perhaps to rue any occasion on which that commitment had been strained or broken. There were the star-shaped medals, which served as badges of membership; the readings from animal-welfare movement texts; and the booklets of "Band of Mercy Melodies," from which selections would be sung at each gathering.

During his months in New Orleans, Angell went doggedly from classroom to classroom—taking care to visit Black schools as well

Band of Mercy promotional image.

as white ones—leaving a trail of newly formed Bands behind him. By the spring of 1885, nearly four thousand clubs would be in operation, representing tens of thousands of young members.

In our current era, we have become skeptical about both the wisdom and the efficacy of organized moral education in any form, but Americans of the nineteenth century believed fervently in it. Indeed, the rise of public schools themselves, in the early part of the century, was driven as much by their potential moral function as by any practical knowledge they might instill; at a time when children had begun leaving their hometowns more often, sometimes as teenagers, elementary schools were seen as a venue for making sure they found a correct moral path at their most impressionable age. The sense of childhood as the moment when proper character could be deliberately encouraged had become a great article of faith, animated by an abundance of horticultural metaphors: "The germs of morality must be planted in the moral nature of children, at an early period of their life," wrote Horace Mann, America's most influential educational thinker of the period. "In that genial soil they will flourish," he went on, "like those pasture oaks we see, scattered about the fields of the farmers, which, striking their roots downward into the earth as far as their top-most branches ascend into the air, draw their nourishment from perennial fountains, and thereby preserve their foliage fresh and green, through seasons of fiery drought, when all surrounding vegetation is scorched to a cinder."

For Mann and other believers in public schooling, the list of virtues that schools could instill was a long one. Under Mann's strong influence, Massachusetts adopted education laws requiring teachers to "impress on the minds of the children and youth committed to their care and instruction, the principles of piety, justice and a sacred regard to truth, love to their country, humanity and universal benevolence, sobriety, industry, frugality, chastity, moderation and benevolence, and those other virtues which are the ornament of human society."

With Bands of Mercy, it is perhaps easiest to think of its educational philosophy as two-pronged: reward and punishment, carrot and stick. The carrot, so to speak, was in tickling children's instinctive desire to belong. Adults spurred the Bands into creation, but the

pose was that children were in charge—a rare sort of empowerment
in that era—and the young members were encouraged to think of
themselves as bound to one another by more than just their love of
animals. The Reverend Mr. Timmins, in an overwrought memoir
about starting up the program in America, recounted a story about
a "big young man" in one school who was rudely skeptical about
joining the new club. Timmins convinced him to join by describing the Band in remarkably gang-like terms: "[I]f a rough, cruel
man came in here and ill-treated you, we would instantly step in
and protect you," the minister said. Indeed, the term "Bands" itself
was clearly intended to have a thrilling, martial cast to it; hence,
too, the medals and the stirring anthems. One of the hymns that
Angell wrote for the American songbook took the form of a military march, with words such as "marching along, we are marching
along / our army of mercy shall right every wrong."

The pledge, meanwhile, provided the stick, in how it provoked
a child's fear of damnation. In the American clubs' meetings, children were asked to reckon publicly with their missteps, whether
through self-disclosure or at the insistence of others; the center-
piece of each meeting was the "report of each member," which
invited the young attendees to declare "what you have done cruel,
or to stop cruelty," or "what you have seen anyone else do cruel."
In the event of an accusation being leveled at another member, the
accused was given the right to reply. (Children were also given a
safer option, to simply say what they had "read about animals or
good deeds.")

The Bands were ecumenical in nature, cutting across lines of
creed, but Angell was pointed in reminding his young charges about
the spiritual implications of the promise they had made: "Remember, children, whenever you may be tempted to take without cause
the innocent life of any creature, that there is present, everywhere,
that great and pure Spirit upon whose mercy you depend, and who
knows every wrong that you may inflict on the humblest of his creatures." Angell worked hard to invest the star-shaped badge with a
spiritual significance, printing the words "Glory to God" prominently near its center and warning children to "not think lightly of
it." The badge was made of humble materials, he allowed, yet was
that not also true of the American flag, or the wooden cross upon

which Jesus was crucified? The Band of Mercy badge was nothing less, Angell wrote, than "the symbol of the rising of another star of Bethlehem to shed healing light on the nations, and on all God's dumb creatures as well."

Even as Angell propagandized the clubs to America's children, he began weaving a mythology around them to adults. *Our Dumb Animals* began to fill with stories of young people moved to carry out bold deeds to protect animals. WHAT A CHICAGO "BAND OF MERCY" SCHOOL GIRL DID, read the headline on the front page of the June 1884 issue—a story reprinted from the *Chicago Daily News,* recounting how a little girl had stood up to a teamster with an overloaded coal cart. Flashing her Band of Mercy star, the girl commanded the driver not to hit his horses anymore, "casting a pleading glance in imitation of the arts of more mature woman-hood." The chastened driver acceded to her plea, and wept—or so the newspaper reported—as the girl strode away.

· · ·

As Henry Bergh headed into his seventies, his ideas about improving human behavior allowed for little carrot—Bergh was all stick, the consequence of his many years spent prosecuting the victimizers of animals, and now of children, in the nation's largest city. In the early days of 1881, at a public event, he had offered a startling dia-tribe about why America should adopt the whipping-post as pun-ishment; he particularly praised the bastinado, the agonizing form of foot-caning used in Egypt. "It is a charming style of whipping," Bergh said, "and makes the recipient cry out lustily that he will not do so any more, and he generally keeps his word." At that point, Bergh said, he had spent sixteen years "looking after the welfare of what are called the lower animals, but I have a greater respect for them than I ever had before I had an opportunity of comparing them with some of the base and miserable samples of humanity that I have met in these courts."

He even made noises about taking a bill to Albany allowing public floggings, which he felt would be just the thing to punish men who abused women and children. This kind of eye-for-an-eye, bloodthirsty approach to justice proved very popular with the press, then as now, but it was off-putting to many of the reform-minded citizens—women especially—who had long been the animal-welfare movement's core supporters. As the *Brooklyn Union* noted, "There is something melancholy in the picture of Mr. Bergh on the warpath for gore, a personified Society for the Enforcement of Cruelty to Wife-beaters."

Bergh's most dramatic fight of that year would be against the city's well-heeled pigeon shooters. As Ernest Freeberg recounts in his fine recent biography of Bergh, he had made a serious strategic error in 1875 when passing a bill against dogfighting and cockfighting, blessing a legislative bargain that specifically exempted pigeon shooting by "incorporated sportsmen's clubs" from the bill's strictures. This meant that in the spring of 1881, when the New York Sportsmen's Association readied plans for an epic shooting match in Coney Island that June, Bergh could only bluster at them.

On the day of the event, Bergh sent a gang of small boys to hand out a pamphlet he had written about pigeon shooting called "So-Called Sport and Its Victims." In it, Bergh exhorted readers to "abolish this cruel and unsportsmanlike pastime" and recast the impulse to hunt live game as a kind of psychotic break: "A practical marksman requiring only recreation, sallies forth in search of amusement. Suddenly he experiences a strange desire to kill—to destroy a hapless being and disfigure the scene which lies like a dream of Paradise before him." Few of the assembled sportsmen seemed chastened by the diagnosis. An hour or so into the carnage, Bergh and some of his officers demanded to be let onto the field to monitor the proceedings, but instead he was ushered to the spectators' gallery, where he was forced to watch the slaughter from afar.

Afterward, some newspapers took Bergh's view of the affair: "The feathers of the slain pigeons covered the ground like snow," a *Herald* writer said, while the *Star*'s correspondent wrote of seeing birds "dying by slow degrees in awful agony"—a sight that left the writer with a "choking in the throat, half grief, half indignation." Bergh took this public outrage as an opportunity to revisit his push for a ban on pigeon shoots, and the following year he pressed Theodore Roosevelt, then a twenty-three-year-old state legislator, to take up the cause, but Roosevelt couldn't even convince his colleagues to hold a hearing.

The years 1884 and 1885 found Bergh contending with such issues as a rat-killing ferret exhibition at Madison Square Garden and the practice of applying red-hot shoes to horses' hooves, and of clipping their coats, neither of which practices are necessarily injurious to them. He became a strident opponent of Louis Pasteur and vaccination, and took on more quixotic fights with P. T. Barnum. But even when confronting evident outrages, as in his fight against cruelty at the horse races at Jerome Park, Bergh hit the same wall that he had in Albany in his attempts to shut down pigeon shoots. The city's power elite had cheered Bergh's attempts to prosecute workingmen who beat horses in the streets, but by the 1880s they had little appetite for taking on the wealthy hunters and horse-race devotees who thumbed their noses at the animal crusade.

Beyond that, the nature of power in America's cities was changing. Beginning in the early 1880s, the rise of the steamship led to an enormous new wave of immigrants, particularly from Italy and Eastern Europe, and their numbers only strengthened the hand of the working-class political machines that had little use for genteel reform causes. Moreover, the new arrivals brought with them a familiarity, even a comfort, with some of the most intense forms of labor agitation that then were convulsing Europe; Americans could not help but imagine that the bloody tenor of the Great Railroad Strike of 1877—in which tens of thousands of workers had burned buildings and trains, and railroad bosses responded with deadly violence—would only worsen in the years to come. Newspapers began following the speeches of visiting anarchists and socialists with lurid fascination. The most sinister of the visitors was Johann Most, a German anarchist who arrived in New York in December 1882 and went on to give frequent speeches in the city and around the country. Most told a crowd of New York socialists that "the best thing one can do with such fellows as Jay Gould and Vanderbilt is to hang them on the nearest lamp-post," and read out a resolution exhorting the audience to "kill, destroy, annihilate your aristocracy and bourgeoisie to the last man."

For figures like Henry Bergh and George Angell, born a half century or less after 1776, the Anglo-American tradition that dominated their conception of the nation—a tradition that also, it should be noted, had birthed the ideas that animated their movement, ideas that flowed predominantly from English thinkers like Humphry Primatt, William Wilberforce, and Frances Power Cobbe—was in danger of disappearing.

Besides labor agitation, the other urban bugbear of the patrician imagination during the 1880s was crime. In point of fact, the urban crime rate on a population basis was falling in many cities, including New York, as the city swelled with new arrivals, but newspapers were filled with horror stories of murder and mayhem. There was no denying that poverty, especially among the newcomers, was widespread and crushingly deep; a sociologist of the period estimated that a quarter of New York households lived on less than $500 a year, or around $15,500 in today's money. All that poverty became increasingly visible as density swelled to unheard-of levels: New York tenements would often pack more than a hundred souls onto a 100-by-25-foot lot. Even as the rich got richer, they could not insulate themselves from all the ways the city was changing, and increasingly it spoke languages they did not understand.

It made perverse sense that even the bullfight, that symbol of Mediterranean savagery, now threatened to find a beachhead in the United States. In 1880, Bergh had successfully appealed to William H. Vanderbilt, the owner of Madison Square Garden, to quash a proposed bullfight by Angel Fernandez, a Spanish torero. He further humiliated Fernandez, who put on his show in a lesser venue far uptown, by showing up with seventy policemen and forcing Hernandez to eliminate all violence from his demonstration. But in 1884, Dodge City, Kansas, hosted a Mexican bullfight on the Fourth of July, and this one Bergh was powerless to stop—twelve bulls met their end in the ring, and Bergh sent an apoplectic note to the Kansas governor, declaring that Dodge City "unblushingly announces to the world that the tastes and habits of the heathen and savage are to be inaugurated upon its soil." Early the following year, while Angell was at the exposition in New Orleans, he learned that the Mexican delegation planned to stage a similar series of events for fairgoers, but he prevailed on Louisiana's governor, Samuel McEnery, to forbid them.

The transformation of America was provoking a bitter defeatism in Bergh: In March 1883, he wrote a dyspeptic letter to George L.

Clarke, the president of Rhode Island's SPCA, in which he blamed his recent failures in Albany on the influx of immigrants. "In presence of the continually augmenting product of the scum and dregs of the human race banished to our State by foreign governments," he griped,

> it is next to impossible to get any just and civilizing law enacted. Italian banditti—Russian nihilists—and Irish dynamiters—are rapidly infusing their barbarous ideas and practices into the policy of State and Metropolitan government, and it seems to be a mere question of time when the purely American character will be a thing of the past.

But Angell, as ever, met the moment with more faith, believing that he and his allies had assembled just the right moral materiel with which to beat back the anarchist advance. In September 1883, he sent a letter to the *Journal of Education* entitled DYNAMITE OR HUMANE EDUCATION,—WHICH SHALL IT BE? "I wish to submit to intelligent readers these propositions," he wrote.

> *First:* Great and dangerous conflicts between capital and labor are threatened in this country.
>
> *Second:* Crimes of violence and a spirit of lawlessness have grown here wonderfully in the past twenty years.
>
> *Third:* About one-half the people of this country, rich and poor, attend regularly no church, nor do their children attend any Sunday school.
>
> *Fourth:* A Nihilist lecturer recently stated to a large audience in Tremont Temple, Boston, that there were then about four hundred schools in Europe (he did not say how many in America) whose only object was to teach the use of explosives, and that two ounces of an explosive he then had, placed at the entrance of Tremont Temple, would destroy the life of every person in that building!
>
> *Fifth:* The coming conflicts in this country must be fought in one of two ways: either mercifully with ballots and other humane measures, or brutally with bullets, incendiary fires,

and all those destructive appliances which modern science has put into the hands of those who are being educated to use them.

Sixth: Those who are to fight these battles, on one side or the other, are in our public schools to-day, and we are educating them.

Seventh: The quickest and most hopeful way of reaching the masses, and leading them to settle political and social questions in merciful ways, is through immediate and widespread humane education in our schools.

Eighth: No man or woman can find in the world a cheaper, quicker, or more effective way than through the Bands of Mercy, designed for the protection of both human beings and the lower animals, with their simple machinery, badges, and cards.

Angell saw the Bands of Mercy as the solution for crime, too, delivering a speech on the subject in 1884 to the national association of public school superintendents entitled "The New Order of Mercy; or, Crime and Its Prevention." In it, Angell marshaled some dubious statistics about the effects of teaching animal welfare: He cited a supposed survey of two thousand U.S. prison inmates in which only twelve reported their families having ever owned a pet, and a study finding that after seven thousand English children were "carefully taught kindness to animals," none were subsequently arrested for any criminal offense.

More revealing, in Angell's rhetoric, was his attitude toward the homes from which public school children were coming. "There are hundreds of thousands of parents among the depraved and criminal classes of this country," Angell said, and "hundreds of thousands of homes where the name of the Almighty is never heard except in words of blasphemy." But, he went on, "there is not a child in one of those homes that may not be taught in our public schools to feed the birds, and pat the horses, and enjoy making happy all harmless creatures it meets on the street, and so be doing acts of kindness forty times a day, which will make it not only happier, but better and more merciful in all the relations of life." Angell was articulating an idea about kindness that mirrored Bergh's ideas about cruelty.

.   .   .

Angell, like the revivalist preachers who circulated around the nation in waves of great awakenings, believed he could save an entire country's soul, that his gospel could touch every heart. Despite his advanced age, he would spend the next decade trying to fulfill that vision—and his campaign would succeed beyond any reasonable expectation, in large part because George Angell was not an entirely reasonable man.

The greatest impediment, though, was that the country was just so big in every sense, with so many unlit interiors. When Angell left New Orleans in mid-March 1885, he traversed the Florida Panhandle's four hundred miles to Jacksonville, the state's biggest city, and spent four weeks in the area. He helped to found a new state SPCA as well as a local chapter in nearby St. Augustine, which then had become a popular destination for wealthy New Yorkers—his lady co-conspirator in Florida was one such snowbird, a woman named Sarah B. Hills, who owned property in the area. As he had done in Louisiana, he traveled from classroom to classroom, starting up Bands of Mercy in both the white and Black schools. "I am quite pleased with my success in Florida," Angell wrote the Massachusetts SPCA as he planned to return home to Boston, crediting Hills's "persistent and unceasing efforts to overcome the unusual difficulties which have rendered all similar attempts in this city and State failures."

Yet out of his sight, south of Jacksonville, there stretched the rest of Florida in all its swamp and splendor—tens of thousands of square miles, boasting few human habitations of much size but countless species of animals that existed nowhere else in the country. It was a place beset by unscrupulous hunters, whose depredations were difficult for an animal-protection law in Tallahassee or society in Jacksonville to stop. As early as the 1830s, John James Audubon had noted that Florida's herons were being "shot in great numbers while sitting on their eggs, or soon after the appearance of their young," in order to harvest their plumes for ladies' hats or other ornamental purposes. Not long after Angell left Florida with a sense of triumph, the naturalist W. E. D. Scott made a trip along the state's Gulf coast near Tampa Bay and found rookeries that, just six years earlier, had been resplendent with herons but were now entirely devoid of them; hunters, he was told, were routinely descending on the breeding grounds, shooting the birds as they nested, pulling off plumes from the back, head, and breast and leaving the bodies for the buzzards.

And why should they care about the tragic waste? There was too much money to be had in scale and speed, and they were hardly the only ones to see it: In the 1880s and 1890s, the abattoirs of Chicago and the laboratory tables of the medical researchers, among other institutions, would create demands for animal bodies at astonishing scale—with rewards so great as to make caring inconvenient.

Jumbo's enormity was exceeded only by
P. T. Barnum's ambition to profit from it.

Chapter 11

HERE COME THE ELEPHANTS!

The blaring of bugles, the banging of drums, the beating of many heavy hooves: These thrilling sounds sent the townsfolk of Lancaster, Pennsylvania, scrambling from buildings onto sidewalks, and from sidewalks into streets. Patient citizens who had been waiting for hours, strategically occupying the stone curbs with the best views of North Queen Street, were swarmed by late arrivals: clerks from nearby storefronts who had abandoned their counters, residents of nearby villages, farmers who had taken leave of their flocks and fields, and a multitude of eager children—from the youngest, standing on tiptoe clutching their mothers' hands, to the oldest, fearlessly clambering up lampposts and onto canvas awnings barely able to hold their weight. The craning heads poking out of every upstairs window had the first glimpse of the banners at the front of the procession as it wound through Centre Square. Barnum's circus had come to town.

Lancaster was the sixth stop on the 1885 summer tour of what was officially billed as P.T. BARNUM'S GREATEST SHOW ON EARTH & THE GREAT LONDON CIRCUS COMBINED WITH SANGER'S ROYAL BRITISH MENAGERIE & GRAND INTERNATIONAL ALLIED SHOWS, but this was often shortened to "Barnum and London Circus" or just "Barnum's," even though Barnum had two partners, James A. Bailey and James L. Hutchinson. On posters and handbills, in circulars and newspaper ads, the production's advance team promised a profusion of amusements: two dazzling daily performances under the big top, a diverse display of animals originating from all corners of

the earth, a sideshow exploiting possessors of unusual (and sometimes unfortunate) human traits, an (overtly racist and exoticizing)
Ethnological Congress of Savage Tribes, and a Roman-style hippodrome in which an inventive variety of races took place (men
on horses; women on horses; monkeys on horses; men on cattle,
on camels, on elephants; ridiculous wheelbarrow races and earnest
reenactments of ancient chariot contests). By the time the special
train pulled into town at 5 a.m. on Wednesday, May 6, local antici-
pation had reached such a pitch that a crowd of spectators was
already waiting on the train platform to watch the wagons unload
and make their way to the lot, north of the town center, where the
tents and ticket booths would be readied for the exciting events of
the day.

During decades past, when circuses traveled from town to town
in lumbering horse-drawn wagons, the parade had coincided with
the journey's end. On the edge of the village, the arriving company
would brush the accumulated road dust from the animals and vehicles, slip into costume, take up musical instruments, and process
through the population center to the still-vacant site of the show.
If the spectacle in the streets proved sufficiently dazzling, an audience might follow, ticket money in hand. After American circuses
adapted fully to the railroads—beginning with Barnum's 1872
Great Traveling World's Fair and Greatest Show on Record—the
parade evolved into an explicitly promotional pageant, occurring
after arrival and setup in advance of the day's first performance.

Barnum's circus procession rolled into Lancaster's downtown
at 9 a.m., exactly as advertised. Behind the lead riders threading
their way through the throng of spectators up North Queen Street
trooped a six-horse team pulling a twenty-piece military band atop
an ornately carved and painted wagon. Fifty uniformed equestrians
followed, in formation. Then came rolling cages filled with fear-
some predators—lions, tigers, panthers, leopards, and bears—and
their trainers; a display of chiming church bells; a gigantic globe;
a rhinoceros; a score of ladies sitting sidesaddle; jockeys on race-
horses; Roman and Moorish chariots; a military-style band; costumed representatives of various global ethnic traditions waving
to the crowds from decorated drays; one-humped and two-humped
camels; a marimba band; a hippopotamus; an out-of-season Santa

Claus; zebras in harness; polar bears and sea lions splashing in wheeled water tanks; and a colossal steam calliope. This feast for the eyes (and nose!) with its noisy soundtrack of merry music, rumbling wagon wheels, utterances of animals, clattering chains, clanging bells, and marching feet prepared the people of Lancaster for the most astounding attractions of them all, arriving near the end of the procession. Because the city's skittish equines might be caught off guard, mounted men made their way through the crowd, loudly bellowing a warning:

"Gentlemen, hold your horses, here come the elephants!"

Horses secured, Lancaster's downtown vibrated with the approach of the mighty megafauna. Resplendent in plumed head-dresses and draped with luxurious tapestries, ridden by costumed mahouts, or surrounded by stern stewards wielding menacing metal-tipped sticks, the great gray giants made their shuffling way through the exhilarated city. Eight little elephants trotted forward at the front of the herd, obeying their human handlers. Behind them plodded nine prodigious pachyderms, notably more sullen and submissive than those preceding. Heavy iron chains, fastened to some of their feet, dragged between the beleaguered-looking beasts, scraping the pavement with every step. Bringing up the rear were a dozen more behemoths, some chained, some free (yet eyeing their drivers warily), some harnessed to a gilded chariot from which circus performers smiled and waved to the enraptured crowd.

How small the storefronts of North Queen Street must have looked behind such colossal creatures as these! How exciting a juxtaposition between the familiar, if drab, features of a stolid industrial town and the extraordinary exotic animal attractions of the Greatest Show on Earth. The biggest North American cities of the era were beginning to have zoos, but more modest settlements could only hope to be visited by a circus such as this. Lancaster was, by all accounts, thoroughly thrilled by Barnum's marvelous menagerie moving through its main thoroughfares. Before the day was out, a reporter for the *Daily Intelligencer*'s evening edition had declared that "no such collection of wild animals in open cages and on foot was ever seen in our streets."

Thousands followed the procession onto the circus grounds, where, after paying fifty cents (children half price), ticketholders perused the exhibit tents until showtime. Sipping lemonade and snacking on peanuts, they wandered right up to waiting wonders such as the hirsute "Jojo the Russian Dog-Faced Boy" and the only partially de-pigmented "Sacred White Elephant, Toung Taloung" from Burma. Animals in the menagerie tent could be observed closely and sometimes touched or fed, while the humans on display in the sideshow might be engaged directly in conversation, induced to perform their specialties, or pressed to sell a photographic *carte de visite*. In the museum tent, a movable collection of natural and manmade artifacts, born out of the ashes of Barnum's last brick-and-mortar museum, was available for inspection. Before the beginning of the matinee, attendees had already been presented with a multitude of marvels such as were, until recently, unprecedented here in America's heartland.

There were more astonishments ahead. Once seated on benches under the enormous canvas of the performance tent, circus-goers would experience an entertainment extravaganza. Acts were staged simultaneously across three center rings and one raised stage, constantly competing with one another for audience attention. There were tightrope walkers, trapeze artists, clowns, contortionists, equestrians, and acrobats. At one moment during the production, Miss Zamamoto "mounted and descended ladders barefoot upon sword blades" in one ring; Leopold and Wentworth demonstrated gymnastic prowess on the parallel bars in another; the third ring offered a trio of entertainments: Herr Drayton performing his "Cannon Ball Act," Crossley and Elder pursuing "Scottish pastimes and Caledonian sports," and Gus Hill undertaking his "Champion Club Swinging Act," while on the stage, Ashley and Hess exhibited "wonderful illustrations of roller skating." One thrill closely followed another. The Human Fly flew, the Snake Charmer charmed, and Professor Charles White put his performing stallions through their paces. After balancing precariously near the top of the tent on a swaying perch, the versatile Mademoiselle Zarah descended swiftly on a slender wire, fastened only by her teeth, then, once safely back on the ground, introduced the audience to her flying flock of trained doves.

Punctuating the show, and eventually providing its finale, were appearances by the enormous, engaging animals who were the principal attraction—of this and every other circus of the era. Even here, among the elephants, there were specialties on display. "Tom Thumb," the world's only "dwarf clown elephant" (named for Barnum's recently deceased protégé and sometime collaborator), provided comical amusement, and the "educated" elephants amazed the audience with coordinated calisthenics. Under the painful threat of trainer George W. Arstingstall's sharp prod, the troop precisely executed bends, twirls, headstands, pinwheels, pyramids, and other decidedly un-elephantine exercises. The blotchy, "sacred" Toung Taloung was a genuine, if unimpressive, variation on the wild-type Asiatic elephant (unlike the painted one offered by a rival circus), but was surrounded by fake worshipful Buddhist monks. The pride of the circus was the infant "Bridgeport," born at Barnum's Bridgeport, Connecticut, winter quarters during February 1882. The little female was only the second (or possibly third) baby elephant born in North America—the previous one, "Columbia," born two years earlier, had belonged to Bailey and Hutchinson's Great London Circus, and Barnum's envy had reportedly led directly to the formation of their three-way partnership.

One elephant towered over all of these, however, both literally and in the public imagination. Jumbo was the undisputed star of Barnum's 1885 show, just as he had been for the previous three seasons, since the day of his arrival in the United States. Although Barnum had exercised his full powers of persuasion to maximize the animal's reputation in America, Jumbo was a true giant—an unusually large African bush elephant who had caused a sensation throughout his life whenever and wherever he was exhibited. His name would go on to become synonymous with superlative size, but in newspaper ads and circulars, on posters and handbills, Barnum and his publicity team called him many other things: "the mighty lord of all beasts," "the largest living quadruped on earth," "monster," "mammoth," and "the towering monarch of his mighty race."

Today, scientists and veterinarians are beginning to understand the ways in which captivity and display disrupt elephants' complex social and foraging behaviors, along with the resulting consequences for their health, fecundity, and psychological well-being. But in the 1880s, as traveling circuses, aided by the capillary-like profusion of railroads around the country, brought exotic animals to an increasingly insulated, urbanized population, Jumbo and other elephants made an astonishing impression that was difficult to resist. They served as ambassadors of the inaccessible animal world, even as they also represented the triumph of human civilization over wilderness; their presence on small-town or city streets embodied globalism, capitalism, and a fun, family-friendly side of technological progress.

That is, an elephant display was a complicated kind of spectacle, one that left the animal-welfare movement—and in particular Henry Bergh, who still saw it as his duty to police P. T. Barnum's excesses—struggling to set norms around how these magnificent beasts should be treated, and indeed whether they should be performing at all.

·   ·   ·

Like all circus and zoo elephants of the era, Jumbo entered captivity early and brutally. Elephants do not readily relinquish their young, and Jumbo's capture in Sudan in 1861 probably occasioned a massacre of his maternal herd. He arrived in Paris still a feeble infant, and he never thrived in the bleak confines of the crowded menagerie at the Jardin des Plantes. When, in 1865, the London Zoological Gardens acquired him in exchange for an Indian rhinoceros, he arrived at his new home in deplorable condition, according to Matthew Scott, the English zookeeper who would care for Jumbo tenderly (if often improperly) for the rest of his troubled life.

Over the next seventeen years, Jumbo became a fixture of the London Zoo, maturing slowly from a juvenile to an unusually leggy adolescent within the confines of a solitary cell and a barren iron-fenced yard. Although a female African elephant, Alice, was added to the collection not long after Jumbo, the two animals enjoyed only limited contact and Jumbo's immediate companions remained overwhelmingly human: zoo staff and visitors—particularly children, who would be permitted, for a fee, to ride a dozen at a time in a carriage perched upon his back. Offerings of oranges, alcoholic beverages, and sweet rolls supplemented his principal diet of hay and oats. Because of his gentleness toward very young children and his benign tolerance of the cruel pranks inflicted by older ones, Jumbo became widely known in Britain as "the children's friend" and the "people's pet."

With adolescence came changes in Jumbo's behavior that deeply worried the zoo's superintendent, Abraham Bartlett. Raging with increasing frequency at night (possibly provoked by the pain of a toothache caused by his too-soft diet), Jumbo severely damaged the reinforced walls of the elephant house as well as his own tusks, fracturing them at the level of the skull. Fearing that Jumbo might go on to rampage during daylight hours, putting visitors at violent risk, Bartlett obtained permission to procure a powerful elephant gun and kept it nearby as a fail-safe. Alternately dreading being the man who allowed an out-of-control animal to maraud a mobbed exhibit or the man responsible for the murder of the famous friend of British children, Bartlett was extremely relieved when he received an offer to purchase Jumbo from America's most famous showman.

For the modest price of two thousand British pounds, the London Zoo sold towering, twenty-one-year-old Jumbo to Phineas Taylor Barnum, who, within days of the sale, sent his agents abroad to collect his prize. After failing to persuade Jumbo to enter a large wooden shipping crate at the zoo, the circus men tried to induce the elephant to walk to the waterfront. He refused to cooperate, resisting all attempts to lead him out through the Zoological Garden gates. In doing so, day after day, in full view of a growing crowd of curious spectators, he awoke widespread public protest against his forced emigration from Britain. Letters poured in to editors of London's newspapers, to supervisors of the Zoological Gardens, and to P. T. Barnum. "Dear Mr. Barnum," read one, "Please do not take Jumbo to America. I think it will be cruel if you do take him where he begs so hard not to be taken. There are plenty of other elephants—will not one of them do you instead?—one that does not mind going. If you will let Jumbo stay, I am sure the English children will thank you." Pointed questions about Jumbo's planned departure for America were raised in the British House of Commons, and Queen Victoria reportedly took a discreet interest in the matter herself. A lawsuit (ultimately unsuccessful) to block the sale worked its way through the Chancery Court. Meanwhile, weeks went by as Jumbo continued to balk at walking into his wooden box.

Barnum evinced no hurry, seeming to delight in every demonstration of affection, anger, or anguish from Britons distressed over Jumbo's departure. He and his publicists kept Americans abundantly apprised of the ongoing uproar abroad, while his men in London maintained a steady, gradual effort to teach Jumbo to voluntarily enter his shipping container. Success was eventually achieved with the help of keeper Matthew Scott—who, it was decided, would accompany the elephant to the United States rather than remaining behind in Britain. After Scott came on board, as if by magic, Jumbo went into the box, the box went onto the boat, and the boat went across the Atlantic. Three weeks later, still in the wooden crate, Jumbo arrived at the Castle Garden pier in New York City. He was heartily greeted by a beaming Barnum, Bailey, and Hutchinson, a handful of VIPs and newspapermen, and a cheering crowd of thousands. Through a heavy rain, eight straining horses and two Asiatic elephants muscled Jumbo's crate up Broadway to Madison Square Garden, where the 1882 season of the Greatest Show on Earth was just getting started.

Jumbo immediately became the star of the show, drawing thousands every afternoon and evening to the packed arena, where he promenaded near the beginning of every performance. Barnum estimated that within ten days of his arrival in America, he had recouped the entire $30,000 it had cost (taking promotion, personnel, transport, and litigation into account) to bring Jumbo to the United States. As the circus completed its Manhattan run and headed out to tour the continent, the circulars, pamphlets, and posters that plastered every destination along the route would emphasize the elephant's unusual size.

Even so, Barnum and his partners were consistently cagey about Jumbo's exact measurements. When one reporter asked how big the elephant was, Barnum declared he was so big he displaced six hundred Irish immigrants from the boat that brought him to America. When asked about the length of Jumbo's trunk, Barnum compared it to the length of a full-grown crocodile. Jumbo's weight was likened to a boxcar full of iron tailings. Jumbo's footprints were so large, one of the show's press agents claimed, they resembled the "indentation" that would be made by a fat man falling from a tall building. Barnum, Bailey, and Hutchinson firmly believed that Jumbo's height and weight were best left to the imagination of a public who wanted to be wowed. (In point of fact, the numbers were probably impressive, particularly for a still-growing young adult, but still short of superlative for the species.)

Jumbo and trainer (likely Matthew Scott).

Jumbo crisscrossed the country in a brightly painted, oversized custom railcar that also contained accommodations for Matthew Scott. Despite his star status, Jumbo was rarely seen anywhere unshackled. A *New York Times* reporter noted that Jumbo was burdened with "immense chains encircling his legs in such a manner that his stride was shortened and locomotion made difficult." Even under the inhibiting influence of these fetters, Jumbo was considered much too mighty to risk any form of misbehavior. Throughout his travels, on the way between circus engagements or around the hippodrome track, Jumbo was accompanied by several stout handlers ready with whips and prods to goad him whenever the gentler persuasion of Scott proved insufficient. George

Arstingstall, the head elephant trainer of the Greatest Show on
Earth, wouldn't have it any other way. "Mr. Arstingstall has very
fixed opinions about elephants," Hutchinson told one newspaper
reporter. "He has no faith in the good effects of being kind to them,
and never attempts to romp with them."

Jumbo's 1882 arrival in America found Arstingstall at the peak
of his pachyderm-persuading powers. A trim, handsome Virginian
with intense eyes and an abundant mustache, he had, though still
in his thirties, already been training wild animals for more than
two decades. As a teenager, not long after graduating from a public
primary school in his home state, Arstingstall signed up with the
popular Dan Rice Circus. Though inexperienced, he took charge
of a troupe of trained bears that had formerly belonged to Grizzly
Adams. He later transferred his talents to the Mike Lipman Colossal Circus, handling their so-called "sacred bull," before briefly
transitioning to hot air ballooning. A long fall brought his short
stint as an aerialist to an end; Arstingstall returned to wild animal training as the safer career choice, and traveled to Europe to
exhibit lions, tigers, and hyenas. In 1876, Arstingstall joined the
Great London Circus, where he turned his attention to the enormous animals that would eventually make him famous. His supervisor there, Stuart Craven, had embraced a humane philosophy of
elephant training, but Arstingstall had his own ideas.

"I will tell you something about training elephants," Arstingstall
said to a *St. Louis Daily Globe-Democrat* writer in August 1879.
"An elephant is a treacherous, cunning, and very intelligent animal," capable of forming strong social attachments—just not to
humans. Therefore, "in handling elephants, fear is the only instinct
to cultivate in them. Kindness, such as you would extend to a dog
or a horse, does them no good. They are liable at any time to harm
you if they are not kept in subjugation. They must be punished
immediately after the offense, whatever it may be, is committed.

"Teaching an elephant a trick is exactly like teaching any other
animal," he went on, with evident bravado. "It only requires mastery of the brute. Put a bell in the grasp of an elephant's trunk and
teach him that every time he drops it he will be prodded, and he
will quit dropping it."

As the Great London's elephant herd grew under the ownership of Bailey and Hutchinson—primarily through import of new animals from Asia, but also with the enviable birth of baby Columbia—so did Arstingstall's reputation as an all-around elephant man. Now heading up a team of trainers and keepers, "Professor" Arstingstall relished the role he claimed for himself as America's foremost elephant expert, providing public comment not only on behavioral topics, but also natural history, husbandry, and veterinary medicine. Despite his constant, candid commentary on the elephantine applications of corporal punishment, it was only after Barnum's circus combined with the Great London show that Arstingstall's methods attracted the attention of Henry Bergh.

.   .   .

A few years beforehand, the relationship between Bergh and Barnum had taken a surprisingly congenial turn. It began in March 1879, when Bergh investigated a report published in the *New York Sun* that a keeper employed by Barnum had shoved a red-hot poker into the trunk of a misbehaving male elephant named Emperor. Bergh spoke with staff and inspected the tip of the trunk himself before pronouncing the accusation to be false. "Why, it requires but one sober thought to convince a person that it would be an impossibility for a man to thrust a red-hot iron up the proboscis of an elephant," Bergh told a reporter for the *New York Evening Express*. "The man who once attempted it would be most apt to see more of the elephant than he desired, and enough to last him the small remnant of life that would be left in him. It is perfectly preposterous that such a cruelty could be perpetrated upon an animal armed with such a tremendous engine, constantly swinging to and fro."

Perhaps Bergh really failed to imagine how a hot iron might be applied to an intransigent elephant's trunk—but a few days afterward, Bailey himself described its use to a *Sun* reporter as not only practicable, but *necessary*. "When an elephant has once felt the smart," he explained, "the mere approach of an iron is enough to tame him." The ASPCA would later make an arrest in the incident, but Bergh's initial reaction signified a shift in his stance against

Barnum—by erroneously offering the benefit of the doubt, Bergh was squandering a crucial opportunity to improve the lot of the nation's elephants.

Several months later, Bergh was consulted by a nascent Connecticut chapter of the SPCA: Who did he think should sit on their board? His unexpected reply: Phineas Taylor Barnum, "for his generous and sympathetic instincts towards the lower animals." Historians disagree about what caused Bergh to warm toward his rival: Had a sincere friendship (or "frenemy"-ship) developed between the two men? Was Bergh succumbing to a corrupt hope that Barnum's wealth might find its way into SPCA coffers? Or did he recognize that Barnum's spectacles awoke an interest in, and sympathy for, the animals they featured? It seems most likely that Bergh, who believed as passionately as Barnum did that all publicity is good publicity, came to feel as though he and his rival were partners in the project of bringing attention to the anti-cruelty cause.

Barnum enthusiastically accepted the board seat, embracing his founding role in the local society and proudly referring to himself thereafter as the "Bergh of Bridgeport." Both he and his young second wife, Nancy Fish Barnum, remained active in the organization for years to come.

Even so, despite this softening in the relationship between Barnum and Bergh—and despite the entreaties of Bergh's critics, who implored him to confine his crusade to domestic species—Bergh continued to take an active interest in the performing and wild animals on display in his city. As he declared to the press, "If I had my way, there would never be a zoological collection in the world. I can see no benefit to humanity, no advantage to art, nor any promotion to science in the confinement of a miscellaneous herd of dumb brutes." Bergh might have made examples of any number of exotic animal exhibitors, but he continued to single out Barnum—and he continued to make headlines for doing so.

As in the often-recounted (by Barnum) dispute over the feeding of snakes, Bergh's critiques of his popular rival sometimes demonstrated an inferior understanding of the basic needs of animals rather than a superior concern for their welfare. (In another of Barnum's favorite anecdotes, Bergh demanded he "furnish the rhinoceros with a tank of water to swim in, when such a proceeding would have killed it.") On other occasions, Bergh seemed to be taken in by the stagecraft in Barnum's animal performances.

One of the more infamous such incidents occurred only weeks after Barnum was nominated for the Connecticut SPCA board. In the spring 1880 season, "Salamander the Fire Horse" featured prominently among the season's promoted attractions. Trained in Germany, the little black stallion would, the posters promised, enter the circus ring amidst a shower of exploding fireworks, then fearlessly fly through several hoops of fire before exiting the arena unscathed.

After hearing a report that an attendant in the first performance had mistakenly dropped a hoop on the horse, causing Salamander's mane and tail to appear to be aflame, Bergh demanded a halt to all future performances on animal cruelty and human safety grounds. It was "simply abominable," he wrote to Barnum, "that the public cannot be provided with amusement by your show without inflicting torture upon an animal." In response, Barnum initially tried to reason with Bergh, making clear that the hoops were lit with harmless "chemical" fire, but Bergh refused to relent. Barnum vowed to defy Bergh's order and would himself introduce the celebrated steed back into the circus arena. He advised Bergh to respond as he saw fit.

The stands were packed when Barnum stepped into the ring the following week, before excited spectators, eager newspaper reporters, unsmiling ASPCA agents, and a sizable contingent of New York police officers ready to make an arrest. "Either Mr. Bergh or I must run this show, and I don't think it will be Mr. Bergh," the showman thundered. "I know more about animals than he knows." Barnum then detailed, at some length, his history with the head of the ASPCA, before commencing a demonstration of the flaming hoops course. As Salamander looked on dispassionately, the rings were ignited and Barnum and several of the show's clowns hopped blithely through them. Superintendent Hartfield of the ASPCA, after inspecting the hoops himself and conceding them to be innocuous, made apologies for his (absent) boss, and withdrew.

Salamander the Fire Horse retained his moniker, and his popularity, even after Barnum had revealed the secret behind his act. That seemed to confirm, once again, Barnum's belief that audiences desire nothing more than to be close to a controversy. Barnum savored his latest victory, but in a letter to the *Evening Post* some days later, he commended Bergh's good intentions. "We should remember that no man is perfect, and that, with all his faults and shortcomings, Henry Bergh, President of the Society for the Prevention of Cruelty to Animals, is to be honored and respected for his unselfish devotion to such an excellent cause."

.   .   .

Bergh continued, fitfully, to criticize the treatment of the animals performing under Barnum's big top. Eventually, Bergh's eye for abuses settled on the handling of elephants by George Arstingstall and the other trainers. On April 1, 1883, the following item (headlined "Bergh and the Elephant") appeared in the *New York Herald:*

> While witnessing the performance of the elephants at Barnum's circus yesterday afternoon, Mr. Bergh noticed one of the keepers prodding the animals with an instrument about thirteen inches long, made of hard wood, on the end of which is a sharp pointed steel hook. Not wishing to make a demonstration during the performance Mr. Bergh waited until the animals were taken from the ring, when he seized the weapon and, after warning the keeper against using such instruments again [*sic*] the future, on pain of being prosecuted, took it to the society's museum, where it is now among others of a similar character.

The object that Bergh seized from the handler (likely Arstingstall, or his assistant Bill Newman) was an elephant hook—also known as an elephant goad, bullhook, or ankus—an ancient tool of elephant subjugation that is still in use today. Its sturdy handle, of variable length, can be made of any resilient material: wood, metal, ivory (adding elephant insult to elephant injury), or, more recently, plastic or fiberglass. Handlers might use this blunt end for beatings, particularly when outside of the public eye. The diverging points of the device's metal tip are oriented so that a painful stimulus may be inflicted through either pushing-stabbing or pulling-hooking movements. Applied to the tender skin around the elephant's ears, eyes, trunk, mouth, feet, or anus, the hook provides aversive motivation without visible violence, and so has been a favorite of circus trainers and others who wish to compel elephants to perform unnatural behaviors without appearing to abuse them.

Arstingstall, with his view that elephants could not be trained by kindness, had never been bashful about the painful properties of the bullhook: "They want to know that you are master all the time, and the elephant-hook has to be in constant use," he was recalled later to have said. He had provided a close-up demonstration of the instrument's power to a group of journalists who, at Barnum's invitation, had gathered to see Jumbo's final appearance in New York City in the spring of 1882. A reporter from *The New York Times* described the scene:

> Jumbo was in his quarters on the Madison-avenue side of the Garden, and near him was a stand laden with apples, pea-nuts and buns. At this stand he cast a wistful look, and at the same time seemed to recognize the fact that Mr. Arstingstall had not lost his steel hook, which he is quick to jab into the trunk or sides of refractory elephants. Jumbo meekly followed Mr. Arstingstall to the track in the Garden.

After bowing to circus-goers, Jumbo and the other elephants processed through Manhattan, then boarded a Hudson River ferry, still accompanied by the reporters. As the vessel churned toward New Jersey, Jumbo became restless, jostling the other elephants packed in behind him. "The elephant keepers were startled," the *Times*'s report continued:

> Prodding Jumbo with the hook, striking him with the whip, and pleading with him, seemed to have no effect upon him. When it seemed almost probable that some of the smaller elephants would drop into the river, Jumbo suddenly checked himself and started forward. The shouts of the keepers were loud and prolonged, and the evidently frightened beast stood still in the centre of the boat, while neighborly elephants rubbed up against him.

Bergh ordered Arstingstall and the other handlers working for Barnum and London to neither use nor carry the elephant hook while supervising their charges. Arstingstall vigorously objected to the new rule, insisting, in an impassioned letter to Bergh, that the instrument was only rarely used, and then only in extreme cases of elephant misbehavior. Even then, no real harm results, the trainer maintained, as the pointed tip protrudes only three-quarters of an inch, while the elephant's tough hide measures two inches thick. Arstingstall predicted that the elephants would immediately detect the absence of the ankus in the handlers' hands and take devilish advantage of the situation, lapsing into unruly and dangerous behavior. He pleaded with Bergh to permit him and his men to carry and display their hooks, even if they were forbidden from using them, in order to protect themselves and innocent audience members from grievous harm. Bergh refused any compromise, and so, reluctantly, the goads were given up.

In the days that followed, Arstingstall and the two assistant trainers stood in the center of Madison Square Garden, wearing a brace of revolvers with which to discourage any animal attempting to rampage through the arena. Because a handgun might do little more than annoy an elephant, heavily loaded rifles, "ready for instant use on the least sign of an elephantine outbreak," were placed near the ring where the giants pirouetted and made pyramids at the center. Even these precautions failed to reassure the handlers who worked under Arstingstall and the other trainers. Several seasoned men refused to continue elephant work without adequate means of "self defense."

On the morning of April 4, inside the elephant quarters, a fight broke out between two of Barnum and London's mightiest males, Pilot and Albert. Newspapers reported that Pilot, in the throes of a springtime hormonal surge, kicked Albert in the eye, provoking a prodigious pachyderm battle that violently shook the supports of the venue, threatening its collapse. Assistant trainer Newman rushed into the fray, separating the elephants with heavy blows to both. Pilot then lifted up Newman with his trunk and flung him into a corner, from which he emerged mildly concussed and missing two teeth.

Pilot was tied down and beaten at length, but failed to signal submission, and so, by the order of uncompromising circus partner James Bailey, the thirty-year-old bull was condemned to die on the grounds that an elephant that refuses to submit to human authority is likely to kill a human at its next opportunity. Before dawn on April 5, Arstingstall loaded a large navy revolver and placed its muzzle between the forelimbs of the recumbent Pilot, still helplessly bound by heavy ropes. Arstingstall fired twice into the elephant's chest, and once into the area beneath his searching left eye, then stood back to observe the effect of his bullets. After several minutes, Pilot convulsed briefly, and then lay still.

Hours later, Pilot's mammoth form, still slumped on the floor of the elephant quarters, underwent a meticulous dissection in situ, supervised by the president of the American Veterinary College. Several veterinary surgeons and butchers provided assistance to Professor Liautard. "[T]he young surgeons showed great interest in the unusual opportunity to study anatomy which the melancholy fate of Pilot afforded," reported the *New-York Tribune* on April 6.

Pilot's execution was treated lightly by other local newspapers the following day. After briefly describing the unfortunate circumstances of the captive animal's life and death, a *Times* writer joked: "He had no regard for religion or morals; he played marbles on Sundays in his youth and drank beer in maturity, and in every way has made a horrible example of himself for little pachyderms who read elephantine Sunday-school books to profit by." This was akin to satirizing contemporary descriptions of criminal personalities, in which the *Times* was appealing to the Victorian prescriptive of harsh punishment for violent or anti-social human behavior.

Bergh was horrified. In a letter to Barnum, leaked (apparently by Barnum himself) on April 8, Bergh condemned the killing of Pilot as "wanton, cruel, and uncalled for," writing, "I have just learned with regret that a gigantic and wonderful creature has been 'disciplined' to death within the walls of your arena for presuming, possibly, to disobey its master's orders while either being abused or suffering from some other of the numerous ills to which all flesh is heir."

According to a paraphrase in the *New-York Tribune,* Bergh said "that if for any real or supposed advantage to science or pleasure these creatures should be taken from their native homes they should be kept in a zoological garden rather than in an itinerant show," and recommended that the Greatest Show on Earth "should not be patronized by respectable and humane citizens who go thither with their children in quest of pleasure." For all his muddledness on the issue of animals in the entertainment industry, Bergh here had achieved a moment of clarity—about the entire enterprise of displaying captive wild creatures for human enjoyment, and about performances coerced from circus elephants in particular.

Barnum's response was typical bluster: "Mr. Barnum says in reply that as the animal was worth $10,000 it is not likely that he would have inflicted upon it any unnecessary violence," a *Tribune* writer noted. "Had Pilot been a man and had he been killed under similar circumstances the courts would have said that the act was done in self-defense." In a telephone interview published the same day, Barnum took a more sarcastic tone, declaring, "I never get angry with enthusiasts any more than with drunkards. Mr. Bergh lives on emotion. I live on judgment as well. He has attacks of male hysterics. . . . He is simply intoxicated with emotion." For a temperance man like Barnum, this characterization must have been intended as a low blow. Still, he generously allowed that Bergh's society had done roughly as much as his Greatest Show on Earth "to ameliorate the savage instincts of mankind."

Public opinion tended, as usual, to side with Barnum. "It is much to be regretted that the zeal of Mr. Bergh and others," *The Brooklyn Union* remarked a day later, "seems sometimes to excite a morbid condition of judgment the effect of which is to bring them into ridicule and reproach, and impair their usefulness. A mad elephant is not to be argued with or cajoled, and when, in the opinion of those who have made his character a study, the lives of persons who come near him are endangered, it is time for him to die."

By the middle of April, Bergh had lost the debate not only over Pilot's death, but also over the use of the elephant hook in the circus ring. "Mr. Bergh yesterday came to his senses and permitted the keepers to resume their use of the prods," trumpeted a Connecticut paper. "Mr. Bergh overstepped the mark. The prod is less painful to an elephant than a spur to a horse, and besides is necessary in case the elephants grow obstreperous. In case of a stampede and a loss of life, Mr. Bergh would have found himself in a very uncomfortable predicament. Bergh had better leave Barnum alone in the future."

The ASPCA president seemed to take this advice to heart. When, in the spring of 1885, during the annual residency of the Greatest Show on Earth at Madison Square Garden, the names of Henry Bergh and P. T. Barnum appeared together in an article about the use of elephant hooks, Bergh was defending the showman against abuse allegations in the *New York Dramatic Times*. In response to a previous editorial suggesting that Bergh had been swayed by flattery to collude with Barnum, Bergh wrote, indignantly, that he was persuaded by Barnum some years previous that the punishment inflicted by bullhooks is not excessive, and is necessary to protect the public from harm that might otherwise result from the animals' unchecked aggression. Bergh went on to applaud the Barnum and London show, describing it as unequaled in all the world. No wonder the editor of the *Dramatic Times* remained unconvinced.

"What does not appear to strike Mr. Bergh," commented the editor, who was perhaps unfamiliar with Bergh's previous declarations, "is that all this wanton forbidding cruelty to the dumb brutes is exercised for no commendable purpose at all."

.   .   .

By summer, the Barnum and London Circus, which had begun its 1885 tour so auspiciously with a record-breaking six-week stand at Madison Square Garden and a series of successful road dates such as the one in Lancaster, began having trouble with its elephants. On July 18, while waiting for his cue to enter the ring in Nashua, New Hampshire, Albert, the former rival of Pilot, became incensed by another passing male and lunged toward him. Keeper James Sweeney forcibly intervened, and Albert tossed and trampled the overmatched young man, before ducking under a tent flap and escaping into the road with George Arstingstall, and his elephant hook, in furious pursuit.

Sweeney died early the next morning in his bed aboard the circus train as it rumbled toward the show's next engagement in Keene, New Hampshire. There, Barnum and his partners invited the local militia to form a firing squad and kill Albert before a crowd of eager spectators, sparking a trend that would last well into the twentieth century of making a public spectacle out of executions of "bad" elephants. Although the event was widely discussed, Bergh withheld comment—even after encouragement from editors at *The Brooklyn Daily Eagle,* who wrote, "We have not any doubt that elephants who kill keepers are justified, humanely speaking, if they are sane, and that elephantine madness is one of the direct conse-quences of a miseducation of a non educable brain. This being so, that part of a circus which involves the exhibition of elephants in idiotic exercises is unwarrantable and cruel, and demands repres-sion. Here is a case in which Mr. Bergh may rightly interfere."

More misfortune lay ahead as the tour continued across the continent. On the evening of September 16, after completing their circuit under the big top in St. Thomas, Ontario, keeper Matthew Scott led his longtime companion, Jumbo, together with the dwarf elephant, Tom Thumb, along what was supposed to have been an idle track toward the waiting circus train. An unscheduled freight unexpectedly advanced on them from behind, slowly but inescap-ably, their way to safety blocked on one side by a resting train and on the other side by a steep embankment that Jumbo balked at descending. The first impact knocked Tom Thumb down the slope, fracturing his left hind limb. Then, as Scott, at the last instant, flung himself out of harm's way, Jumbo's huge hindquarters absorbed the train's full force, derailing the steam engine and pinning the gasping giant against the tracks.

A reporter on the scene described the sorrowful result:

When the noise and confusion had somewhat ceased so that an examination could be made of Jumbo, it was apparent that the hand of death was upon him. But Jumbo looked more majestic than ever before! The king of Afric's forests met the King of Terrors undaunted. He gave one groan after being struck. Then he assumed an attitude of determination, which he maintained till the sands of his life ran out and he was dead. Long after life was extinct his keeper, who brought him from the Zoological Gardens in London, lay on his body and wept.

A day later, Barnum's agents supplied a grander account: As the screaming locomotive bore down on the trio, it was said, Jumbo neglected his own escape in order to rescue his "protege" Tom Thumb. In this telling, Jumbo wheeled about, faced the oncoming engine, and trumpeted alarm to his fellow elephant. When the panicked pygmy pachyderm failed to clear the track, Jumbo grasped his friend around the middle with his trunk and hurled him clear from danger—only an instant before being struck head-on himself. Further embellishments followed. In the following week's version, Jumbo saved Tom Thumb *and* pushed Matthew Scott to safety before bravely making a doomed charge at the oncoming locomotive.

Barnum, as usual, took a philosophical position. "The loss is tremendous," he told reporters, "but such a trifle never disturbs my nerves. Have I not lost a million dollars by fires, and half as much by other financial misfortunes? But long ago I learned that to those who mean right and try to do right, there are no such things as real misfortunes. On the other hand, to such persons, all apparent evils are blessings in disguise."

And indeed, to Barnum, it was. Henry Augustus Ward, a well-respected natural historian (trained by Louis Agassiz) known for his museum-quality taxidermy mounts, had committed himself in advance to the formidable task of preserving Jumbo in the event of the animal's untimely death. Now, instead of one Jumbo, Barnum would have two—the skin and the skeleton, each preserved separately under Ward's supervision. Barnum unveiled the results at a press banquet held near Ward's laboratory in Rochester, New York. Attending members of the media beheld the spectacle of double Jumbo while enjoying a fine dinner capped by an unusual dessert: gelatin made from the ground-up ivory of Jumbo's truncated tusks.

Jumbo's remains rejoined the Greatest Show on Earth at Madison Square Garden that spring, and toured with the show in special conveyances designed to accommodate his increased (and inflexible) postmortem height. In a poignant touch, Barnum purchased Alice, the elephant's former companion at the London Zoo, to present as "Jumbo's widow." Wearing a black veil, accompanied by Matthew Scott and several more elephants as handkerchief-waving "maids-in-mourning," Alice paraded around the circus ring behind the body of her "beloved."

If Bergh felt sorry for Albert, Jumbo, or the other circus elephants who continued their suffering in the coming years, history does not say. When Bergh himself died, in 1888, of pneumonia, among the most conspicuous mourners in attendance at St. Mark's Church was the showman P. T. Barnum—who, calling at the ASPCA offices on the previous afternoon, had expressed his "regret at the loss of one whom he considered among his oldest and dearest friends."

Before the rabies vaccine, loose dogs—and their
bites—were a source of urban terror.

Chapter 12

AN EYE ON YOUR DOG

On April 15, 1886, when fourteen-year-old Amalia Morosini swung open the front door of her family's stone mansion in the exclusive Riverdale-on-Hudson section of the Bronx, she was expecting to see Finette—her beloved brown-and-white English setter, who regularly slept just outside the door on a mat. Amalia didn't realize that the canine greeting her on the porch that morning was an altogether different animal. When she reached out to pet the slender dog's head, the difference became disastrously clear; the girl was brazenly bitten on the bridge of her nose.

In the ensuing pandemonium, the biter turned and fled the porch, sprinting onto a neighbor's property. There, it approached two local dogs, a Newfoundland and a Scottish terrier, provoking a melee that drew in at least one other dog, a spitz. The high-pitched howls of canine battle attracted an excited human audience from neighboring estates. When a coachman pointed out the interloper—crying, "Look out for that dog. He's mad"—a mob armed with pistols, shotguns, and pitchforks converged in pursuit of the retreating cur. The group tracked it down and killed it, ignoring the long-held wisdom that the only reliable way to confirm rabies in a biting dog was to lock it up for several days and watch for the disease's ravaging signs—madness, paralysis, drooling, haunting vocalizations, and rapid, inevitable death. The result of their impatience was a bloody canine carcass and a dangerous uncertainty about the long-term health of the young Miss Morosini.

Amalia was the youngest daughter of Giovanni P. Morosini,

the former bodyguard and later business partner (in one of the Gilded Age's most improbable bootstrap rags-to-riches stories) of Jay Gould, notorious robber baron of the railroads. Along with their grand home, extensive art collection, and stable full of fine horses, the Morosini family took tremendous pride in their pack of purebred canines—pointers, setters, fox terriers, fox hounds, Newfoundlands, and collies, some twenty animals in all. The Morosini dogs were normally given the run of the property, but on this particular morning, the coachman had confined Finette and her companions to prevent them from mixing with mongrels recently seen trespassing on the grounds.

Following the bite, initially described as superficial, Amalia's mother hurriedly transported the girl to her father's office in Manhattan, where the dermatologist L. Duncan Bulkley was summoned to examine the injury. The physician treated the site aggressively, cauterizing the entire area where the dog's teeth had torn the flesh. The swift application of caustic chemicals or a red-hot iron to the site of a bite wound had been known for centuries to lower the likelihood that rabies or some other infection would develop in its aftermath, but it was far from foolproof. Even after subjecting their youngest daughter to this potentially disfiguring procedure, Amalia's parents faced the possibility that weeks or months later she might develop the horrible symptoms of hydrophobia—as rabies then was sometimes called—a cruel disease that few, if any, survived.

Peace of mind for the Morosinis would be hard to come by. Science was still struggling to explain why some bite victims eventually developed hydrophobia while others didn't. Were all aggressive dogs capable of causing the condition or only some of them? Were all bite recipients susceptible or only certain ones? Determined to receive the informed advice of New York City's most eminent rabies expert, Amalia's parents arranged for the body of the offending canine to be rushed to the pathology laboratory at the American Veterinary College, and to the waiting knives of Dr. Alexandre Liautard and his students.

.   .   .

In 1886, the American Veterinary College was flourishing. It remained the preeminent such institution in the United States, but it no longer lacked for peers. The New York College of Veterinary Surgeons had regrouped since Liautard's departure and continued to produce a small class of trained graduates every year. Successful veterinary colleges had been established at Harvard and the University of Pennsylvania, and in the cities of Minneapolis and Chicago. Agriculturally focused land-grant universities, too, began offering veterinary coursework and degrees.

Under Liautard's leadership, the American Veterinary College continued to set the standard for the training of American veterinarians. Admission to the school was now restricted to applicants with academic credentials or successful performance on an entrance examination. To accommodate an increasing number of students from all over the United States, the college had hired additional faculty and expanded its lecture, laboratory, and clinical facilities. To graduate, pupils had to complete a rigorous two-year course of study, and pass oral, written, and practical examinations.

At the 1883 commencement ceremony, Liautard and other faculty members had shared the stage with a host of distinguished guests, among them Henry Bergh, as the famous Reverend Henry Ward Beecher addressed the graduating students. "Human life may be of more importance than the life of an animal, and yet the veterinary surgeon may rank as high as him who ministers to humanity," began Beecher, before citing Darwin's well-known theory placing humans in close kinship with non-human creatures. In their embryonic forms, Beecher pointed out, the man and the dog were indistinguishable. It was later in life that their differences became plain—not necessarily in man's favor. The dog "knows more through instinct, than many men through reason and common sense. Yet, I grieve to say, in all scripture there is no praise for dogs. If they perish, alas! what becomes of their owners?"

Beecher concluded his remarks with a few kind words for the twenty-two young men then embarking upon their professional lives: "This is an age of humanity. Men are sensitive to suffering as they never were before. Cruel laws are passing away, and even cruelty in slaughtering animals is discountenanced. Do not let any man look down on you because he ministers to mankind while you minister to suffering brutes. Let your names be remembered for your fidelity, your humanity, and your science." After the speeches, music filled Chickering Hall as the graduates—including Dr. Samuel K. Johnson, whose valedictory speech that evening was judged to be "one of the best ever delivered before a class of young medical students"—celebrated.

A quarter century before, when Liautard emigrated from France, he was one of just a handful of "educated" (at least by his exacting standards) veterinarians in the country. Now, thanks to colleges like his, there were hundreds, putting their skills to work on behalf of the nation's animals. The year after graduating, the young Dr. Johnson, together with another graduate, S. S. Field, converted a former boarding stable on West 25th Street into the New York Veterinary Hospital, an institution for the care of both horses and dogs. On the first floor, past the client waiting room and a pharmacy, sat the roomy stalls for horses, separated from the front by sliding doors that—according to the *New York Dial*, in a glowing review of the new establishment—"keep from the eyes of all visitors all unpleasant sights, and protect their noses from any malodorous smell."

The upper floor tended to the canine patients. Photographs taken some years later show a separate waiting room for dog owners, with stately furniture and a wall of glass medicine bottles, and a treatment room with examination tables and kennels, not terribly unlike what one might see in small veterinary clinics today. A long, narrow room was set aside for suspected rabid dogs, with capacity for seven. On Wednesday afternoons, Drs. Johnson and Field offered a free clinic for New Yorkers who could not afford to pay.

Modest though such facilities were, their rise represented a crucial turning point for the rapidly developing field, with the effects felt all around the country. In 1887, a reporter from the local paper in Leavenworth, Kansas, was surprised to hear that the town now had a veterinary hospital; he headed down the street from the newspaper's offices, passed a hay market, and entered what looked like a livery stable, to find that it had been converted into a state-of-the-art clinic for horses and dogs. The reporter was particularly impressed to see the pharmacy, with its "stock of medicines sufficient almost to start a small drug store," as well as the array of surgical instruments, many of which had been invented by the two founders themselves—one of them, a Dr. Ayers, having recently graduated from the American Veterinary College.

The largest and best appointed of the new hospitals were those attached to the veterinary colleges. The one at the University of Pennsylvania, at the corner of 36th and Pine Streets in West Philadelphia, advertised itself at its founding in 1885 as the largest in the nation, rivaled worldwide only by the hospitals in Paris and Budapest. That same year, the hospital at Harvard, on Village Street in Cambridge, Massachusetts, had space for thirty-two horses, thirty dogs, and a few cattle, and estimated that it had seen two thousand cases since its founding two years earlier. To serve the community, it had established a subscription system whereby those making a regular payment of support could have their large animals hospitalized for a flat fee of one dollar per day, dogs for fifty cents.

In extending their care to dogs, these early veterinarians were acknowledging how much owners valued their pets—and reinforcing it, too, giving owners an outlet for their burgeoning love and concern. Even then, the existence of dog hospitals gave rise to the kind of anxious hypochondria on an animal's behalf that today's vets know all too well. In 1888, a *Brooklyn Daily Eagle* reporter noted that "slight indispositions" had begun sending dog owners into conniptions: "A cough, a refusal to take food, or the snapping of the animal at a stick will cause them to run at once to the dog doctor, when by a little judgment they might cure the trifling malady themselves." The *Daily Eagle* writer met an Angora cat in one local clinic whose owner had paid for a special coal fire, to keep the beloved animal warm night and day.

This new valuing of pets, it should be noted, was both emotional and financial. In 1886, a court in Cambridge delivered what might well have been the nation's first legal judgment against a veterinary hospital. The plaintiff was a South Boston baker who brought his beloved brindle bulldog to the clinic at Harvard. When a doctor tried to administer medicine to it, it snapped at him, slipped out of its collar, and ran down the stairs and out the open front door, never to be seen again. The baker testified that the dog was worth $200; the court awarded him $20.

Among the wealthy in particular—those like the Morosinis, with
the means to obtain expensive dogs and care for them—dogs had
become not just family members but fashion items. Up and down
the social ladder, the ladies and gentlemen of New York evinced a
great fondness for promenading around the streets with their pampered canine companions. "Fifth Avenue is given over between the
hours of twelve and one to dogs and brisk moving women," a *Daily
Eagle* correspondent noted in 1885. "It is considered rather English
to go out in a tailor made dress at that hour and stride rapidly up
and down the avenue, with an eye on your dog and a whip in your
hand." A few years later, a *Sun* story reported that ladies "walk in
the avenue with their dogs in leash beside them, and their nurses
follow leading the children, or more frequently promenade in a different direction."

Increasingly, the dogs at the ends of those leashes boasted of
pure bloodlines. The arrival of the Westminster Dog Show in 1877
had coincided with a rise in appreciation, even a kind of fetish, for
the multiplying welter of official breeds. Society reporters could
now comment on trends in canines much as they did on hat styles
or hem lengths. *Harper's Bazaar* noted in 1887 that the "coming
dog" was the black and tan, while the pug, long a favorite of high-
style ladies, was getting the heave-ho. The following year, the *Sun*
hailed the ascent of the Yorkshire terrier, noting that "Japanese
pugs" (what today are called Japanese chins), fox and Skye terriers,
and Maltese and King Charles spaniels were also on the upswing.

In these ascending tastes, nineteenth-century Americans were
enacting a new, modern phase in a practice that stretched back millennia. Since its domestication in Asia more than fourteen thousand years ago, *Canis familiaris* has not only provided humans
with companionship but also performed vital services across
various societies: guarding homes, herding livestock, killing pests,
hunting game, pulling cargo, supporting soldiers, producing meat
and fur. Selective breeding for traits that enhanced the dog's func-
tionality in a particular role (often in a specific, regional setting)
led to the development of distinct types. At least as far back as
the ancient world, humans developed sturdy dogs for pulling sleds;

imperturbable dogs for the front lines of battle; observant, agile dogs for maneuvering sheep; keen, disciplined dogs for pointing out, flushing, chasing down, or retrieving game; and small, sweet dogs for warming ladies' laps. Cats entered into the domestication relationship later, and perhaps less completely, than did dogs, but after dispersing geographically from the early agricultural societies of the Middle East, at least sixteen geographic types emerged, distinguished from random-bred cats mainly by external physical traits: coat color, length and softness, and structure and proportion of the face and body.

By 1886, the American Kennel Club recognized twenty-eight varieties of man's best friend, residing everywhere from Washington to Winnipeg. For that year's Westminster dog show, prominent kennels all over the world sent specimens of setter, pointer, Saint Bernard, collie, spaniel, mastiff, hound, toy, and terrier for the judges' inspection. Of the many "famous dogs" expected, noted *The New York Times,* the English setter Rodrigo—from Tennessee's Memphis and Avent Kennels—was among the most celebrated; a few months earlier, a rapturous local reporter in Memphis had called him "undoubtedly the dog of the period" and the "grandest English setter in the world." As for cats, though Madison Square Garden wouldn't host its first show for them until later in the 1890s, breeds like the Maine Coon, Manx, Siberian, Siamese, Angora, and Abyssinian were gaining popularity among feline fanciers. Complaining about the rise of purebred pet fascination, a writer for *Century Magazine* intoned that year: "Luxurious self-gratification, the accompaniment of our growing wealth, is ever seeking new methods for the exhibition of its passing whims and fancies. While in one direction the resources of art and science are exhausted to minister to its wants, in another the animal world is ransacked to pander to its bizarre and eccentric longing for novelty."

As dogs became fashion items, their well-heeled owners naturally wanted them kept in the best possible style. Multiple newspapers ran accounts about wealthy society matrons hiring maids or nurses to care for their animals. A reporter in 1887 claimed there were "dozens" of such dedicated caretakers, and reprinted a want ad for one: "a maid for a pet poodle, who understands thoroughly how to wash and dress, feed and nurse dogs, and the care of their

wardrobes. Must be pretty, gentle and refined. Wages $20 a month."
Similarly, in 1888, the *Sun*'s report on fashionable canines described
how the adoration of them could extend even after death:

> A pet dog belonging to a wealthy lady died during her absence
> from home and was buried by the servants under her hus-
> band's direction in the flower pot. Arriving home the day suc-
> ceeding the burial, the lady ordered the dog disinterred; his
> body was bathed, laid in state in an elaborate coffin, and a
> noted artist was sent for to come and paint his portrait. The
> artist reports a solemn scene. The lady was in tears beside the
> little coffin, refusing to be comforted.

The upper crust's mania for dogs grew so intense that it became
hard to separate fact from fiction. A reporter for New York's *Sunday Star* went to the Westminster show in the spring of 1885 and
relayed a story he allegedly heard from a groomer there, about a
society affair the man had recently worked on West 49th Street; he
called it a "poodle party," though the thirty-six dogs there were
of many breeds. Cards of invitation were sent out, the groomer
claimed, with the party's total expense running to perhaps a hundred dollars, or more than $3,000 in today's money. Was this tale
real, or the reporter's comedic invention? It's hard to say, but we
do know that less than twenty years later, the New York society
denizen Harry Lehr really did throw a "dog's dinner" at a mansion
in Newport, Rhode Island, with a special meal prepared for the
animals: stewed liver and rice, shredded dog biscuit, and a fricassee
of bone.

And what to make of contemporary reports of a canine *tailor*—a
man who supposedly made bespoke doggy clothes of the finest
materials, along with copious accessories to match? So claimed
this 1887 newspaper story: "The reporter was shown little smoking
caps with tassels, which he was assured were worn by many dogs at
home, curious little blankets of plush and velvet, cloth and richly
wrought in silk, and even little white silk nightcaps, which are worn
by delicate pet dogs during cold weather."

Anyone who has ever implored a dog not to shake off a Hallow-
een costume may find cause to question this account, but there can

be no doubt that the culture of pampered pet-keeping that Americans indulge in today had its birth in the high society of the 1880s. If some of these stories were inventions or exaggerations, they made it into newsprint only because they were plausible extrapolations of something that was apparent on the avenues.

.　　.　　.

These new attitudes toward dogs made the decade's rabies outbreaks even more wrenching, not just for dog-bite victims and their families, like the Morosini clan, but for every canine lover in the city. Every act of aggression made a dog suspect, but the only effective "test" of the era was observing over several days whether its neurologic derangements progressed to death (or didn't). In the meantime, it was not always possible to distinguish a rabid dog from an angry, frightened, injured, or irritable one. It was popularly believed, even by some physicians, that *any* dog inflicting a damaging bite was rabid. Veterinarians endeavored to systematically describe the sequence of physical changes peculiar to a dog suffering from rabies, but most of these were observable only in a still-living patient. A postmortem examination of a rabid dog might provide useful clues, but did not necessarily produce findings differentiating it from a non-rabid dog.

Rabies' reign of terror, however, was about to come to an end. In 1885, several months prior to Amalia's injury, the famous French scientist Louis Pasteur had announced the first successful trial of immunization against rabies, administered as a series of thirteen injections over eleven days into the skin over a patient's abdomen, following the bite of a rabid dog. Pasteur had developed the treatment by the careful attenuation, in the laboratory, of the viral agent of infection—weakening it enough to provoke immunity without (much) risk of causing death. The rabies vaccine was the first human vaccine to be created in a medical laboratory. (The only previous use of immunization in humans involved the strategic induction of infection with smallpox or a related animal virus to produce immunity to more serious disease caused by natural infection.)

The medical community outside of France was slow to embrace

Pasteur's therapy. Nineteenth-century technology did not permit the culturing, on biological media, or the visualization, under the microscope, of a virus. Viruses, as such, were not really understood to exist in this era, and even the germ theory of disease, which Pasteur's earlier work with bacteria had provided much of the evidence for, was not widely agreed upon. In the United States, many physicians still believed in the miasma theory, which held that "bad air" gave rise to illness. Other doctors viewed the rabies vaccine as a risky procedure against something that was not necessarily infectious in nature or even a genuine medical malady, but rather a psychosomatic disorder.

But at least one medical practitioner in 1886 New York energetically promoted Pasteur's ideas about germ theory, rabies, and vaccination—the same one who would be tasked with providing a postmortem examination of the brown-and-white dog that bit Amalia Morosini.

Of all the contributions Alexandre Liautard made during his long, consequential career in veterinary medicine, establishing the *American Veterinary Review* was arguably the most important, as it ushered in an era of scientific, evidence-based practice to the field of animal health in the United States. The U.S. Veterinary Medical Association (USVMA) had founded the monthly journal in 1877 as its official organ, placing it under Liautard's editorship. He would later own it, and it would remain under his control until the organization bought the publication back in 1915. Within the pages of the *Review,* Liautard published a lively mix of scientific papers (including translations of articles from European journals), case reports, correspondence, professional news, and strongly worded editorials. Its independence from its parent organization allowed the journal to stake out bold and potentially unpopular opinions about veterinary ethics, education, scholarship, leadership, and science.

As editor, Liautard highlighted the era's most exciting biomedical research frontier: investigation into microbial causes for disease. The seventh issue of the *Review,* published in September 1877, featured Liautard's translation of Alfort pathologist Henri Bouley's recent remarks before the French Académie des Sciences, in vigorous support of Pasteurian germ theory. Like his German scientific rival, Robert Koch, Pasteur was then engaged in the study of anthrax, an economically important disease of livestock that occasionally took human lives. Bouley declared the question of the disease's origins settled, in favor of contagious microbes:

> Admitting that contagion is the most essential distinctive characteristic of anthrax, and knowing the agent-instrument of its transmission, M. Pasteur, it seems to me, has given a perfectly exact definition of the disease, where he defined it by the agent itself, the bacteridie, which is found in all species identical to itself, by the properties it possesses, from whatever species it may proceed, to develop in all anthrax, characterized in each one respectively by its proper symptomatic conditions.

The scientific debate between the contagionists (Pasteur, Koch, Lister) and the anti-contagionists, who believed diseases arose in animals and people independently of the presence of microbes, was centered in Europe, where scientific experiments were being energetically carried out at universities and other government-sponsored research institutions. Laboratory science had yet to find large-scale financial support in the United States, where it remained more of a genteel hobby, and so, even as the United States produced more and more technological advancements during the nineteenth century, its scientific contributions lagged.

The *Review*'s early coverage of germ theory research provided American veterinarians with an unusually positive perspective on the controversy being bitterly debated across the Atlantic. Many (but not all) prominent American physicians still favored miasmatic and zymotic (the interaction of external environmental and internal bio-enzymatic factors) explanations of disease, and arguments both for and against germ theory were published in the nation's medical journals and popular periodicals. Largely due to the editorial influence of Alexandre Liautard, veterinarians who subscribed to the *American Veterinary Review* were presented with an overwhelmingly pro-contagionist viewpoint.

According to the calculations of historian John D. Blaisdell, Louis Pasteur's work was published and discussed more often than that of any other individual in American veterinary journals of the 1880s. The *Review* and its on-again, off-again competitor, the *Journal of Comparative Medicine and Surgery,* followed Pasteur's experiments investigating microbial causes for anthrax, chicken cholera, hog cholera, and swine fever. When Pasteur and his collaborators devised methods of weakening some of these veterinary pathogens in order to induce immunity to natural infection in susceptible animals—creating the first modern vaccines—American veterinarians were kept closely abreast of his breakthroughs.

Liautard declared himself to be a germ theorist early on. In an 1880 editorial, he made his opinion on the matter clear, and pointed out the practical importance of Pasteur's scientific discoveries:

> The believers in the spontaneity of the development of contagious diseases have found in M. Pasteur a powerful opponent, who slowly, but surely, demonstrates by undeniable proofs that the virulent properties of those affections is due to the presence of microscopical organisms. A few years ago it was his wonderful discovery of the causes of the contagious disease of the silkworm; later, the evident proof of the bacteridæ as causes of carbuncular affections, and now it is his demonstration of the ætiology of chicken cholera, an affection which destroys so many of our valuable poultry, and brings on ruin to large poultry breeding establishments.
>
> But this last discovery goes farther. With some restrictions, justified by the limited number of experiments yet made, he shows that chicken cholera is not only due to the presence of a microbe, developing itself in the organism of the hen, as was already demonstrated by Perroncito and Toussaint, but that it can be prevented by inoculation . . .

When, at last, Louis Pasteur turned his attention to rabies, the *American Veterinary Review* provided veterinarians with timely news of each advancement. Unlike the bacterial pathogens he had been studying until then, rabies could not be seen under a light microscope or cultured on a glass plate; it could only be grown and observed in the bodies of animals. So his laboratory experiments necessarily entailed the death of numerous rabbits, dogs, and other

"M. Pasteur in the Laboratory," 1885.

mammals. To ensure the passage of virus from one animal to another, Pasteur and his disciples developed the technique of infection through cerebral inoculation: drilling a small hole in the skull of an anesthetized animal, so that infectious material (nervous tissue from a previously infected animal) could be applied directly to the dura mater covering the brain. This method provided reliable virus transmission from one experimental subject to the next, leading directly to the development of Pasteur's life-saving vaccine. Descriptions of the process, however, detailed in journal articles and summarized in newspapers around the world, would fuel the outrage of anti-vivisectionists.

Liautard nonetheless continued to express unequivocal enthusiasm for Pasteur's work. At a USVMA meeting in 1884, not long after Pasteur had announced successful induction of immunity to rabies in vaccinated dogs, Liautard presented a paper, later reproduced in the pages of the *Review*, summarizing recent advances in the scientific understanding of infectious diseases. "The days of guess work and unsustained, though more or less plausible hypothesis, are gone by. The theories of spontaneous growth, of the climateric influences, and the old errors of hygiene, have vanished in the presence of the truths which have become the offspring and reward of close observation and rigid experiment; of microscopic research, and of practical medicine, as tested in the laboratory." Experiments on animals, including dogs, were essential to the labo-

ratory testing of Pasteurian theories on germs, immunity, and vaccination against disease.

For Liautard, Pasteur's scientific methods were clearly justified
by the promise offered by their fruits. With particular respect to
his rabies research, Liautard saw benefits ahead for both dogs and
humans:

> This disease, so terrible in its aspect and results, so treacher-
> ous in its development, and so insidious that its name alone is
> almost a synonym for a frightful death, has now lost a great
> deal of its character by the recent discovery which we also owe
> to Pasteur and to his collaborators. And when we consider
> that we are on the point of mastering it, of protecting from
> its attacks an animal which is often almost a member of our
> households, and thus in many instances of protecting our-
> selves, and perhaps preventing its development in the unfortu-
> nate human being who may have become inoculated with it.

To Liautard, it was clear where the sympathies of the profession
should lie. "Of the value of these results we veterinarians will be
able to judge appreciatively, and we shall, no doubt, take advantage
of them," he wrote. "Of course, much remains to be done. This is
only one first step, and it most probably means the ultimate slow
stamping out of hydrophobia."

.   .   .

When the remains of the brown-and-white dog arrived at the American Veterinary College, the faculty and students were prepared.
Systematic, thorough postmortem examination of large and small
animals was as fundamental to the school's clinical mission as it
was to the training of new veterinarians. As professor of anatomy,
Liautard regularly demonstrated the fundamentals of normal and
pathologic anatomy on the bodies of animals that had died in the
college's care and on others presented to the institution expressly
for that purpose. His practiced procedure of necropsy (veterinary
autopsy) sought to leave no organ unturned in the search for a
diagnosis.

The meticulous examination of the Morosini dog produced a small handful of abnormal findings beyond those associated with canine- and human-inflicted violence. These included a mild congestion of the throat and several organs; an empty, retracted bladder; and the presence of a single, large bird feather within the stricken dog's stomach. Based on these observations, along with descriptions of the dog's behavior leading up to its demise, the examiners arrived, tentatively, at a diagnosis of rabies. The feather, in particular, seemed to satisfy the simple rubric described by Henri Bouley, whose paper on hydrophobia Liautard himself had translated and published in 1884: Bouley had contended (erroneously) that the sole postmortem sign of canine rabies was the presence, in the stomach, of "substances of no alimentary value." Liautard urged Amalia's parents to book immediate passage across the Atlantic, so that the girl might receive Pasteur's vaccine in his Paris laboratory before symptoms of hydrophobia set in—which, in the case of a facial bite, could happen in a matter of days.

The Morosinis accepted Liautard's recommendation with some ambivalence, still in doubt that Amalia's health was in danger. The family expressed no lack of confidence in Pasteur's remedy, but questioned the need for it. "Mr. Morosini does not regard the danger to his daughter as great," a family friend told a reporter for the *New-York Tribune* on the eve of the family's departure. "If there should be any evil results from the dog's bite, he would be unable to forgive himself for neglecting any reasonable or possible precaution. It is for this reason, and not from any fear, that he takes his daughter to Paris."

While the American medical community at that time was deeply divided about the safety and utility of rabies vaccination, the larger population was considerably less so. Hardly any Americans had as yet received Pasteur's vaccine, but the nation's newspapers breathlessly followed the progress of the handful of patients who had traveled to Paris to receive the breakthrough treatment.

Of particular interest were a group of four school-age, working-class boys from Newark, New Jersey, who had been viciously attacked by a rampaging dog on the morning of December 2, 1885. The dog was killed on the spot. A prominent New Jersey physician recommended the boys' immediate departure for France, and called for public donations to help defray the costs of their passage. Contributions large and small poured in from neighbors, friends, fellow schoolchildren, collections made by local labor groups, and checks written by captains of industry. Local and far-flung newspapers, particularly *The New York Herald,* devoted dozens of columns over several weeks to the effort to deliver the boys to Pasteur's laboratory, melodramatically dwelling on the dangers they faced without medical intervention. The vaccine procedure itself was detailed by reporters on the scene, and the boys' reactions ("It doesn't hurt a bit") were dutifully recorded and cabled back to rapt American readers. Upon their return, the thriving children enjoyed so much celebrity that a Bowery theater engaged them for several weeks to appear before paying audiences—who lined up by the thousands to lay eyes on the four young medical marvels.

American newspapers found an enthusiastic readership for their overwhelmingly positive portrayal of the Newark boys' vaccine experience. Historian Bert Hansen notes:

> While many aspects of the rabies-cure coverage were adventitious, the editors were happy to exploit two inherent features of this story that always evoke strong human interest: children and dogs. The added factors of helpless victims, good Samaritans, community fund-raising, a perilous voyage, a noble (and conveniently distant) hero, divided opinions among local authorities (who could therefore be interviewed and quoted at length), and a potentially happy ending were of great value as well.

The Newark boys' story helped to shape American optimism about research-driven medical progress at the end of the nineteenth century. Hansen asserts that "[w]hen American newspapers and magazines devoted extravagant attention to the first Americans treated with Pasteur's brand-new rabies 'cure,' they were not simply reporting an event with broad human-interest elements, they were also elaborating a story of medical discovery as something useful and exciting to ordinary people." Enthusiasm for scientific medical interventions generally, and the rabies vaccine in particular, persisted even when, months later, it was revealed that two additional Newark children and several canines—bitten on December 2 by the same rampaging dog—remained just as healthy as the vaccinated group. Meanwhile, from Europe came news of the deaths of three out of sixteen Russian peasants who, after suffering a rabid wolf attack, traveled to Pasteur's laboratory from Smolensk for treatment. Experts who doubted the benefits of the vaccine (or who didn't believe that rabies was infectious in nature or deadly in result) seized on these circumstances as evidence that the cure was worse than the disease. The popular perception of Pasteur's vaccine remained overwhelmingly positive in spite of this.

And so, on the morning of April 22, Amalia, her fashion-crazed older sister, Giulia, their parents, and their physician, Dr. Busteed, boarded the luxury steamship *Germanic* (then among the world's fastest liners), bound for Europe. An hour before setting off, Mr. Morosini told a *Herald* reporter that the family had not told Amalia the reason for the trip, and had no intention of doing so in advance of their arrival in Paris.

· · · ·

Alexandre Liautard and his colleagues, having discharged their duty in the postmortem room, elected, "in view of the present advanced state of medical science," to pursue the Morosini matter one step further. Using the experimental methods honed in Pasteur's laboratory, the veterinarians sought to *scientifically* confirm the dog's diagnosis of rabies.

The resulting paper, written up by American Veterinary College house surgeon Dr. James A. Walrath, detailed a cerebral inoculation procedure in which a portion of the Morosini dog's brain stem was applied to the exposed brain of an anesthetized healthy dog. Walrath described the surgery's outcome, observed over the following weeks in heartbreaking but definitive terms. According to Dr. Walrath, the recipient dog recovered well from anesthesia

Alexandre Liautard,
circa 1890.

and surgery, quickly resuming a normal attitude and appetite. His sutured wound gradually healed. But on the fifteenth postoperative day, caretakers noticed the dog becoming more subdued, and, at the same time, "more than usually affectionate toward the house surgeon." The following day, the first signs of so-called "dumb" rabies became apparent: the dog's jaw slackened, hanging limply as abundant saliva poured forth. Symptoms progressed to more generalized loss of function, including paralysis of the hind limbs, on days 17 and 18. The dog finally succumbed to his illness before the morning of the nineteenth day. An autopsy performed on the second dog echoed the one done on the first, showing pronounced congestion of the dog's throat, and bedding material (hay and straw) present in the throat and stomach. The bladder was empty and firmly retracted into the pelvic cavity. A diagnosis of rabies was thus confidently pronounced—for both the Morosini dog and the pitiful subject of the experiment.

On day 17, convinced of the subject dog's clinical course, Dr. Liautard sent a cablegram to Pasteur confirming a diagnosis of rabies in the Morosini dog. He received a reply two days later: Miss Morosini's treatment had already commenced. At the point when Liautard's message reached Paris, the girl had just received her third dose of vaccine.

"We may therefore conclude," Liautard told the *Herald* on May 19, "that the young lady is now alright." However, he cautioned, if Amalia had waited for the confirmatory test result before departing for the ocean voyage to Paris, she would not necessarily have been saved. "M. Pasteur says he will not guarantee a cure if the patient delays coming to him after the 36th day." Liautard considered Miss Morosini's escape from terrible disease and death to have been a narrow one.

Liautard was enthusiastic about the lifesaving potential for humans of confirmatory rabies testing in animals. Americans who lacked the resources of the Morosini family could hardly afford to pursue rabies vaccine treatment based on the mere possibility of infection. Testing would determine the need, on an individual basis, for rabies vaccine after a dog bite. However, given the time involved in cerebral inoculation testing—more than two weeks, in the Morosini case—and the necessity for early administration of vaccine to effectively prevent hydrophobia, rabies vaccine needed to be available for administration immediately upon confirmation of the result. It was therefore critical, Liautard argued, to establish an American institute for the provision of Pasteur's therapy on the near side of the Atlantic. He called upon the United States government to fund the creation of a Pasteur Institute in New York City, to ensure timely vaccine treatment for people bitten by animals confirmed to be rabid.

Did Liautard have any personal qualms about the use of a healthy dog in his experimental rabies test? If so, they went unrecorded. Quarantine and observation of a living canine rabies suspect would remain the preferred indicator of the need for human rabies treatment following a bite. Liautard expressed little patience for those who summarily killed dogs involved in biting humans. But in cases where the suspect dog was already dead, Liautard seemed willing to put more, perhaps many, animals through cerebral inoculation as a confirmatory test—at least, once human rabies immunization became locally available, and a more definite diagnosis of canine rabies would have meaningful implications for human lives.

When Liautard was announcing the success of his dog-based diagnostic, he was also putting forward a more visionary idea for applying Pasteurian science to the prevention of rabies deaths—both canine and human. To the *Herald* reporter, Liautard predicted that the rabies vaccine's best application might be as a prophylactic in dogs, given in advance of virus exposure to protect and preserve canine health. The possibility of human rabies exposure from these dogs would thereby be eliminated. It needn't be optional; indeed, it shouldn't, in order to have the greatest effect. The reporter noted in his piece that the professor "seemed to think that it was possible in the future to have a law compelling all owners of dogs to have their animals inoculated for rabies as a preventative."

.　　.　　.

For a decade or so, America's animal-welfare movement and its new, scientific approach to veterinary medicine—as embodied in the figures of Henry Bergh and Alexandre Liautard, who began their work on behalf of the nation's animals at roughly the same time—had seemed fully aligned in their values and goals. But the work of Louis Pasteur drove a wedge between their two worlds, one that arguably persists in the present day. Presented with medical advances in which some animals have died, even suffered, in order that future animals (and humans) might live healthier lives, Liautard and his allies threw in their lot with the scientists: "[E]xperiment on animals is absolutely indispensable, both for the good of animals and of man," wrote one veterinarian in *American Veterinary Review* in 1885. "Every advance in knowledge is a benefit to all." But Bergh, like many animal activists today, threw in his with the camp that refused to see such research as justified.

As early as 1880, years before Pasteur began the experiments that would lead to the rabies vaccine, it was clear that his revolutionary advances in immunology would present the perfect storm for the anti-vivisection movement. In that year and the one that followed, he announced the successful development of vaccines against chicken cholera and anthrax, both of which had inevitably involved experimentation on animals, but the results of which were now poised to alleviate the suffering of countless animals in the future. From then on, it was Pasteur's name, more than any other, that sprang to the lips of educated defenders of animal research— such as Charles Darwin, who cited Pasteur as his primary example in an April 1881 letter explaining why he declined to support a total ban on the practice.

And from then on, whether anti-vivisection activists admitted it to themselves or not, it became their goal to discredit Pasteur's work. Such a task was made easier by the unnerving, unnatural quality of vaccination itself, the underlying concept of which bothers people even today. Then, the germ theory was still in its infancy, and many educated people had trouble accepting that all these various maladies were caused by these tiny, hypothetical-seeming pathogens; that a brew of such pathogens, cooked up in a lab, should be injected into healthy humans or animals carried with it a whiff of the satanic.

Henry Bergh had never been America's most vehement opponent of animal research, but he was among the first to take up the fight against Pasteur and vaccination. Rather than celebrating the arrival of a medical technology that would save thousands of animal lives a year, Bergh responded with derision, including in a bitter anti-vaccine screed, "The Lancet and the Law," published by the *North American Review* in February 1882, which mingled Bergh's disapproval of Pasteur's methods with his distrust of their fruits. Calling vaccination a "hideous monstrosity," he attempted to dismiss a century's worth of benefits from smallpox immunization, and then sniped at Pasteur's efforts to create comparable miracles for animals:

> [A]s though vaccination's twin sister, vivisection, were not sorely enough afflicting the lower animals, Monsieur Pasteur is now doing his best to inoculate them with diseases peculiar to the human family. That he will succeed in this, both his enemies and his friends believe; but there is just one consideration which he seems to have overlooked, namely, that when he shall have reduced all our food-animals to the same diseased condition to which the human race has been brought by the practices of Jenner and his disciples, we shall all probably have become vegetarians, and then Pasteur's occupation will be gone! That his process deteriorates the constitution of animals cannot be disputed.

As Pasteur's discoveries multiplied, Bergh and other antivivisection activists dug in their heels. In October 1885, when the world was captivated by the debut of the human rabies vaccine, Bergh co-founded the American Anti-Vaccination Society, to make "the evils of vaccination" more widely known to the public.

This put him on a collision course with Liautard. Beginning in May 1886, Liautard was heatedly denounced by Dr. Edward Charles Spitzka, a prominent neuroanatomist, surgeon, and psychiatrist, who told a *Tribune* reporter he found Liautard's conclusions "laughable." A few months later, at the Hall of the Academy of Medicine in New York, Spitzka presented the results of his own experiment on six healthy dogs, in which he applied, through cerebral inoculation, a variety of odious substances* in an attempt to

---

* These were: first, an emulsion made up of preserved brain tissue from a man who had reportedly died from hydrophobia almost four weeks earlier, along

demonstrate that the introduction of *any* foreign material into the canine braincase would cause the symptoms observed by Liautard and his colleagues. Reading his paper at the Academy of Medicine on June 10, Spitzka declared that his results supported his theory that rabies was a psychological, rather than a physiological, disorder. Although all but one dog had survived relatively mild neurologic illnesses following his experimental treatments, Dr. Spitzka claimed that the symptoms manifested by his subjects typified what Liautard and other contagionists called "rabies." He invited the physicians, scientists, and journalists in attendance to inspect for themselves the five survivors, which he set loose in the room to mingle freely with the audience. After concluding his official remarks, Spitzka chloroformed one to death, and separated the brain from the skull for display.

Bergh sided with Spitzka in this debate, telling the *Times* that Spitzka was "aiming to show what I believe, that there is no such specific disease as hydrophobia. He wants to demonstrate to people who will stop to think that the transmission of rabies from animals to man is a fallacious theory, and that while people may die of fear they are not in danger if they will rid their minds of silly notions on this subject." Remarkably, Bergh was even sanguine about the sacrifice of canine life involved in Spitzka's experiment: "If he can show this, and can correct popular impressions upon this subject, and thereby prove that Pasteur is a humbug, I shall not consider the sacrifice of a few dogs a great price to pay for this object."

That same summer, Bergh disavowed the germ theory along with the lifesaving benefits of inoculation—particularly as performed by Pasteur. "There seems to be no end to fanatics now that find a microbe for every disease. It will probably end with their finding one for delirium tremens. It is not at all improbable that this germ theory will extend its antics to every form of disease," he com-

---

with fresh brain from a rabbit that had died of a fungal infection soon after receiving a cerebral inoculation of tissue from the same human brain immediately after the man's death; second, an intact piece of spinal cord from a healthy calf, twenty-eight hours after slaughter; third, a chopped-up piece of the same cord; fourth, an emulsion of calf spinal cord; fifth, fifteen cubic millimeters of common yellow soap; sixth and finally, ten drops of stale horse urine.

plained to a writer for *The Kansas City Times*. "There is no proof that Pasteur has ever cured a patient of hydrophobia, for there is no proof that he has ever had a hydrophobia patient. He has bulldozed his countrymen; his government has subsidized him; and the people take what he gives them. He has insulted common sense."

.　　.　　.

Spitzka and Bergh would be proven wrong, of course. Liautard's cerebral inoculation test, eventually perfected using rabbits and guinea pigs rather than dogs, became the standard method for the postmortem diagnosis of rabies until the 1903 discovery of bright-staining microscopic structures in infected brain cells. Its wide use by health departments, hospitals, agricultural institutions, and veterinary colleges throughout the United States and around the world revealed rabies to have a complex epidemiology affecting wild animals and livestock species, disrupting old narratives focused on vicious dogs and hysterical humans. Moreover, despite Bergh's misgivings, it was cerebral inoculation testing that provided proof that not every biting dog was actually rabid.

Meanwhile, Pasteur's rabies vaccine successfully stood up to larger and larger trials, particularly after his post-exposure treatment protocol was refined based on additional experiments involving human patients and, of course, animal subjects. Liautard and several like-minded colleagues in public health and medicine eventually succeeded in opening a durable Pasteur Institute in New York City in 1890; Liautard served as the institution's consulting veterinary surgeon. The domestic preparation and administration of rabies vaccine substantially improved its accessibility to Americans who needed it.

Altogether, the availability of effective testing and treatment for rabies did much to diminish the fear and drama surrounding the dread disease. Newspaper reports of rabies outbreaks in U.S. cities appeared less and less frequently following the implementation of Pasteur's innovations. American veterinarians, largely due to the efforts of Alexandre Liautard, led the medical community in embracing the rational, scientific approach to rabies that allowed this to happen.

It wasn't until the twentieth century, however, with the rolling out of mandatory canine vaccination laws in most U.S. states, that our contemporary, untroubled relationship with dogs really came into being. As Liautard had predicted more than half a century earlier, prophylactic vaccination of dogs would prove to be the best way to prevent rabies in both the dogs themselves and the human beings who lived alongside them. Thanks to rabies vaccination (and other veterinary therapies like deworming and flea treatments), the dog's place in the American home would become fixed. And veterinarians—who would see their livelihoods threatened by the decline of the working horse—found new occupation in vaccinating and healing increasing numbers of beloved pets.

For animals, realization of the benefits of the Pasteurian revolution was still decades away, but the Morosini family seemed to be enjoying its full fruits in the late spring of 1886. On the evening of June 13, a few days after Spitzka's demonstration at the Hall of the Academy of Medicine, Amalia Morosini stepped lightly from the *Germanic* onto New York's teeming waterfront. She was overheard saying to her friends waiting on the pier that she had never felt better in her life. A *Herald* reporter noted, "The young lady, indeed, looked as if she had never known a moment's sickness."

Late-nineteenth-century fashions favored hats
festooned with feathers—and whole birds.

Chapter 13

FOR THE BIRDS

Chilled by choppy, gray-blue waves, the March winds that rustle Cape Cod's brittle beach grass don't carry with them the warmth or fragrance of springtime, even as the days grow longer and the midday sun slowly rises in the sky. But by late April, the breezes blowing from the south deliver spring in its most marvelous form— hundreds, then thousands, then tens of thousands of small black- and-pale-gray orange-billed shorebirds. Swooping down on their elegantly tapered wings and forked tail feathers to alight on every available surface, the common tern arrives, after a long journey from South America, to its ancestral breeding grounds on the Cape and its surrounding islands. The chattering mass of birdlife blankets the sparsely vegetated, stony and sandy substrate above the tideline.

Tern pairs form, or re-form—the species is highly monogamous but the sexes winter separately—through acrobatic courtship flights, high above the beaches. On the ground, the enamored male circles his mate with head low, tail high, and wings thrust stiffly sideways, while the female tilts her beak skyward, seemingly embarrassed by his gratuitous display. He feeds her fish recently snatched from the sea, and the two prepare a simple ground nest site in close proximity to their neighbors', where she will deposit a small clutch of speckled, conical eggs. After three weeks of incubation, mostly (but not exclusively) by the female, the semi-precocial chicks burst forth, covered in fluffy black-streaked down, and ready, within hours of hatching, to stand on spindly orange legs and gaze warily at the world through open eyes.

Doting tern parents alternately supplement their babies' body heat in the nest and hunt food for the hungry hatchlings. Offshore, where clouds of terns hover overhead, the ocean teems with tiny fish, brought near the surface by pelagic predators. (Fishermen have long prospered by directing their boats toward columns of the flocking birds.) Terns plunge beak-first from the air to catch their quarry just beneath the surface of the waves. Ferrying small silvery fish, one by one, back to the nesting grounds, common terns continue to provision their offspring even as the chicks become more mobile and independent, wandering, then fluttering, away from the nest to explore the outer edges of the colony. The chicks' adventuring renders them vulnerable, but adults of both sexes demonstrate a fierce willingness to act in defense of unfledged young, alone or collaboratively in screeching mobs.

Although a variety of animals (rats, raccoons, mink, gulls, herons, owls, and others) might make a meal of a tern egg or chick, the species that most imperiled the survival of the common tern in Massachusetts during the second half of the nineteenth century was the usual one, "the greatest of all destroyers," in the memorable phrase of ornithologist William Brewster: human beings.

By the 1880s, the tern, like so many species of American birds, was being slaughtered wholesale for the cause of fashion. As urban populations swelled and a growing middle class discovered conspicuous consumption, women had adopted more elaborate modes of dress. Grand new department stores and elegant boutiques attracted female shoppers with ready-to-wear styles, mirroring those featured in the new breed of fashion magazines. Cheap immigrant labor and technological improvements in textiles and garment construction made à la mode clothing and accessories newly affordable, while expanded global trade in specialty items like Chinese silks, French lace, ivory buttons, and Arctic furs made them increasingly sumptuous. Compared to earlier eras, the feminine aesthetic that prevailed on U.S. city streets in the 1880s was fanciful, elaborate, and over the top.

Above her bustled, ruffled, flowing skirt, tight, corseted bodice, ruched sleeves, and high, brooched collar; atop her discreetly made-up countenance and her carefully coiffed updo—the crown of every late-nineteenth-century lady's look was an artfully arranged hat, the bigger, usually, the better, because it allowed for more extravagant adornment. Bunches of ribbons, beaded butterflies, fake leaves, and fabric flowers bedecked brims of woven straw or woolen felt. Feathers frequently festooned hats, too, alone or in combination with other elements. The contrasting stripes of a pheasant's flight feather; the eye-catching iridescence of a peacock's tail; the profuse abundance of an ostrich plume; the spare, ephemeral arc of a heron aigrette—feathers were thought to add a gentle, organic grace to a Victorian woman's sculpted form.

Nestled among the forget-me-nots and feathers, taxidermied birds and bird parts took her look to another level. Multiple hummingbirds, warblers, or finches might be posed as though flitting as a flock through a miniature hat-top garden. Milliners placed larger specimens singly: perched, sitting atop a decorative nest, or spread out over the forward crown. Owls' heads stared from some arrangements; brightly colored songbird breasts thrust out from others. A mania for "Mercury wings" attached a pair of outstretched avian arms to the side of many fashionable heads.

In a letter to *Forest and Stream* published in 1886, Frank Chapman, a young New York City ornithologist, enumerated all the avian embellishments that he observed on ladies' headwear over the course of two late-afternoon strolls through a fashionable uptown shopping district. Out of many hundreds of hats he saw, he calculated that 77 percent featured feathers, birds, or parts thereof—the majority having been so "mutilated" they could not be identified. He nonetheless recognized forty separate North American native species, ranging from the exceedingly familiar (four American robins, five blue jays, nine Baltimore orioles) to the somewhat more esoteric (Acadian owl, swallow-tailed flycatcher, two ruffed grouse). The most frequently espied species was the cedar waxwing (twenty-three), but right behind it, at twenty-one each, were the northern flicker and the common tern.

On and around Cape Cod, no one watched the tern's decline with more sorrow than William Brewster, who was emerging as a singular leader within his generation of American ornithologists. In 1873, he had co-founded the Nuttall Ornithological Club (named after Thomas Nuttall, the Englishman who had authored the first field guide to North American birds). At first consisting of a few childhood friends meeting weekly in Brewster's Cambridge, Massachusetts, attic, the organization grew to include a number of local and corresponding bird enthusiasts: museum curators and academics as well as hobbyists, taxidermists, specimen traders, and undergraduates (including Theodore Roosevelt, then at Harvard)—most of them young and, according to club policy, all of them male. The club's *Bulletin,* launched in 1876, became the first ornithological journal in the United States. Under the editorship of Joel A. Allen, the conservationist visionary, contributors shared anatomic and field notes on known species, announced the discovery of previously unknown types, and furnished lists of birds observed in particular locations.

"The Terns of the New England Coast," one of hundreds of articles Brewster wrote for the journal and its successors, went beyond a mere description of the birds' field characteristics and life histories. He discussed, chillingly, the terrible effect on regional tern populations of egg-collecting and hunting by humans. In the aftermath of one visit by hunters to a Massachusetts breeding colony on Muskeget Island, off the coast of Nantucket, Brewster observed that "many a poor bird is seeking its missing mate; many a downy little orphan is crying for the food its dead mother can no longer supply; many a pretty speckled egg lies cold and deserted. Buzzing flies settle upon the bloody bodies, and the tender young pine away and die." He mourned that

> [a] graceful pearl-tinted wing surmounts a jaunty hat for a brief season, and then is cast aside, and Muskegat [*sic*] lies forgotten, with the bones of the mother and her offspring bleaching on the white sand. This is no fancy sketch; all over the world the sad destruction goes on. It is indeed the price of blood that is paid for nodding plumes.

It should be noted that some small fraction of the destruction at Muskeget had been carried out by William Brewster himself. His pilgrimages to the island were made to collect terns, not simply to admire them. (He argued that one could do both: "One who has never held in his hand a freshly killed tern can scarcely imagine its wonderful beauty.") Until the introduction of prism binoculars in the 1890s, the scientific study of birds relied upon the inspection of their dead bodies. Brewster and his fellow bird enthusiasts listened to their subjects, watched them from a distance, shot them, raided their nests, dissected their insides, and stuffed their skins. Brewster offered no apologies to the terns, writing, "Science may be, nay, certainly is, cruel at times, but not one tithe of the suffering is caused by her disciples that the votaries of the fickle goddess Fashion yearly sanction."

By the mid-1880s, Brewster had headed up the founding of a national group for the study of birds, the American Ornithologists' Union (AOU). The problem of declining species was just one of its many concerns, but in 1886—thanks to a different, more populist attempt to advocate for birds, launched by the wealthy young publisher of *Forest and Stream,* George Bird Grinnell—the stars aligned for the nation's ornithologists, conservation advocates, and animal-welfare activists to make a concerted effort to save bird species from extinction. It ultimately would be a short-lived campaign, but it laid the groundwork for a more durable movement that would exist by century's end.

.   .   .

It was in February 1886, a couple of weeks after its grim survey of ladies' hats, that *Forest and Stream* put a historic notice on its front page. "Very slowly," an editorial declared, "the public are awakening to see that the fashion of wearing the feathers and skins of birds is abominable. There is, we think, no doubt that when the facts about this fashion are known, it will be frowned upon and will cease to exist. Legislation of itself can do little against this barbarous practice, but if public sentiment can be aroused against it, it will die a speedy death."

The notice proposed the creation of a new society to arouse that sentiment: the Audubon Society, named after the artist and naturalist John James Audubon, "a man who did more to teach Ameri-

cans about birds of their own land than any other who ever lived."
While *Forest and Stream* was a magazine targeted very much at
men (A WEEKLY JOURNAL OF THE ROD AND GUN was the manly tag-
line below the title), the editorial made clear that the work of the
Audubon Society would first and foremost need to convince the
nation's women; it hoped that "if the subject is properly called to
their notice, their tender hearts will be quick to respond."

The author of this text was Grinnell, now thirty-six, who had
only in recent years arrived at what would become his profound,
lifelong calling as a publisher and activist in the nascent cause of
conservation. As it happens, he had a personal connection to the
Audubon family, having grown up in northern Manhattan on land
parceled off by Lucy "Minnie" Audubon, the painter's wise widow,
who still lived nearby. Minnie kept her land as a wild sanctuary,
which allowed young George Bird—the middle name, bizarrely
providential in retrospect, was pure coincidence, having been the
surname of his father's cousin and longtime business partner—to
grow up with a reverence for nature. Another bit of bizarre providence arrived in his life not long after he returned to New York from
his buffalo hunt in 1873, in the form of a banking panic that put
the nation's economy into a tailspin: While the family was nearly
ruined, it sent his father, George Blake Grinnell, into early retirement, freeing his son to pursue his passions with what remained of
the fortune.

Most of those passions (and, soon enough, some of the fortune) flowed through *Forest and Stream,* which had been founded
amid the 1873 panic by a newspaper editor named Charles Hal-
lock. Grinnell, then twenty-four, began contributing occasional
pieces that same year; he became the magazine's natural history
editor in 1876, and took over the whole enterprise in 1880, at the
age of thirty. By then, the bird cause clearly weighed on him. At the
founding of the AOU in 1883, he was one of a very few amateurs
invited to become members. That fall, he published an editorial
called "Spare the Swallows," a popular victim on ladies' hats but
one that played an important role, Grinnell pointed out, in con-
trolling insects on farms. A *Forest and Stream* issue in August 1884
included "The Sacrifice of Song Birds," a front-page editorial full
of rhetorical thunder:

The destruction of American wild birds for millinery purposes has assumed stupendous proportions. The unholy work
gives employment to a vast army of men and women, and
this army wages its campaign of destruction with a diabolical
perfection of system. From Florida to Maine the bird butchers are shooting, netting, snaring and poisoning, seven days in
every week and every week in the season.

The same issue had a "Natural History" column that put numbers
and figures to this industry of death, describing in particular how a
single village in Long Island was sending thousands of birds every
week to New York City taxidermists. "Now what is the public, and
especially the great army of bird lovers in the United States, going
to do about this?" Grinnell asked.

With his announcement of February 1886, he was providing one
answer. The Audubon Society was essentially a society based on
a moral promise, in that all members committed themselves "to
prevent, so far as possible (1) the killing of any wild birds not used
for food, (2) the destruction of nests or eggs of any wild bird, and
(3) the wearing of feathers as ornaments or trimming for dress."
Over the first six weeks, Grinnell received commitments from new
branches all around the country, and in June, he proudly reported
that the total roll of Audubon Society members had grown to
10,000, and declared—with what would prove to be considerable
overconfidence—that "song bird feathers have had their day as hat
decorations."

Grinnell knew that the animal-welfare movement would provide him with an obvious set of allies in his new society, and it was
hardly a surprise that the most vocal support came from George
Angell. This wasn't just because Angell, more than Henry Bergh or
any other movement leader, ranked humane education at the top of
his list of priorities. It was also because Grinnell's Audubon societies, whether he realized it or not, shared some interesting DNA
with Angell's Bands of Mercy. By the summer of 1886, when Grinnell numbered Audubon members nationwide at 10,000, Angell's
three-year-old campaign had *hundreds* of thousands of children
participating, in more than 5,000 clubs nationwide. In his appeals
on behalf of the new Audubon clubs in *Our Dumb Animals,* Angell

pointedly expressed hope "that every one who joins them will be led to go still further and form or join a 'Band of Mercy.'" Wittingly or no, Grinnell was tapping into one of the fundamental ideas surrounding moral transformation in the 1880s, one that Angell had spent three years popularizing: a belief in public pledges and self-declarations as a means of prompting upright behavior.

More broadly, the Audubon Society hoped to channel a pool of feminine social energy whose growth was then much in evidence. All around the country, women were joining clubs to support political causes—particularly temperance and women's suffrage, movements whose leadership and memberships overlapped to a degree often forgotten today—as well as ones with charitable aims, such as the National Women's Relief Society and the American Red Cross. There was also a boom in societies for professional women, most notably Sorosis, begun in the 1860s by a group of New York women writers. By the 1880s, there were Sorosis chapters all around the country, along with a welter of other groups focused on female success, the Association for the Advancement of Women and the Young Ladies' National Mutual Improvement Association among them. In 1885, the novelist Gertrude Garrison went to Sorosis' seventeenth anniversary banquet at Delmonico's and was overwhelmed by the collection of attendees: "representative women, superior women, aspiring, striving women." She continued: "The average mind has not yet brought itself to acknowledge that women have a right to organize for their own improvement. It will permit them to meet together and scrape lint for almshouse patients, earn money to convert heathen, or sew for the ragged children of drunkards, but it can't reconcile itself to women's clubs for purposes that are not benevolent." That whole spectrum of clubs, from the fervently crusading to the defiantly selfish, grew exponentially, including two at the decade's tail end—the National Council of Women, in 1888, and the General Federation of Women's Clubs in 1889—whose mission was to help all these clubs coordinate with one another.

Such was the spirit in the air when Grinnell started up his new organization in early 1886, hoping to attract women away from the milliners' shops and toward the cause of bird protection. That same summer, the Chicago writer Rose Elizabeth Cleveland, in

"The Woman Behind the Gun," cartoon from *Puck*.

her magazine *Literary Life,* demonstrated the power of the appeal, describing how a "dear personal friend" impressed on her the necessity of forswearing avian fashion and joining her local Audubon chapter. "I confess this appeal moved me more than any other," she wrote, because her friend "represents a class who are known by the somewhat vague term of 'society women!'" She went on, rather grandiosely:

> [The] espousal of such a cause as this represented by the Audubon Society by such women is very significant and very hopeful, not only for the birds, but for the women; and if for the women then for the men, for society, for the state, the church, the world, the universe.

Earlier in the year, the American Ornithologists' Union had put forward a "model law" that states could pass to protect local birds, and under pressure from the new societies, New York had already enacted a version of it, prescribing punishment of five to thirty days in prison and/or fines of $10 to $50 for killing any "wild bird other than a game bird"; it also offered a bounty of half the levied amount to whoever brought the case, essentially encouraging vigilantes to bring charges against hatmakers and fashionable ladies. That November, a reporter contacted a number of the city's milliners and found them deeply aggrieved: The new law, said one, "was got up by a lot of cranks, who like to see their names in the papers. If these people want to be really charitable why don't they turn their attention to humanity?"

.   .   .

In February 1887, with Grinnell's society now boasting 20,000 members in 400 different towns, he debuted a publication for it: *The Audubon Magazine.* Though its printed format was very different from *Our Dumb Animals,* there was a clear resemblance in the content, which included, among other categories, news of the movement, hortatory essays, and uplifting fictional tales. George Angell, Henry Bergh, and Caroline Earle White were all now numbered among the organization's honorary vice presidents, and one of the first issues detailed White's personal efforts to rescue the terns of Muskeget, which was near her and her husband's summer home on Nantucket.

With the new magazine, it was clear Grinnell understood that he needed to reach women and families above all, a very different audience from *Forest and Stream*'s. *Audubon,* a manifesto in the first issue announced, "will aim to be practical, instructive and helpful; but it will never be prosy. With inspiration drawn from the great book of nature, how can its pages have other than variety, freshness and charm?" As a family magazine, it went on, "each number will be prepared with special care that there be for young readers a full share of entertainment." And so there were fables like "The Two Princesses," in which two royal sisters, loath to be separated from each other by their impending marriages, are saved by a magical swallow; or "Charley's Wonderful Journey," a Lewis Carroll–like tale about a little boy who dreams of talking to animals.

As in *Our Dumb Animals,* women writers themselves came to the fore. A bracing essay on "Woman's Heartlessness," by Celia Thaxter—the daughter of a New Hampshire lighthouse keeper who by then had achieved some renown as a poet—railed against the "indifference and hardness" she had experienced in trying to engage fellow women on the subject of bird fashion: "Not one in fifty is found willing to remove at once the birds from her head, even if languidly she does acquiesce in the assertion that it is a cruel sin against nature to destroy them." On a less strident note, the children's author Henrietta Christian Wright contributed "Princess Ruby-Throat," a fantastical tale that reimagined the whole world of backyard birds as a realm of fairies and magic.

Much of *The Audubon Magazine* was devoted to essay-length appreciations of individual bird species, many of them penned by a twenty-four-year-old ornithological prodigy named Florence Merriam (who later, taking her husband's name, would become known as Florence Merriam Bailey). Her father, Clinton Merriam, had served in Congress between 1871 and 1875 and developed an interest in the natural world that he instilled in his daughter and also his son, C. Hart Merriam, who himself became an eminent zoologist and a major figure in conservation. Florence's passion, though, was for birds, and the announcement of the Audubon movement changed her life.

Florence Merriam, Smith College yearbook photo, 1886.

At the time, she was a student at Smith College, and she immediately helped to found a society there and then proceeded to use it to upend attitudes around campus: Seventy students joined, out of a total enrollment of only three hundred or so. Just a few months in, a professor reported that two-thirds of the college's students had stopped wearing birds on their hats; one of Northampton's hatmakers came to campus and asked if the administration had handed down an edict to that effect, given how many young women had brought in their hats for retrimming. In the summer of 1886, the naturalist John Burroughs came to teach for three days, and he took the young women up nearby Mount Tom to catch "the contagion of the woods." As Merriam recounted in *Audubon:* "With gossamers and raised umbrellas we would gather about him under the trees, while he stood leaning against a stump, utterly indifferent to the rain, absorbed in incidents from the life of some goldfinch or sparrow, interpreting the chippering of the swift as it darted about overhead."

For Merriam, this experience launched what would become a lifelong career as an observer, cataloger, and extoller of avian life in America. Her signed essays about different species began running in *Audubon* in its fifth issue, June 1887, inaugurating a series called "Fifty Common Birds and How to Know Them." "When you have saved a man's life you naturally take a new interest in him," she began,

> and feel that you would like to know him; and so it is with the birds the members of the Audubon Society have been trying to rescue. You are so in the habit of discriminating between men, and studying their individual peculiarities, that it appears a comparatively easy matter to know them; but with birds the case is entirely different. There are so many kinds, and yet they seem to look and to sing exactly alike. Your task seems a hopeless one at the outset. After a little, a new world of interest and beauty opens before you, but at first the difficulties you meet are almost overwhelming.

Having thereby brought the novice into her confidence, she proceeded in the preface to lay out some basics of birding: when to go out, how to look, how to listen. Unlike other (so-called scientific) ornithologists of her day, Merriam wasn't preoccupied by questions of taxonomy or nomenclature that relied on comparisons across a series of stuffed specimens. She demonstrated instead how much insight might be gained from contextualized observations made in the field.

After the preface, she began her catalog of common birds. The robin: "He is nine to ten inches long, and as he is a general favorite, and has the courage of his conviction that man is a 'good fellow,' he fares very well, and keeps fat on cherries and strawberries if the supply of fish worms runs low." The chickadee: "When he is happy, he is the best company one could hope for, on a winter's walk; when he is busy he seems the realization of perpetual motion; and when he gives up his ordinary pursuits and prepares to rear a family, he goes to work in the same generous fashion." The meadowlark: "The famous song of the European lark may be superior to that of our own, but the mournful melody of the meadowlark is full of poetic suggestions. He is the hermit thrush of the meadows, as solitary and pensive where the light-hearted bobolink's song jostles the sunbeams, as the lonely hermit is in his dusky forest cloister."

The poetry, the anthropomorphism, the evoking of individual personalities for species—here, *The Audubon Magazine* hoped, was the antidote to the brutality of the era's fashions, in which these delicate and irreplaceable creatures had been reduced to mere decoration.

.   .   .

While sightseeing in Kentucky and Ohio during the second decade of the nineteenth century, land surveyor David Thomas noted frequent encounters with wheeling flocks of vibrantly colored, vociferous parakeets overhead. A natural history enthusiast more inclined toward the gentler subject of botany, Thomas documented the birds' voracious feeding habits and voluble social behaviors without affection. "[T]hough they have become so familiar; and though they excel all the birds of this country in beauty of plumage," he wrote, "their scream is so discordant, and their fierceness of disposition so apparent, as to preclude every sensation of attachment."

Twelve inches from hooked beak to pointed tail, feathered in brilliant green and gold with a sunny red-orange face, the Carolina parakeet (or parrot) ranged across much of the eastern half of the present-day United States, preferring the thickly wooded bottomlands of great river valleys where hollowed-out trunks of mature cypress trees provided commodious communal roosting and nesting sites to the highly sociable species. Gregarious groups of up to a few hundred hurtled through the forest en masse, fleetly flying in tight formation between packed treetop perches. Able to eke out a living in temperate climes (unlike all but a few other parrots) *Conuropsis carolinensis* subsisted largely on wild seeds but occasionally raided grain fields and fruit orchards, playfully laying waste to crops and enraging farmers, who retaliated by killing the birds in great numbers; the parakeets had a habit of hovering around their stricken companions, which made them easy rifle marks.

Not all observers were disposed to dislike the birds. Audubon remarked in 1827 that "the richness of their plumage, their beautiful mode of flight, and even their screams, afford welcome intimation that our darkest forests and most sequestered swamps are not destitute of charms." He wistfully noted that those charms were becoming more difficult to experience. "Our Parakeets are very rapidly diminishing in number; and in some districts, where twenty-five years ago they were plentiful, scarcely any are now to be seen," he wrote, but admitted, "Their flesh is tolerable food, when they are young, on which account many of them are shot."

Habitat destruction and diseases introduced by Europeans (and their poultry) probably did more to depopulate the Carolina parakeet than the predations of farmers and hungry wildlife portrait painters. Like the bison and the passenger pigeon, parakeets had disappeared from most of their former haunts by the 1880s. Rather than ranging up the Eastern Seaboard to Pennsylvania, and across the great midwestern river drainages, the birds were reduced to small remnant populations, most of them in Florida. Before the end of the century, the ornithologist Amos W. Butler would write, "It is but natural to think that the extinction of these birds is but a question of a few years."

While commercial hunters would take any chance they got to shoot these last few birds to sell for millinery ornaments—how lovely those flashy feathers must have looked sticking out of a hatband!—the most ardent stalkers of the parakeets clinging to survival in Florida's least accessible swamps were none other than the scientific ornithologists. They knew that the Carolina parakeet was headed for extinction, but they couldn't help but serve their own true passion, which was cataloging, observing, and taxonomizing avian life in America. Minute differences in morphology or coloration were often all that separated one species or subspecies from another, so researchers relied on comparisons between the taxidermied remains of related birds, collected across varied geographic locations or spans of time, to correctly classify their subjects of study.

And so, when 1886 saw the dawn of the bird protection movement in America, the scientific ornithologists played an awkward
role in it. They had seen the problem earlier than anyone else: Ten
years earlier, when Joel Allen penned his pioneering series of articles on looming American extinctions, he had written extensively
about the threat to birds. And in 1884, during the second day of the
American Ornithologists' Union's second meeting, Brewster had
stepped forward to "call attention to the wholesale slaughter of
birds, particularly Terns, along our coast for millinery purposes,"
and proposed the formation of a six-member committee "for the
protection of North American birds and their eggs against wanton
and indiscriminate destruction."

The scientists also brought some rhetorical fire when they cared
to. The same month that Grinnell started the Audubon Society, the
editor of *Science* offered the pages of his widely read journal to
broadcast the ornithologists' concerns. A sixteen-page supplement
to the February 26, 1886, issue, prepared by the AOU's bird protection committee, laid out the case for avian conservation, attempting
to objectively demonstrate the breadth and scale of the slaughter.
Allen, in his own urgent essay, quoted an unnamed writer to illustrate what he called the "aesthetic" consequences of avian mass
extinction: "a garden without flowers, childhood without laughter,
an orchard without blossoms, a sky without color, roses without
perfume, are the analogues of a country without song-birds."

Allen and the AOU called on all Americans, but especially "the
dead bird-wearing gender," to change the laws, habits, and fashions
contributing to bird depopulation. "Surely those who unthinkingly
have been the cause of a great cruelty will not refuse their influence in abating it, now that they are awakened to the truth." In the
same package in *Science,* the AOU printed its model law for states
to enact, making it the first group to envision a legal system for
protecting American birds.

Later, though, as the Audubon movement attempted to take
flight, the AOU did not maintain its sense of urgency. An *Audubon
Magazine* subscriber who picked up the AOU's journal, *The Auk,*
during those months would have been perplexed at how uncon-
sumed the scientists seemed with the disappearance of their subject
matter. Rare was the *Auk* article that did not involve its author

shooting a bird, or multiple birds; indeed, many articles consisted of long lists of bird species the author had shot somewhere, merely to document that it could be found there (for now). Even in articles that took population decline as their subject—like W. E. D. Scott's dire April 1887 account of rookeries in southern Florida, which detailed the devastation that hunters had wrought on what once had been enormous populations of egrets and other herons—the author set to shooting as soon as the opportunity presented itself.

Perhaps it was true, as the AOU's protection committee sanguinely stated, that the birds shot for ornithological research were "relatively few in comparison to the number destroyed for millinery and other mercenary purposes,—so small as to not materially affect the decrease of any species." But the cognitive dissonance was not lost on readers, and it demonstrated the rhetorical limitations of a public appeal for animals that seemed to see no tragedy in any individual death. It also opened up the scientists to the charge of hypocrisy—which became a source of great controversy in the ornithology world, especially around the question of amateurs and their right to harvest specimens for study the way that professionals did. Amateurs were particularly rankled by the permit system created by the model law, as it was passed in New York: Any killing of non-game-bird species in the state now had to be authorized by a panel of experts, based at the American Museum of Natural History, to determine that the rationale was properly scientific. The law even required that permit holders offer up financial bonds before collecting specimens, to cover their liability in the event of prosecution. Heated letters to *Ornithologist and Oölogist,* a publication favored by amateurs and taxidermists, accused the AOU of trying to shut young ornithologists out of the profession. Allen, who personally oversaw the museum's panel, wrote a passionate riposte noting that of the first twenty permits, granted as of early 1887, only five had gone to members of the AOU, and eleven to applicants who did not even consider themselves ornithologists.

For all of his farsightedness on the problem of conservation, Allen clearly had no appetite for pursuing it at the expense of his research. During 1888, *The Auk* was essentially silent on the issue of bird protection, and Allen, the publication's editor, confined his own articles to the minute parsing of dead bird specimens, seaside sparrows sent from Florida and titryas acquired from Ecuador, cataloging their variations, monastically taxonomizing these delicate creatures whose presence in American life was increasingly threatened.

. . .

By the beginning of 1889, nationwide membership in Audubon societies was approaching 50,000, but not nearly enough of them had subscribed to *The Audubon Magazine* to cover its expenses. It seemed far from clear that the whole effort was making a difference: For all the conversion stories from the first few months—all those local hatmakers, supposedly stunned by a sea change in demand— the fashion industry seemed to be redoubling its interest in bird slaughter. "We learn from sources that are unfortunately but too reliable," Grinnell wrote in late 1888, "that the Parisian mondaines or demi-mondaines, who dictate the fashions to the women of the civilized world, have decided that feathers are to be *de rigueur* this winter." He went on:

> Phenomenal as has been the growth of the Audubon Society, its fifty thousand members constitute less than one in a thousand of our population; and widely although we have advertised the movement, the Society with its methods and aims is probably not known to one in a hundred of the people of the United States. We have about a thousand Local Secretaries in as many towns; outside those towns very few people have heard of the Society, and even in the large towns in which we have the greatest number of members, the Society is wholly unknown in many cases to the great majority of the people.

What was needed, Grinnell went on, was a "machinery" that could bring the message to a greater number of Americans, which was a task (it went without saying) that a startup magazine like *Audubon* would be hard-pressed to achieve. Meanwhile, he ruefully noted, these questions of taste were being arbitrated by a "small coterie of American women, numbering at most only a few hundreds": that is, "the acknowledged social leaders in our principal cities," women for whom "the reintroduction of feather millinery in Paris would afford an opportunity for a splendid triumph."

In other words: Mass political organizing is hard to do, and after trying his hand at it for two years, Grinnell gave up. After New York, only Pennsylvania succeeded in passing a version of the AOU model law, in 1889. That was also the year that *The Audubon Magazine* disappeared, and the notices for the society disappeared from *Forest and Stream* as well.

It can't have been entirely a coincidence that by then Grinnell was getting involved in a different kind of conservation society, targeted at a much smaller group of people and based on a far less idealistic theory of social and political change. At a dinner in December 1887 at the Madison Avenue home of Theodore Roosevelt's sister Edith, the future president, Grinnell, and ten other men had decided to start a club to advocate for the interests of enlightened hunters. At a subsequent dinner the next month, this one at Pinard's on 15th Street, the twelve settled more of the details. Membership would be restricted to a hundred men in total, all of whom, as Grinnell noted in an item in *Forest and Stream,* must "have killed one or more varieties of North American large game with the rifle." More than that, they would be men "of high social standing," as well as "of intelligence and education."

At this point, Roosevelt's political career was stalled, after he finished third in the New York City mayoral race in 1886. Nevertheless, he and the other men around those tables were men of status indeed—one might even call them masculine analogues to that "small coterie" of women whose control over tastes in fashion Grinnell described so ruefully. Along with the future president of the United States, who became president of the new club, other founding members included Albert Bierstadt, the famed landscape painter; the wealthy industrialist Heber R. Bishop; the former treasury secretary Benjamin Bristow; and the AOU co-founder Daniel Elliot; as well as scions of a number of the storied New York families, including John Jay Pierrepont, Rutherford Stuyvesant, and a few more Roosevelts for good measure.

They called their new society the Boone and Crockett Club, and it was the opposite of an Audubon Society in every way—aimed at a tiny elite rather than everyone, at men instead of women (its first

stated principle being to "promote manly sport with the rifle").
Indeed, it bore more resemblance to the AOU, not just in its elitism
but in its attitude toward killing the animals whose numbers they
hoped to preserve—a stance that essentially became, in large part
through Roosevelt's outsize influence, the attitude toward game
animals that persists among American hunters today. Killing, in
the vision behind the Boone and Crockett Club, was not merely a
precondition for membership or (as with the AOU's ornithologists)
a necessary evil, but rather the stated purpose of the group; these
men wished to save big-game animals so that they could continue
shooting them.

Nowhere here was an attempt to imagine their suffering—no
children's fables anthropomorphizing a caribou or moose, as *The
Audubon Magazine* or *Our Dumb Animals* might have done, no
analogizing of their wounds to those of humans. Instead, the animals were recast as noble competitors to the sporting men, who in
turn needed to prove themselves *worthy* of their quarry. By their
second meeting, in the spring of 1888, the founders had refined the
requirements of entry from those who had "killed one or more varieties of American large game with the rifle" to those who had done
so under the terms of "fair chase," which the group defined, first
and foremost, as still-hunting—meaning only wild game, stalked
on foot in its own habitat. They also took care to define specific
techniques as unfair, like the use of traps, or shooting animals from
a boat as they swim in the water, or "fire-hunting" (using lights at
night to catch animals off guard), or "crusting" (hunting on snow-
pack thick enough to support hunters but not the big game, which
would fall through in the chase and become easy targets).

Sensible as these limitations sounded, it was an exercise in ratio-
nalization to imagine a struggle between man and beast as "fair,"
as improvements in firearms made hunting big game easier with
each passing year. And, of course, these rules of so-called fair
chase created a justification for rationing the killing of ever-scarcer
animals in exactly the way that suited the wealthy white outsider,
rather than the Indian nations that still hunted game (at least in
part) for sustenance.

In April 1889, a few native groups were to conduct an annual
hunt on the outskirts of Yellowstone National Park, then less than

twenty years old, to obtain meat to dry for the rest of the year. But at Grinnell's urging, the Boone and Crockett Club asked the secretary of the interior to outlaw the hunt—indeed, to order that the Indians would "not be permitted to leave their reservations in large parties, except when in charge of some reliable white man." The club argued that the Indians "destroy great quantities of game without regard to the game laws," and "cause incalculable damage to the forests of the continental watershed by the fires which they start." Here was the ultimate fruition of the conflicting attitudes toward Indian stewardship that Grinnell had shown as a younger man: Over the coming decades, both he and Roosevelt would deepen their sentimental attachment to Indians and their disappearing culture, even while doing little of substance to stop, let alone reverse, their dispossession.

Between the big-game hunters of Boone and Crockett and the scientists of the AOU, one could see a pattern emerging: Those who best understood the grim trajectory of American wildlife seemed to care above all about being allowed to continue to harvest scarce animals for their own purposes. And this, in the end, is what sealed the fate of the Carolina parakeet. As the conservation historian Mark V. Barrow notes, it had entered a death spiral: "a decrease in the number of parakeets served to increase their value to collectors, whose predations further decreased the remaining population."

In the spring of 1889, Frank Chapman—the young ornithologist who had tallied for *Forest and Stream* the bird carcasses adorning New York ladies' hats—set off to find this exceedingly well studied bird, which he and every other bird lover understood to be teetering on the very brink of extinction. He had to have his own.

He was on a collecting trip in Florida's Indian River region when he and his guide saw the telltale flash of green feathers in the distance. It took two days for them to track the birds down and kill four, and then another two days to bag an additional five. "I shall make no further attempts to secure others," Chapman wrote in his journal, "for we have almost exterminated two of the three small flocks which occur here, and far be it from me to deal the final blows. Good luck to you poor doomed creatures, may you live to see many generations of your kind."

Two days later, encountering the third flock, he shot six more.

BLACK BEAUTY

HIS GROOMS AND COMPANIONS

THE "UNCLE TOM'S CABIN" OF THE HORSE

George Angell's brazen act of literary piracy created a titanic bestseller.

Chapter 14

A GREAT PREACHER

For more than twenty years *this thought* has been upon my mind.

Somebody must write a book which shall be as widely read as *"Uncle Tom's Cabin,"* and shall have as widespread and powerful influence in abolishing cruelty to horses as Uncle Tom's Cabin had on the abolition of human slavery.

Many times, by letter and word of mouth, I have called the attention of American writers to this matter and asked them to undertake it. At last the book has come to me—not from America, but from England, where already over *ninety thousand copies have been sold.*

—George Angell, *Our Dumb Animals,* March 1890

With every passing year, George Angell's schemes for teaching kindness seemed to multiply almost heedlessly. There was *Our Dumb Animals,* whose monthly circulation had risen to 75,000, the highest since its inaugural issue of 1868, and which continued to publish a mix of moral instruction and sentimental storytelling tailor-made for family reading. There was the welter of essays, pamphlets, and placards that the Massachusetts SPCA printed and sent off to libraries, legislatures, colleges, and Sunday schools, all around the nation. The group regularly awarded prizes at agricultural fairs, honoring improvements in the treatment of horses and livestock; it handed out 5,000 placards of "advice and warning" to local teamsters and 1,000 copies of an essay on horseshoeing to local blacksmiths. In 1889, Angell founded a national group, the American Humane Education Society, to fund the printing and distribution of humane tracts on a profusion of subjects. Even more dramatic in terms of outreach, of course, Angell had taken his appeal directly to America's children through the Bands of Mercy crusade; by 1890, six years in, more than 7,000 such clubs had formed around the United States, encompassing an estimated 500,000 members.

Still, two years after Henry Bergh's death—news of which, owing to a March 1888 snowstorm that shut down telegraph lines, reached Boston too late for him to travel to the funeral*—Angell felt that the campaign for animals could use an *Uncle Tom's Cabin*. To be sure, this was a yearning that channeled the myths more than the facts around Harriet Beecher Stowe's 1852 anti-slavery novel. *Uncle Tom's Cabin* was indisputably a sensation, selling 300,000 copies in its first year and remaining an unprecedented bestseller through the remainder of that decade—a decade, of course, that also saw the rise of the Republican Party and of a willingness to shed blood to end slavery. But the role that Stowe's sentimental tale played in spurring that sea change had become mythologized over time, as the memory of the complex, contingent, and unglamorous political maneuvering of the 1850s faded to a gauzy retrospective sense of moral awakening. In 1881, Frederick Douglass would write of *Uncle Tom's Cabin* that "nothing could have better suited the moral and humane requirements of the hour. Its effect was amazing, instantaneous, and universal." (This post hoc literary reputation building would reach its apotheosis even later, with a tale in which President Lincoln himself supposedly declared to Stowe, "So you are the little woman who wrote the book that started this Great War." This story first surfaced in 1896, not long before Stowe's death, in an *Atlantic Monthly* article; its account,

---

* In conspicuous attendance at Bergh's funeral was P. T. Barnum, who himself died three years later, having made provision in his will for a monument to Bergh to be erected in Bridgeport, Connecticut.

sourced to Stowe's daughter, had the president asking, "Is this the little woman who made the great war?")

No doubt Angell, after decades of trying to foment his own mass moral awakening, could not help but contrast its progress with this idealized vision of the 1850s, in which a novel prodded millions to goodness. More than sixty years after the founding of the RSPCA in London, and a quarter century after Bergh had put the suffering of working horses at the center of the ASPCA's mission (and its logo), urban horses continued to suffer. Enforcement against the most brutal assaults on horses by their drivers had had some effect, but the vogue for carriage horses, despite (or perhaps because of) their anachronistic quality in a new era of steam engines and street-cars, had only increased among the wealthy, who favored many of the irresponsible practices that reformers had decried for decades. Most prominent among these was the check rein, an apparatus that wrenched the equine neck into an abysmally upright position, lending horses an air of martial nobility at the cost of tremendous pain to them. George Angell's Massachusetts SPCA had inveighed against the check rein in the first issue of *Our Dumb Animals* in 1868, and Angell had subsequently written a whole pamphlet on the subject, but to little effect.

At some point in early 1890, one of Angell's humane corre-spondents, a New York philanthropist named Georgiana Kendall, forwarded him a copy of *Black Beauty*, a slim novel published thir-teen years earlier in England. Its author, Anna Sewell, had been a housebound woman in her fifties, living in the village of Old Cat-ton, near Norwich, suffering through the terminal stages of what contemporary biographers suspect was lupus. Despite the spare simplicity of her prose—which would eventually ensure its status as a classic for many generations of children—the drafting of *Black Beauty* took Sewell more than five years, owing to a long stretch of particularly severe illness during which she could dictate only small snippets to her septuagenarian mother, Mary. "Years went on, and no progress was made, except in her mind, where many pictures were clearly drawn and stored away in her memory," Mary recalled of that period. Significant progress resumed in 1876, when Anna recovered enough to begin writing in her own hand again, and by the end of the following year the book was finished. Infamously, a

local publisher paid a onetime fee of £20 for it, with no provision
for royalties, and by the following year Anna was dead; not only
was she unable to witness her little book's success, but her family
wound up seeing no share of the soon-considerable proceeds.

The book had been a modest success in England but had found
no publisher in America—until it struck Angell like a thunder-
bolt. He made immediate plans to print it in large quantities with
no regard for the British publisher's copyright, selling it at a fee
small enough to ensure the widest possible audience. In his first
edition of *Black Beauty,* a preface laid out his bare-bones business
model: "Through the kind gifts of friends I am enabled to pay $265
for having [the book] electrotyped, and through the kindness of
another friend am enabled to print a first edition of ten thousand,
at the marvelously low price of twelve cents each—to which must
be added, when sent by mail, eight cents for postage, etc." For context, twenty cents in 1890 was the rough equivalent of $6 in today's
money, an impressive deal for a brand-new book.

And in the months that followed, Angell marshaled his entire
humane enterprise to promote and celebrate this singular little
novel—which represented, both in its details and in its motivations,
the apex of a singularly late-nineteenth-century notion about how
to mold behavior for good through the power of imagination.

.   .   .

Black Beauty has often been described as the first "animal autobiography," but in reality it represented the fruition of a lineage of
first-person animal tales stretching back at least a century, most of
them children's fables. In England, the first-person animal genre
can be traced back at least to a two-volume children's book from
1783 called *Life and Perambulation of a Mouse,* by Dorothy Kilner,
and other whimsical efforts followed over the years, some from the
perspective of cats (*Marvelous Adventures,* 1802, and *The Adventures of Poor Puss,* 1809) and one in 1857 called *Rambles of a Rat.*

As we've seen, *Our Dumb Animals* undertook a lengthy offer-
ing in this vein in 1868, a multi-part serial entitled "The Story of a
Good and Faithful Horse." In 1871, the publication gave space to
"Rob," a thirty-year-old horse who explained to readers the brutal

future faced by those of his species no longer able to work. In both cases, one suspects that Angell played some role in the tale's construction; his yearning for a definitive animal novel might well have been motivated in part by an appreciation of how difficult the task was to pull off. The attempts at the genre in *Our Dumb Animals* were characterized by listless, florid prose, as if to bully a reader through sheer verbiage into entertaining the notion that a horse's thoughts might merit moral consideration.

By contrast, *Black Beauty* is simple and lean in its construction. The tale advances through chapters that seldom run much past a thousand words, delivering efficient morals about cruelty and kindness with a minimum of treacle or clutter. A bracing set piece is presented in chapter 2, "The Hunt," about a hunting accident witnessed by the narrator in his youth. A horse and a rider die in the incident, and the tragedy of each passing is marked and mourned by the horses who look on. The human victim, we learn, was the only son of their owner, Squire Gordon, the "pride of his family," while the equine victim, a "good bold horse" named Rob Roy, is shot dead before the narrator's eyes; Black Beauty's mother "never would go to that part of the field afterwards." And then, at the spare chapter's end, a different group of horses enter the scene:

> Not many days after, we heard the church bell tolling for a long time; and looking over the gate we saw a long strange black coach that was covered with black cloth and was drawn by black horses; after that came another and another and another, and all were black, while the bell kept tolling, tolling. They were carrying young Gordon to the churchyard to bury him. He would never ride again. What they did with Rob Roy I never knew; but 'twas all for one little hare.

After Black Beauty's idyllic foalhood at Birtwick Farm, his story becomes the bildungsroman of a working-class horse. Beginning at the age of four, when Squire Gordon first puts a bit in his mouth, the narrator moves through a checkered career of both upward and downward mobility, encountering humans who treat him well and poorly in turn. First, there is the aristocratic Lord W——, who is kindly to his horses even as his wife is cruel. Then, the narrator is sold to a London stable that rents him out, thereby putting him at the mercy of a wide array of drivers, such as the Cockneys who, "instead of starting at an easy pace as a gentleman would do, generally set off at full speed from the stable yard; and when they want to stop, they first whip us and pull up so suddenly, that we are nearly thrown on our haunches." His next owner, Mr. Barry, is well tempered, but the groom—given the Dickensian moniker Alfred Smirk—is a neglectful layabout. Eventually Black Beauty winds up in the hands of Nicholas Skinner, the worst of the worst, a man with "black eyes and a hooked nose" and a voice "as harsh as the grinding of cart wheels over gravel stones." Skinner works the narrator nearly to death, until he is saved in the book's last pages through a final sale to the kindly Farmer Thoroughgood.

All the while, Sewell seeds her tale with specific judgments on the various maltreatments of working horses. Ginger, an older equine at Squire Gordon's farm who previously was a coach horse, offers an indictment of the check rein straight from the horse's mouth: "Fancy now yourself, if you tossed your head up high and were obliged to hold it there, and that for hours together, not able to move it at all, except with a jerk still higher, your neck aching till you did not know how to bear it." Similarly, an old horse named Oliver inveighs against the docking of tails: "I was tied up, and made fast so that I could not stir, and then they came and cut off my long beautiful tail, through the flesh, and through the bone, and took it away." When Ginger asks why, Oliver exclaims: "For fashion!" and adds: "There was not a well-bred horse in my time that had not his tail docked in that shameful way, just as if the good God that made us did not know what we wanted and what looked best." The climactic scene of Beauty staggering under an unmanageable load could have been ripped straight out of Henry Bergh's crusades against the horsecar lines:

> I was struggling to keep on, goaded by constant chucks of the rein and use of the whip, when, in a single moment—I cannot tell how—my feet slipped from under me, and I fell heavily to the ground on my side; the suddenness and the force with which I fell seemed to beat the breath out of my body. I lay

perfectly still; indeed, I had no power to move, and I thought now I was going to die.

The book's detailed accounts of suffering have prompted some scholars to wonder if Sewell drew direct inspiration from *Uncle Tom's Cabin,* which was widely read in England as well. In a 1997 paper, the academic Robert Dingley went so far as to propose a nearly one-to-one parallel, seeing Lord W—— as analogous to Mr. St. Clare, who in Stowe's book purchases Tom; both, Dingley points out, are aristocratic figures, civil to a degree that their cruel wives are not. Then, following "this period of relative, though uneasy, prosperity," Dingley notes, Tom and Beauty both move "toward a condition in which they are no longer regarded as sentient beings by the uncaring men who purchase them." This spiral culminates with Simon Legree and Nicholas Skinner, respectively, barbaric men who work the heroes nearly to death, until salvation arrives in the form of two benevolent, final owners.

Such superficial plot similarities aside, however, *Black Beauty* and *Uncle Tom's Cabin* could not be more dissimilar in the manner of their telling. Stowe's prose is overwrought and lugubrious, as is her plot, in marked contrast to that of Sewell, who writes at a canter: Tom's miseries at the hands of Simon Legree, for example, extend over countless thousands of words to consume the last quarter of *Uncle Tom's Cabin,* whose total word count is three times that of *Black Beauty,* while Skinner's purchase, ownership, and sale of Beauty all transpire over a handful of pages as Sewell races toward her happy ending. Absent from Sewell's book, too, is Stowe's religious fervor; as the literary theorist Jane Tompkins has noted, the anti-slavery message of *Uncle Tom's Cabin* is inseparable from its relentless Christian allegory and eschatology, as Stowe "speaks to her audience directly in the way the Old Testament prophets spoke to Israel, exhorting, praising, blaming, warning of the wrath to come."

Over time, *Black Beauty* has become classified as a book for children, but it was not written as one, and our present-day difficulty in seeing it as suitable for grown-ups—or, for that matter, in seeing *Uncle Tom's Cabin* itself as an important work of literature, rather than a lamentable exercise in sentimentality—is the product of a uniquely twentieth-century understanding of what storytelling is for. Most college-educated adults today have been raised, to some degree or other, on notions of artistic value that denigrate instruction, formula, and emotion in favor of ambiguity, complexity, and sangfroid. But this was not the dominant perspective of 1852, or 1877, or even 1890 (though by then, the seeds of the twentieth-century attitude had begun to germinate). As Jane Tompkins notes, "The implantation of virtue was the primary goal of nearly everything nineteenth-century Americans read: textbooks, novels, poems, magazine stories, or religious tracts." Fiction as an imaginative *machine* for instilling virtue was a primary mode in which adults of that era read novels, why they praised them, why they shared them with others. When George Angell brought *Black Beauty* to America as a method of moral transformation, he was not tilting at windmills but channeling what remained one of the highest literary aspirations of his age.

.   .   .

The reception from American readers was everything Angell could have hoped for—a trajectory he documented in *Our Dumb Animals* month by month in the hope that the publicity of success would spur still more success. It did. The English sales figures, which at first had served to endorse the book's quality ("already" more than 90,000), were quickly eclipsed. Two months in, Angell himself had printed 60,000, and was launching a new, even cheaper edition, printed on thinner paper and sold at half price: just ten cents delivered and six cents if purchased in person at the Massachusetts SPCA offices. By July, the total had reached 90,000, and by October 156,000, well past the total sold in England over the course of thirteen years.

Notices in newspapers were glowing. A rave appeared in *The Critic,* a New York journal of book criticism, sandwiched between notices of new Balzac and Schopenhauer translations. The *New York Commercial Advertiser*'s reviewer experienced the novel as a kind of supernatural visitation: "I sat down to read it last night and did not move from my chair until it was finished," he wrote. "I have no space to chronicle all that 'Black Beauty' said to me of his varied experiences in life of high and low degree. After he had told all of his pathetic story, I turned into my bed in the small hours of the night, and when I was asleep he stood there still." The *New York Parish Visitor* likened the book's equine narrator to a man of the cloth, in an item entitled A GREAT PREACHER. "We do not often speak of preachers by name," the paper wrote,

> nor as a rule do preachers care to be paraded before the public in the columns of any of our papers. But in the present case we think we are justified in making an exception.
>
> Everything about the preacher—his race, his color, his appearance, and the subjects of discourse, as well as the audiences to which he speaks, are so unique, peculiar, and strange, and yet so real, and what he says so practical and telling, that we wish all our readers to hear him.
>
> He is of the equine race, in color black, of the dumb-animal persuasion, and his name is Black Beauty. *Thousands upon thousands have heard him, and wish everybody else to hear him.*

Marketing *Black Beauty* became Angell's life, and in the fall he announced that he was suspending all of his speaking engagements. He began to arrange for translations into German and French, and letters poured in proposing other translations as well. Some correspondents offered money to help build a monument to Anna Sewell, which eventually would come to fruition as a drinking fountain for horses in Ansonia, Connecticut. Other letter writers offered testimonials, claiming that the book was already leading to better treatment of horses across the nation. A reader from Chicago wrote in:

> I stopped an expressman who had a starved-looking horse, and asked him if he would read "Black Beauty" and lend it to his friends. He promised he would, and I sent him a copy. A few days after, on a hot day, I was passing his stand, and saw that he had a cabbage-leaf over his horse's head to protect it from the sun, while he was sitting on the sidewalk, reading "Black Beauty."

Among Angell's correspondents were some of the nation's moral luminaries. Henry Ward Beecher's widow, Eunice, made bulk orders to distribute among her friends. Willard Mallalieu, a bishop of the Methodist Episcopal Church in New Orleans, wrote Angell to "most earnestly wish the book might be read by every boy and girl, and every man and woman in Christendom," while John Williams, the Catholic archbishop of Boston, wrote to congratulate Angell on the new Italian translation of *Black Beauty* and "hope that its kind teachings may be extended to all nations." Scores of university presidents wrote in as well: from Johns Hopkins, the University of Texas, Amherst, Williams, and Wesleyan, among other schools.

Many of Angell's correspondents were civic leaders in communities around the country, placing orders of hundreds of copies to distribute in their hometowns. Bulk buyers often had the specific intention of giving them out to horse drivers. Angell's longtime benefactor Emily Appleton, who had been so instrumental in the Massachusetts SPCA's founding, paid for 1,600 free copies for drivers in Boston. In Plainfield, New Jersey, the local Band of Mercy vowed to give the book to "every driver of a grocer's delivery wagon, every hackman, every cartman, and teamsters of every name."

With success came certain headaches. Angell ruefully looked on as two New York publishers rushed out knockoff editions, which Angell warned readers of *Our Dumb Animals* not to purchase— not only were they printings of inferior quality, but they "leave out all the humane pictures and information which constitute an important part of our book, substituting advertisements of corsets, medical discoveries, pills, etc., etc." Meanwhile, Sewell's original British publisher, Jarrold & Sons, sent outraged letters to Angell, demanding royalties for all the tens of thousands of copies he had sold. Angell's response was to harp on their villainy in having paid Sewell such a meager fee, and also to appeal to his readers' anti-British jingoism.

Angell claimed that at his low prices, none of the thousands of dollars he was pulling in were being banked as profit, and his insistence that this publishing effort was a moral crusade, not a business, seemed genuine. In his broadside against Jarrold & Sons in *Our Dumb Animals,* he donned the garb not merely of patriotism but of religion, repeatedly invoking Jesus's exhortation in Mark 16 to "Go ye into all the world and preach the Gospel to every creature." Indeed, by this point Angell had embraced a number of religious metaphors that some of the book's most fervent fans had offered—calling it, for example, "The Gospel of Dumb Animals." And he happily reprinted speculation from a newspaper in Topeka, Kansas, that *Black Beauty* was on track to "outsell all other books that have ever been published except the Bible."

.　　.　　.

Sacrilegious comparisons to the Good Book aside, Angell was no doubt aware that his tally of 371,000 copies, in less than a year, surpassed the first-year sales figure for *Uncle Tom's Cabin;* at times he allowed himself to lump in an estimate of copies sold by his two hated New York competitors in order to cite a figure of more than half a million. His Bands of Mercy movement continued to grow, too, with lists of newly formed Bands filling pages of *Our Dumb Animals* in tiny type; the December 1891 issue listed more than 400, bringing the total of Bands in America up to more than 11,000—a jump by more than half since the arrival of *Black Beauty.*

By then, these two projects of Angell's, the book and the Bands, had become essentially coequal prongs of a moral campaign aimed directly at children—an unprecedented new moment in the history of the American animal-welfare movement, and certainly the most remarkable aspect of that movement nationwide during the early 1890s. Despite the declaration, on its first appearance, that *Black Beauty* was appropriate moral fuel for readers of any age, over its first year its reputation as a children's book began to coalesce, especially as animal-welfare supporters around the country made bulk orders on that basis. Perhaps the proudest developments that *Our Dumb Animals* reported were the decisions taken by school boards around the country to adopt the text in classrooms. In the summer of 1890, when the National Educational Association convened its annual meeting in St. Paul, Minnesota, Angell had five thousand copies sent along for the delegates.

To Angell, it all fit together. As he declared in his 1884 address about the Bands of Mercy and crime, humane education could

mold people to become "better and more merciful in all the relations of life." Vicariously experiencing Black Beauty's good and ill
treatment at the hands of the humans in his life would train young
readers to treat their own horses, dogs, and livestock more mercifully; it would also teach them to treat friends, classmates, and even
strangers with kindness as well.

One of the most revealing looks at Angell's philosophy of
humane education is an address he prepared for Boston elementary school students, one he delivered over the years to scores of
classrooms all across the city. Nearly 12,000 words in length, the
address must have been hard to get students to sit through, but
Angell did his best to engage his young listeners. He told personal
stories about his own childhood—he said that as a boy he talked
constantly to the animals he met on the street, adding, "I didn't
care half so much what the people thought, as I did what the *horse
or dog* thought"—and about his founding of the Massachusetts
SPCA, the fatal horse race to Worcester, the largesse of Emily
Appleton.

Mostly, though, what he did was string together animal tales, of
the kind found every month in the pages of *Our Dumb Animals*. He
used them in his address to build a homespun vision of the animal
kingdom that put human behavior toward them into sharp relief.
In many ways, it was an enchanted sort of vision—Angell's stories
often featured animals who rewarded their friends, or lashed out at
their enemies, or generally displayed a remarkable level of wisdom.
But he clued children in to how perceptive animals actually could
be: "These lower creatures know the tones of your voice," he said,
"and they know just as well as you do when you talk kindly."

One can see, in the accretion of his tales, that he believed humane
education about animals could become, when cleverly elaborated,
a full moral education. He dramatized the rewards of being kind,
describing for his young listeners the adulation heaped on a Parisian schoolboy who gave a hungry dog his own dinner, and the
medal and standing ovation that the local SPCA awarded the boy at
its annual meeting, in the great hall of the Sorbonne. This, in turn,
led Angell to a nifty articulation of the Golden Rule: "I hope you
will always do to every half-starved dog or cat, or other creature

you may happen to meet, exactly what you would like to have done if you were half starved yourself."

His remarks were slyly canny on the dynamics of human affairs, particularly about the ways in which children might persuade grown-ups to be kind to their animals. "I tell all the boys and girls, when they see a real miserable looking horse on the street, one that they really pity, if they will only say, in the kindest tone, four words so the driver can hear them, 'I pity that horse.'" He went on: "That horse will be better taken care of very soon, for no man will care to drive a poor horse many days through the streets of a city where sixty thousand boys and girls are ready to tell him, every time he stops, that they pity his horse."

Most moving of all, to contemporary ears, is Angell's invocation of the power of animals to improve our lives. "It may be worth a thousand dollars to you some time, if you remember what I am now going to tell you," he said,

> and that is, that if you ever see the time when you feel as though you hadn't a friend in the world, and wish you were dead, go and get some pet that you can talk to and love and care for—if it is only a little bird—and you will be astonished to find the relief and happiness it will bring into your life.

Ironically, Angell's best argument for humane education as the key to moral behavior was one that would dissipate in the decades to come. The nineteenth-century world of his childhood, and even of his young listeners' childhoods, teemed with horses in the streets and other animals scrambling about underfoot. All that ambient animal life presented children with the *opportunity* to be cruel, or kind, in a profoundly teachable way. In an essay called "Thoughts for Teachers and Clergymen," published in *Our Dumb Animals* in December 1891, Angell made his case for this idea: "Please think and tell me if you can find a better way under heaven for making children merciful," he wrote, "than by teaching them to be constantly doing kind acts and saying kind words to God's lower creatures, by whom they are surrounded, and which they are meeting on the streets and elsewhere a hundred times a day."

But, of course, the disappearance of many of those animals from city streets had already been foreseen. The February 1892 edition of *Our Dumb Animals* showed off a lavish engraving of "the carriage of the future," an electric motorcar puttering down a country road with no horses in sight. The great replacement of horses was vividly under way on the nation's streetcar lines, hundreds of which had now begun experimenting with electric models—a development that Angell celebrated, too, publishing a comedic poem in the March 1892 issue that was narrated from the perspective of a working horse:

> *I'm the happiest horse in town to-night!*
> *I go with flying feet*
> *For I have seen the gladdest sight*
> *'Way down on Boylston Street.*
> *And what it means I know full well;*
> *And when I've said my say,*
> *Down where I dwell, at the Horse Hotel,*
> *There will never a horse say "neigh."*
>
> *I know I'm right; and now for the sight*
> *On Boylston Street I saw—*
> *A street-car with a brilliant light,*
> *But never a horse to draw.*
> *It rolled along, now fast, now slow,*
> *Steady and straight on the track;*
> *But what made it go, I'm sure I don't know—*
> *There was no horse, front or back.*

Angell thought interacting with animals made children humane, but neither could he mourn the thought of a world in which animals, at least those other than pets, could inhabit a separate sphere of their own. Such cognitive dissonance is especially understandable when it comes to the horse, a creature bred to work for human beings but one whose burdens in human society have been so frequently and famously cruel. Should a love of horses make us want to see them laboring all around us, treated well, or desire instead to free them from all labor? This question is still debated today, such as in the fight taken up by animal-welfare advocates in New York City (including by Bill de Blasio, while mayor) to ban horse-drawn carriages from Central Park, alleging that the horses are poorly treated. However one feels about that issue, a fact seldom raised in the debate is that for thousands of New York children, the park carriages will offer their only sight of a horse in any given year, if not perhaps their entire lifetime—a state of affairs that, even if good for the horses, might not necessarily be auspicious in the long term for young New Yorkers' tenderness toward animals. A comparable irony surrounds Bergh's notion of "cruelism" as regards that other set of now-absent animals, the ones we eat. On the one hand, personally witnessing a cow cruelly slaughtered might prompt a child to cruelty later in life, but on the other hand, it might spur her to vegetarianism; meanwhile, we now live in a world in which the entire scene takes place miles away from us, outside our notice.

As for *Black Beauty*, the decline of the working horse has turned it into a very different kind of children's classic than it was in the 1890s. Then, it dramatized the thoughts and feelings, the joys and sufferings, of a workaday beast of burden that children saw all around them. By the mid-twentieth century, *Black Beauty* had become a nostalgia trip into a lost world, one in which horse power, and not internal combustion engines, moved people and their cargo to and fro. And the novel's end—which in its day depicted a workingman's retirement, of the sort that readers might genuinely wish, albeit in vain, for the horses they saw in the street—today feels like a fantasy story: A creature beloved, but seldom seen, is returned to the idyll he came from, a pastoral realm of horses that most boys and girls can only imagine. "My troubles are all over, and I am at home," Black Beauty says at the book's conclusion, describing a scene not unlike a Christian vision of death and salvation. "Before I am quite awake, I fancy I am still in the orchard at Birtwick, standing with my old friends under the apple trees."

Armour's facilities were so enormous that one packing
house boasted of a "half mile of hogs."

Chapter 15

THE SLAUGHTER
FACTORIES

His name was Hickory Nut, and for a shining moment in fall 1891, he was a star: the paragon of everything a modern beef steer was supposed to be.

A two-year-old Hereford, Hickory Nut was not necessarily more handsome than the other hundred or so head of cattle on display in Chicago's Exposition Building, competing in the city's annual Fat Stock Show. His red-and-white coat may not have shone brighter; his manner may not have been more regal. No, what drew the judges' admiration was his weight, a prodigious 1,029 pounds, and, more important, the rapidity with which he had gained it—1.71 pounds per day over his short lifetime. This latter statistic allowed Hickory Nut to carry the contest over Captain, his 1,704-pound short-horned rival, whose demonstrated gain was only 1.61 pounds per day. Declaring Hickory Nut the overall "grand sweepstakes" champion, the judges awarded his owner, W. S. Van Natta of Fowler, Indiana, nearly $1,000 in prizes.

A colossus made of meat—shaped like a modern refrigerator turned on its side, appendaged by a bulging brisket, short, tapered legs, a thin, tasseled tail, and a compact triangular head crowned by upturned horns—the Hereford steer, one of several "improved" cattle breeds popular in late-nineteenth-century America, embodied a profound transformation in the bovine animal, which the rise of the Union Stock Yards and the centralized, corporatized meat industry had helped bring about.

Certainly a Hereford bore little resemblance to the aurochs, the large, leggy wild ancestor of domestic cattle that ranged across the temperate grasslands of Asia, Europe, and North Africa. Two separate domestication events—one in the Middle East and one on the Indian subcontinent—transformed the fierce aurochs into tractable livestock useful for their hides, horns, meat, and (probably later) milk. Their strength pulled plows, their waste fertilized fields. Domestic cattle spread with the advent of agriculture throughout the ancient world, and became so indispensable to what Europeans thought of as civilization that Columbus carried a small number of them on his second voyage from Europe across the Atlantic, in 1493. From colonists to cowboys, settlers of North America depended on cattle. The animals that survived to provide even a bit of milk or meat were the ones that were bred. The early American cattle herd was a heterogeneous, scraggly bunch. Early-nineteenth-century farmers, particularly the more prosperous ones, began importing breeding stock from Europe and establishing bloodlines that would better meet the demands of the American agricultural landscape. Cattlemen carefully selected animals for their fortitude, fecundity, and, especially, efficiency: making a lot of meat from a minimum of locally available forage and feed.

Over the course of the 1870s and 1880s, a few economic forces converged to create some radical shifts in how beef cattle were fed and slaughtered. As the livestock and meatpacking industries grew and centralized, prices paid per pound began to drop, and buyers could be choosier about the steers they were willing to buy. Armour & Company and the other meat giants wanted "prime" beef, marbled with fat, which corn feeding produced more reliably; also, while pasture-fed steers were ready to take to market only at certain times of the year, a corn-fed steer could be sold anytime. As the 1880s progressed, livestock growers began to sell off their steers earlier and earlier in life: Because the weight gains of intensive feeding taper off after the animals' second year, it was more profitable to sell them at two years old or even younger, a trend that came to be known as "baby beef."

Thus had Hickory Nut, by the time of his triumph, lived out the meager life now allotted to beef cattle in America: a two-year race to put on phenomenal weight, increasingly crowded into feedlots instead of roaming in pasture, and then a rail trip to a date with death in the city. Most of the millions of animals now making that journey were expiring in the slaughterhouses of Armour and the other meatpacking giants. Hickory Nut, however, saw his end at the Fat Stock show, the day after his victory, cut up by a local butcher, Louis Pfaizer, in front of an audience for what was to be the steer's final, posthumous competition: as a dressed carcass. He lost.

.   .   .

As the meatpackers transformed American beef cattle, they also transformed Chicago. After the announcement that it had been selected as home to the 1892 World's Fair—officially dubbed the Columbian Exposition, to mark the 400th anniversary of Columbus's arrival in the New World—East Coast commentators reacted with scorn. "What will Chicago do with an undertaking so various and so colossal?" the Boston *Sunday Herald* asked, and went on:

> She can have a hundred, perhaps a thousand, acres of a cattle show; the herds and kine of the prairies can be lassoed, if necessary, until their numbers surpass the imaginary herds the poet saw upon a thousand hills. There will be beef on the hoof and beef in cans, pickled beef and dried beef, lard of all degrees of spuriousness and butter all oleomargarine. There may be sausage raw and pig's feet cured; but, after all, even with her stockyards, her odorous creek and antiquated bridges, her sloughs that perfume the night air with poison, and her elevators that occasionally let their walls fall apart, she is not quite ready to make, without outside help, an adequate world's fair to represent the progress of mankind for three [*sic*] centuries.

It was a cruel caricature of a burgeoning metropolis of two million, which by then boasted most of the trappings of urbanity—world-class universities, an opera house, an orchestra. But there was no escaping the uncanny degree to which livestock and the killing thereof dominated the city's economy. By then, an estimated one-quarter of Chicago's workers were directly or indirectly employed in the animal business. The city's total livestock trade, worth less than $43 million in 1866, had ballooned by 1892 to nearly $254 million, or nearly $8 billion in today's money. For well over a decade, much of the nation's beef had been slaughtered in Chicago, first traveling in canned form and now, increasingly, in the form of "dressed beef" traveling in refrigerated train cars.

Perhaps due to the mockery, when the fair opened six months late, in May 1893—bad weather had compounded the difficulties of erecting the ambitious two-hundred-structure "White City"— tributes to the livestock industry were relatively sparse inside the various halls. Armour & Company, along with the other large meatpackers, did set up an exhibit in the grand Agricultural Building, but they also turned Packingtown into a tourist destination in its own right, for any fairgoers who cared to make a side trip down from Jackson Park to the Lake district. Throngs of them did. Specially for the fair, Armour had established a visitor's department, the garrulous head of which spoke eight languages, in order to better handle the surge. The company set up shuttle services from nearby train stations, and created an illustrated souvenir book that described the work of its packing plants in loving detail. All of this helped burnish the industry's public image, as well as that of the handful of men who controlled it and profited from it, men whose personal fortunes had grown to rank among the city's largest.

None of these fortunes loomed larger than that of Philip D. Armour. The same year as the Exposition, he had endowed and opened the Armour Institute of Technology, which offered degrees in mechanical and electrical engineering and enrolled local students at no charge. His firm by then employed 12,000 people, who made more than $6 million a year in wages. It owned 4,000 railway cars for moving its goods about the country, all extracted from the roughly four million animals that its factories slaughtered and processed each year.

The firm's staggering ambition was a natural outgrowth of Phil Armour's own work ethic. He awoke at 5 a.m. every morning, ate breakfast at 6 a.m., and strode from his fashionable but unostentatious manse on Prairie Avenue—a South Side boulevard that had come to be called "Millionaire's Row"—to begin work at his downtown Chicago headquarters by 7 a.m. He would arrive to find an ox horn newly filled with fresh-cut flowers, along with all of the telegrams and reports from Armour & Company's far-flung offices that had come in overnight. For the next eleven hours, until 6 p.m., he worked tirelessly. Co-workers marveled at his command over the minutiae of each of the business's myriad departments, each of its regional sales offices. "When he wanted to take up a matter," the *Chicago Tribune* recounted, on the occasion of Armour's death in 1901, "he called the man at the head of a department to him, paid close attention to what he had to say after a few questions, and then gave his instructions. So perfect was the discipline of the machine that employees no more thought of violating his instructions than of considering a change in the law of gravitation."

Philip D. Armour, 1895.

Unlike his fellow "beef barons" of the period, Gustavus Swift and Nelson Morris, Armour had spent a lifetime in the meat business without learning to butcher animals himself. "If you showed me a piece of meat," he once said, "I could not tell you what part of the bullock it came from." What he possessed instead was an unparalleled instinct for a different kind of killing, the sort carried out in financial markets. His short-selling coup during the Civil War was the first of many times he used a combination of intuition and raw purchasing power to bend commodity exchanges to his will: cornering wheat, propping up pork. He famously led the industry in its decades-long campaign against the railroads, which in the late 1860s, seeing that a nation-wide move from shipping livestock to shipping packed meat would cut considerably into their revenues, had joined forces and refused to carry the latter at fair prices; by the late 1880s, it was the packers themselves who owned and controlled the refrigerated cars that transported their wares, and they essentially dictated the price at which the railroads would haul them. Before an economic panic swept the nation in 1893, Armour somehow had the foresight to stash away eight million dollars' worth of gold in his vaults.

And Armour saw, as keenly as any tycoon in the nation, how the speed and reach of the railroads and the astonishing growth in the nation's population could be harnessed to build a company of unprecedented scale. In the 1970s, when the business historian Alfred D. Chandler published *The Visible Hand,* his definitive account of the rise of the American corporation in the late nineteenth and early twentieth centuries, one of the few organizational charts he chose to reproduce was that of Armour & Company, spread out over two pages, a remarkable document of bureaucratized killing. Much of what its array of boxes and links depicts is the elaborate system of regional offices that Philip Armour had set up beginning in 1884, which had ballooned to more than forty by 1890—distribution hubs capable of pushing his products into every household in the nation. This network allowed the firm to reduce to fourteen days the average period that elapsed between purchasing an animal and recouping cash from its meat, in transactions from coast to coast.

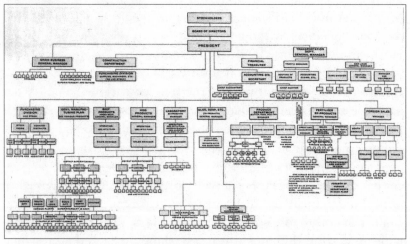

Organizational chart, Armour & Company, early 1900s.

The chart also reflects just how many different products Armour & Company had learned to derive from its millions of living inputs. In the 1870s, the firm began making sausage with the meats that were too unappetizing to eat in other forms. In 1880, it began manufacturing oleomargarine—ancestor of the vegetable-oil-based butter substitute we know today—using beef suet that until then had been discarded. In 1885, the firm purchased a local glue factory as a way to make money from hooves; by the mid-1880s, Armour was turning blood and bones and other scrap into fertilizer, a line of business that was taking off at the time of the Exposition. Soon the firm would be turning bones into buttons, combs, pipe stems, and chessmen, stretching intestine into strings for violins and tennis rackets.

This was the machinery of death that an estimated 10,000 fairgoers came to Packingtown every weekday to witness in 1893, during the five-month run of the Exposition. In our present day, it is often remarked that the cloistered nature of industrial animal production helps blind us to its inherent cruelties—an obscurity that major animal producers often work hard to perpetuate, especially where the cameras of animal-rights activists and investigative journalists are concerned. But at the tail end of the nineteenth century, at the exact place where these industrial-grade patterns of cruelty were being created, the companies threw open their doors and invited the public in. The reaction, by and large, was not revulsion but a strange sort of fascination.

. . .

The term "slaughterhouse" was widely employed to describe the places in which Armour and the other packing barons killed animals, but as a few outside observers noted, these structures bore no resemblance to the slaughterhouses (or, in the French term, *abattoirs*) then operating throughout Europe, where the slaughtering process had become increasingly standardized and government-run at the urging of public-health officials. European slaughterhouses were single-story buildings with copious ventilation and a floor designed expressly for the purpose of dispersing blood: watertight and convex, with an efficient drainage system.

By contrast, the slaughterhouses of Chicago were better thought of as slaughter factories. These were grim, poorly ventilated buildings of four to six stories each. The killing tended to take place at the top, and then, with the help of gravity, the animal's carcass moved downward through the building, essentially being disassembled and sorted into all its various saleable parts: the cuts of meat but also the hide, the fat, the organs, the bones, all directed through chutes and other means to the departments of men who handled, packaged, or rendered them.

The killing process for pigs was an industrial-grade version of the slaughtering machine that first came into use in the 1860s. Each pig was hoisted up and bled out, then deposited in scalding water to soften its bristles for scraping. From there, the carcasses were chilled for forty-eight to seventy-two hours before workers moved them to an elaborate cutting operation, itself spread out over multiple floors: Hams and shoulders were removed on the top floor and then sent through chutes down to the floor below, where all the various cuts were prepared, with the trimmings then sent to an even lower floor for sorting.

With cattle, the process was comparable but even more complicated, because so many more by-products had to be prepared for shipment, particularly the delicate and valuable hides. The profusion of by-products led to an astonishing degree of specialization: One federal survey from around the turn of the century found that a single Chicago meatpacking facility was processing more than 100 cattle per hour, utilizing 157 men in some 78 different occupations. The animals were stunned with blows to the head and sent tumbling down onto a lower platform, where they were hoisted up with ropes for killing and bleeding out. At that, the various disassemblers could set to work: the "headers," who cut the hide from around the head; the "leg breakers," who took off the hind feet; the "breast sawyers," who cut the breastbone; the "caul pullers," who removed the valuable fatty membrane from around the organs; the "fell cutters" and "rumpers," who removed the hide from the hind end; the "gutters," who took out the organs; and on and on. All the work of this sorting process would be sent down to the lower floors: heads and feet to the bone house, fats to the oil house, the tripe and tongues and hearts and livers to their various curing cellars or cooling houses.

And the visitors came to watch it all—this despite the fact that the animals themselves would often give the lie to the efficient, painless killing process that the companies had supposedly created. Sometimes a cow, despite having been stunned, would tumble down and take to its feet in a desperate attempt to escape. As for the pigs, there was little doubt that some of them were surviving past the initial steps that were supposed to put their miseries to an end. This allegation surfaced in public in 1880, in a broad exposé of cruelty at the Yards by the *Tribune*. "[N]ot infrequently," the reporter noted, "a hog reaches the scalding-tub before life is extinct; in fact, they sometimes are very full of life when they reach the point whence they are dumped into the seething tub. It would be any easy matter to so arrange the rail that a hog which still lived could be laid to one side for a few minutes until life ceased to exist; but no such provision is made."

In one of the most disturbing passages in *The Jungle*, Upton Sinclair's deeply reported 1906 novel that would bring the nation's attention to abuses in the meatpacking industry, the narrator describes the din of the hog-killing floor:

The uproar was appalling, perilous to the eardrums; one feared there was too much sound for the room to hold—that the walls must give way or the ceiling crack. There were high squeals and low squeals, grunts, and wails of agony; there would come a momentary lull, and then a fresh outburst, louder than ever, surging up to a deafening climax. It was too much for some of the visitors—the men would look at each other, laughing nervously, and the women would stand with hands clenched, and the blood rushing to their faces, and the tears starting in their eyes.

Meantime, heedless of all these things, the men upon the floor were going about their work. Neither squeals of hogs nor tears of visitors made any difference to them; one by one they hooked up the hogs, and one by one with a swift stroke they slit their throats. There was a long line of hogs, with squeals and lifeblood ebbing away together; until at last each started again, and vanished with a splash into a huge vat of boiling water.

· · ·

Where, one might wonder, was the Illinois Humane Society, which George Angell had helped set up in 1871, inspired above all by the maltreatment of livestock at the Union Stock Yards? The most straightforward explanation is that, beginning in 1880, the meat-packers succeeded in co-opting it. That year, Phil Armour's name first showed up on the humane society's board of directors, and he and his fellow packers aligned themselves with the society on a high-profile issue—the use of iron spikes or brads in driving hogs and cattle during transportation—agreeing to penalize sellers twenty-five cents for every ham found to have been bruised by this prac-tice. The Humane Society heralded the news in its annual report under the header THE AWAKENING OF THE PACKERS AND PROVISION MERCHANTS. "More valuable allies than these could scarcely have been hoped for," gushed the society's president, John G. Shortall. "Let us hope for a long continuance of this unity of commerce and humanity in a common defense."

Like Henry Bergh, Shortall was part of the same urban elite as the captains of industry he was supposed to be regulating. But unlike Bergh, whose wealth came from inheritance, Shortall had scrapped his way to the top, a fact that perhaps explains how easily he aligned himself with Chicago's largely self-made tycoons. Born in Dublin in 1838, Shortall emigrated to the United States with his family when he was still a boy. After his parents died, he spent three of his teenage years working for Horace Greeley at the *New-York Tribune,* then followed Greeley's famous advice to young men and headed west in 1854, landing in Illinois. Soon, Shortall had begun a new career in the business of real-estate "abstracts," i.e., research documents used to establish a history of ownership for legal pur-poses, and by the early 1860s had become the lead partner in a firm, Shortall and Hoard, that produced such reports. A partic-ular windfall arrived with the Great Fire of 1871: Thousands of original deeds to downtown real estate burned up with the build-ings whose ownership they proved, but the ledgers of Shortall's firm were salvaged—when Shortall and a friend forced a wagon driver at gunpoint to load them amid the inferno and take them to safety. It was these ledgers, along with the records of two other firms (which quickly agreed to merge with Shortall's firm, forming a highly profitable monopoly), that established the chains of own-ership that permitted the city's landowners to rebuild.

Shortall made his residence on Millionaire's Row, five blocks up

Prairie Avenue from Phil Armour's home. He became famous for his parties, held in a resplendent oblong drawing room with fine art bedecking the custard-colored walls, bric-a-brac made of gorgeous Bohemian glass, a Venetian mirror hanging over the Dutch fireplace. Like Armour, Shortall made a habit of walking to work each day, though on a considerably less punishing schedule than the meat baron's: He would emerge at 10 a.m. with his long-haired collie, and man and dog would stride off together to the Humane Society's offices, returning at 4 or 5 p.m. The two were a notable sight around town, in part because of the beauty of the dog, but also because of Shortall's own smart attire; as a local newspaper noted, "He wears a high hat and collar, with just the suggestion of crimson at his throat, brick brown English gloves, a smart little business suit of Scotch cheviot and is as handsome as a picture in his long Inverness coat, the cape of which goes flippitty-flap as if in sympathy with the playful brute at his side."

In 1893, when Shortall wanted a new building for the Humane Society, who was there to open his wallet but Phil Armour, pitching in $2,500, or more than $70,000 in today's money. And when Armour died, eight years later, the society published an encomium to the nation's largest butcher in its annual report—helping to launder Armour's posthumous reputation, washing away the blood of the countless millions of animals so cruelly disassembled in his slaughter factories.

John G. Shortall, 1892.

Beyond the question of Shortall's personal sympathies, there were also structural impediments that kept the Illinois Humane Society from serving as a meaningful check on animal cruelty in the packinghouses. The enforcement model that Henry Bergh had innovated, which spread to societies around the country, relied heavily on incoming tips from citizens—do-gooders who witnessed, say, an overloaded horse team on a streetcar line or a maltreated calf in a butcher's wagon. By contrast, at the stockyards and in the packinghouses, the vast majority of the human witnesses to the fate of animals were ones with great disincentive to speak out.

Then there was a basic jurisdictional issue: Unlike in the streets of the city, humane monitoring of Union Stock Yards and Packingtown was technically controlled by the state of Illinois, which funded a "humane agent" to oversee both locations; it was only a gentleman's agreement between the Humane Society and the state that gave the society informal supervision over the agent. By all accounts, the first one, a red-headed, freckle-faced Irishman by the name of John McDonald, did a good job of keeping the cruelty to a minimum. A former prison warden, McDonald was generally seen as an honest broker, even as he was famous for his rough treatment of anyone he saw mistreating animals inside the yards; Shortall liked to tell the story of when McDonald, after rounding a bend to see a drover maliciously whipping some sheep, gave the man "such a pommeling that his mother would not have known him."

After several years, the penitentiary lured McDonald back with a larger salary, and subsequent humane agents became lightning rods for controversy. In the society's papers from this era—which have been preserved in two archives, one at the University of Illinois at Chicago and the other at the Abraham Lincoln Presidential Library in Springfield—there are folders full of correspondence about William Mitchell, who served as humane agent for much of the 1880s. Multiple drovers at the yards wrote letters to Shortall decrying him as lazy and incompetent, and the governor, Richard J. Oglesby, expressed alarm over how many complaints he was receiving about Mitchell. But Mitchell stayed on, and when he was reappointed ten years later, it was thanks in part to a petition supporting him, signed by a number of luminaries at the yards—among them, notably, P. D. Armour and Gustavus Swift.

That last fact cannot help but color one's interpretation of an incident from January 1888, when Edwin Bergh (one of Henry's nephews) of the ASPCA sent Shortall a letter, repeating a claim that echoed the *Tribune*: that hogs being slaughtered in the meatpacking houses were often still alive, and thereby "sensible of suffering," during the scalding process. Shortall passed Bergh's note along to Mitchell, asking him to investigate. Mitchell wrote back and flatly denied the charge: "I beg leave to state that all hogs that are slaughtered in the abattoirs in & around the Union Stock Yards are always dead before they are plunged into the scalding tubs."

Despite the fact that this particular allegation would surface over and over again, to the point that it must have had some truth to it, Shortall seemed content to let the matter rest.

·   ·   ·

Perhaps the most remarkable fact about the correspondence of the Illinois Humane Society during this period is how little of it involved livestock. Here was an organization devoted to animal welfare in the backyard of the nation's exploding, heavily concentrated animal industry, with tens of millions of livestock animals passing through the Chicago area each year; and yet weeks go by in the archives without a single letter drawing the society's attention to the treatment of even one of them.

Beyond the jurisdictional issues in the Lake district, another reason for this involved a transformation in the group's mission that had taken place in 1877. Unlike the pioneering East Coast SPCAs founded by Bergh, Angell, and White, which remained devoted solely to animals and left it to other groups to handle child protection, the Illinois society was the first that decided to take on the task of protecting children as well. This would prove to be the more common approach nationwide: By 1908, when there were 354 anti-cruelty organizations in the United States, the majority of them would be hybrid organizations like Illinois's, with most of them taking on the name "humane society" to connote this dual function.

As the Illinois society's agents began intermixing the two streams of work, the consequences were profound. In part, that was because the needs of children were so great in urban America of the 1880s, with all the deprivations of poverty and neglect that Jacob Riis exposed to such galvanizing effect in *How the Other Half Lives*. But it was also because the public's attention to child suffering was acute, and easily aroused; the group's archives from the era are stuffed with handwritten letters from Chicagoans raising concern about specific children in their neighborhoods, a mix of good-faith concerns and rank busybodyism. The Humane Society's agents investigated every one, scrawling quick summaries of their findings on the backs of the original complaints. A select few from one agent's files in 1883 and 1884:

I wish to call your attention to a colored family at 651 W. Madison St. second floor. They have a child about four years old. They abuse him terribly. [*On the reverse, the agent's note: "Investigated and found no cruelty."*]

There is a family on the sidewalk at No. 152 W. Fulton they have been put out for not paying rent they are both drunkerds of the worse kind they have two small children that needs seeing to [*"I found that James Welch was looking for rooms, Mrs Welch was sober and the children looked comfortable"*]

The name of mother means patience and love as I understand it, but their is one at 624 W. Superior St. that seems to think the more she beats her boyes the better. I can hear the blowes almost any hour of the day it is so dreadfull [*"Investigated and found no cruelty"*]

Humain Society I wish you'd come and investigate a case widow woman and 2 children She is a Drunkist and leaves here children all day without food and often returns after midnight drunk and with men and whips her children shamfully without cause [*"Drinks some but children healthy. Gave her a reprimand."*]

As his agents were recalibrating their work to cover children as well as animals, Shortall pursued his own pet issues around child protection. He spent countless hours engaged in a vituperative, multi-year campaign against public performances by children, firing off fevered warnings to any impresario who planned to showcase underage actors on the stage and sending agents to shut down an 1892 dance performance by a seven-year-old prodigy from Chile. Another preoccupation was the carrying of young children on bicycles, an offense for which Shortall authorized his agents to arrest parents. "It is not alone the possibility of an accident that jeopardizes the welfare of the infant," Shortall told a local paper, "but the injurious results to the immature child of spinning along at a rapid rate of speed."

The decision to take on child protection was not without controversy in Illinois, as Shortall would acknowledge: "It was feared that with a horse and a child at the same time calling for help, the horse would be likely to suffer, at least by delay." But he always insisted that the fear about "delay" had been unfounded, that the efforts on behalf of children had not harmed those for animals. That may well be the case; but the inclusion of children changed the whole context of the work, making it harder for animals to rate consideration.

As we have seen, the most visionary flashes of insight on the part of the era's great animal advocates arrived in moments when they felt called to follow their principles to logical conclusions, even if underappreciated at the time—such as Bergh's probing thoughts about turtles, or the long process undertaken by White and the Women's Branch to make the killing of urban strays, the very definition of animals no one cared for, as painless as possible. Even when the impulses of these figures led them onto questionable moral terrain (as in some of the efforts against animal research) or even to absurdity (as with Bergh's most ill-informed or ill-advised campaigns against Barnum), they nevertheless made radical progress conceivable, by opening Pandora's boxes of moral obligation—loosing into the world ideas about the evil of pain and suffering that, once thought, could no longer be unthought.

The Humane Society model, by contrast, pulled toward respectability and nowhere else. In its twinning of innocents, children and animals, it steered straight into the hearth-and-home vision of family life that dominated so much sentimental art of the period: the child and the puppy, both wordless and blameless, both requiring (and capable of repaying) love and attention, not merely freedom from pain or hunger. At this moment, when the movement was going all in for *Black Beauty* and the Bands of Mercy, it had begun to seem as if the ultimate purpose of humane education was not to ameliorate the lot of animals but merely to ennoble the children.

·　　·　　·

The most uncomfortable fact about the slaughterhouses, though, is how many people witnessed their savagery and found it not just educational but thrilling. The most vivid and vexing description comes from Rudyard Kipling, who visited Chicago in 1889 as part of an American tour, chronicling it in dispatches for the colonial newspaper in India (*The Pioneer*) where he had been working as an editor. Having begun his travels in San Francisco and headed eastward, he declared Chicago to be the first "real city" he encountered—"the other places do not count"—but added that, "having seen it, I urgently desire never to see it again." He railed against its polluted air and water, its uninspiring architecture ("interminable vistas flanked with nine, ten, and fifteen storied houses . . . no colour in the street and no beauty"), its residents' gauche obsession with discussing wealth and success.

Kipling ended his journey at the packinghouses, which, he noted, had become a popular tourist destination. He went to see the killing of pigs—they dropped into the boiling vats "still kicking," he observed—and the slaughter of cattle, which "were slain at the rate of five a minute, and if the pig men were spattered in blood, the cow butchers were bathed in it. The blood ran in muttering gutters. There was no place for hand or foot that was not coated in thicknesses of dried blood, and the stench of it in the nostrils bred fear." Amid this scene, he caught sight of another visitor, "a young woman of large mould, with brilliantly scarlet lips, and heavy eyebrows, and dark hair that came in a 'widow's peak' on the forehead. She was well and healthy and alive, and she was dressed in flaming red and black." He continued:

> She stood in a patch of sunlight, the red blood under her shoes, the vivid carcasses tacked round her, a bullock bleeding its life away not six feet away from her, and the death factory roaring all round her. She looked curiously, with hard, bold eyes, and was not ashamed.

It was an indelible vision of humanity untroubled by violence toward animals. Kipling's angel of death had achieved the mental state that Sinclair's visitors, in his roughly contemporaneous reporting for *The Jungle*, were attempting to reach—those men "laughing nervously," and the women with "the blood rushing to their faces, and the tears starting in their eyes." But what, exactly, were all of these visitors trying to access in themselves? The Chicago historian Dominic Pacyga—who notes that local schoolchildren were taken to the slaughterhouses for decades, as recently as the 1950s—has described the purpose of this spectacle as "the presentation of the modern," reflecting the rising attitude that brought hundreds of thousands of people to witness the miracles of the World's Fair and the savagery of the meat industry nearby: the knowledge of what so-called progress looked like, but also a desensitization to its less salubrious side, and to the idea that some level of violence might be necessary for its continuance.

All around, one could see this hard-bitten, unsentimental view of suffering and violence rising. Certainly this sense was intruding in the 1880s and 1890s around the question of labor, among the nation's business owners—whose Pinkerton strikebreakers thought nothing of killing scores of people in the course of keeping plants open, as they did in Homestead, Pennsylvania, in 1892—as well as among certain labor activists who, in thrall to the anarchist "propaganda of the deed," saw murder as a small price to pay for a more just future. It was also plain as day in the far-flung empires that European nations and, increasingly, the United States were building and maintaining with great violence, as inventors of the period diligently devised ever more deadly armaments (dynamite, the Maxim gun, smokeless powder) to be deployed in the service of colonial warfare. By the end of the decade, when Kipling sent his infamous poem to Theodore Roosevelt, exhorting him to take up "the White Man's Burden" and colonize the Philippines, one could positively smell the slaughterhouse blood in his phrase "the savage wars of peace."

The slaughterhouse tourists were catching up with John Call Dalton and the sangfroid of the scientists, those for whom abstract future gains required a certain toll in blood, and perhaps even a willingness to shed it oneself. To these rising moderns, Frances Power Cobbe's uncomprehending moral diagnosis of the vivisectionist—that he is "anxious to relieve the sufferings of unseen, and perhaps unborn, men and women," but "cares in comparison nothing at all for those agonies which are endured immediately under his eye"—

would become a kind of compliment, a clear-eyed description of the temperament the moment required; indeed, one can see how neatly Cobbe's formulation applies to all the "isms" that would turn the twentieth century into an unprecedented bloodbath. It was a manner of thinking that violated, even disproved, the fundamental tenet of the animal-welfare movement: its bedrock faith in an intrinsic human decency to be appealed to, a childlike state of simple recognition between creatures that could be accessed in our moment-to-moment interactions with animals, and with one another, if only we let ourselves tap into it.

This, perhaps, is the best explanation for why the humane movement could not confront the slaughterhouses: The reality of them simply could not be reconciled within their worldview.

As the World's Fair approached, Shortall poured himself into fair-related initiatives: erecting a "humane" exhibit at the Liberal Arts Building (the exhibit was later "awarded honorable mention, with diploma and medal," he noted proudly in the next year's annual report), and organizing a Humane Congress to be held over three days at the Memorial Art Palace, a newly constructed building in Grant Park downtown that now houses the Art Institute of Chicago. Leafing through Shortall's correspondence from 1892 and 1893, one sees how the logistics of the conference multiplied, as societies from around the nation and the world sent their RSVPs (George Angell regretfully declined, while Caroline Earle White agreed to come) and travel and lodging had to be arranged—a vivid reminder of how the institutional bureaucracy of activism can consume the time and headspace that might otherwise flow to the activism itself.

The event, which took place October 10–12, 1893, was stimulating. Representatives from Turkey, France, Italy, and Japan spoke about the challenges of animal protection in their home countries. Multiple speakers, including Shortall and White, read papers on the evils of vivisection. Others expounded on the mistreatment of cattle in transit, out on the plains, at sea—the naturalist William Hosea Ballou noted that because vessels flying any flag other than the American one were considered foreign soil, federal laws about livestock transportation did not apply. A Hindu priest, B. B. Nagarkar of Bombay, came to speak about his religion's rev-

erence for animals, noting archly to the Chicago audience: "You
have in this country laws which discriminate between the killing of
animals cruelly and killing them kindly. This the Hindoo cannot
understand. To kill an animal by any means is to him cruelty, and
your laws seem but a contradiction of terms."

The disconnect that the priest saw was one that pervaded so
much of American society, and Chicago in particular—nowhere
more vividly than in the slaughterhouses, of course. But the
gulch in sensibility could be seen a different way by simply opening the *Daily Inter Ocean,* Chicago's business-minded broad-
sheet, during the days of the conference. There, a regular feature
called "The World of Trade" tallied up all the relevant economic
indicators—"The grain markets were rather slow but irregular. . . .
The Kansas report made the crop 24,000,000 bu, or 5,000,000
bu more than a month ago. . . . The railway and miscellaneous
bond market was irregular and some heavy advances and declines
were made. . . . Dry goods market shows no improvement in the
main. . . ."—and in its middle sat an unceremonious chart called
LIVE STOCK RECEIPTS, tabulating in rows and columns the various
animals that had passed through the city in the previous days:
21,876 cattle on Monday the 9th, 151,212 hogs on Tuesday the
10th, and so on.

Unlike corn or bonds, these were living creatures. To reduce them
to cold hard figures was, in a sense, the logical correlate of learning to tolerate, at least for a half hour on a slaughterhouse tour,
the sights and sounds of their killing. Cow by cow, pig by pig, all
that blood and din was necessary to keep the numbers rising, and
to think otherwise was not just sentimental; it was old-fashioned.

Professor William H. Keen's Clinic
Jefferson Medical College Hospital
December 10th 1902.

Techniques used in the surgical theater were
developed and practiced on live animals.

Chapter 16

THE ZOOPHILISTS

In the mid-1890s, a *Philadelphia Inquirer* piece described a new esprit de corps that had emerged among the city's medical students. The newspaper gave it a name: the "amphitheater habit," which described the addictive thrill of assuming one's seat in a surgical theater, waiting to see what pedagogical delights might lie in store. The *Inquirer* included a sketch of a theater at the Jefferson Medical College in Philadelphia, with its ring of seats rising almost to the ceiling and its tables piled with what the writer called "a most appalling array of glittering surgical instruments"—not just knives but "saws, drills, flesh hooks, tourniquets, everything that money can buy that is calculated to expedite scientific work upon suffering humanity."

In March 1895, the head of surgery at the college, William Williams Keen, planned to give his amphitheater audience quite a show. For a difficult case of paralysis—a man had lost the use of one leg, after severing some nerves behind the knee in an accident—Keen devised a radical operation: If the man's severed nerves could not be repaired during surgery, Keen would try grafting in a nerve from a donor dog, which he would acquire from the local animal shelter.

Keen's reputation as a surgeon was by then titanic. During the Civil War, he and two other army surgeons—including the physiologist S. Weir Mitchell, John Call Dalton's protégé, who himself had set up shop in Philadelphia—developed pathbreaking methods of treating gunshot wounds. In 1893, it was Keen who had been selected to lead a secret mission to excise a cancerous tumor from the jaw of President Grover Cleveland, a procedure that was successfully and stealthily performed aboard a yacht owned by one of the president's wealthy friends. Despite the removal of five teeth and much of his upper jaw, Cleveland recovered well and denied all rumors of an operation.

One could hardly blame Keen for believing, a year and a half later, that he could operate on anything. There was a significant catch to his plan, though. Getting a dog from Philadelphia's shelters would mean tussling with the city's most formidable animal advocate, Caroline Earle White. Through her role as the head of the Women's Branch of the Pennsylvania SPCA, White retained a close command of the city's animal shelters, and in the previous twenty years, she had shifted her focus to become the nation's most prominent foe of animal research, establishing a national organization based in Philadelphia, the American Anti-Vivisection Society (AAVS), to lead the fight for new laws restricting the practice.

Keen and White had tangled before, on multiple occasions. Early in her animal-welfare campaign, she had spent two hours in his office attempting to bring him over to her side on the vivisection issue, prompting him (as he later recalled it) to proclaim, "I regard it as a scientific, moral, and Christian duty to obstruct and nullify, to the extent of my influence and ability, your efforts to hinder experimental research on animals." After the founding of the AAVS, the two delivered dueling addresses on the subject at the Woman's Medical College of Pennsylvania, one of the few such institutions in the country. It seems likely that Keen came up with his notion of a canine nerve transplant, at least in part, as a provocation to his longtime adversary. On the morning of March 6, he sent the hospital's superintendent, George Bailey Jr., to the shelter in order to ask for a dog. Predictably, Bailey was rebuffed, and Keen received a note from White that same afternoon, explaining that the shelter had a blanket policy of refusing to give up animals to medical experimentation.

But this was Keen's trap, because the operation he was proposing—in which a successful outcome would mean, hypothetically, that a man could regain his ability to walk—was arguably therapeutic in nature, not experimental. He wrote to White laying out his intentions and asking, once again, for her cooperation in furnishing him with a dog. In the event that the dog's nerve would be required, he explained, the animal would "have precisely the same care that the man will before the operation, and after I have taken out the nerve I shall continue the anaesthetic to the dog until he is dead." Keen invited a representative of the Women's Branch to be present in the room during the procedure.

The feud between the two eminent Philadelphians was a microcosm of a bitter divide in elite society on both sides of the Atlantic. White spoke on behalf of a small but growing movement of people, including some physicians, who believed that the cruelty of medical experiments on live animals could not be justified under nearly any circumstances. Keen channeled the rising elite of the nation's medical establishment, who saw research on animals—and the right to carry out such research with no restrictions—as central to the medical revolutions taking place before their very eyes. It was an unresolvable clash of values: the profound suffering of research animals, on the one hand, pitted against the incremental but undeniable gains in medical knowledge, on the other.

But from a twenty-first-century vantage point, what is perhaps more interesting is how much the debate revolved around what we today call "alternative facts." Keen and his faction consistently overplayed the utility of animal experiments, just as they did the gains happening then in medicine writ large, and they dissembled around the plain fact that the vast majority of animal experiments were mere demonstrations, carried out in the course of medical instruction. White and her allies went even further in their wishful departures from reality, refusing to acknowledge that animal research had led to any progress, and carrying out elaborate self-deceptions and indulging in tortured logic to convince themselves of the contrary. All the motivated untruths, half-truths, and omissions were channeling some deeply held faiths on both sides: about the future of medicine, the prerogatives of medical researchers, and the fundamental relationship between morality and science.

.   .   .

When White founded the American Anti-Vivisection Society, which began with a public meeting in February 1883, in Association Hall on Chestnut Street, a tension was present from the beginning: Did the new society argue for the *total* abolition of vivisection, or merely the restriction and regulation of it? White's model and idol, Frances Power Cobbe—to whom she had paid a visit in London, in the months leading up to the event—had staked out the more radical position, and White confided to her fellow founders in private that this was her belief, too: Medical research on living animals should be entirely banned.

But she worried that this would alienate potential allies, especially given how unsuccessful the campaign against vivisection in America had been to date. Perhaps White, in rejecting a stance that would tar doctors like Keen as moral reprobates, was influenced somewhat by her social station in Philadelphia: Her husband was one of the city's most prominent lawyers, a major figure in Catholic social circles, an intimate of Republican politicians. When President Rutherford B. Hayes visited the city in 1878, Caroline was one of a handful of women who escorted his wife, Lucy, around the city, showing her (in the *Inquirer*'s formulation)

"public institutions where woman's work is nobly exemplified." White's connections to the Philadelphia elite had helped her found the Pennsylvania SPCA, and then carry out an unparalleled reinvention of the city's animal shelters; one can imagine why, on the question of animal research, she imagined that a more friendly approach would help bring the medical elite to the table.

Having chosen the moderate path, White and the organization soon adopted a more moderate name to match: the American Society for the Restriction of Vivisection. This was the name under

Caroline Earle White, undated photograph.

which the group pursued its first legislative push, attempting to persuade the Pennsylvania legislature to pass a law curtailing animal research. The bill was fairly modest in its aims, requiring that anyone engaging in vivisection—which it defined as the "cutting, wounding, or other surgical or medical treatment of a living animal" or "the artificial production in such animals of painful disease for the purpose of physiological research"—apply for a license, and document all their experiments for the purposes of transparency.

After presenting their bill to the state House of Representatives in January 1885, White and her colleagues were persuaded to meet with a representative of the city's research community, Dr. H. C. Wood, to discuss a compromise. The original bill had empowered county treasurers' offices to dole out the licenses, but Wood proposed instead that a medical institution, the College of Physicians of Philadelphia, ought to control the process. And he persuaded the activists to soften a provision banning vivisection for demonstration purposes, adding an exception for medical schools.

Wood pronounced himself pleased with the amended bill and even had it printed up himself, sending it back to White's society for approval. Plans were made for a group of society members to jointly present the new bill in Harrisburg with Wood and S. Weir Mitchell, who also supported the compromise—or so White and her colleagues were led to believe. But the anti-vivisectionists were about to receive a lesson in hardball politics. Having made no preparations to support their cause before the assembled legislators, they looked on in horror as Wood and Mitchell both declined to speak in favor of the bill. Wood even had the temerity to stand and deliver a pro-vivisection oration, declaring (as the society recorded ruefully in its next year's annual report) that the practice "had accomplished marvels in aiding the progress of science and the medical art, and denying that any good reason existed for such a law. In short, if he had gone before the committee for the express purpose of defeating the bill, he could scarcely have expressed his sentiments more strongly against it." The bill died an ignoble death.

Such underhanded tactics no doubt helped to solidify, in White's mind, the sense that compromise with these men was impossible. One imagines her mind casting back to Cobbe's essay on the "Moral Aspects of Vivisection," which the Women's Branch had printed up back in the 1870s, with its rhetoric about animal research representing "a backsliding in feeling and moral aim almost measureless in the depth of its descent." Even so, she still declined to advocate for a complete ban on animal research—in the fall of 1885, when

Keen wrote and asked her to clarify her stance on this question, she sent an aggrieved response: "Have we not within a few months changed our name for the explicit purpose of showing that we are not working for the total suppression of vivisection and are we not people of honor? . . . No! my dear Sir, the weapons of fraud, deceit and misrepresentation are used on your side, not on ours."

Yet her rhetoric on the evils of vivisection grew ever more strident. In early 1886, delivering her address to the Woman's Medical College of Pennsylvania—responding to Keen, who had delivered his pro-vivisection speech the previous fall—she sketched out a lineage of sinister "Vivisectors" that lumped Keen and his present-day allies in with the most infamous medical butchers of Europe, like François Magendie and Moritz Schiff, who allegedly killed some 14,000 dogs in the course of his experiments. Echoing Cobbe, she spoke acidly of the moral degradation of all the men in this tradition: the "almost indescribable barbarities which are the natural result of unchecked experimentation upon animals, and which will always be the result, to a greater or lesser extent, where men are left at full liberty to carry out their investigations in any manner they please, free to gratify every caprice of a sometime morbid fancy, every experiment suggested by an unnatural and diseased curiosity."

In May 1887, White finally bowed to the wishes of many of her more radical members, and put forward a proposition to reorient the group's mission to explicitly support abolition—going back on the assurance she had sent to Keen less than two years before. H. C. Wood's great betrayal in Harrisburg loomed large in her explanation of why, but her grievance at the medical community went further than that: "With some few noble exceptions," she noted, in her address explaining her evolved position, "the medical profession has, in spite of the moderation of our demands, treated us with indifference, holding itself entirely aloof from us, and yielding us not the least encouragement." Worse, she pointed out, the moderate stance had given the doctors an opening for a pernicious form of argument:

> Our opponents can say to us, with truth, "You acknowledge that you are in favor of Vivisection to a certain extent;" and

when we would indignantly disclaim such a supposition, they can reply, "Why, of course you do; you ask for a license for vivisectors, and you say that your Society is for the restriction of vivisection; then you acknowledge that it is right to a certain extent, or you would not say the restriction but the cessation, of vivisection, in your title and in your charter. Now then, *you* think it allowable to a certain extent, and *we* think it allowable to a greater extent, and we have just as much reason to claim that we are right as you have."

By the same token, White explained, she rejected another moderate position that certain activists were taking, in support of a ban only on *painful* experiments. Could they really trust researchers to hold to such a compromise? "Is it probable that a scientist," she asked, "absorbed in the investigation he is pursuing, just on the brink, as he may often fancy himself to be, of making some discovery, will stop every few moments in order to administer another dose of the anaesthetic, thus interrupting himself and jarring upon his delicate perceptions, which are worked up to the utmost point of tension? The idea is truly absurd!"

No, the only path forward was total abolition. "It is true that the prospect of our obtaining a law which should secure this end seems very far off," White acknowledged, but "it does not seem any more hopeless than did the abolition of Negro slavery in this country sixty years ago, yet how soon was it accomplished!"

Almost certainly the decision was a strategic one for the (re-renamed) American Anti-Vivisection Society, regardless of the underlying merits of the position: Activist groups, then as now, thrive when they channel the passions of the most committed. After its charter was amended, the society received a letter from a local physician named Matthew Woods, asking to join. "As an Association having for its object merely the restriction of barbarity, I could not have become a member," the doctor wrote, "but since you are making an effort to have it abolished altogether I will consider it a great honor to be permitted to work with the Society in its effort to accomplish this." In short order, Woods became the AAVS president, a move that reflected not merely the utility, in a public fight again the medical profession, in having a bona fide doctor at the helm, but also the fact that the anti-vivisection cause had begun to make genuine inroads with America's doctors. This fact could also be seen in the growing anti-vivisection advocacy of Dr. Albert Leffingwell, who beginning in the 1880s had published a series of essays on the subject in popular magazines, recounting the worst horrors of Magendie and Bernard (and their American acolytes, Dalton and Flint) and expressing doubts that any practical gains from animal research were worth the moral cost involved.

In the early 1890s, the AAVS, together with sister chapters in various states, made a renewed push for legislation. Another bill went before the Pennsylvania legislature in 1893, and activists succeeded in getting it through the state senate, but it died in the lower chamber. Washington State activists fared similarly, pushing a bill through the legislature, only for the governor to veto it. The modest success was Massachusetts, which in 1894 passed a law banning vivisection from the Boston public schools—that is, the grade schools, hardly the greatest users of the practice.

Still, by 1895, a project carried out by the American Humane Association—organized by Woods, Leffingwell, and a minister named Titus Munson Coan—showed just how far the campaign against animal research had gone in swaying opinion within the medical field. As part of a broader survey on vivisection attitudes, the group polled physicians in Massachusetts and New York and found that only 19 percent of them supported the status quo of unregulated research practices; a nearly equal number of them (18 percent) favored the total abolition of vivisection, with the majority favoring restrictions based on utility of the experiment, the use of anesthetics, or both.

W. W. Keen must have been especially vexed to see the statement that Dr. Theophilus Parvin, a towering Philadelphia figure of an earlier generation who until recently had himself presided at Jefferson Medical College, gave along with his response—one that, the survey committee noted, seemed to summarize the majority position of their medical respondents. "Should the law restrict the performance of vivisection? I think it ought," Parvin had written. "That restriction ought to forbid all experiments without worthy objects, and in every case, so far as possible, the animal during and subsequent to the operation must be preserved from pain. . . .

I cannot think that vivisections done for teaching purposes, simply showing what has been proved time and again upon hundreds and thousands of victims, are justifiable unless anaesthesia is employed, *to not merely mitigate, but to completely abolish suffering of the animals.*"

And Keen no doubt was horrified to see that some physicians, in backing the position of total abolition, were edging toward a view that animal research had given literally no benefits to medicine: that it "serves no purpose that is not better served after other manners" (as Dr. James Garretson, from a rival medical college in Philadelphia, opined), or that it "has opened up no new views for the treatment and cure of diseases" (as Dr. Forbes Winslow, of London, wrote). In these opinions they echoed the high dudgeon of Dr. Matthew Woods, who declared, in a thunderous oration soon after ascending to the presidency of the AAVS, that "the progress of medicine is *retarded* by the methods of the vivisector."

.   .   .

In fact, animal research and medical progress continued to be intimately bound up together—though the relationship between the two was complex, just as it remains today. In Keen's 1885 address to the Woman's Medical College, later reprinted in *Popular Science*, he enumerated some of the recent benefits as he saw them. The first, and perhaps most instructive, was pharmaceutical testing. "Who would think it right," Keen asked the students, "to put a few drops of the hydrochlorate of cocaine"—then a miracle local anesthetic that, he noted, had been essentially unknown a year before—"into the eye of a man, not knowing what frightful inflammation or even loss of sight might follow? Had one dared to do it, and had the result been disastrous, would not the law have held him guilty and punished him severely, and all of us said Amen?" The only reasonable moral approach, Keen said, was to try drugs first in animals, and he rattled off a list of other medications whose safety and efficacy had been proven only through this method.

Then he turned to his own specialty of surgery, dwelling on the abdomen in particular. "The spleen has been removed, part of the stomach has been cut out for cancer, part of the bladder has been dissected away, the entire gall-bladder has been removed, and several inches of the intestine have been cut out, all with the most remarkable success," he declared. "To all of these, experiments upon animals have either led the way, or have taught us better methods." While he did not linger on that last point, it was key to understanding Keen's strident feeling that even regulation would be a grave mistake. The most commonly supported restriction was to ban classroom demonstrations of results already proven—but as Keen well knew, surgeons-in-training of that era were not just witnessing demonstrations on research animals but *participating* in them to build up skill, practicing the same techniques that they would soon be attempting on humans.

From there, Keen toured through a whole host of other research areas, where both specific studies and broader practices on animals had led to medical advances in humans—treatment of heat stroke, the effects of removing an unhealthy kidney, and many more—before coming around to the remarkable research being done by Louis Pasteur and others in the field of bacteriology, the revolutionary consequences of which would become clearer still during the decade following his address.

Set against all that evidence, how could the anti-vivisection faction claim that animal research was a dead end? In part, they convinced themselves of this position with a textual reliquary of sorts that they had assembled over decades, anti-vivisection remarks attributable to various prestigious men of science. In some cases, these were idiosyncratic practitioners like Lawson Tait, an eminent British surgeon who opposed vivisection on moral grounds and also believed it unnecessary to advance the field; in others, it was outsiders to medical research such as Charles Darwin or Charles Alexander Gordon, the honorary physician to Queen Victoria, both of whom expressed negative opinions of vivisection without much familiarity with how it was being used day-to-day in medical colleges. Other textual snippets were drawn from famous historical vivisectors themselves, like a stray remark of Claude Bernard's from late in his career that his "hands were empty of results," or a similarly late assertion from Charles Bell, demurring that despite the many animal experiments involved in his pioneering work on the nervous system, they did not deserve primary credit for the advance.

Beyond that, the halting nature of medical progress allowed the anti-vivisectionists to cast doubt on nearly any claimed advance from animal research, both in their own minds and in the public discourse. Keen's address to the women's college moved systematically from one branch of inquiry to another, laying out what vivisection was revealing in each area, but in her response, Caroline White attacked each example with whatever rhetorical weapon came most readily to hand. That heat-stroke research on rabbits? The temperature they were exposed to was too high, obviating the relevance to humans, she claimed. That research on the effects of removing a kidney from dogs? It had already been shown that humans could survive nephrectomy just fine, White countered, so the animal research was unnecessary. The playbook was simple and effective: Any animal experiment that wasn't futile could instead be decried as superfluous, and vice versa.

Ironically, perhaps the best argument wielded by the anti-vivisectionists of the 1890s had in a sense been handed to them by the *inadequacy* of animal research throughout history. Over the centuries, in their zeal to use animals to understand human physiology and treat human maladies, researchers had tended to neglect the systematic study of how humans and animals differ, and how animals differ from one another, in their physiology and response to various treatments—the discipline called comparative medicine. What do animal studies tell us about humans? As we now know well, the answer is always *It depends,* which is why even today, success in the former so often can lead to heartbreak in the latter. Listening to Keen's address, the women in the audience might well have imagined dogs to be perfect stand-ins for people in the vast majority of experiments, while White argued the opposite: that the action of drugs "is often so different in men and animals that experiments upon the latter form a most misleading method of research." She went on:

You have, doubtless, all heard of how many substances that are poisonous to man are innocuous to certain animals; how horses can take large quantities of antimony, dogs mercury, goats tobacco, mice hemlock, and rabbits belladonna, with perfect impunity. Supposing that any physiologist, reasoning after Dr. Keen's fashion, and having tried belladonna upon rabbits or mercury upon dogs, should have given these substances, without any hesitation, to human beings, would not the consequences have been much more deplorable than trying the hydrochlorate of cocaine upon the eye of a man before testing it upon an animal?

White and the anti-vivisectionists were sparing in their use of religious language, but on this question of animal similarity to humans, the question of divine intention was never far from the surface. The assumption that human resemblances to animals were only superficial, and thus impossibly futile to plumb, helped underscore the activists' portrayal of vivisectors as tragic figures who (in Woods's words) "sacrifice their better feelings to plow, bore and cut through the living tissues of God's sentient creation in quest of this *ignis-fatuus*"—will o' the wisp—"which ever evades them." The anti-vivisectionists believed that useful medical research could be carried out only on humans themselves, a notion that Keen saw as monstrous but that White saw as a divinely mandated fact, and one that even offered a novel form of theodicy: "Divine Providence has, we believe, ordained that in some of the many accidents which so often, unhappily, befall mankind, a legitimate means can be afforded for wresting the secrets of Nature from her grasp and increasing our knowledge of physiology," she told the medical students.

By the early 1890s, it was clear that bacteriology, and in particular the work of Pasteur and his various disciples, offered a devastating rebuttal to the notion that God had ordained the futility of animal research. Keen's address to the women's college happened just months before the earliest American dog-bite victims, including Amalia Morosini, traveled across the ocean for rabies inoculation at Pasteur's hands. Even a few months later, when White's response was delivered, the efficacy of the treatment could still be reasonably doubted. But in the subsequent years, as the data became inarguable and acceptance of the method spread, it prompted profound cognitive dissonance in the AAVS and its allies around the world. There was no question that Pasteur's methods qualified as unacceptable vivisection by their standards: To harvest his rabies vaccine, he had routinized a process of exposing live rabbits to the virus via trepanation, i.e., boring into the skull. This forced vivisection's foes to hold on for years to the notion that the resulting vaccine was unreliable, if not outright dangerous.

By 1895, as Keen prepared to send his next letter to White in the matter of the shelter dog, the safety and efficacy of the rabies vaccine was no longer in serious question, and Keen could crow about multiple new treatments devised through similar methods. Scientists from Germany and Japan had developed a process for creating an antitoxin against diphtheria, then a common and deadly infection, that involved injecting

William W. Keen

live horses with the bacterium and harvesting a serum from their blood. And a researcher at the Pasteur Institute in Paris had developed a vaccine against cholera, one of the developing world's greatest killers, through a series of experiments on live guinea pigs. If White had had her way, Keen pointedly noted in his letter, neither of these advances would exist. "In your misguided zeal for dogs," he wrote,

> you are guilty, in my opinion, of cruelty to this man [Keen's patient] and cruelty to all mankind, because you thwart scientific progress under the guise of love for animals. You would condemn to the tortures of disabilities of accident and disease people who have been happily rescued by the more humane scientists in my profession.
>
> You will pardon me if I write earnestly. It is because I feel deeply the injury you are trying to inflict upon the human race. Happily, the common sense of the community does not allow you to have your way, as they prefer the devotion of my own profession to the welfare of mankind, to your devotion to dogs in preference to men.

After sending off this letter, Keen supplied the full correspondence to the press, whose reaction confirmed his belief that the general opinion was in his favor, not White's. The item was picked up as far away as South Carolina, where a Charleston paper covered it with this headline: DOG OR MAN? MRS. WHITE DECIDES FOR THE CANINE.

.   .   .

Later in life, Keen assembled an entertaining collection of invective that anti-vivisectionists had hurled at him. "I hope your mother if she is living will die in the most terrible torture, and if she is dead that her soul will never know rest for having given life to such a vile monster as you," one anonymous letter read, after he had published a pro-vivisection article in *Ladies' Home Journal.* "When your time comes to die," another letter read, "every cry of pain and anguish that you have been the cause of producing in these helpless creatures will follow you to the depths of hell." In the same essay, Keen compiled a list of clauses that anti-vivisection literature used to describe medical research labs: "scientific hells," "torture houses," "temples of torment." Since the early essays of Frances Power Cobbe, anti-vivisectionists had claimed that animal research destroyed the moral fiber of the medical men who practiced it, but Keen cited all this intemperate rhetoric in order to throw the same accusation back at them. "Can a cause which so seriously injures the character of its advocates that they indulge in this prolific vocabulary of vituperation," he wrote, tongue only partly in cheek, "by any possibility have an uplifting influence?"

In the minds of Keen and other passionate defenders of animal research, the hate mail only solidified their sense of the anti-vivisectionists as "antis" (a shorthand term the defenders took to using) above all. But the movement and its culture did put forward a positive vision, a fascinating blend of modern and anti-modern attitudes that touched on far more than just the narrow question of animal research, or even animals at all.

The clearest place to see it was in the *Journal of Zoophily,* which the AAVS began publishing in 1892. In both its purpose and its name, *Zoophily* was clearly inspired by *The Zoophilist,* the newspaper of Frances Power Cobbe's Victoria Street Society in London, but the tone and approach were far different. While the British publication crackled with Cobbe's brand of fiery intellectual debate, its American cousin was more sedate and pastoral. Much like *Our Dumb Animals, Zoophily* offered a miscellaneous collection of items, which included notes on the society's legislative progress (or lack thereof, as the case tended to be) and dramatic accounts of vivisectional cruelty, but it also offered genuine uplift: inspiring items on the humane treatment of animals and even, in the age of *Black Beauty,* some fiction.

Even more interesting were the movement's attempts to claim the mantle of science on its own, idiosyncratic terms. A section called "The Library" rounded up relevant reading, pointedly drawn from enemies as well as allies—it wanted to make a clear show of the fact that anti-vivisectionists could understand and rebut anything that the medical establishment put forward, even as it placed more humanistic texts on equal footing. In the first issue, the three books considered were a guide to good writing, a collection of anti-vivisection essays, and a two-volume chemistry book based in part on animal research. This last book provided the opportunity for a master class in passive aggression: "Dr. Chittenden (who, by the way, is not a doctor of medicine) has given us two very valuable works. The observations due to experiments not connected with animal torture are particularly trustworthy and suggestive . . ."

In a section entitled "Natural History," *Zoophily* embraced the same gentle, more observational approach to describing the animal kingdom that the writers in *The Audubon Magazine* had, an American literary tradition stretching back at least to Thoreau. The first item in the first section, "The Gold-Crested Wren," read as follows in its entirety:

This lovely little bird is so small and light that it can cling suspended on the end of a single narrow leaf, or needle of pine, and it does not depress the least branch on which it may alight. The Gold Crest frequents the loneliest heath, the deepest pine wood and the immediate neighborhood of dwellings indifferently. A Scotch fir or pine grew so near a house in which I once lived that the boughs almost brushed the window, and when confined to my room by illness it gave me much pleasure to watch a pair of these wrens who frequently visited the tree. They are also fond of thick thorn hedges and, like all birds, have their favorite localities, so that if you see them once or twice in one place you should mark the tree or bush, for they are almost certain to return. It would be quite possible for a person to pass several years in the country and never see one of these birds. There is a trick in finding birds' nests and a trick in seeing birds. The first I noticed was in an orchard; soon after I found a second in a yew tree close to a window, and after that constantly came upon them as they crept through the brambles or in hedgerows, or a mere speck up in a first tree. So soon as I had seen one I saw plenty.

Note the contemplative tone, with its easy slide in and out of the first person ("so near a house in which I once lived," etc.). The whole mode seemed to assert—in the face of a rising scientific establishment that wanted to generate knowledge through a rapacious, cruelly extractive approach to animal life—an opposing, more humble and meditative attitude. In *Zoophily*'s "Natural History" section, a reader might find an Italian naturalist studying the hibernation of a dormouse—not through vivisection, but through tender observations of its sleep habits ("As the winter grew intensely cold, the times of perfect repose, during which no breathing could be perceived, became much longer, sometimes more than twenty minutes"); or a disquisition on how fishes breathe in cold conditions that treats the question as a "matter of common observation," something that "anyone who has caught fish through ice three feet thick on Maine ponds" can understand; or an essay by Minnie Ward Patterson, a Michigan poet of some renown, in which she and her children discover a beetle in their flower garden and set to documenting some tests of its remarkable strength.

In understanding the culture of the anti-vivisectionists, it is important to understand it as largely a women's movement. It is no accident that Keen and White delivered their dueling addresses to the students of the Woman's Medical College; Keen would have fairly suspected that they, far more than his male students, were susceptible to the arguments of his adversaries. Women were the imagined readers of *Zoophily*, just as they were of *Our Dumb Ani-*

mals and *Audubon,* and they were also the acknowledged leaders of the movement on both sides of the Atlantic. In the 1860s, when White led the founding of the Pennsylvania SPCA, it was universally understood that she would step aside for male leadership, but by the 1880s, elite culture had shifted to the point that that was no longer necessary. Her longtime friend and ally Mary F. Lovell, who had been instrumental in the Women's Branch, took an active role in the AAVS as well, and the two women essentially ran the group and its agenda, even during the years when they recruited male presidents.

The sense of anti-vivisection as a women's cause had only grown over time. In its early years, the AAVS's executive committee had a roughly even balance of men and women, but by 1895, the group's composition was seventeen women and three men, and the AAVS had even joined an agglomeration of women's groups, the National Council of Women, as a member organization. That year at a NCW convention in Washington, D.C., White and Lovell both gave speeches in which they attempted to convince the delegates to join their cause, reciting the worst crimes of the vivisectionists and counterposing them with Christ's teachings. "Will you, with the chivalry which belongs to good and true womanhood side with the suffering and helpless?" Lovell implored, while White upped the spiritual ante considerably: "Remember that if you are convinced of the cruelty and unjustifiability of vivisection, and do not help us as far as you can to put it down and banish it from our midst, that at the last great Day of Judgment you may be held as accessory to the criminality."

In emphasizing a harmony that had to exist between scientific reality and Christian morals, their vision aligned closely with that of another prominent women's movement of the era, "scientific temperance," which believed strongly (and somewhat a priori) that alcohol and tobacco were irredeemably poisonous to the human body. Over the course of the late 1880s, led by the former schoolteacher Mary Hunt, the movement's activists—including Lovell, in Pennsylvania—pressured state after state to adopt laws mandating that particular textbooks on human health, some of them heavily edited by Hunt herself, be taught in primary schools. A *Popular Science* review of one of them, *Our Bodies and How We*

Live, noted that 67 of the book's 412 pages dwelled on alcohol in some way, such that "no topic or discussion is free from allusions to it." Moreover, as the reviewer noted, the scientific content of the book's proclamations was rather thin. On the growth of the bones: "It is the testimony of sagacious physicians that alcoholic drinks and tobacco tend to check the growth of the bones. . . . A well-developed form is something to be prized. No wise boy or girl will risk attaining it by indulging in filthy or injurious habits while young." On physical fitness: "Alcohol and tobacco act as poison to the nerve force which controls the muscles, and thus lessen the amount of muscular power and endurance."

It is easy to look back on these exercises in moralized science as the nadir of unscientific thinking. But of course, science itself can have its own preconceived notions that take decades or centuries to shake, as the natural world stubbornly fails to conform to the generalizations made about it. Throughout the 1890s, the German bacteriologist Robert Koch was engaging in his futile attempt to create a tuberculosis vaccine, inspired by the astonishing success of vaccines against rabies and cholera. (Does one microscopic pathogen behave the same way as another? *It depends.*) And meanwhile, the women who nodded along to the proclamations of White and Lovell would have understood well that the new era of medicine could feel like a cruel, inhuman, unfeeling practice, as the family physician was replaced by the "scientist at the bedside"; a pamphlet with that title, published by the Victoria Street Society in London and written by the pioneering woman doctor Frances Hoggan, described how hospitals had begun to see patients as merely a "greater or lesser quantity of material," with "the poor, and especially the women of the poorer classes . . . sure to be the greatest sufferers." This shift was symbolized, viscerally, by the rise of the speculum among gynecologists, who used it to conduct a more effective examination but at the cost of turning women's most intimate encounter with the health-care system into a highly alienating experience.

On the merits, the moralized notions of these late-nineteenth-century women got many things right that the scientists got wrong. Tobacco *was* a far greater enemy of human health than the scientists understood, and the effects of alcohol (especially in women) are only having their proper reckoning today, in terms of understanding the life-years lost. As for animal research, many of the results touted by Keen and his ilk were every bit as misleading as White charged, in terms of their implications for treating humans. The depressing fact was, and remains, that the genuine benefits of animal research have come only through staggering amounts of trial and error, of yearslong efforts stuck in unproductive alleyways, with tens or hundreds of thousands of animals expended in experiments that yield nothing—or, as the case may be, less than nothing. For every Pasteur, whose sacrifice of thousands of animals can be credited with saving countless human (and animal) lives, there were scores of scientists who killed comparable numbers to no good end.

Ultimately, this grim reality supplied both the best argument against vivisection *and* the best argument against its regulation, for it was difficult to devise a regulatory regime that would lessen the animal toll without unintentionally ensnaring the Pasteurs in red tape along with the failures-to-be. To support animal research was to embrace not only the useful sacrifices of animals but the countless useless ones, too, as the necessary price of innovation. It was a tradeoff that W. W. Keen was more than willing to make, and indeed to describe as "more humane" than the alternative, but one can hardly blame White and her allies, then and now, for regarding it as a dubious moral calculation.

.   .   .

There is no evidence that Keen ever carried out his experimental surgery on the paralyzed man. As White acidly noted in one of her letters to him, he almost certainly could have found his animal nerve donor through some other means: "In view of the fact that considerable numbers of dogs are kept, as we have heard, at the various medical colleges for the purposes of extermination, I must acknowledge my surprise that you should have applied to a Society such as ours, for one of those under our charge." It is telling that Keen, having grandstanded about White's "thwart[ing] scientific progress under the guise of love for animals" and then leaked all the letters to the press, apparently did not follow through on his benevolent impulses.

And it's a good thing, too, because the operation he proposed would have been a total failure. Even today, there is no animal tissue that can be reliably grafted into human patients—what science calls xenotransplantation—without rejection by the human host. Keen almost certainly would have known the disappointing history of those attempts going back more than a century: blood from various animals, corneas from pigs, skin from sheep. In the late twentieth century, scientists would famously attempt to transplant whole organs from primates, including kidneys and hearts, with no success. In 2022, a team from the University of Maryland transplanted a heart from a genetically modified pig into a dying cardiac patient; they hoped the ten tweaked genes in the porcine donor would be sufficient to fool the human immune system, but the recipient survived for only two months. Victory may yet come, but in the meantime, xenotransplantation offers another example of an animal research practice that has killed thousands of creatures over centuries with very little to show for it.

W. W. Keen proposed to throw yet another dog on that pyre, either because he genuinely believed he might succeed where others had failed, or—more likely—to score a rhetorical point in his battle with the anti-vivisectionists. He spent decades more fighting that battle, and winning it, helping rally against furtive attempts at national legislation and helping to block the cause from being discussed at an international humane congress in 1910. As he noted contentedly in his memoirs: "In season and out of season, I have been ever on the alert to find a joint in their armor which I could pierce, and my efforts have not been altogether in vain."

The pet cemetery symbolized the transformation of the
companion animal into a member of the family.

Chapter 17

DIED BELOVED

On a hillside in Westchester County, twenty miles or so north of New York City, lie three acres of proof that the human-animal bond can transcend life itself. Founded in 1896, the Hartsdale Pet Cemetery is America's oldest resting place for domestic animals, and on a recent visit, its current proprietor, Ed Martin, showed us around the most historic part of the site, shaded by old trees and suffused with decades of love and grief. A prodigious fifty-ton mausoleum, erected in 1917 by one M. F. Walsh, houses the remains of her pets Sally and Toodles. Nearby, a marble headstone sports a marvelous relief of a terrier named Babe, clad in a bow tie, a carved ball lying before it, nevermore to be chased. Equally poignant is the marker for a collie belonging to Annie De Voe, a Manhattan boarding-house owner, which reads:

OUR SYDNEY
DIED SEPT. 4, 1902
AGED 16 YRS.

BORN A DOG
LIVED LIKE A GENTLEMAN
DIED BELOVED

Lost to time is the photograph that once adorned the headstone's center, which showed, according to a waggish news account a few years after the burial, "the late lamented gazing soulfully into the whitherward."

The cemetery began as a collaboration between a Hartsdale land-owner, Emily Berthet, and the veterinarian Samuel K. Johnson—Liautard's enterprising former student, who established the New York Veterinary Hospital on 25th Street soon after graduating and turned it into an enduring institution, complete with his own line of patent medicines. So it perhaps made sense that he would be the first to see how a veterinary practice could profitably expand all the way into the hereafter. Bereaved owners would bring the deceased to Johnson's hospital, where it would be sealed into a zinc-lined box and sent by train upstate. Upon the pet's arrival in Hartsdale, a short journey by horse cart would take it to Berthet's property for burial. In the earliest days, prices ranged from $5, for the interment of a small pet, up to $15—more than $500 in today's money—for a large grave, which could be filled over years with a family's furry loved ones. (Some of the cemetery's tombstones attest to this super-saver approach, their long rosters of names demonstrating just how many dogs or cats a single human can be forced to grieve in a lifespan.)

Less is known about Berthet, who made her primary residence on 129th Street in Manhattan but kept a dwelling on the seventeen-acre Hartsdale property, three acres of which she fenced off for the cemetery. Mary Thurston, the cemetery's present-day historian, says that the earliest known pet burial on the site was Berthet's own cat Fuzz, buried there in 1887 or 1888, soon after she acquired the site. Thurston believes that Berthet originally dreamed of starting a pet burial ground much closer to the city—pointing to an 1896 newspaper interview in which an anonymous New York woman describes her active preparations to start a canine cemetery near the famous Calvary cemetery for humans, in what is now Queens. "I love dogs, and it is as much on this account as it is that I need a vocation that I have gone into this business," the unnamed inter-viewee told the reporter—a business, she added, that "at present is perhaps unusual, but which in the future, I am sure, will become just as much an institution as the burial of human beings."

That woman was right, of course. Pet cemeteries remain rela-tively few when compared to their human counterparts, but they are indeed a permanent institution in American life, with more than a hundred of them around the country. Today, the cheapest plot and burial at Hartsdale begin at $2,500, in addition to the cost of a tombstone. In that transaction, and in the other ways we now memorialize our departed pets—the sentimental portraits, the urns for cremains, the final footprints imprinted in clay, or (in a recent trend) the remembrance tattoos, marking owners with an indelible symbol of grief—we can see the outlines of the industry the unnamed New York matron envisioned. With its arrival in 1896, the pet cemetery symbolizes the transformation of the American dog or cat into a bona fide member of the family, a companion whose passing can shake us to our core and whose memory must be honored. As the anonymous woman put it that year, with only a bit of hyperbole, "A man or woman who is sincerely attached to a dog is as anxious that he shall have decent burial or disposition after death as if it were a case of a child." She added: "This may seem absurd to people who cannot enter into the feeling of attachment that exists between dogs and their masters, but it is true, nevertheless."

It took thirty years to get there—from 1866, when New York killed stray dogs by drowning them in an East River tank, to 1896, when the ASPCA, in its brand-new shelters in Manhattan and Brooklyn, euthanized the unclaimed animals in humane chambers along the lines of those used in Philadelphia; from downtown dogfights and heedless horse abuse in the street to dog shows and horse ambulances and veterinary hospitals. Those three decades also saw a steady rise in the work of animal-welfare organizations: A few years from the century's end, when the nation had grown to forty-four states, cruelty was being policed in thirty-nine of them, as well as the District of Columbia, by SPCAs or humane societies (the holdouts all being relatively new admittees to the union—Nevada, North Dakota, South Dakota, Idaho, and Wyoming).

The American Humane Association took the trouble to tally, based on all its member groups' reports for the year, the full law-enforcement activity being carried out by all those chapters nationwide, and the numbers were impressive for a nation of fewer than 75 million people: "Children relieved from distress or rescued from evil surroundings, many of them placed in homes, beneath whose fostering care they may grow toward manhood and womanhood, for the past year 28,446; animals relieved from suffering and cruel treatment, 125,093; persons prosecuted for offences against children and dumb beasts, 7,733; the total number of cases of all kinds investigated for the year, 98,507." The AHA also printed a world-wide roster of societies in the back of its annual report, showing how far the movement had spread beyond its English roots: Besides the many groups in the British Isles and throughout Western Europe, there were now societies in Algeria, South Africa, Argentina, Brazil, Australia, New Zealand, Tasmania, and elsewhere.

The new type of goodness was a selective benevolence. Animals no longer present in daily life had increasingly become an abstraction—sometimes to be fretted about, as in the case of certain wildlife threatened by human rapaciousness, but more often, as in the case of food animals, to be forgotten about. In 1896, much like today, self-conceived animal lovers put Armour's "dressed beef" on their dinner plates (or spread its "butterine" on their bread, or washed with the firm's cow-fat-based "Family Soap") without a thought for the animals from which these products were derived, or the brutal assembly-line process by which they were killed and rendered. That was now transpiring at a great distance, literally and metaphorically. Animal lovers could look about themselves with satisfaction because the cruelty was happening elsewhere.

·　　·　　·

The attitudes about animals that were most in motion, in 1896, were those concerning wild animals, and the role that modern Americans should take in their study and preservation. Gone were the days when a showman could, with unencumbered conscience, wrest a series of doomed whales out of the St. Lawrence and into a tiny enclosure in lower Manhattan, or pretend that such experiments in for-profit menagerie-making were actually an edifying exercise in "natural history." Circuses like Barnum's were still moving animals of all sizes and descriptions around the country, but a new generation of more scientific, more conservation-minded individuals were already puzzling over the question of how to responsibly bring wild animal species to the public. In 1896, the modern

answer to that question began to take shape—thanks to a letter that arrived in the very first week of January, in Buffalo, New York.

Addressed to a forty-one-year-old naturalist, taxidermist, author, and, more recently, real-estate speculator named William Temple Hornaday, the letter contained a surprising proposition. "I know that you have for some time retired from scientific life and have taken up active business, but the opening that presents itself for renewed scientific work in this City seems to me such a promising one that I trust it may cause you to give it serious consideration," wrote Columbia University paleontologist Henry Fairfield Osborn, on the advice of his scientific colleagues Joel A. Allen and C. Hart Merriam. Writing on behalf of the executive committee of the New York Zoological Society, Dr. Osborn expressed his sincere hope that Hornaday would agree to be considered for the directorship of an ambitious new zoo planned for the north of the city.

Embittered by a previous experience conceiving, securing funding, and creating a scheme for the National Zoo in Washington, D.C.—only to be forced out by a scientist-administrator who didn't share his expansive vision—Hornaday replied to Osborn's letter with guarded interest. "If it is your desire to secure the services of a man who is technically scientific,—an 'investigator,' a linguist, and a describer of new species,—then I am not the man for you," he cautioned. "[S]uch as they are I have my powers! I believe I am in touch with the general public, and know how to serve out popular natural history, for the millions, even though I cannot interest and instruct the technologists. I believe that if I have one mental gift that I prize, it is the creative faculty,—the power to originate."

Hornaday's "power to originate" had already taken him from a rustic midwestern boyhood to national prominence in the natural history profession. At age nineteen, his formal education, at Iowa State Agricultural College, concluded without a degree when he departed for an apprenticeship at Ward's Natural History Establishment in Rochester, New York (where Jumbo would later be stuffed). There, he learned the art of taxidermy so thoroughly that he was soon dispatched to collect his own specimens in Florida, Cuba, Barbados, Venezuela, India, Sri Lanka, and Borneo. "Fight in the Treetops," a naturalistic diorama painstakingly constructed from the fruits of those travels, depicting a moment of heated battle between an orangutan and a gibbon against a backdrop of rainforest vegetation, established Hornaday's reputation as an artist working in the medium of animal skins.

Appointed chief taxidermist in 1882 by the United States National Museum (then a branch of the Smithsonian Institution) in Washington, Hornaday thrived in his elevated position, growing and maintaining the National Museum's collection of taxidermic displays, creating large on-site exhibitions and preparing smaller traveling exhibits, which he accompanied to various U.S. cities. His museum work left him ample time to write for children and adults on animal-related topics, including, in 1885, a well-received book recounting his specimen-hunting adventures. In 1886, after reading an article describing the destruction of the North American bison, Hornaday quickly arranged a series of hunting trips to Montana, determined to obtain twenty high-quality hides for the Smithsonian collection—if he could find twenty buffalo left in the wild to kill. With some difficulty, he accomplished his objective, noting on his return trip that the expedition (which he liked to call the "last scientific buffalo hunt") had been undertaken "just in the nick of time," as the magnificent megafauna were just then on the brink of extinction.

The monumental diorama Hornaday would craft from the skins of the bison killed on that hunt, a grouping of six individuals, ranging from a spindly-legged calf to a magnificent bull he had bagged himself, became his greatest achievement as a museum taxidermist. While he spent his days piecing together his mammalian masterpiece, Hornaday worked in his after hours on a different kind of document on the disappearing species: a monograph entitled *The Destruction of the American Bison,* which detailed the habits, historical abundance, and human-caused devastation of the herds, recounting, with evident regret, the missed opportunities to preserve the imperiled species. He made no apologies for killing some of the last buffalo left on the plains, but underwent an awakening to the peril faced by North American wildlife. This moment marked the beginning of Hornaday's career as a conservationist, and led to him taking a professional interest in the preservation of living animals in captivity. He made his proposal for a Smithsonian Institution zoo not long afterward. His vision for a humane, educational, conservation-focused National Zoological Park would someday largely be realized, albeit without Hornaday's ongoing leadership. After his bitter standoff in 1890 with the Smithsonian's ruling secretary, Hornaday abandoned natural history in the nation's capital for real estate in upstate New York.

One month after Osborn's letter, while in town interviewing with the New York Zoological Society's executive committee, Hornaday visited the South Bronx, one of three locations under consideration for the new park. As he marveled at the unspoiled wildness of the site—glacier-carved ridges, rocky escarpments, verdant meadows, virgin forest, a coursing river, and a clean, clear lake—his vision for the future Bronx Zoo began to come into focus. "As I walked over the ground, again and again," he remembered later,

> and tried to imagine what would happen there if Noah should arrive with his arkful of animals and turn them loose, I saw the bison and the antelope seeking the rolling 20-acre meadow in the southeastern corner; the deer, elk, moose, and caribou scampering for the open sun-lit woods all along the west, where grass and shelter could be found together; the bears and foxes hiding in the rock ledges; the mountain sheep clambering to the top of the highest point of rocks, and the beaver scuttling into the deep, secluded pool where there are trees to be cut, and dams without number to be built.

The zoo Hornaday imagined, the zoo he would endeavor to build after his April 1896 appointment as director of the New York Zoological Park, used the native features of the South Bronx to create leafy, craggy, stream-fed enclosures for the animals on exhibit. He supposed, not unreasonably, that animals housed in a more naturalistic environment would behave more naturally. The pronghorns would graze, the prairie dogs would burrow, and the pintails would paddle around their pond. He wished, wherever possible, for the barriers between man and beast to be invisible, while most zoos continued to display animals in sparsely furnished cages. Rather than having visitors peer between iron bars at stressed-out animal inmates performing stereotypical behaviors or, worse, pelt them with pebbles or peanuts to provoke a personal response, Hornaday

hoped that those coming to the Bronx Zoo might experience animals similarly to how they would if they came upon them in the
wild. In so doing, they might have the opportunity to appreciate
the special qualities of each species, and foster a feeling for how
they fit into nature.

Like Noah, Hornaday saw his mission as one of preservation:
species imperiled by the catastrophic consequences of human
excesses could be protected from harm and encouraged to procre-
ate. Under his leadership, the Zoological Society made preservation and captive breeding explicit objects of their enterprise. "As
the vertebrate fauna of the world decreases," read the "Statement
of Plans and Purposes," a summary of Hornaday's philosophy that
prefaced the society's first annual report, "the need for collecting
and propagating living animals under protection becomes more
imperative. No civilized nation should allow its wild animals to
be exterminated without at least making an attempt to preserve
living representatives of all species that can be kept alive in confinement." Someday their offspring, like those of Noah's charges,
might repopulate the land where their ancestors formerly thrived.
It was an urgent proposition. "Throughout the entire continent of
North America, nearly every wild quadruped, bird, reptile, and
fish is marked for destruction," the society warned. "Apparently no
species is too large, too small, too worthless, or too remote to be
sought out and destroyed by gun, trap, net, or poison."

Hornaday knew that the animals native to North America and
elsewhere wouldn't have a future unless humans were taught to
value them in their wild state. "Unless we can create a sentiment
which will check this slaughter," argued the purpose statement, "or
devise laws for those who do not respect sentiment, the bones of
our now common types will become as rare as those of the dodo
and the great auk; and man will be practically the sole survivor
of the great world of life." Although Hornaday, and the society,
acknowledged the provision of public amusement as a major point
of any zoo, he sought to put education at the center of the New
York Zoological Park's mission, in the hope that the destruction of
animal life might be "checked by the spread of an intelligent love of
nature and its products." Through explanatory scientific labeling
of living exhibits, provision of an on-site library, and encourage-

ment of visual artists working from life to create two- and three-dimensional representations of resident beasts, the new zoo aimed to influence city-dwellers to value wildlife that they might otherwise never encounter face-to-face.

With the zeal of Barnum, Hornaday sought to create a big animal-based attraction of broad appeal. Within a week of accepting the position of director, he promised *The New York Times* he would deliver "a great institution for popular education in zoology, free as air, wherein the most interesting of the living of this continent, and others also, will be brought together and displayed under such pleasing and beautiful conditions that the study of zoology will become the most popular recreation of Greater New-York." Unfortunately, also like Barnum, Hornaday incorporated entertainments involving trained animals into his vision, in order to widen the appeal of the park. "Wild animal performances are no more cruel or unjust than men-and-women performances of acrobatics," he declared later. In an especially reprehensible (and also Barnum-esque) move, Hornaday exploited a Congolese Pygmy man, Ota Benga, displaying him in the primate house until an outraged group of African American clergymen forced him to stop.

Hornaday's vision of what a zoo could and should be, both for its animal inmates and its human visitors, still persists and is being perfected today. Not only do the National Zoo in Washington and the Bronx Zoo still bear his imprint, a hundred years after his retirement, but so too does any zoological park where the animals are displayed amid natural vegetation and coursing waterways, or are accompanied by plaques describing the natural history and conservation status of the species. Improvements in the provision of intellectual and social enrichments for animals build on his legacy, even as the hope that most captive breeding programs will lead to re-establishment of healthy wild populations has, for some time, seemed impossibly optimistic.

Eventually, Hornaday would shift his efforts from the preservation of captive wild animals to the conservation of animals in the wild, beginning with buffalo. In 1905, with Ernest Baynes and Theodore Roosevelt, he would found the American Bison Society, an organization dedicated to the survival of the wild buffalo. Two years later, fifteen captively bred Bronx Zoo bison would be

shipped to the Wichita Mountains Wildlife Refuge and Game Preserve in Oklahoma, the first native wild animal reintroduction in
North America. In the following years, additional animals would
be released in Montana, South Dakota, Nebraska, and elsewhere.
While still managing day-to-day operations at the Bronx Zoo, Hornaday increasingly made time to advocate for the establishment
of wildlife refuges, the safeguarding of fur seals, and protections
for migratory birds. His impassioned 1913 book, *Our Vanishing
Wildlife: Its Extermination and Preservation,* would exert a profound influence on the twentieth century's American conservation
movement.

.   .   .

Over the course of 1896, as plans for Hornaday's zoo began to come
together, the Audubon movement—largely snuffed out after George
Grinnell's abandonment of it in 1889—also re-ignited. In this case,
the spark was lit not by a letter but by a published article detailing
the bloody scene at a Florida heronry in the wake of a hunt, and
it prompted deep disgust and dismay in thirty-eight-year-old Harriet Hemenway. As a wealthy member of Boston's social elite, Hemenway frequently attended the lectures, performances, and parties
where feathers festooned women's heads, and as the daughter of an
abolition activist, she was quick to spot an opportunity to push for
moral progress. Clutching the clipping, Hemenway hurried across
Clarendon Street, in the city's Back Bay neighborhood, to confer
with her similarly well-connected cousin, Minna Hall.

Over tea, the two hatched a plan to prevent the inhumane slaughter of herons and other birds for the hat trade. Like the preserva-
tionists of the previous decade, Hemenway and Hall believed that
educating women about the cruel origins of their precious plumes
would help convince many to give them up, in favor of more benign
bows and baubles. But unlike Grinnell and his friends at the American Ornithologists' Union, they understood how much more compelling the message would be coming from females at the forefront
of fashion, and they determined to leverage their own social status
to persuade Boston's leading ladies to forswear their feathered hats.

Today's readers would think twice (we hope) about bedecking

themselves in fancy feathers, but it is worth pausing to appreciate what makes them so dazzling. A marvel of flexible, lightweight resilience, the pennaceous feather covers and contours the bird, providing protection against environmental elements and forming wing and tail surfaces for flight. Pigments and proteins embedded in each feather's microstructure—central rachis, radiating barbs, branching barbules—produce saturated color and shimmering iridescence, especially during breeding season, when many birds molt into a flashier feather-look in order to attract mates. Some species don't stop at a brighter wardrobe, but add additional feather elements to elevate their sex appeal. (Accessorize, accessorize, accessorize!) From peacock tails to quetzal streamers and puffin tufts, avian evolution often favors fanciful feathering for birds looking for love.

Egrets are no exception. When these willowy white herons prepare to breed, males and females sprout specialized filoplumes that flow behind them like a bridal veil, each a subtle work of art: a filamentous, arcing rachis, mostly bare, with a few, fine barbuleless barbs extending from its slender shaft. The effect enraptures bird and human alike. In 1872, the often-quoted British writer John Ruskin described the breeding egret: "Perfectly delicate in form, snow-white in plumage, the feathers like frost-work in dead silver, exquisitely slender, separating in the wind like the streams of a fountain, the creature looks like a living cloud rather than a bird."

Their exquisite plumage, and their habit of nesting near one another in crowded colonies, made egrets sitting ducks for the millinery feather trade—still flourishing a decade after the collapse of Grinnell's Audubon Society. In the midst of the economic depression that followed the Panic of 1893, wholesalers paid as much as thirty-five dollars per ounce of aigrettes, as the birds' breeding plumes were called, when an ounce of gold cost twenty. Since each adult egret produced only forty to sixty diaphanous plumes, many had to die to satisfy market demand. Hunters swarmed the southern swamps searching for the birds' remaining breeding colonies, hoping to make their fortune harvesting herons by the hundreds.

Middlemen shipped the precious plumes to London, Paris, and New York, where they were sorted, bundled, cleaned, and sometimes dyed before resale to milliners. During the winter of

1895–96, fashion favored mixed sprays of aigrettes and ostrich feathers secured by jeweled clasps or fancy bows. These served as an adornment for crushed turbans, ribboned hats, and prettily coiffed bare heads. Under the headline "The Importance of the Frolic Feather in This Season's Fashionable Frippery," one widely syndicated style writer complained, "Gladly would I write of aught save feathers, but how may one evade the fact? Thrust upon us every day in a new and more extravagant form, not to be ignored, catching the dullest eye, insisting, exhorting, commanding. The fact is that feathers rule the roast—or roost."

Hemenway and Hall were mounting a new attempt to dethrone them. Their effort began with the Blue Book, a catalog of the Boston-area elite, from which they compiled a list of prominent women likely to wear plumes in public. Next, the cousins planned a series of exclusive tea parties, inviting their bird-bedecked society sisters to partake of their impeccable hospitality as they plied them with arguments to abandon their objectionable headwear. Tea party by tea party, hundreds of wealthy and powerful Boston Brahmin women were persuaded to wear only feather-free fashions.

Harriet Hemenway

A few weeks later, in early February, Hemenway, Hall, and a contingent of their early converts formally founded the Massachusetts Audubon Society (named, like its predecessor, for the artist) and installed William Brewster, the ornithologist, as its president. The organization quickly expanded its activities from society tea parties to the publication of pamphlets, circulars, calendars, and bird identification charts. Although significant national-level victories were still years away, a shifting of the conversation about aigrette-wearing was already taking place. Newspapers now made frequent note of the cruel excesses of the millinery feather trade: "The mania for egret plumes is still so great that it seems to exceed the former one for wearing the bodies of birds," wrote a *Boston Globe* reporter in March. "Any observant person who notices these plumes waving, not singly, but often in clusters, on the heads of so many women must know that the slaughter has not been thousands, but millions." When another article discussing avian hat ornaments failed to mention their unpleasant origin—or the movement afoot to end their use—the society was quick to issue a reproach. "To the Editor of the [*Boston Evening*] *Transcript*," began their pointed letter, printed on October 24, 1886:

> Will you kindly allow the Massachusetts Audubon Society to correct some statements made in an article entitled "Use of Birds in Millinery," published in the Transcript of Oct. 17?
>
> While there may be a large call for feathers this winter, the fact that over one thousand persons, mostly in and about Boston, have joined our society and agreed not to wear or encourage the use of feathers of wild birds is evidence that there must be some decrease in the demand.

One year after its founding, the group had successfully lobbied the state to pass a law prohibiting the sale of wild bird feathers. As the society racked up accomplishments under its male leadership, Hemenway and Hall continued to involve fashion leaders in the dissemination of their message. In 1897, the club persuaded actress Martha Morton to insert a few words on behalf of birds into a play she was performing in at the Tremont theater. By the end of 1897, Pennsylvania, New York, New Hampshire, Illinois, Maine, the District of Columbia, Wisconsin, New Jersey, and Colorado had formed state Audubon chapters of their own, and Rhode Island, Ohio, Iowa, and Indiana were well on their way to doing the same.

The cousins applied the stick as deftly as the carrot in service of their cause: They regularly resorted to social censure to discourage the display of hat feathers. In a 1909 letter, Hall would scold Helen Herron Taft for wearing plumes to her husband's presidential inauguration. The long-lived cousins would both remain active in the Massachusetts (and, eventually, the National) Audubon Society into the middle of the twentieth century, each becoming well known for her independence, outspokenness, and defiance of convention—in politics and philanthropy as well as in fashion.

.   .   .

At seventy-three years of age, George Angell was, by 1896, the grand elder statesman of the campaign for animals in America. And yet for him, the cause of mercy was never about just domestic animals, or charismatic wild animals, or even animals at all. It was about everything.

This was why, during the first months of that year, the readers of *Our Dumb Animals* found that the lion's share of the publication was devoted to Angell's passion against war. The occasion was a diplomatic crisis then brewing with Great Britain, over a border dispute between British Guiana and Venezuela. President Grover Cleveland's secretary of state, Richard Olney, had determined that under the Monroe Doctrine—that seventy-five-year-old declaration of hemispheric supremacy—the United States held the unilateral right to arbitrate such disputes. Rhetoric with Britain had ratcheted up to the point that Congress was appropriating $100 million for a military buildup. In a rapid-fire series of dyspeptic, italics-strewn items, Angell gnashed his teeth at everyone agitating for war:

> *If we could have our way* war should never be declared except by a majority vote of the whole nation—wives and mothers should have the right to vote—and all men, *whether in the United States Senate or elsewhere,* who should seek to plunge us into an un-christian and un-holy war should be denounced *as public enemies* in every pulpit and newspaper, and on every platform of the land.

If we had the power we would send all those army and navy officers *who are so anxious to get the poor fellows under their command into a fight,* out into our Indian Territory to fight *each other,* and have a suitable force stationed near to *hang the survivors.*

We notice in the newspapers that a Congressional chaplain prayed *the Lord* the other day to *make this nation quick to resent insult.* This chaplain may have thought that he was praying *to the Lord* but he was really praying to a *very different individual.*

He railed against the Monroe Doctrine itself, calling it "perfect nonsense," and in response to Theodore Roosevelt's saber-rattling on the subject, he published two items lampooning "Ranchman Roosevelt" (who was then emerging as a national political figure), reminding his animal-loving readers of a series Roosevelt once published in which he admitted to having allowed cattle on his ranch to starve to death in winter.*

In response to Angell's diatribes, the *Chicago Tribune* called him "a fair illustration of the nonsense a man can utter when he has wheels in his head." The San Francisco *Examiner* described his articles as "wild-eyed treason." *The Sacramento Bee* reported that because of Angell's "sneering" about the Monroe Doctrine, local public schools had prohibited those issues of *Our Dumb Animals*— which the *Bee* described, in a headline, as "A Paper Which Seeks to Plant the Seeds of Disloyalty in the School-rooms of the Country."

To be sure, during the months that Angell's antiwar fever consumed him (the crisis would cool as the year progressed, with the border conflict amicably settled the following year), the animal cause was not absent from his thoughts. He had begun to agitate

---

* It was not to be Angell's last, or most consequential, fight with Roosevelt. Angell's contempt for the rising politician's pro-war politics, especially his theatrics with the "Rough Riders" in Cuba, combined with his love of big-game hunting, resulted in so many anti-Roosevelt missives in *Our Dumb Animals* that the paper was banned, for a time, from the Washington, D.C., schools.

George Angell,
undated photograph.

on the vivisection cause, offering a bounty of $100 for anyone who
provided evidence of cruel animal experimentation in Massachusetts; perhaps as a result of this offer, he also aired a report—from
a "perfectly reliable authority"—that medical students at Boston University were being required to "operate on many cats and
dogs," but had been "cautioned not to talk on the subject with outside parties." He inveighed, month after month, against the equine
check rein and the docking of tails. He evangelized his Bands of
Mercy, the roster of which now stretched past 25,000.

He had even found a successor to *Black Beauty.* In 1893, his
American Humane Education Society held a prize competition,
offering $200 to the three best novels about kindness and cruelty.
One of the twenty-one entries came from a thirty-two-year-old
writer in Nova Scotia—herself, like Angell, the daughter of a Baptist preacher—named Margaret Marshall Saunders, who had been
inspired by Sewell's novel to try her hand at a similar story with a
canine narrator. The result was *Beautiful Joe,* a highly fictionalized
reimagining of a story of terrible cruelty that Saunders had heard
about: a dog in Ontario whose owner treated it brutally, even cutting off its ears and tail, before it was rescued by a kind family.

Unlike in Sewell's tale, the dog's deliverance comes very early
on, with the rest of the story given over to his happy new family,

and to the quaint dramas faced by domestic animals in small-town Canada. Even so, the formal debt to *Black Beauty* was so explicit that *Beautiful Joe*'s narrator makes a puckish reference to it in the first chapter: "I am an old dog now, and am writing, or rather getting a friend to write, the story of my life. I have seen my mistress laughing and crying over a little book that she says is a story of a horse's life, and sometimes she puts the book down close to my nose to let me see the pictures." After winning one of the $200 prizes, *Beautiful Joe* was published later in 1893, with a dedication to Angell. By the end of 1896 it had sold 200,000 copies. It would go on to become the first book by a Canadian author to surpass a million copies in sales.

Still, Angell's moral fervor just couldn't be confined to animals alone. Even as the year went on and war fever subsided, he could be found announcing the results of a new writing prize, $100 for the "best plans of settling the difficulties between capitalism and labor." He railed against the nation's growing concentration of wealth and the rise in social tensions it was engendering; more than a century before Bernie Sanders's crusade against billionaires, Angell declared that every millionaire (a net worth equivalent, today, to less than $34 million) was a policy failure:

> We think a peaceful way out of this great national danger may be found through *limiting the amount of property which any one person shall be permitted to hold* and compelling all over that sum to be given to charities, or by severe taxation paid into the public treasury, for public improvements or otherwise.
>
> If this be declared unconstitutional then *change the constitution.*
>
> But what shall the limit be?
>
> Well, we think that a million of dollars is about as much as one person should be permitted to hold.

He fumed at the unrepresentative nature of the U.S. Senate, noting that "little states of some 50,000 or more population have the same power to enact or prevent the enactment of laws as the great states of New York and Pennsylvania." He floated a version of what would eventually become the New Deal, saying, "A million men could be easily employed today at fair wages on needed public improvements, and there is plenty of money to pay them *only it is not rightly divided*."

No doubt Angell had seen enough to know that none of his causes were advancing in lockstep, if they could be said to be advancing at all. He knew that the nation's moral landscape could wither in places even as it flourished in others. He pleaded for the restriction of vivisection at colleges, knowing full well that the powerful presidents of Harvard and other prestigious schools were fighting hard against him. He seemed to understand that on the matter of militarism and the Monroe Doctrine, the raw passions of the American public ran against his pacifism. Even the check rein, the easiest thing in the world for a horse owner to forswear, persisted purely out of a stubborn allegiance to fashion among the urban elite.

All Angell could do was implore his readers, hope for the best, and stay focused on persuading the generations to come. "One thing we must never forget," read an item he placed in the magazine over and over again—seemingly as a reminder to himself; he was, after all, getting on in years—was *that the infinitely most important work for us is the humane education of the millions who are soon to come on the stage of action.*" If the issues are different today, the invocation is a wise one, in times of advancement, stagnation, or even reaction: Look to the future. For what else, in the end, is there to do?

"The victims of the pot and pan— / Went forth against the tyrant man."

Afterword

THE EXPLODED CIRCLE

George Thorndike Angell breathed his last in the early hours of March 16, 1909, at the age of eighty-five. He died, as one newspaper put it, "in the harness": still in command of the Massachusetts SPCA, of the American Humane Education Association, and of *Our Dumb Animals,* despite the ravages of kidney disease and a failing heart. In his funeral procession the following Saturday, two columns of working horses tromped behind the hearse, thirty-six of them in all, a mourning rosette affixed to each of their bridles—the animals themselves seeming to recognize, *The Boston Globe*'s reporter observed, that "something out of the ordinary was taking place."

Angell had lived to see nearly a decade of the new century, one from which those working horses—the inspiration for so much of his work, and that of Henry Bergh, Caroline Earle White, and the rest of the founding generation of animal activists—would soon disappear. In 1899, Alexandre Liautard's *American Veterinary Review* had dismissed any thought of the horse's displacement by the car: "As a pleasure vehicle it may be possible to pass over good roads with speed and comfort in the automobile," an editorial scoffed, "but when the novelty wears away it will lack the life, interest and pleasure of man's best friend." And yet in the year 1917, mere months after White passed away at age eighty-three at her residence on Nantucket, the last horsecar was retired in New York; horsepower, the force that ran the nineteenth-century city, was quickly being relegated to the status of metaphor.

·   ·   ·

We have tried to make the case here that three decades, from 1866 to 1896, saw the birth of the modern attitudes of Americans toward the animals in their midst. But we would be remiss in not noting some of the twentieth century's most important milestones in that evolving relationship. Four in particular stand out to us:

1900: The Lacey Act, passed at the urging of the new generation of Audubon societies and other conservation activists, created stiff federal penalties for the trade in birds and other game that had been illegally captured or killed, providing the crucial missing piece in a nationwide legal regime to protect threatened species. Later that year, the elevation of Theodore Roosevelt to the presidency, after the assassination of William McKinley, would eventually result in the setting aside of enormous public lands for those species to at least attempt to hold on: 230 million acres in all, spread over scores of new parks, protected forests, and animal preserves.

1906: Though the fairness of Upton Sinclair's portrait of the meatpacking industry was hotly contested (and remains a controversial subject to this day), *The Jungle* provoked a flurry of congressional investigations and hearings in the months after its publication. This resulted, that same year, in the passage of the landmark Federal Meat Inspection Act, which created much stronger oversight of the sanitary conditions in which American livestock were slaughtered, while doing essentially nothing to regulate the cruelty of the killing process. Sinclair, a committed socialist, had hoped his book would lead to outrage over the treatment of workers by Armour & Company and the other packing giants, and was chagrined to see how wholly the response to his book focused on the issue of meat safety—famously quipping, "I aimed at the public's heart, and by accident I hit it in the stomach," a witticism that could just as easily have applied to the novel's failure to move Americans on the issue of cruelty to animals in slaughterhouses.

1933: This was the year that the Jackson Laboratory in Bar Harbor, Maine, released a price list for an unusual line of products, one that augured a wholesale transformation in the world of medical research: ten different "stocks" of standardized, inbred lab mice, sold at ten cents apiece with a money-back guarantee. Arguments centered on cruelty had not, in the main, persuaded researchers to abandon experimentation on dogs and other beloved animal species, but the rise of genetics—alongside an understanding that genetic variation in study subjects could skew the validity of trial results—made it no longer scientifically acceptable to carry out experiments on just any old animal from the city pound. Thanks to the deft inbreeding techniques of the Jackson Lab's murine maestro, Clarence Cook Little, these mice lines (particularly the one called "C57Black," known today as Black-6 after the slot that it occupied on Little's price list), were hardy, predictable, and phenomenally prolific at multiplying, perfect for fueling the meteoric rise in scientific experimentation over the course of the twentieth century. Today, well over 90 percent of all laboratory animals are mice or rats, a nonstop rodent bloodbath that horrifies some animal-rights activists but has mostly brought down the temperature on the nation's "vivisection" debates.

1947: Edward Lowe, working at his father's construction-supply business in South Bend, Indiana, suggested to a friend that she try filling her "cat box"—which some die-hard cat lovers had begun using, generally filled with sand or dirt, to allow their pets to relieve themselves indoors—with an unusual clay product he had lying around. The result was remarkable, absorbing the cat urine and its odor without dirtying cat paws. So Lowe began marketing the pebbly clay, now known as fuller's earth, under the brand name Kitty Litter. The rise of the modern litter box ultimately is what convinced millions of Americans to bring cats inside, helping to put the cat on equal footing with the dog as a beloved family pet. (In the spirit of equal time, though, it's also worth mentioning another development of the post–World War II era, one that helped strengthen the bond between Americans and dogs: the rise of mandatory rabies vaccination—Alexandre Liautard's great idea—which soon eradicated the canine rabies strain in the United States, removing an ancient and justifiable source of anti-dog sentiment.)

There are many other milestones, closer to our own day, that we could list—for example, the book *Animal Liberation* by the philosopher Peter Singer, published in 1975; the birth of the "no-kill" animal-shelter movement, jump-started in 1989 when San Francisco, in cooperation with its local SPCA, set a goal of 100 percent adoption rates; the shockingly effective anti-fur campaigns carried out by People for the Ethical Treatment of Animals (beginning around *1990*)—all the way up to the *2016* decision by Ringling Brothers and Barnum & Bailey to finally stop exhibiting elephants.

But all of these developments seem to have cemented the pattern, the selective care for certain species and not others, that was plainly visible way back in *1896*. America's adoration for dogs and cats has deepened to the point that we will spare no expense for their health and well-being; even euthanasia, long blessed by animal activists (including Singer) as an acceptable solution for suffering or neglect, is now met with some hesitance as pets continue to approach the moral status of people. Charismatic wildlife species, likewise, command legislative action and huge streams of donations to groups that advocate for them: to save the whales, or the sea turtles, or the polar bears. Even the wolf, so long a target of extermination in the United States, has become a darling of conservation activists who fight to preserve its tenuous numbers and its fragile right to roam, despite the demonstrable harm to the interests of human ranchers.

Meanwhile, per capita consumption of pork—harvested from an animal every bit as intelligent as a dog, if not more so—is roughly equal to what it was in *1965*. Those pigs are slaughtered, it must be said, in a manner considerably less savage than the one practiced in *1890*s Packingtown: Thanks to the Humane Slaughter Act (*1958*), federal law now requires that animals be "rendered insensible to pain by a single blow or gunshot or an electrical, chemical or other means that is rapid and effective, before being shackled, hoisted, thrown, cast, or cut." With pigs, this is generally done either with electrocution or by suffocation in a carbon-dioxide chamber; with cattle, the method of choice is the captive-bolt gun. (Per capita beef consumption is significantly down since the 1960s, but consumption of chicken has skyrocketed—an animal, notably, whose killing is not covered by the Humane Slaughter Act.)

If the conditions of its death have improved, the living conditions of the American food animal remain grim. Despite years of promises by meat producers and corporate customers to end the practice, many sows are still kept almost permanently in seven-foot-by-two-foot "gestation crates," too small to turn around in. Dairy cows, which naturally live to the age of twenty on average, are stimulated to produce so much milk that they generally are no longer useful after three to four years, a life of incessant milking that ends in premature slaughter. The rise of concentrated animal feeding operations (CAFOs) has doomed millions of pigs, cattle, and chickens to entire lifespans spent cheek by jowl in the stench of their own waste—waste that also threatens the health of nearby communities and ecosystems.

As of this writing, America is home to roughly 99 million cattle and 74 million pigs: populations that exceed those of dogs and cats (84 million and 60 million, respectively, in the most recent AVMA survey) in scale, but the welfare of which commands so much less of our moral attention. It's not that they're less intelligent, or less capable of suffering. It's not that we *owe* them any less; our patterns of consumption lead to their existence and their treatment. We simply don't care enough about them—at least not yet.

.   .   .

It can be easy to be pessimistic about humans' capacity for moral transformation. Social scientists often find, in interviews with individual subjects, that no amount of reason and evidence will unsettle their instincts about right and wrong, even when those instincts manifestly result in prejudice or hatred toward others. In explaining such resistance, often these experts will invoke evolution, pointing out that the human brain was forged in an era marked by tight kinship bands and deep mistrust of outsiders. The psychologist Jonathan Haidt, who has become the nation's most persuasive commentator on the limits of persuasion, has compared our deeply ingrained moral attitudes to an elephant atop which our conscious power of reasoning is merely a tiny rider, lacking much ability to steer the ancient beast that bears us along.

Yet on larger timescales than the typical research study can capture, we know that moral change *does* happen, often at profound scale and remarkable speed. To some degree, this is merely a function of replacement, as humans mired in old attitudes die off. But often we see profound change that sweeps up individuals of all ages, as evidenced by the thirty-point swing in just twelve years (to 70 percent in 2021, up from 40 percent in 2009) in support for gay marriage in America. It's arguable that the rise of an animal-welfare consciousness in America between 1866 and 1876—aided, of course, by the development of the idea in England and then Europe over the preceding decades—represented a shift of similar breadth and speed.

How can humans, so often impervious to persuasion in the short term, succumb so wholly to new norms in a matter of years? Whatever the underlying psychology might be, it's worth observing that these shifts, at least after they happen, are codified through analogies that would have seemed impossible or offensive beforehand, much as a comparison of animal suffering to human suffering might feel to certain readers today. "If men can vote, why shouldn't women?" "If the nation welcomes immigrants from Europe, why not those from Asia or Africa?" "If businesses should be legally forced to serve people of all races, why not also require that they accommodate people with disabilities?" In the analogies they contain, such questions often have been seen as laughable or offensive until they become urgent and then, finally, irresistible. The so-called Golden Rule—*Do unto others as you would have others do unto you*—has been formulated in countless ways across different eras and cultures, and one way of seeing the history of moral change is as the continual erasing, and more capacious redrawing, of the line that defines which "others" are worthy of consideration.

This metaphor of an expanding "circle" of care dates back at least to Humphry Primatt in 1776 ("our Love and Mercy are not to be confined within the circle of our own friends, acquaintance, and neighbours . . . but are to be extended to every object of the Love and Mercy of GOD *the universal parent*"). A century later, the same metaphor was adopted by William Edward Hartpole Lecky in his two-volume tome from 1869, *A History of European Morals from Augustus to Charlemagne*. Surveying the two millennia that separated the beginning of his study period, in the Roman empire, and the time of his writing, Lecky perceived a steady growth in consciousness among individuals and societies alike. At first, Lecky writes, "the benevolent affections embrace merely the family," but "soon the circle expanding includes first a class, then a nation, then a coalition of nations, then all humanity, and finally, its influence is felt in the dealings of man with the animal world."

In our own time, the metaphor has been picked up by Peter Singer, the thinker who has done more than any other to advance the idea of animal rights. In his book *The Expanding Circle*, which takes Lecky's passage as its epigraph, Singer declares that excluding animals from our moral consideration is as abhorrent as excluding people of other races. He goes on: "The only justifiable stopping place for the expansion of altruism is the point at which all whose welfare can be affected by our actions are included within the circle of altruism. This means that all beings with the capacity to feel pleasure or pain should be included; we can improve their welfare by increasing their pleasures and diminishing their pains." To Singer, extending our circle to animals means that even if we don't see their interests on the whole as equal to those of humans, we must count their pain and suffering to be just as pressing a moral concern as ours.*

What would it take to inaugurate a *new* new type of goodness, one that convinced Americans to take seriously their responsibility to the nation's food animals? The obvious answer would be to convince people to "expand their circle" yet more, to encompass species they might hitherto have considered to lie beneath moral notice. Science might help: more research, for example, that confirms the intelligence of pigs (British psychologists recently taught some to play video games), or close observational studies that show the biomarkers of stress and suffering they express while in factory-farm conditions. Analogy, as ever, could be invoked for emotional impact: What if you yourself, or your children, or your dogs and cats, were forced to live and die the way America's pigs do?

But it's also worth acknowledging how the metaphor of the circle has become strained since Lecky's day, as the world has become radically more populous, interconnected, and complex. Yes, one reason why some of our "circles" do not yet extend to pigs, the

---

* We do not embrace this position, even as we respect its severe logic. It's true that Singer's strident principles were what allowed him, writing in the 1970s, to perceive and call out the monstrosity of industrialized livestock production long before other animal advocates were willing to do so. But there are other issues around which a certain degree of "speciesism" seems to us unavoidable—particularly medical research on animals, which under some conditions cannot yet be replaced by alternatives.

way they do to dogs or cats, is ingrained prejudice just waiting to be overcome: those selective attitudes toward certain species that we have inherited as a culture, which can dissipate as our so-called circles expand. But another, more vexing reason is that the animals our society treats the most cruelly tend to be those that now live at an enormous remove from us, physically and in other senses as well—and crucially, the link between our actions and their suffering has become more distant too, more indirect, more mediated. It is a supercharged version of a problem that began with the Union Stock Yards and the rise of the Chicago meatpacking industry, where actions that once would have been performed in one's community, forcing one (for better or worse) to witness them, are now performed many hundreds of miles away at staggeringly greater scale.

On Henry Bergh's theory of cruelism, this shift could be seen as progress, but in reality, it has made the task of engaging consciences more difficult. For when livestock become mere industrial inputs housed far from human society, not only does the incentive toward cruelty increase, our individual responsibility becomes simultaneously thinner and wider. All the dairy products consumed by an eighteenth-century farm family would often have derived from a single cow, one whose treatment they personally oversaw and bore full moral responsibility for. But the half gallon of milk you buy at the supermarket will mingle the output of many cows, often from multiple farms, all of them totally outside your realm of experience. Over the course of a year, it would be reasonable to assume that thousands of cows created the milk that goes into the food you eat: the foam on your latte, the cheese in your burrito, the whey in your processed supermarket items. Even vegans arguably bear some responsibility for propping up the animal economy, if they patronize businesses that also sell animal-based products: Once the problem is understood systemically, there is no limit to how many degrees of culpability the moral ledger can tally. And this in turn leads to a debilitating moral fatigue, as the burden of adding up tiny fractions of responsibility for so many distant animals becomes too hard to process.

Needless to say, this problem is not confined to animal welfare. The most vivid version of it revolves around climate change. No one could doubt that our "circles" of moral concern include our own descendants, but when it comes to the climate issue, millions of Americans are acting in ways that threaten the well-being of their own great-grandchildren, if not their grandchildren, some of them already living. This willful disregard can't be entirely blamed on the effects of fossil-fuel propaganda and misinformation: Even those of us who "believe the science" often struggle to act as if we do. Neither can this dissonance be chalked up, at least not entirely, to the sacrifices involved in forswearing carbon-emitting behaviors. Much like the distance (in all senses of the word) that exists between a hamburger order and the suffering of a hypothetical cow in a feedlot somewhere in the country, the distance between that hamburger and a deadly future heat wave in South Asia—roughly one-seventh of all carbon emissions worldwide, it's estimated, can be traced back to meat production, barely less than the global total for every form of transportation combined—is hard for us to bridge in our minds.

Climate change is commingled, as well, with the catastrophic state of the world's wildlife populations. For all the attention paid to polar bears and wolves, a recent University of Arizona study analyzed data about 538 different plant and animal species from hundreds of sites around the world and determined that nearly half of them were in danger of climate-related extinction. A 2019 research effort found that wild North American birds— some of the same species that powered the birth of the Audubon movement—had seen their populations plummet by a third in just fifty years, an estimated decline of 2.9 billion birds in all. Right under our noses, scientists are warning of an "insect apocalypse": involving, for example, a 90 percent drop in U.S. butterflies in two decades, and an 87 percent decline in one formerly common bee species, the rusty-patched bumblebee. If the problem of extending our "circles" to a boundless multitude of distant food animals is hard enough, it's harder still when we are asked to ponder the consequences of human action on species we know nothing about, the roster of their names too long to digest, let alone memorize.

.   .   .

The new type of goodness that spread in the late nineteenth century was all about expanding the circle. The new type of goodness we need today has to *explode* the circle, in a sense. Because the worst problems we face are systemic in nature, we need a morality to match, one that allows us to attach gut-level moral urgency to our marginal roles in an infinitude of injustices, for which the line between cause and effect is hard to trace.

The most profound thinker on this problem is Dale Jamieson, a professor of environmental studies at New York University, whose book *Reason in a Dark Time* offers a bracing diagnosis of the moral bind that humanity finds itself in on the climate issue. In an interview at his office, Jamieson pointed out that there's a long tradition across cultures of forgiving even direct *second*-order consequences of human behavior—as in the Catholic doctrine of "double effect," first articulated by Thomas Aquinas in the thirteenth century: "Nothing hinders one act from having two effects, only one of which is intended, while the other is beside the intention." Under this doctrine, as long as that first, intended effect is moral, then the act can be permissible, even if that second effect would normally cause the act to be forbidden—and even if that collateral effect is fully foreseeable.

Moreover, it's a relatively short stretch of human history in which moral dilemmas have even been *perceived* as systemic. As the historian Peter Bernstein lays out in his book *Against the Gods: The Remarkable Story of Risk,* the Western intellectual tradition took centuries to push past an ingrained sense of individual, divinely ordained fate in order to develop the concepts of risk and probability, which in turn were necessary to allow the kinds of statistical investigations that underpin our current ways of understanding the world. Not until the nineteenth century did those techniques allow for the birth of statistical forms of public-health research, the early version of what we now call epidemiology.

Our academic modes of systematizing human society are all roughly of similar vintage: economics, political science, social psychology, and the other "social sciences" didn't really coalesce until the early twentieth century. And meanwhile, of course, everything *became* more interconnected over the course of that century, as economies and communication technologies grew ever more nationalized and then, soon, globalized. That is: Even as it's taken centuries to awaken to the systemic nature of some social problems, other problems have become truly systemic only in recent decades. And then there are the problems like climate change, which it took an unfathomably complicated global economy to create in the first place.

From a moral perspective, one vexing feature of systemic cause-and-effect relationships is that they tend to expose everything we do to moral judgment—or even what we *don't* do, because we contribute to systemic problems by doing nothing. A reluctance to accept this kind of moral logic is especially pronounced in the contemporary West, Jamieson observed in our interview: Historically "there's a public sphere, and there's a private sphere, and the government has no business in intervening in the private sphere," he says. "But one of the problems with climate change—and generally these kinds of globalized problems we have—is that they're actually driven by things that we do in the traditional private sphere. Right? About what we eat, and what we consume, and how we get from one place to another. And that's part of the profundity of the challenge, and also makes it very difficult for government to regulate the behaviors that drive climate change."

If understanding problems as systemic before the twentieth century was far rarer than it is today, campaigns of *activism* against systemic problems, ones that took their systemic nature into account, were vanishingly uncommon. A notable exception, which Jamieson sees as an important case study for climate activists, was the campaign against slavery that began in the late eighteenth century. In particular, he zeroes in on the "blood sugar" campaign in England, in which abolitionists persuaded some 300,000 Britons to join a boycott of the nation's largest import because it was harvested by enslaved people in the West Indies. As an act of consciousness-raising, it was remarkable: hundreds of thousands of consumers forgoing sugar to protest brutality against people whom they didn't know at all, who weren't even being brutalized nearby, who really were an abstraction in much the same way that distant food animals or the future victims of climate change are abstractions to us today.

Does systems-driven moral thinking really have a chance? As we write, in the long shadow of the COVID-19 pandemic, it's possible to see the case for optimism. After all, on its way to killing millions of people worldwide, the pandemic presented us with a set of systemic moral problems every bit as complicated and tangled as those surrounding climate change—some involving weighing the risk to ourselves and our loved ones, but many of them about weighing the risk our actions pose to people we will never meet or know. Think about the kind of reasoning that so many of us began to internalize as we weighed our daily affairs: Even if *I*, given my risk factors (age/vaccination status/general health), needn't worry too much about dying from a COVID infection, nevertheless my decision to head out into a public space, unmasked or even masked, might cause me unwittingly to transmit the virus to someone else, who in turn might transmit it to others.

It was a far cry from the reaction to the Spanish flu a century ago. True, there were widespread school closures around the nation, and public-health ads with slogans like SPIT SPREADS DEATH or STAY AT HOME—IT HAS NEVER BEEN EASIER TO SAVE LIVES. But those attempts hardly penetrated to the degree they have today, when epidemiological language has become common parlance—consider the brief ubiquity of "flatten the curve," a catchphrase about a line graph—and many Americans wound up arguing for stricter public policy than the experts did. (In January 1919, a San Francisco alderman was probably being only a little hyperbolic when he estimated that "91½ percent" of local residents disapproved of reinstating the city's mask mandate.)

For all the callousness that some Americans displayed about the novel coronavirus and its consequences, it's far more remarkable to think about how many other Americans managed to internalize the complex chain of moral logic it demanded. And it's a chain that, once constructed in your mind, is hard to sever: Whether you're thinking of buying a hamburger, on the one hand, or throwing a party in a pandemic, on the other, forcing yourself to think hard about the suffering that might thereby result—days or months or even years down the line—makes it difficult to look at that decision in quite the same way again.

.   .   .

The dislocations of the pandemic taught Americans something else very important, too: All around the country, they learned to value animals as never before. Millions of households adopted dogs during lockdown, flooding veterinary clinics with patients. Pet-related businesses took off, reporting billions of dollars in new spending—on toys, beds, and coats; on grooming, walks, and boarding; on crates, carriers, and strollers; on dental chews for cats' teeth, CBD chews for dogs' anxiety; on GPS activity monitors, to track pets' whereabouts and count their steps.

Within the pet food industry, no segment grew faster than "fresh" dog food—companies like Freshpet, Ollie, Nomnom, and Just Food for Dogs, which offer "human-grade" foods for beloved pups instead of kibble or cans. Prices from one of the leading brands, The Farmer's Dog, run to $3 per day for a small dog to as high as $10 or more for a large one, delivered to one's door in customized plastic pouches that come preprinted with the animal's name: "Rex's Beef Recipe, Packed with ♥." In a comical inversion of the age-old debate on animal research, The Farmer's Dog touts that its foods are "tested on humans."

Even more comical, if you stop to think about it, is the company's name. In the eighteenth century, most owned dogs *were* farmer's dogs, working animals that herded livestock and scared birds away from crops. In exchange, in addition to the porridge and other inexpensive, vegetarian foodstuffs that pre-modern dogs tended to be fed, they might have enjoyed some scraps of animal protein the family didn't want—a tradition that carries on today in the form of commercial dog foods, which make use of the meat by-products that supermarkets can't sell. But as The Farmer's Dog understands, there are pet owners, most of whom live far from farms in every sense, willing to pay handsomely for the myth of a different kind of farmer's dog: one who gets "human-grade" foods cooked especially for him, which means animals killed specifically for him; one whose gastronomic needs deserve to be filled at a cost of hundreds of dollars a month, to say nothing of his grooming, boarding, walking, and more.

Far be it from us to say that any dog is cared for too much. But owners who spend $10 per day on dog food—which exceeds what the poorest 20 percent of American households spend on groceries—might reflect on whether their communities might also benefit from similar largesse. When it comes to many of today's pet owners, it seems, the question isn't whether dogs and cats fall inside their circle of affections; it's whether enough of their fellow humans do, in an era of technology-driven isolation and alienation. Indeed, "expanding our circles" today might require inverting the old analogy, in a whole new spin on the Golden Rule: *Love thy neighbor as thy pet.*

Better still, we might use our own reservoirs of pet love—the deep adoration we feel for the animals we're privileged to live with—as well-springs from which to love, and to aid, all those distant, unseen animals we know only as abstractions. Such animals include the sows in "gestation cages" and all the other food animals mired in feedlot existences that, while stopping well short of illegal cruelty, can hardly be regarded as happy lives, as well as the wildlife species threatened by habitat destruction and climate change, so numerous and far-flung that we may never learn the full list of species snuffed out. Any new type of goodness takes a new kind of mental discipline, an insistence that we recode everyday actions that once seemed innocuous—whether flogging a horse or ordering a hamburger—as intolerable acts of cruelty, because they will result in the suffering of sentient creatures. Just as our powers of imagination were capable of such a leap in 1866, they are capable of the more difficult leap we face today. It is time, once again, to put them to work.

of Cruelty to Animals, Susanne Whitaker at the American Veterinary Medical History Society, Jaimie Fritz at the American Kennel Club, and Jonathan Walford at the Fashion History Museum in Cambridge, Ontario. Thanks, also, to the staffs of the Abraham Lincoln Presidential Library, the Temple University Special Collections Research Center, the Historical Society of Pennsylvania, the New-York Historical Society, the Columbia University Health Sciences Library, NYU's Lillian and Clarence de la Chapelle Medical Archives, the New York Public Library, and, last but not least, the Brooklyn Public Library system and its interlibrary loan staff.

And finally, thanks and love to our friends and family—especially our son, Emmett, who has had to listen to us talk about the animals of nineteenth-century America for a significant portion of his (otherwise fairly happy) childhood.

ACKNOWLEDGMENTS

First and foremost, we're indebted to our editor at Knopf, Jon Segal—friend of authors and animals alike—who understood this project from the very beginning and never flagged as its ally and counselor. Thanks, too, to his assistants, Sarah Perrin and Isabel Ribeiro, as well as to the whole Knopf team: Susanna Sturgis, Amy Brosey, Romeo Enriquez, Michael Collica, Elora Weil, Demetri Papadimitropoulos, Emily Murphy, and more.

Our agent, Elyse Cheney, gave crucial guidance all along the way, and helped crystallize for us the book we wanted to write. Some friends helped us with invaluable advice and early reads—in particular, Caleb Crain, who was kind enough to look at many of our chapters at a moment when we weren't entirely sure where the project was going. Laurel Frydenborg and Heather McCurdy each lent a veterinarian's eye; Steven Johnson helped us think through some of the big ideas, and Josh Kendall helped us make some key decisions.

The three years during which we researched and wrote this book were thrown into chaos by the COVID-19 pandemic, and we're deeply grateful to everyone who helped us get access to source materials during this historically difficult moment for libraries and archives: Rob Halpin at the Massachusetts SPCA, Christina Perella at the Historical Medical Library of the College of Physicians of Philadelphia, Leela Outcalt and Christina Chavez at the Museum of the City of New York, Dan Harper at the University of Illinois Chicago, Rebecca Goldrick at the American Society for the Prevention

NOTES

Introduction: A New Type of Goodness

3 **"loud rushing roar"**: Alexander Wilson, *Wilson's American Ornithology* (Boston: Otis, Broaders, and Company, 1840), 400.

3 **"the trampling of thousands of horses"**: James Fenimore Cooper, *The Chainbearer* (London: Richard Bentley, 1845), 107.

3 **"a hard gale at sea"**: John James Audubon, *Ornithological Biography, or an Account of the Habits of the Birds of the United States of America* (Philadelphia: E. L. Carey and A. Hart, 1832), 324.

3 **"The sound was condensed terror"**: Quoted in A. W. Schorger, *The Passenger Pigeon: Its Natural History and Extinction* (Madison: University of Wisconsin Press, 1955), 189.

4 **"a scene of uproar"**: Audubon, *Ornithological Biography*, 324.

4 **Mark Twain, in a memoir**: Mark Twain, *Mark Twain's Autobiography*, vol. 1 (New York: Harper & Brothers, 1906), 114.

4 **stewed with salt pork**: Mrs. D. A. Lincoln, *Mrs. Lincoln's Boston Cook Book: What to Do and What Not to Do in Cooking* (Boston: Robert's Brothers, 1894), 262–63. See also Mrs. S. T. Rorer, *Philadelphia Cook Book: A Manual of Home Economies* (Philadelphia: Arnold and Company, 1886), 200–202.

4 **Trappers devised a spring-pole apparatus**: Charles D. Stewart, "The Pigeon Trap," *Wisconsin Magazine of History* 24 (September 1940): 20–24.

4 **Packs of pigeons were lured**: F.E.S., "Netting Wild Pigeons," *Forest and Stream* 43 (July 14, 1894): 28. See also William Brewster, "The Present Status of the Wild Pigeon (*Ectopistes migratorius*) as a Bird of the United States, with Some Notes on Its Habits," *The Auk* 6 (October 1889): 285.

4 **Once captured**: Brewster, "Present Status of the Wild Pigeon," 288. See also F.E.S., "Netting Wild Pigeons," 29.

4 **But quite a few**: Schorger, *Passenger Pigeon*, 157–66.

4 **Often these shootoffs**: "Mr. Bergh and the Pigeon Shoot," *Brooklyn Union*, June 22, 1881, 2.

5 **"A man will sit up all night"**: *Our Dumb Animals*, February 1879, 67.

5 **"for the purpose of a target"**: *Our Dumb Animals*, March 1879, 76.

5 **He attended a meeting:** George Thorndike Angell, *Autobiographical Sketches and Personal Reflections* (Boston: Franklin Press, 1884), 63.

5 **Soon thereafter, Angell secured:** Ibid.

5 **and soon after the turn:** Joel Greenberg, *A Feathered River Across the Sky* (New York: Bloomsbury, 2014), 170–73.

6 **On an evening in that same spring:** *Our Dumb Animals,* April 1879, 82.

6 **A mere decade later:** Ibid.

6 **The Massachusetts SPCA now had:** Ibid.

7 **in the state of New York:** American Society for the Prevention of Cruelty to Animals, *Fourteenth Annual Report (for 1879),* 13.

7 **"hell of horrors":** *New York Herald,* March 29, 1879, 8.

7 **"It may almost be said of Henry Bergh":** "Henry Bergh and His Work," *Scribner's,* April 1879, 872.

8 **a dissolute and sinful young man:** Rev. Abial Fisher, "George Angell," in *Annals of the American Pulpit,* vol. 6 (New York: Carter and Brothers, 1860), 599.

8 **rendering him so lifeless:** Angell, *Autobiographical Sketches,* 1–2.

8 **Under the influence of his first wife:** Fisher, "George Angell," 600–601.

9 **he carried a piece of paper:** Angell, *Autobiographical Sketches,* 2.

9 **"It has long been my opinion":** Ibid., 7–8.

10 **Passing by a cattle market:** Ibid., 8.

10 **"If any man believes":** Speech reprinted in *Our Dumb Animals,* April 1879, 82. Repunctuated for clarity.

Chapter 1: Kindling Kindness

17 **From their nesting place:** Llewellyn M. Ehrhart, William E. Redfoot, and Dean A. Bagley, "Marine Turtles of the Central Region of the Indian River Lagoon System, Florida," *Florida Scientist* 70 (Autumn 2007): 430–31.

17 **To turtle hunters in southern Florida:** J. M. Murphy, "Turtling in Florida," *Outing* 17 (November 1890): 98–101. See also "Taking the Green Turtle—How He Is Caught, Handled, and Sent to New-York," *New York Times,* May 17, 1885, 6.

18 **On their backs:** Donald C. Jackson, interview by the author, August 14, 2018.

18 **a dish so prized:** William Grimes, *Appetite City: A Culinary History of New York* (New York: Farrar, Straus and Giroux, 2009), 79–80.

18 **"Cut off the head":** *Cassell's Dictionary of Cookery* (London: Cassell, Petter, Calpin & Co., 1883), 1019.

18 **docking at nearby Pier 22:** "Cruelty to Animals," *The World* (New York), May 31, 1866, 2.

18 **Two hundred fishing boats:** "The Markets of New York," *Harper's New Monthly Magazine,* July 1867, 235.

20 **"eat without pleasure":** Steven Nadler, ed., *Cambridge Companion to Malebranche* (Cambridge: Cambridge University Press, 2000), 42.

20 **"the poor beetle that we tread upon":** William Shakespeare, *Measure for Measure,* Act 3, Scene 1, lines 88–90. For these literary citations, we are indebted to Rod Preece's splendid sourcebook, *Awe for the Tiger, Love for the Lamb: A Chronicle of Sensibility to Animals.*

20 **"such a tender feeling for my horses":** Molière, *The Misanthrope and Other Plays* (New York: Signet Classics, 2005), 154.

21 **"the Love and Mercy of God"**: Humphry Primatt, *A Dissertation on the Duty of Mercy and Sin of Cruelty to Brute Animals* (London: R. Hett, 1776), iii.

21 **"Love is the great Hinge"**: Ibid., 1.

21 **This, increasingly, was the God**: See Jeffrey W. Barbeau, *Religion in Romantic England* (Waco, TX: Baylor University Press, 2018), xvii–xxxvi; see also James Turner, *Reckoning with the Beast* (Baltimore: Johns Hopkins University Press, 1980), 1–14.

22 **"benevolence and compassion"**: Turner, *Reckoning with the Beast*, 6.

22 **"no less sensible of pain than a Man"**: Primatt, *Duty of Mercy*, 13.

22 **"It has pleased GOD"**: Ibid., 11.

22 **"For the same reason"**: Ibid., 12.

23 **"I am to ask your Lordships"**: *Cruelty to Animals: The Speech of Lord Erskine Taken in the House of Peers* (Edinburgh: Alex. Lawrie, 1809), 2.

24 **"Almost every sense bestowed"**: Ibid., 3–4.

25 **"a three-pounder in weight"**: Clara Morris, "Riddle of the Nineteenth Century: Mr. Henry Bergh," *McClure's*, March 1902, 417.

26 **one estimate in the 1830s**: Timothy J. Gilfoyle, *City of Eros* (New York: W. W. Norton, 1992), 52.

26 **bequeathed to us the word "hooker"**: Irving Lewis Allen, *The City in Slang* (New York: Oxford University Press, 1995), 184–86.

26 **The captain of one Bergh-built craft**: Zulma Steele, *Angel in Top Hat* (New York: Harper & Brothers, 1942), 16.

26 **During the two days of bullfighting**: Henry Bergh, "Correspondence of the Mirror," *The Evening Mirror* (New York), June 16, 1848.

26 **"[N]ever before has a similar"**: "ASPCA Founder Henry Bergh Travel Journal, Part Three: Spain and France Continued," 44. Digitized by North Carolina State University Libraries.

27 **"At the instant that the bull"**: Bergh, "Correspondence of the Mirror."

27 **"Whenever the bull tore out"**: Quoted in *The Daily American* (Nashville), November 18, 1880, 3.

27 **A manager of Booth's Theater**: "Christian Bergh's Son," *New York Times*, March 18, 1888, 11.

27 **A rare success came in 1858**: Edward P. Buffet, "ASPCA General History of the Society, Part One," 56. American Society for the Prevention of Cruelty to Animals Archive, N.C. State University Libraries' Digital Collections: Rare and Unique Materials, https://d.lib.ncsu.edu/.

28 **"I have been in the publishing business"**: "A Poem by Henry Bergh," *New York Times*, November 30, 1880, 5.

28 **"Encouraged by my success"**: *Philadelphia Press*, quoted in *The Indiana Herald*, November 5, 1884, 2.

29 **it employed five regular inspectors**: "Royal Society for the Prevention of Cruelty to Animals," *The Standard* (London), May 21, 1861, 3.

29 **he began an evolution**: See, for example, Tim Hutchinson, "The Theological and Political Evolution of Henry Ward Beecher," unpublished master's thesis (University of Arkansas, 1990); retrieved from https://scholarworks.uark.edu/etd/2596.

29 **a sermon on "The Love of God"**: Henry Ward Beecher, *Sermons*, vol. 1 (New York: Harper & Brothers, 1868), 35–52.

30 **"The best way to cure":** Lydia Maria Child, *The Freedmen's Book* (Boston: Ticknor and Fields, 1865), 98.

30 **In 1853, a vegetarian banquet:** "Vegetarian Festival," *New York Times,* September 5, 1853, 1.

31 **"teamster who goads with whip and curse":** "Cruelty to Animals," *New York Times,* August 14, 1862, 3.

31 **one of them showed several men:** *Frank Leslie's Illustrated Newspaper,* October 28, 1865, 1.

31 **"Shall we ever have among us":** *Frank Leslie's Illustrated Newspaper,* December 9, 1865, 179.

Chapter 2: Animal New York

35 **The urban dairy horse:** Ann Norton Greene, *Horses at Work: Harnessing Power in Industrial America* (Cambridge, MA: Harvard University Press, 2008), 22. See also "The Milkman's Horse and Wagon," *The Milk Dealer* 2 (May 1913): 10–12; and A Milkman, "Milk—From the Depot to the Consumer," *Scientific American* 22 (January 15, 1870): 45.

35 **Millennia of selective breeding:** Greene, *Horses at Work,* 13–14. See also Debbie Busby and Catrin Rutland, *The Horse: A Natural History* (Princeton, NJ: Princeton University Press, 2019).

36 **On February 9, 1866:** "Brooklyn—Runaway Accidents," *The Sun* (New York), February 9, 1866, 4. See also "Four Runaway Horses—Several Persons Seriously Injured," *Brooklyn Daily Eagle,* February 8, 1866, 3.

37 **Paradoxically, the opposite was true:** Greene, *Horses at Work,* 4–9.

37 **As the metropolis spread:** George Rogers Taylor, "The Beginnings of Mass Transportation in Urban America: Part 1," *Smithsonian Journal of History* 1 (Summer 1966): 37.

37 **Private horse-drawn carriages:** Ibid., 40–41. See also Clay McShane and Joel A. Tarr, *The Horse in the City* (Baltimore: Johns Hopkins University Press, 2007), 55.

37 **Intracity mass transit:** McShane and Tarr, *The Horse in the City,* 57–63.

38 **By 1866, tracks had been laid:** Ibid., 63–65.

38 **"Thirty seated, forty standing":** "Street-Car Salad," *Harper's Weekly,* March 23, 1867, 189.

38 **Alongside these passenger vehicles:** "The Position of the Horse in Modern Society," *The Nation,* October 31, 1872, 277.

38 **Those tasked with driving:** Hilary J. Sweeney, "Pasture to Pavement: Working Class Irish and Urban Workhorses in Nineteenth Century New York City," *American Journal of Irish Studies* 11 (2014): 134–35. See also McShane and Tarr, *The Horse in the City,* 39.

39 **The *Sun* reader:** "American Geographical and Statistical Society—Cruelty to Animals," *The Sun,* February 9, 1866, 4.

39 **Despite a lashing winter storm:** Edward P. Buffet, "Bergh's War on Vested Cruelty," vol. 1, 163. American Society for the Prevention of Cruelty to Animals Archive, N.C. State University Libraries' Digital Collections: Rare and Unique Materials, https://d.lib.ncsu.edu/.

39 **host of competing entertainments:** "Amusements," *New York Times,* February 8, 1866, 7.

39 **Bergh began by acknowledging:** Buffet, "Bergh's War on Vested Cruelty," vol. 1. See also "Society for the Prevention of Cruelty to Animals," *New York Herald,* February 12, 1866, 2; and "Cruelty to Animals," *New-York Commercial Advertiser,* February 10, 1866, 4.

40 **By the end of the evening:** "A New York Society for the Protection of Animals," *Evening Post,* February 9, 1866, 2. See also "Cruelty to Animals," *New-York Daily Tribune,* February 9, 1866, 4.

40 **Within several weeks:** Buffet, "Bergh's War on Vested Cruelty," vol. 1. See also Bernard Unti, "The Quality of Mercy: Organized Animal Protection in the United States, 1866–1930," PhD diss. (American University, 2002), 79.

41 **Nine days later:** Unti, "The Quality of Mercy," 81.

41 **The maximum penalty:** Ibid., 82.

41 **The very night of his return:** "Humanity in New-York," *New-York Daily Tribune,* March 16, 1878, 3. See also Zulma Steele, *Angel in Top Hat* (New York: Harper and Brothers, 1942), 1.

42 **he quickly adjusted his methods:** "Henry Bergh and His Work," *Scribner's,* April 1879, 879.

42 **His second attempt:** "Cruelty to Animals—First Case of Punishment Under the New Law," *New York Times,* April 13, 1866, 8. See also American Society for the Prevention of Cruelty to Animals, *First Annual Report* (New York, 1867), 47.

42 **Picking up momentum:** American Society for the Prevention of Cruelty to Animals, *First Annual Report* (New York, 1867), 47.

42 **Bergh quickly came to relish:** "Henry Bergh and His Work," 874.

43 **Some of the poorest residents:** Andrew A. Robichaud, *Animal City: The Domestication of America* (Cambridge, MA: Harvard University Press, 2019), 167–70.

43 **Besides pulling wheeled conveyances:** Ibid., 160–64.

43 **Even as the expanding metropolis:** Catherine Brinkley and Dominic Vitiello, "From Farm to Nuisance: Animal Agriculture and the Rise of Planning Regulation," *Journal of Planning History* 13 (May 2014): 113–35.

43 **Before refrigeration:** "Abbatoirs—History of New-York Slaughter-Houses," *New York Times,* April 1, 1866, 3.

43 **food animals raised elsewhere:** Brinkley and Vitiello, "From Farm to Nuisance," 113–35. See also "Cattle Driving in the Streets," *Frank Leslie's Illustrated Weekly,* April 28, 1866, 81.

44 **Awash in blood:** "Board of Health," *New York Times,* March 13, 1866, 1.

44 **Strays were ubiquitous:** Katherine C. Grier, *Pets in America: A History* (Orlando, FL: Harcourt, 2006), 80–81.

44 **Neutering of pet species:** Ibid., 277.

44 **"DWELLERS IN FIRST WARD":** "A Big Problem in Cats," *New York Times,* March 16, 1893, 5.

44 **In 1866, the same year:** "The Dog Pound," *New York Times,* June 18, 1866, 8.

45 **Excrement was everywhere:** Joel A. Tarr, "Urban Pollution—Many Long Years Ago," *American Heritage,* October 1971, https://www.americanheritage.com/.

45 **On the poorer streets:** Brinkley and Vitiello, "From Farm to Nuisance," 113–35.

45 **The stench of animal slaughter:** "Sanitary Condition of the City," *New York Times,* August 21, 1856, 1.

45 **So did the precarious circumstances:** McShane and Tarr, *The Horse in the City,* 49–50.

46 **Some adults, too:** Jack William Berryman, "Anglo-American Blood Sports, 1776–1889: A Study of Changing Morals," master's thesis (University of Massachusetts, 1974), 51.

46 **Christopher Keybourn:** Bronwen Dickey, *Pit Bull: The Battle Over an American Icon* (New York: Alfred A. Knopf, 2016), 25–28. Luc Sante, *Low Life: Lures and Snares of Old New York* (New York: Vintage Books, 1991), 201.

47 **The saloon's location:** Luc Sante, *Low Life,* 106–7.

47 **Customers entered a gas-lit bar:** "Religion in Kit Burn's Dog Pit," *New-York Daily Tribune,* September 22, 1868, 2. See also Edward Winslow Martin [alias of James Dabney McCabe], *The Secrets of the Great City: A Work Descriptive of the Virtues and the Vices, the Mysteries, Miseries and Crimes of New York City* (Philadelphia: National Publishing Company, 1868), 388–90.

48 **"The performance":** Edward Winslow Martin [alias of James Dabney McCabe], *The Secrets of the Great City,* 389.

48 **The *Tribune* reporter:** "Religion in Kit Burn's Dog Pit," 2.

48 **"Two huge bull-dogs":** Edward Winslow Martin [alias of James Dabney McCabe], *The Secrets of the Great City,* 389–90.

49 **A scheduled fight:** "Religion in Kit Burn's Dog Pit," 2. See also "Kit Burns' Dog Paradise in Water Street," *Frank Leslie's Illustrated Weekly,* December 8, 1866, 181.

50 **In addition to prosecuting cases:** American Society for the Prevention of Cruelty to Animals, *First Annual Report, 1867* (New York: ASPCA, 1867), 47–57.

50 **as recorded by a reporter:** "Cruelty to Animals," *The World* (New York), June 1, 1866, 8.

51 **a question of classification:** Ibid.

51 **When the legal circus:** "Police Intelligence—The Turtle Case at the Tombs—Justice Hogan Dismisses the Complaint," *New York Herald,* June 3, 1866, 5.

51 **Nowhere on the docket:** American Society for the Prevention of Cruelty to Animals, *First Annual Report, 1867,* 47–57.

51 **In November of that year:** "A Degrading Amusement," *New York Herald,* November 20, 1866, 7.

51 **Bergh's initial attempts:** Ernest Freeberg, *A Traitor to His Species: Henry Bergh and the Birth of the Animal Rights Movement* (New York: Basic Books, 2020), 79–80.

51 **After considerable agitation:** Martin and Herbert J. Kaufman, "Henry Bergh, Kit Burns, and the Sportsmen of New York," *New York Folklore Quarterly* 28, no. 1 (1972): 15–29.

51 **eight arrests were made:** "Water Street Sports in the Tombs—Mr. Bergh on Their Trail," *New York Herald,* December 3, 1866, 5.

52 **According to *The New York Times:*** "The Tombs—Before Justice Dowling, Dog Fanciers in Trouble," *New York Times,* December 3, 1866, 8.

52 **After the passage:** "Cruelty to Animals," *New-York Tribune,* May 16, 1866, 4.

52 **The *New-York Atlas:*** "Cruelty to Animals," *New-York Atlas,* June 9, 1866, 4.

52 The *Times* offered: "Cruelty to Animals—First Case of Punishment Under the New Law," *New York Times,* April 13, 1866, 8.

52 Its support for the cause: "The Society for the Prevention of Cruelty to Animals," *New York Times,* June 6, 1866, 4.

53 best known during the Civil War: Harold Holzer, *Lincoln and the Power of the Press* (New York: Simon & Schuster, 2014), 488–508.

53 Now, with the postwar humane energy: *The World,* November 3, 1866, 5.

53 The most ambitious (and disgusting): "Prevention of Cruelty to Animals—Great Mass Meeting at Union Square," *New York Herald,* May 13, 1866, 6.

54 "cannot resist the inclination": "Cruelty to Animals," *The Sun* (New York), February 14, 1866, 2.

54 By the time of the society's: American Society for the Prevention of Cruelty to Animals, *First Annual Report* (New York, 1867), 71–76.

54 In 1866, she was: *Constitution, Address, and List of Members of the American Association for the Promotion of Social Science* (Boston: Wright & Potter, 1866), 89.

54 she was a donor: *Proceedings of the First Anniversary of the American Equal Rights Association* (New York: Robert J. Johnston, 1867), 80.

Chapter 3: Under the Knife

58 As the medical students looked on: See Austin Flint Jr., *The Physiology of Man* (New York: D. Appleton and Company, 1873), 189–202; see also John Call Dalton, *A Treatise on Human Physiology* (Philadelphia: Henry C. Lea, 1871), 464–73.

58 In the mid-1860s: William G. Rothstein, *American Medical Schools and the Practice of Medicine* (New York: Oxford University Press, 1987), 92.

58 "the refined, well-educated": Ibid.

58 In 1854, Dalton had been: John C. Dalton, "On the Movements of the Glottis in Respiration," *American Journal of the Medical Sciences* (July 1854): 75.

59 Flint, a decade younger: Austin Flint Jr., "Experimental Researches into a New Excretory Function of the Liver," *American Journal of the Medical Sciences* (October 1862).

59 "in a tiny suite of rooms": S. Weir Mitchell, "Memoir of John Call Dalton," in *Biographical Memoirs,* vol. 3 (Washington, DC: National Academy of Sciences, 1895), 185.

59 with his nose in the *Arabian Nights:* Ibid.

59 He was a skilled rider: Ibid.; John Call Dalton, *John Call Dalton, M.D., U.S.V.* (Cambridge, Mass.: The Riverside Press, 1892), 5–6, 103–5.

60 "Of all the horrible pangs inflicted": "Cruelty to Animals," *New-York Commercial Advertiser,* February 10, 1866.

60 "Gentlemen, as the animal cost me": Quoted in *John Bull* magazine, February 28, 1825, 67.

60 "cut up Dumb Animals Alive": A. W. H. Bates, *Anti-Vivisection and the Profession of Medicine in Britain* (London: Palgrave Macmillan, 2017), 18.

61 "kept alive so long": Letter to *The Herald,* reprinted in *Brooklyn Union,* February 13, 1867, 1.

61 **a demonstration innovated by Dalton:** See "On the Cerebellum, as the Centre of Co-ordination of the Voluntary Movements," *American Journal of the Medical Sciences* (January 1861): 83; see also Dalton, *A Treatise on Human Physiology*, 443–48.

61 **"As the subject of vivisection":** John Call Dalton, *Vivisection: What It Is, and What It Has Accomplished* (New York: Baillière Brothers, 1867), 1.

62 **As early as 450 BCE:** Andreas-Holger Maehle and Ulrich Tröhler, "Animal Experimentation from Antiquity to the End of the Eighteenth Century: Attitudes and Arguments," in *Vivisection in Historical Perspective,* ed. Nicolaas A. Rupke (New York: Routledge, 1987), 15.

62 **Not long thereafter, Galen:** Anita Guerrini, *Experimenting with Humans and Animals* (Baltimore: Johns Hopkins University Press, 2003), 11–18.

63 **"without pity or compassion":** Ibid., 18.

63 **Following a medieval period:** Maehle and Tröhler, "Animal Experimentation from Antiquity to the End of the Eighteenth Century," 16–19.

63 **In the 1620s, Italian physicians:** Guerrini, *Experimenting with Humans and Animals,* 23–33.

63 **"In the time of Harvey":** Dalton, *Vivisection,* 8.

63 **Harvey, through a series:** Ibid., 15–19.

63 **"experimented on kittens, birds":** Ibid., 19.

63 **Antoine Lavoisier, who in the 1770s:** Ibid., 20–21.

63 **There was the role of the periosteum:** Ibid., 33–35.

63 **the then-novel practice of blood transfusion:** Ibid., 21–25.

64 **encomia both to Charles Bell:** Ibid., 27–31. Dalton also paused a moment to speak to Bell's support, near the end of his life, for the anti-vivisection cause. Bell had used postmortem dissection of human cadavers and experiments on living animals to achieve his results, and he later opined that it was the former, not the latter, to which his major breakthroughs were owed. Dalton dismisses this, saying: "In reviewing, at the present day, the works of Sir Charles Bell and their results, it is evident that everything of value in the physiology of the nervous system which he discovered, viz. the motor character of the anterior roots, and the distinction between the fifth and seventh cranial nerves, he discovered by means of experiment upon living animals."

64 **Dalton, born in 1825:** John O. Green, *A Memorial of John C. Dalton, M.D.* (Cambridge, MA: University Press, 1864), 14.

64 **Flint, in 1836:** Unpublished biography of Austin Flint, Flint family papers, New York University School of Medicine archive.

64 **doctors trained at elite universities:** Paul Starr, *The Social Transformation of American Medicine* (New York: Basic Books, 1982), 47–51.

65 **"the unbiased opinion":** Ibid., 55.

66 **"continuous tradition":** Guerrini, *Experimenting with Humans and Animals,* 71.

66 **"In twenty years":** *Claude Bernard and the Internal Environment: A Memorial Symposium* (New York: Marcel Dekker, 1979), 12–15.

66 **Flint's handwritten notebook:** Unpublished notebook, Flint family papers, New York University School of Medicine archive.

66 **"M. Bernard appears":** Ibid., entry from May 12, 1854.

66 **"illustrated his subject":** Ibid.

67 "The physiologist is no ordinary man": Claude Bernard, *Introduction to the Study of Experimental Medicine,* quoted and translated in Noah K. Davis, "The Moral Aspects of Vivisection," *North American Review,* March 1885, 216.

67 One of Dalton's colleagues: Mitchell, "Memoir of John Call Dalton," 181.

68 "whether the practice of that branch of surgery": "Vivisections—Letters from Henry Bergh and Dr. Dalton," *Buffalo Medical and Surgical Journal,* October 1866, 152.

68 Even so, Dalton was not entirely satisfied: Unpublished notes by Dalton, College of Physicians and Surgeons archive, Columbia University Health Sciences Library.

68 Bernard's famous "red notebook": *The Cahier Rouge of Claude Bernard* (Cambridge, MA: Schenkman Publishing Company, 1967).

69 "The swift certainty": Mitchell, "Memoir of John Call Dalton," 180.

69 "He illustrates his lectures": "Surgery and Medicine in the Metropolis," *New York Daily Herald,* June 30, 1867, 7.

Chapter 4: The Living Curiosities

71 As the vast glaciers: Pierre Béland, *Beluga: A Farewell to Whales* (New York: Lyons & Burford, 1996), 214–15.

72 When the whales are not chasing: Heather M. Hill, Sarah Dietrich, and Briana Cappiello, "Learning to Play: A Review and Theoretical Investigation of the Developmental Mechanisms and Functions of Cetacean Play," *Learning & Behavior* 45 (December 2017), https://link.springer.com/.

72 indigenous people hunted: Marcel Moussette, *Fishing Methods Used on the St. Lawrence River and Gulf* (Ottawa: Parks Canada, 1979), 36–37.

72 When French explorer: Béland, *Beluga: A Farewell to Whales,* 215.

72 Basque sailors joined: Pierre Béland, "The Beluga Whales of the St. Lawrence River," in *Critical Perspectives on Pollution,* ed. Stephanie Watson (New York: Rosen Publishing Group, 2007), 140.

72 French colonists followed: Béland, *Beluga: A Farewell to Whales,* 215–16.

72 "In 1861, I learned": P. T. Barnum, *Struggles and Triumphs; or, Forty Years' Recollections of P.T. Barnum* (Buffalo: The Courier Company, 1881), 561–62.

73 After preparing an eighteen-by-forty-foot tank: Ibid., 563–64.

74 Upon the belugas' arrival: "The Whales," *New-York Tribune,* August 9, 1861, 3.

74 Barnum's advance publicity effort: Barnum, *Struggles and Triumphs,* 564–65.

74 Barnum being Barnum: Ibid., 565–66.

76 And so, Barnum continued: "Distinguished Arrivals—A Gala Day at Barnum's," *New York Times,* June 29, 1865, 2.

76 "NOW IS THE TIME": *New York Herald,* July 2, 1865, 7.

77 Samuel Hurd, Barnum's manager: Philip B. Kunhardt Jr., Philip B. Kunhardt III, and Peter W. Kunhardt, *PT Barnum: America's Greatest Showman* (New York: Alfred A. Knopf, 1995), 192.

77 Police arrived in a brave attempt: "Disastrous Fire," *New York Times,* July 14, 1865, 1.

77 Pandemonium reigned outside: "Conflagrations—The Destruction of Barnum's Museum," *New York Herald,* July 14, 1865, 1.

77 **Thirty thousand New Yorkers:** "Disastrous Fire," *New York Times,* July 14, 1865, 1.

77 **Firefighters raised ladders:** "Great Fire in New York—Barnum's Museum Burned," *Brooklyn Daily Eagle,* July 13, 1865, 3. See also "Disastrous Fire," *New York Times,* July 14, 1865, 1.

77 **Desperation mounted quickly:** Amanda Bosworth, "Barnum's Whales: The Showman and the Forging of Modern Animal Captivity," *Perspectives on History* (April 2, 2018), https://www.historians.org/.

77 **The next day's *New York Times:*** "Disastrous Fire," *New York Times,* July 14, 1865, 1.

77 **Only one animal escaped:** "Great Fire in New York," *Brooklyn Daily Eagle,* July 13, 1865, 3.

78 **"Almost in the twinkling of an eye":** "Disastrous Fire," *New York Times,* July 14, 1865, 1.

78 **When the Ann Street side:** Bosworth, "Barnum's Whales."

78 **Barnum, who traveled:** Barnum, *Struggles and Triumphs,* 640–41.

78 **What was left:** Bosworth, "Barnum's Whales."

78 **The small, staid town:** Robert Wilson, *Barnum: An American Life* (New York: Simon & Schuster, 2019), 9–29.

79 **Barnum's initial entertainment gambit:** A. H. Saxon, *P. T. Barnum: The Legend and the Man* (New York: Columbia University Press, 1989), 68–74.

79 **The turning point came:** Wilson, *Barnum,* 50–57.

79 **The museum edifice:** Barnum, *Struggles and Triumphs,* 131–32.

79 **He put on display:** *An Illustrated Catalogue and Guide Book to Barnum's American Museum* (New York: Barnum's American Museum, 1860s). See also "Disastrous Fire," *New York Times,* July 14, 1865, 1.

79 **He renovated the lecture room:** Saxon, *P. T. Barnum,* 104–7.

80 **"'Humbug' consists in":** P. T. Barnum, *The Humbugs of the World: An Account of Humbugs, Delusions, Impositions, Quackeries, Deceits, and Deceivers Generally, in All Ages* (New York: Carleton, 1866), 20.

80 **The year after he took over:** Barnum, *Struggles and Triumphs,* 130–50. See also Neil Harris, *Humbug: The Art of P. T. Barnum* (Chicago: University of Chicago Press, 1973), 62–67.

80 **"M'lle Jane" was heralded:** *New-York Daily Tribune,* April 29, 1846, 2–3.

80 **Although it would be:** John Rickards Betts, "P. T. Barnum and the Popularization of Natural History," *Journal of the History of Ideas* 20 (June–September 1959): 353–54.

81 **"No Orang Outang ever brought":** "Another Day," *Evening Post,* May 5, 1846, 3.

81 **in 1851, launched:** T. Tufts, *Grand Entrance of the Asiatic Caravan, Museum, and Menagerie of PT Barnum* [Handbill] (Worcester, MA: Barnum's Asiatic Caravan, Museum, and Menagerie, June 11, 1851).

81 **including a mature male Indian rhinoceros:** L. C. Rookmaaker, *The Rhinoceros in Captivity: A List of 2439 Rhinoceroses Kept from Roman Times to 1994* (The Hague: SPB Academic Publishing, 1998), 108.

81 **"the unicorn of the Holy Writ":** *New York Herald,* July 4, 1854, 9.

81 **a pair of giraffes:** *New York Herald,* November 30, 1854, 7. See also *Gleason's Pictorial Drawing Room Companion* 6 (May 13, 1854): 300.

81 **In 1860, Barnum sponsored:** Barnum, *Struggles and Triumphs,* 529–42.

81 **In 1865, the untimely demise:** Ibid., 566.

82 **At its opening in 1859:** *The Grand Aquaria Is Now Open for Public Exhibition!* [Handbill] (Boston: Cutting and Butler's Aquarial Gardens, July 4, 1859).

82 **Glass aquaria held:** "Boston Aquarial and Zoological Gardens," *Ballou's Dollar Monthly Magazine*, July 1862, 6–8.

82 **Cutting trained them himself:** *The Domestic History of the Learned Seals, "Ned" and "Fanny," at the Boston Aquarial Gardens, 21 Bromfield Street* (New York: G. A. Whitehorne, 1860).

83 **Sadly, the ambitious expansion:** "Death of an Inventor in an Insane Asylum," *New York Times,* August 14, 1867, 3.

83 **Remodeled and reimagined:** Jerry Ryan, *The Forgotten Aquariums of Boston* (Pascoag, RI: Finley Aquatic Books, 2011), 45–49.

83 **On July 13, 1865:** "Disastrous Fire—Total Destruction of Barnum's American Museum," *New York Times,* July 14, 1865, 1.

83 **According to the memoirist:** Thomas Floyd-Jones, *Backward Glances: Reminiscences of an Old New-Yorker* (New York: Unionist Gazette Association, 1914), 34–35.

84 **a fire at a medical college on 14th Street:** "The Great Fire," *New York Times,* May 23, 1866, 8.

84 **"There is no study":** *A Brief Biographical Sketch of I.A. Van Amburgh* (New York: Samuel Booth, 1860), v.

85 **Of the nine specimens:** "Elephant Hunting in Ceylon," *New-York Tribune,* May 29, 1851, 6.

85 **"The distinguished African":** "A Distinguished Departure," *New-York Tribune,* April 18, 1855, 7.

85 **the version that burned up in 1865:** *An Illustrated Catalogue and Guide Book to Barnum's American Museum* (New York: Wynkoop, Hallenbeck & Thomas, c. 1864), 102.

87 **Isaac Van Amburgh died suddenly:** *Evansville* (IN) *Daily Journal,* December 6, 1865, 2.

87 **an advertisement from the first:** "Barnum & Van Amburgh's Museum and Menagerie Combination," *Frank Leslie's Illustrated Newspaper,* December 1, 1866, 14.

87 **"shudder and avert their eyes":** "Cruelty to Animals," *New York Commercial Advertiser,* February 10, 1866.

88 **"It may be urged that these reptiles":** "Cruelty to Animals—Interesting Correspondence Between President Bergh, Professor Agassiz, and P.T. Barnum," *The World* (New York), March 19, 1867, 7.

88 **On December 29, the museum's snake tamer:** "A True Snake Story," *New York Commercial Advertiser,* January 3, 1867, 1.

89 **"I do not know of any way":** "Cruelty to Animals—Interesting Correspondence," *The World.*

89 **This, in turn, touched off:** Ibid.

90 **The blaze began early on Tuesday:** "Burning of Barnum's Museum. Total Destruction of the Building and Its Contents," *New York Times,* March 3, 1868, 5. See also Barnum, *Struggles and Triumphs,* 698–700; "Fire in Broadway," *New York Herald,* March 3, 1868, 7; and "Barnum's Museum Burned," *New-York Tribune,* March 3, 1868, 3.

90 As fire spread through the structure: "The Fire Imp," *New York Herald,*
    March 4, 1868, 5.

91 Scores of animals died: "Burning of Barnum's Museum," *New York Times,*
    March 4, 1868, 8.

91 A photograph from the following day: Barnum, *Struggles and Triumphs,*
    700–701.

Chapter 5: To Philadelphia and Boston

93 "the very plainest kind": Zulma Steele, *Angel in Top Hat* (New York: Harper
    and Brothers, 1942), 40.

93 One such pilgrim: Jane Campbell, "Mrs. Caroline Earle White, Reformer,"
    Records of the American Catholic Historical Society of Philadelphia 33, no. 1
    (March 1922): 37.

94 "[A]ll the gentlemen to whom I have appealed": Caroline White to Henry
    Bergh, January 14, 1867, American Anti-Vivisection Society Records, Temple
    University Special Collections Research Center (TUSCRC).

94 She started with her own family: Obituary for Emily Warren Appleton, *Seventy-
    Second Annual Report of the Trustees of the Perkins Institution and Massachu-
    setts School for the Blind* (Boston: Geo. H. Ellis, 1904), 31–32.

94 "If I were a man": White to Bergh, March 23, 1867, TUSCRC.

96 Abolitionist groups routinely met: Edwin B. Bronner, *Thomas Earle as a
    Reformer* (Philadelphia: International Printing Company, 1948), 22.

96 on at least one occasion: Campbell, "Mrs. Caroline Earle White, Reformer," 30.

96 an accounting in 1845: Russell Weigley et al., eds., *Philadelphia: A 300-Year His-
    tory* (New York: W. W. Norton, 1982), 327.

96 "It would make your heart bleed": White to Bergh, March 23, 1867, TUSCRC.

96 A newspaper ad from November 1866: *The Evening Telegraph* (Philadelphia),
    November 13, 1866, 4.

97 "We may be personally defeated": Ann D. Gordon, ed., *The Selected Papers of
    Elizabeth Cady Stanton and Susan B. Anthony,* vol. 4 (New Brunswick, NJ: Rut-
    gers University Press, 1997), 304.

97 "The chief speaker was Lucretia Mott": *The Seneca Falls Courier,* reprinted in
    The Liberator (Boston), August 18, 1848, 6.

98 "no text of Scripture": Ibid., 83.

98 "It is time that Christians": Dana Greene, ed., *Lucretia Mott: Her Complete
    Speeches and Sermons* (New York: E. Mellen Press, 1980), 107–13.

98 she studied Latin: Campbell, "Mrs. Caroline Earle White, Reformer," 47.

98 Astronomy, too, was a passion: Ibid., 46–47, 52.

99 This created no small amount: Ibid., 32.

99 "impression, without making any display": Ibid., 33.

99 "higher law inwardly revealed": Anna M. Speicher, *The Religious World of
    Antislavery Women* (Syracuse, NY: Syracuse University Press, 2000), 81.

99 "two men, equally learned": Ibid., 35.

101 "known to be possessed": *Boston Herald,* February 22, 1868.

101 a compendium a few decades later: *The New York Clipper Annual* (New York:
    Frank Queen Publishing Company, 1893), 70–1.

101 A crowd of racing fans: *Boston Herald,* February 24, 1868.

101 Empire State, who had accomplished: *Boston Herald,* February 22, 1868.

101 At 10:46, the two horses set off: *Worcester Spy,* February 24, 1868, reprinted in *Chicago Tribune,* February 28, 1868, 2.

102 No newspaper ever offered: We base this speculation on the *Worcester Spy*'s citing of the cause of death as "spasmodic colic."

102 the losing horse died in a Boston stable: *Fall River Daily Evening News,* April 16, 1868, 2.

103 one such squib from January 1864: *Massachusetts Ploughman,* January 23, 1864, 1.

103 a tiny item in the *Evening Transcript: Daily Evening Transcript,* August 23, 1852.

103 a small mention in the *New England Farmer: New England Farmer,* November 10, 1860, 3.

103 "In your paper of this morning": *Boston Daily Advertiser,* February 25, 1868.

103 Within twenty-four hours: George Thorndike Angell, *Autobiographical Sketches and Personal Reflections* (Boston: Franklin Press, 1884), 9–11.

104 From there, April was a flurry of activity: Ibid., 12.

104 On May 20, 1868, Angell: Ibid., 13–14.

104 It reprinted the state's new anti-cruelty statute: *Our Dumb Animals,* June 2, 1868, 2–3.

105 "Jewish mode of killing animals": *Our Dumb Animals,* July 7, 1868, 11.

105 One poem, an original penned: Ibid., 10.

105 Another poem, "Little Bell": Ibid., 11.

105 a short story about Flora: Ibid., 13.

105 short piece about the "check rein": Ibid., 10–11.

106 "If thousands of cattle": *Our Dumb Animals,* February 2, 1869, 66.

106 "The Story of a Good and Faithful Horse": *Our Dumb Animals,* September 4, 1868, 28.

107 "[O]ne day in May": *Our Dumb Animals,* October 6, 1868, 35.

107 "I saw poor, hard-worked and half-starved": *Our Dumb Animals,* December 1, 1868, 55.

108 the manner in which the city captured: "Report of the President of the 'Woman's Branch,'" *Second Annual Report, Women's Branch of the Pennsylvania Society for the Prevention of Cruelty to Animals,* 1871, 3–4.

108 In June of that year, the group: "Report of the Shelter Committee," *Third Annual Report, Women's Branch of the Pennsylvania Society for the Prevention of Cruelty to Animals,* 1872, 16–17.

109 "It seems a mockery of Christian charity": *Harper's Weekly,* January 20, 1872, 65.

109 Angell wrote back to White: Bernard Unti, "The Quality of Mercy: Organized Animal Protection in the United States, 1866–1930," PhD diss. (American University, 2002), 168.

110 the word was repurposed in 1870: Robert F. Weir, ed., *Physician-Assisted Suicide* (Bloomington: Indiana University Press, 1997), 38–40.

110 "When a dumb animal is hopelessly": *St. Louis Post-Dispatch,* January 28, 1906, 4B.

111 an event held to mark: "Cruelty to Animals," *The Press* (Philadelphia), April 7, 1870, 6.

112 **"no sooner get hold of a theory or principle":** *New-York Tribune,* reprinted in *Daily Evening Telegraph* (Philadelphia), January 29, 1870, 2.

112 **The yard had been constructed:** Unti, "The Quality of Mercy," 170.

113 **all were fed a healthy diet:** *Frank Leslie's Illustrated Newspaper,* August 30, 1873, 393–94.

113 **the completed euthanasia chamber:** "A Humane Canicide," *Philadelphia Inquirer,* July 29, 1871.

Chapter 6: Meatropolis

115 **consuming fifteen million feet of lumber:** *Appletons' Hand-book of American Travel, Western Tour* (New York: D. Appleton and Company, 1871), 13.

115 **as many as a thousand men:** Jack Wing, *The Great Union Stock Yards of Chicago* (Chicago: Religio-Philosophical Publishing Association, 1865), 15.

115 **fifty linear miles of streets and alleys:** W. Jos. Grand, *Illustrated History of the Union Stockyards* (Chicago: Thos. Knapp, 1896), 15.

115 **roughly five hundred dwellings in all:** Wing, *The Great Union Stock Yards of Chicago,* 17.

115 **some 115,000 souls:** "Chicago," *Atlantic Monthly,* March 1867, 332.

115 **nine different railroad companies:** Wing, *The Great Union Stock Yards of Chicago,* 18.

115 **the future of America's livestock industry:** See William Cronon, *Nature's Metropolis* (New York: W. W. Norton, 1991), 209–10; also Louise Carroll Wade, *Chicago's Pride: The Stockyards, Packingtown, and Environs in the Nineteenth Century* (Urbana: University of Illinois Press, 1987), 41, 47–50.

116 **"A cattle train stops":** "Chicago," *Atlantic Monthly,* 332.

116 **six miles of pipe:** Wing, *The Great Union Stock Yards of Chicago,* 20–21.

116 **capable of sizing up thirty cattle:** "Chicago," *Atlantic Monthly,* 333.

116 **"where the money is paid":** Ibid.

116 **fine mosaic floors:** Wing, *The Great Union Stock Yards of Chicago,* 24–25.

116 **"the most enjoyable retreat":** Ibid., 24.

116 **"no women above stairs" rule:** Dominic A. Pacyga, *Slaughterhouse: Chicago's Union Stock Yard and the World It Made* (Chicago: University of Chicago Press, 2015), 41.

117 **the first practice game:** Pacyga, *Slaughterhouse,* 43.

117 **Within a decade of the yards' founding:** "The Stock-Yards," *Chicago Tribune,* December 23, 1875, 5.

117 **"visiting Egypt, and not the pyramids":** Ibid.

118 **"quite as possible to transact business":** Grand, *Illustrated History of the Union Stockyards,* 15.

118 **One early visitor noted:** Wing, *The Great Union Stock Yards of Chicago,* 24.

118 **"No *man ever had a better mother*":** George Thorndike Angell, *Autobiographical Sketches and Personal Reflections* (Boston: Franklin Press, 1884), 2.

118 **the task of recruiting:** Ibid., 18.

118 **"Must an animal be worked":** *Boston Daily Evening Transcript,* July 16, 1868, 2.

118 **"My time was fully occupied":** Angell, *Autobiographical Sketches,* 19.

119 **"In Cork, I found a hospital":** "Mr. Angell's Letters," *Our Dumb Animals,* June 1, 1869, 5.

119 "I have not seen in Glasgow": Ibid.

119 "I have been three weeks in London": "Mr. Angell's Letters," *Our Dumb Animals,* August 3, 1869, 33.

119 and then Zurich, where: "Mr. Angell's Letters," *Our Dumb Animals,* October 5, 1869, 51.

119 "dragged in, struggling, slipping": "Mr. Angell's Letters," *Our Dumb Animals,* November 2, 1869, 61.

119 a sign at the local zoo: "Mr. Angell's Letters," *Our Dumb Animals,* December 7, 1869, 71.

120 He had been back just a few weeks: Angell, *Autobiographical Sketches,* 37.

120 Dore took a job as a teacher: A. T. Andreas, *History of Chicago,* vol. 2 (Chicago: The A. T. Andreas Company, 1885), 106.

120 dabbling in the cattle industry: Wade, *Chicago's Pride,* 89.

120 So Angell headed west: Angell, *Autobiographical Sketches,* 37.

120 One story, passed along to him: "Letter from a Gentleman of the Chicago Press," *An Appeal in Behalf of the Illinois Humane Society,* March 1, 1871, 2.

120 "a crowd of persons": Angell, *Autobiographical Sketches,* 38.

120 "The cruelties at the stock yard": "Letter from a Gentleman of the Chicago Press."

120 So one morning he threw on: Angell, *Autobiographical Sketches,* 38.

121 "an almost perpendicular descent": George Angell, "What I Saw and Heard at the Chicago Stockyards," *An Appeal in Behalf of the Illinois Humane Society,* March 1, 1871, 3.

121 "*They* don't care": Ibid.

121 One former Texas drover told him: Ibid.

121 Prospective buyers, Angell was told: "The Stock Yards—Letter from a Chicago Stock Reporter," *An Appeal in Behalf of the Illinois Humane Society,* March 1, 1871, 2.

121 By early November, Angell: Angell, *Autobiographical Sketches,* 38.

122 Porter had played a key role: *The Story of the Typewriter, 1873–1923* (Herkimer, NY: Herkimer County Historical Society, 1923), 45–46.

122 negotiating his fee down: Angell, *Autobiographical Sketches,* 39.

122 more than three thousand copies: "The Society's Appeal to the Public," *An Appeal in Behalf of the Illinois Humane Society,* March 1, 1871, 1.

122 In Angell's address: See "Our Fellow Brutes," *The Chicago Republican,* December 7, 1870; also "Cruelty to Animals," *The Times* (Chicago), December 7, 1870.

123 Of the twelve lines: *Facts Respecting Street Railways* (London: P.S. King, 1866), 33–35.

124 That February 14: "A Triumph for Mr. Bergh," *New-York Tribune,* February 14, 1871.

124 During another morning of cold: "Bergh Beaten," *New York Herald,* February 18, 1871; "Mr. Bergh Arrests a Railroad President," *New-York Tribune,* February 18, 1871.

124 the ASPCA made a comparable stir: "The Dog Fighters in Court," *New York Herald,* February 24, 1871.

125 "Twice each week I have occasion": "Bergh vs. Vanderbilt," *New York Times,* August 31, 1871, 3.

125 "At the mines": "Henry Bergh and the Car Horses," *New York Times,* December 26, 1871, 4.

126 **In a pamphlet he distributed:** "Friendly Appeal to Butchers," reprinted as "President Bergh's Appeal to Butchers" in *Our Dumb Animals,* December 1871, 157.

127 **a shocking incident:** "Putrid Beef," *Boston Herald,* April 18, 1871; "Abominations at Brighton," *Boston Daily Journal,* April 18, 1871.

128 **The incident touched off:** "Report on the Sale of Bad Meat in Boston," excerpted as "Transportation of Cattle by Rail," *Our Dumb Animals,* February 1871, 72.

128 **his personal copy of it:** Digitized by MIT Libraries as part of "150 Years in the Stacks," https://libraries.mit.edu/150books/2011/01/17/1871/.

128 **"The flesh of mammalia undergoes":** Augustus C. Hamlin, *Martyria* (Boston: Lee and Shepard, 1866), 83.

129 **Maltreated animals will be flooded:** Contemporary studies that show a link between stress and meat quality include Yonela Zifikile Njisane and Voster Muchenje, "Farm to Abattoir Conditions, Animal Factors and Their Subsequent Effects on Cattle Behavioural Responses and Beef Quality—A Review," *Asian-Australasian Journal of Animal Sciences* (June 2017): 755–64; A. Y. Chulayo et al., "Effects of Transport Distance, Lairage Time and Stunning Efficiency on Cortisol, Glucose, HSPA1A and How They Relate with Meat Quality in Cattle," *Meat Science* (July 2016): 89–96; Filipe Antonio Dalla Costa et al., "How Do Season, On-Farm Fasting Interval and Lairage Period Affect Swine Welfare, Carcass and Meat Quality Traits?," *International Journal of Biometeorology* (November 2019): 1497–1505; Giancarlo Bozzo et al., "Analysis of Stress Indicators for Evaluation of Animal Welfare and Meat Quality in Traditional and Jewish Slaughtering," *Animals* (Basel) (March 2018): 43. For evidence on the other side, see L. Rey-Salguiero, "Meat Quality in Relation to Swine Well-Being After Transport and During Lairage at the Slaughterhouse," *Meat Science* (August 2018): 38–43; M. J. Alcalde et al., "Effects of Farm Management Practices and Transport Duration on Stress Response and Meat Quality Traits of Suckling Goat Kids," *Animal* 11, no. 9 (2017): 1626–35; L. Nanni Costa et al., "Effect of Journey Time and Environmental Condition on Bull Behaviour and Beef Quality During Road Transport in Northern Italy," *Deutsche tierärztliche Wochenschrift* (April 2003): 107–10.

129 **In early 1872, Angell published:** George Angell, *Cattle Transportation in the United States* (Boston: Massachusetts Society for the Prevention of Cruelty to Animals, 1872).

130 **"It is for the interest of shippers":** Ibid., 7.

131 **a typical brine involved:** Wade, *Chicago's Pride,* 9.

131 **Most of the city's packing operations:** Ibid., 66.

131 **he was kicked out:** "Busy Life of Mr. Armour," *Chicago Tribune,* January 7, 1901, 2.

131 **At nineteen, he joined the gold rush:** Cora Lillian Davenport, "The Rise of the Armours, an American Industrial Family," master's thesis (University of Chicago, 1930), 8–9.

132 **eventually hiring round-the-clock guards:** Harper Leech and John Charles Carroll, *Armour and His Times* (New York: D. Appleton-Century Company, 1930), 23–24.

132 **The firm made a killing:** "Busy Life of Mr. Armour," *Chicago Tribune.*

132 **the sixth-largest pork firm:** Wade, *Chicago's Pride*, 65.

132 **the so-called slaughtering machine:** Ibid., 63.

132 **"Everything in and about the establishment":** "The Packing Season," *Chicago Republican,* December 11, 1866, 3.

133 **The sudden hoisting of a pig:** Wade, *Chicago's Pride*, 63.

133 **By 1874, Armour & Company:** Wade, *Chicago's Pride*, 104–5.

Chapter 7: The Horse Doctors

135 **It began in September 1872:** A. B. Judson, "Report on the Origin and Progress of the Epizootic Among Horses in 1872, with a Table of Mortality in New York," *Third Annual Report of the Board of Health of the Health Department of the City of New York: April 11, 1872 to April 30, 1873* (New York: D. Appleton and Company, 1873), 250.

135 **It would start as a dry cough:** A. F. Liautard, "Report on the Epizootic, as It Appeared in New York," *Third Annual Report of the Board of Health of the Health Department of the City of New York: April 11, 1872 to April 30, 1873* (New York: D. Appleton and Company, 1873), 276–77. See also Bonnie R. Rush, "Equine Influenza," *Merck Veterinary Manual,* January 2014, https://www.merckvetmanual.com.

135 **The lymph nodes of the throat:** Liautard, "Report on the Epizootic, as It Appeared in New York," 276–77. See also Rush, "Equine Influenza."

135 **The illness would not prove:** Judson, "Report on the Origin and Progress of the Epizootic Among Horses in 1872," 275.

135 **But they were depressed:** Liautard, "Report on the Epizootic, as It Appeared in New York," 276–77. See also Rush, "Equine Influenza."

135 **Even as Toronto succumbed:** "The Canadian Viceroy," *New York Herald,* October 1, 1872, 3.

135 **Soon after his return:** Quoted in "The Horse Disease. The Canadian Epidemic Spreading at an Alarming Rate. Western New York Affected," *New York Herald,* October 22, 1872, 7.

136 **The New York Times estimated:** "Ravages of the Horse Disease in Rochester," *New York Times,* October 22, 1872, 8.

136 **By this time, reports:** Judson, "Report on the Origin and Progress of the Epizootic Among Horses in 1872," 252–54. See also "The Canadian Horse Disease—Appearance in Albany," *New York Times,* October 23, 1872, 5.

136 **This prompted the ASPCA:** "History of the ASPCA," American Society for the Prevention of Cruelty to Animals, https://www.aspca.org.

136 **The vehicle was a boxy affair:** "The New Ambulance" [image], *American Society for the Prevention of Cruelty to Animals, Seventh Annual Report* (New York: Cushing, Bardua, & Co., 1873), 28.

137 **Liautard was born at home:** Jeanette Mitchell-Vigneron, "Alexandre Liautard (1835–1918), Sa Vie—Son Oeuvre," PhD diss. (Ecole Nationale Vétérinaire D'Alfort, 1982), 17–18.

138 **It was reported that the Imperial Guard:** Francois Bugnion, "Birth of an Idea: The Founding of the International Committee of the Red Cross and Red Cres-

cent Movement: From Solferino to the Original Geneva Convention (1859–1864)," *International Review of the Red Cross* 94 (Winter 2012): 1301.

138 **Uncle Étienne would have:** Colin Robins, "A Note on Veterinary Surgeons in the Crimea," *Journal for the Society of Army Historical Research* 87 (Autumn 2009): 217–20.

138 **Alexandre perhaps envisioned:** Mitchell-Vigneron, "Alexandre Liautard (1835–1918)," 19–24.

140 **In 1832, the editor of *American Turf Register:*** "Cure of Lockjaw in Horses," *American Turf Register and Sporting Magazine* 4 (September 1832): 13.

140 ***The Cultivator* published in 1838:** "Substitute for Spaying," *The Cultivator: A Monthly Publication, Devoted to Agriculture* 5 (October 1838): 140.

140 **Several years later, *The American Agriculturalist:*** "Dogs and Cats," *The American Agriculturalist* 3 (November 1844): 340.

140 **In 1845, *Michigan Farmer* contained advice:** "Diarrhea or Scours in Calves," *Michigan Farmer, and Western Agriculturalist* 3 (May 25, 1845): 24.

141 **Also, since antiquity, experts:** George Fleming, *Horseshoes and Horseshoeing: Their Origin, History, Uses, and Abuses* (London: Chapman and Hall, 1869). See also A. D. Fraser, "Recent Light on the Roman Horseshoe," *The Classical Journal* 29 (June 1934): 690–91.

141 **The role of the farrier:** A. Lawson, *The Modern Farrier* (Newcastle upon Tyne: Mackenzie and Dent, 1828), 30, 75–78, 128, 451.

141 **A remedy for bleeding:** Quoted in J. F. Smithcors, *The American Veterinary Profession: Its Background and Development* (Ames: Iowa State University Press, 1963), 160.

142 **Physicians often could be persuaded:** J. F. Smithcors, "Medical Men and the Beginnings of Veterinary Medicine in America," *Bulletin of the History of Medicine* 33 (July–August 1959): 332–34.

142 **"Good for man and beast":** Quoted in Smithcors, *The American Veterinary Profession,* 187–88. See also *Merchant's Gargling Oil A Liniment for Man & Beast* [advertising card] (Buffalo: Clay & Company, n.d.), https://www.digital commonwealth.org; and *Pain-Killer Almanac & Family Receipt Book* (Cincinnati: J. N. Harris & Company, 1868), 40.

142 **Three veterinary colleges opened:** Everett B. Miller, "Private Veterinary Colleges in the United States, 1852–1927," *Journal of the American Veterinary Medical Association* 178 (March 15, 1981): 583–84.

142 **By 1860, Liautard was in practice:** Mitchell-Vigneron, "Alexandre Liautard (1835–1918)," 34.

142 **The United States Census that year:** Department of Commerce and Labor, Bureau of the Census, "Comparison of Occupations at the Twelfth and Preceding Censuses," *Special Reports: Occupations at the Twelfth Census* (Washington, DC: Government Printing Office, 1904), xxxiv.

142 **Along with building his private practice:** Mitchell-Vigneron, "Alexandre Liautard (1835–1918)," 29–34.

143 **His most durable creation:** Smithcors, *The American Veterinary Profession,* 299.

143 **Forty veterinarians assembled:** Mitchell-Vigneron, "Alexandre Liautard (1835–1918)," 55.

143 **The men hailed from all over:** Smithcors, *The American Veterinary Profession,* 299.

143 **Soon thereafter, Liautard made:** Mitchell-Vigneron, "Alexandre Liautard (1835–1918), 38.

143 **At the reopening ceremony:** A. S. Copeman, *Introductory Lecture Delivered at the Opening of the New York College of Veterinary Surgeons* (New York: M. T. Tyler, 1865), 2–4.

144 **Liautard was not just the college's host:** Mitchell-Vigneron, "Alexandre Liautard (1835–1918)," 38. See also: A. Liautard, "History and Progress of Veterinary Medicine," *American Veterinary Review* 1 (March 1877): 9 (appendix).

144 **When the epizootic swept through:** "The Horse Epidemic," *The Sun,* October 25, 1872, 1. See also "Hippo-Malaria. The Continuance of the Critical Condition of the Tortured Car Horses," *New York Herald,* October 29, 1872, 3.

144 **An illustration from the ASPCA's annual report:** *American Society for the Prevention of Cruelty to Animals, Seventh Annual Report* (New York: Cushing, Bardua, & Co., 1873), 21.

144 **Out in the streets:** "The Equine Influenza," *New York Herald,* October 28, 1872, 13.

145 **Men picked up wheelbarrows:** "The Horse Disease," *Frank Leslie's Illustrated Newspaper* 35, November 16, 1872, 35.

145 **Claiming exorbitant prices:** "The Horse Disease in New York," *Sacramento Daily Union,* November 9, 1872, 8. See also "The Horse Epidemic," *New York Times,* October 30, 1872, 8; and "The Coming Ox," *New York Times,* October 31, 1872, 6.

145 **Steamboats ferried commuters:** "The Horse Epidemic," 8.

145 **Horse-drawn fire engines:** Ann Norton Greene, *Horses at Work: Harnessing Power in Industrial America* (Cambridge, MA: Harvard University Press, 2008), 167–69. See also "The Horse Disease," *Chicago Daily Tribune,* October 31, 1872, 1; "The Horse Epidemic," *New York Times,* October 29, 1872, 5; "An Embargo on Commerce," *The Sun,* October 29, 1872, 3; "Our Noblest Servants," *The Sun,* October 31, 1872, 1; "The Horse Disease in New York," *Sacramento Daily Union,* November 9, 1872, 8.

145 **Some policemen found themselves:** "An Embargo on Commerce," *The Sun,* October 29, 1872, 3.

146 **Complaints about the treatment:** *American Society for the Prevention of Cruelty to Animals, Seventh Annual Report* (New York: Cushing, Bardua, & Co., 1873), 20.

146 **The Third and Fourth Avenue lines:** "The Horse Disease in New York," *Sacramento Daily Union,* November 9, 1872, 8. See also "The Horse Epidemic," *New York Times,* October 30, 1872, 8.

146 **Overloaded cars placed insurmountable burdens:** "Hippo-Malaria," *New York Herald,* 3. See also "Epizootism," *Brooklyn Union,* October 30, 1872, 4.

146 **On the evening of October 30:** "The Horse Disease in New York," *Sacramento Daily Union,* November 9, 1872, 8.

146 **One clue lay in the pattern:** Sean Kheraj, "The Great Epizootic of 1872–73: Networks of Animal Disease in North American Urban Environments," *Environmental History* 23 (July 2018): 495.

147 **Philadelphia was obliged to release:** Jeffrey Michael Flanagan, "On the Backs of Horses: The Great Epizootic of 1872," master's thesis (College of William and Mary, 2011), 13.

147 **Washington, D.C., reported:** "Deserted Streets," *Daily National Republican,* November 5, 1872, 4.

147 **That winter, New Orleans:** "Races Postponed Until Saturday," *New Orleans Republican,* December 3, 1872, 5.

147 **In the West, battles:** John Gregory Bourke, *On the Border with Crook* (New York: Charles Scribner's Sons, 1892), 208.

147 **"I think I had begun":** Quoted in David A. Norris, "When a Plague Tormented America's Horses," Historynet, May 21, 2019, https://www.historynet.com/.

147 **Alexandre Liautard and his colleagues:** "The Horse Distemper," *New York Times,* October 26, 1872, 4.

147 **Modern virologists have theorized:** David M. Morens and Jeffery K. Taubenberger, "An Avian Outbreak Associated with Panzootic Equine Influenza in 1872: An Early Example of Highly Pathogenic Avian Influenza?," *Influenza and Other Respiratory Viruses* 4 (November 2010): 373–77. See also David M. Morens and Jeffery K. Taubenberger, "Historical Thoughts on Influenza Viral Ecosystems, or Behold a Pale Horse, Dead Dogs, Failing Fowl, and Sick Swine," *Influenza and Other Respiratory Viruses* 4 (November 2010): 327–37.

148 **According to a story in *The New York Herald*:** "The Horse Plague," *New York Herald,* October 25, 1872, 3.

148 **A *New York Times* writer observed:** "The Horse Epidemic," *New York Times,* October 24, 1872, 8.

148 **Wealthy newspaper magnate:** "The Mysterious Malady," *New York Herald,* October 27, 1872, 10.

148 **A letter from Union army general:** "A Letter from Gen. Roberts, U.S.A., to Mr. Bonner on the Horse Epidemic," *New York Times,* October 25, 1872, 8.

148 **Letters published elsewhere:** "An Embargo on Commerce," *The Sun,* October 29, 1872, 3.

148 **A *New York Herald* reporter:** "The Horse Plague," *New York Herald,* October 25, 1872, 3.

149 **"The treatment of influenza":** Liautard, "Report on the Epizootic, as It Appeared in New York," 278.

149 **But Liautard went on to describe:** Ibid., 279.

149 **"Experience has taught me":** Ibid., 278.

150 **the fire department had few healthy ones:** *Report of the Commissioners Appointed to Investigate the Cause and Management of the Great Fire in Boston* (Boston: Rockwell & Churchill City Printers, 1873), vii–viii.

150 **some 776 buildings burned:** Ibid., iii.

150 **a false rumor began to spread:** "A Serious Charge," *Our Dumb Animals,* December 1872, 256.

150 **"To societies like ours":** "Lessons of the Horse Malady," *Our Dumb Animals,* November 1872, 248.

150 **"has passed, and left its record":** "The Epizootic Disease," *Our Dumb Animals,* December 1872, 256.

151 **The mule in Louisville:** *Our Dumb Animals,* July 1873, 20.

151 **The dog in Wilmington:** "'Cam,'" *Our Dumb Animals,* July 1873, 10.

151 The mother cat: "My Cat 'Stripe,'" *Our Dumb Animals*, June 1873, 7.

151 The Newfoundland dog: *Our Dumb Animals*, June 1873, 6.

151 The family of geese: "Not Such a Silly Goose After All," *Our Dumb Animals*, August 1873, 22.

151 "As soon as the accident occurred": "An Actress's Love for Her Horse," *Our Dumb Animals*, September 1873, 32.

152 As more rigorous news accounts had noted: "Leo Hudson," *Daily Journal of Commerce* (Kansas City, MO), June 5, 1873, 1.

153 a long species-by-species guide to euthanasia: "How to Kill Animals Humanely," *Our Dumb Animals*, April 1874, 91.

153 the MSPCA began providing hammers: "Killing Animals," *Our Dumb Animals*, May 1874, 101.

153 That same year in New York: Mitchell-Vigneron, "Alexandre Liautard (1835–1918)," 39–42.

153 The hundreds of veterinarians: Smithcors, *The American Veterinary Profession*, 320.

154 He declared that this innovation: "Editorial: College of Veterinary Surgeons of America," *American Veterinary Review* 5 (January 1882): 455.

154 One grocer's reminiscence: Smithcors, *The American Veterinary Profession*, 357.

154 Historian Ann Norton Greene: Greene, *Horses at Work*, 230–34.

155 "It is a fact as strange": "President Bergh's Address at the Opening Exercises of the American Veterinary College," *American Veterinary Review* 2 (November 1878): 349–50.

Chapter 8: Every Buffalo Dead

157 During the Pleistocene epoch: International Commission on Stratigraphy, "International Chronostratigraphic Chart," 2020, https://stratigraphy.org.

157 Thus was exposed: Thomas A. Ager, "Late Quaternary Vegetation and Climate History of the Central Bering Land Bridge from St. Michael Island, Western Alaska," *Quaternary Research* 60 (July 2003): 19–32.

157 These ancestral bison multiplied: Duane Froese et al., "Fossil and Genomic Evidence Constrains the Timing of Bison Arrival in North America," *Proceedings of the National Academy of Sciences of the United States of America* 114 (March 28, 2017): 3457–62.

157 The original combined range: Ben A. Potter et al., "History of the Bison in North America," in *American Bison: Status Survey and Conservation Guidelines 2010*, ed. C. Cormac Gates et al. (Gland, Switzerland: IUCN, 2010), 6–8. See also Andrew C. Isenberg, *The Destruction of the Bison: An Environmental History, 1750–1920* (New York: Cambridge University Press, 2000), 25; and Mary Meagher, "*Bison bison*," *Mammalian Species* 266 (June 16, 1986): 1–2.

158 As enormous as they are: Zak Ratajczak et al., "Reintroducing Bison Results in Long-Running and Resilient Increases in Grassland Diversity," *Proceedings of the National Academy of Sciences* 119 (August 29, 2022): 4–5.

158 The rubbing of their hairy bodies: Alan K. Knapp et al., "The Keystone Role of Bison in North American Tallgrass Prairie: Bison Increase Habitat Heterogeneity and Alter a Broad Array of Plant, Community, and Ecosystem Processes,"

BioScience 49 (January 1999): 39–50. See also Bryan R. Coppedge and James H. Shaw, "Effects of Horning and Rubbing Behavior by Bison (*Bison bison*) on Woody Vegetation in a Tallgrass Prairie Landscape," *American Midland Naturalist* 138 (July 1997): 93–95.

158 **Within the herd:** Dale F. Lott, *American Bison: A Natural History* (Berkeley: University of California Press, 2002), 5–35. See also Tom McHugh, *The Time of the Buffalo* (Lincoln: University of Nebraska Press), 179–98.

159 **Historically, the maneuvering:** Joe C. Truett et al., "Managing Bison to Restore Biodiversity," *Great Plains Research* 11 (Spring 2001): 123–36. See also Zachary Nickell et al., "Ecosystem Engineering by Bison (*Bison bison*) Wallowing Increases Arthropod Community Heterogeneity in Space and Time," *Ecosphere* 9 (September 2018): 1–10; and George C. Frison, "Paleoindian Large Mammal Hunters on the Plains of North America," *Proceedings of the National Academy of Sciences of the United States of America* 95 (November 24, 1998): 14576–83.

159 **Bison numbers had begun their decline:** Andrew C. Isenberg, *The Destruction of the Bison: An Environmental History, 1750–1920* (New York: Cambridge University Press, 2000), 31–92.

159 **Soon the bison slaughter accelerated:** Andrew C. Isenberg, "Toward a Policy of Destruction: Buffaloes, Law, and the Market, 1803–83," *Great Plains Quarterly* 12 (Fall 1992): 227–41.

160 **Guided expeditions on horseback:** Isenberg, *The Destruction of the Bison,* 128–30.

160 **Sometimes passengers would even shoot:** "Buffalo Hunting," *Harper's Weekly,* December 14, 1867, 797.

160 **Newspapers printed stories:** "The Russian Prince," *New York Times,* January 14, 1872, 4. See also "The Ducal Chase," *Kansas City Times,* January 16, 1872, 1.

160 **According to the environmental historian:** Isenberg, *The Destruction of the Bison,* 128–43.

160 **Improvements in tanning technology:** McHugh, *The Time of the Buffalo,* 253.

160 **Standing at a distance downwind:** Richard Irving Dodge, *The Plains of North America and Their Inhabitants* (New York: G. P. Putnam's Sons, 1876), 134–41.

161 **On January 25, 1872, a letter:** "Wanton Butchery—The Evils of Buffalo Hunting—Letter to Mr. Henry Bergh from Kansas," *New York Times,* January 26, 1872, 5.

161 **Over the weeks that followed:** "Buffaloes vs. Indians," *The Baltimore Sun,* January 31, 1872, 1. See also *Philadelphia Inquirer,* January 27, 1872, 4.

161 **Hazen's letter prompted:** "Slaughter of the Buffaloes," *Nashville Union and American,* February 14, 1872, 1.

161 **The same native nations:** Isenberg, *The Destruction of the Bison,* 143–56.

162 **To some U.S. leaders:** Ibid., 128.

162 **"Kill every buffalo you can":** Lieut.-General the Rt. Hon. Sir W. F. Butler, G.C.B., *Sir William Butler: An Autobiography* (London: Constable and Company, 1911), 97.

162 **In his 1872 annual report:** U.S. Secretary of the Interior, *Report of the Secretary of the Interior,* U.S. House of Representatives, 42nd Congress, 3rd Sess., 1872, Ex. Doc. 1 (part 5), vol. 1, 5.

162 General Hazen didn't agree: "Wanton Butchery," *New York Times*, January 26, 1872, 5.

162 *Our Dumb Animals* printed a letter: "The Wanton Destruction of the Buffalo," *Our Dumb Animals*, March 1872, 181.

162 *The Baltimore Sun* editorialized: "Buffaloes vs. Indians," *The Baltimore Sun*, January 31, 1872, 1.

163 sending back thirty-six crates: John Taliaferro, *Grinnell: America's Environmental Pioneer and His Restless Drive to Save the West* (New York: Liveright, 2019), 47–58.

163 "Their mode of life appealed strongly": Ibid., 54.

164 In Grinnell's account of the hunt: "Buffalo Hunt with the Pawnees," *Forest and Stream*, December 25, 1873, 305.

165 "Oh! well may the Indian hunter": "My Dog," *Our Dumb Animals*, November 1872, 247.

165 which the historian Shari Huhndorf: Shari M. Huhndorf, *Going Native: Indians in the American Cultural Imagination* (Ithaca, NY: Cornell University Press, 2001).

165 Improved Order of Red Men: Ibid., 65–78.

166 Grand Order of the Iroquois: Ibid., 66.

166 "[T]here is an inevitable conflict": George Bird Grinnell, "The Natives of the Alaska Coast Region," in *Alaska*, vol. 1 (New York: Doubleday, Page & Co., 1901), 183.

166 At the moment when President Grant: Douglas H. MacDonald, *Before Yellowstone* (Seattle: University of Washington Press, 2018), 28–29.

166 Since the end of the previous century: Mark V. Barrow Jr., *Nature's Ghosts: Confronting Extinction from the Age of Jefferson to the Age of Ecology* (Chicago: University of Chicago Press, 2009), 39–46.

167 his tally of documented extinct species: "The Old 'New' World," *Evening Star* (Washington, DC), June 16, 1873, 2.

167 That January, the *Topeka Commonwealth:* Reprinted as "Tremendous Slaughter of Buffaloes in Southern Kansas," *Chicago Tribune,* February 6, 1873, 8.

168 Allen began collecting animal specimens: Joel A. Allen, *Autobiographical Notes and a Bibliography of the Scientific Publications of Joel Asaph Allen* (New York: American Museum of Natural History, 1916), 1–11, 20–27.

168 He made an additional: Ibid., 27–31.

168 He noted accounts: J. A. Allen, "The Extirpation of the Larger Indigenous Mammals of the United States," *Penn Monthly*, October 1876, 794–806.

168 He dug up accounts: J. A. Allen, "On the Decrease of Birds in the United States," *Penn Monthly*, December 1876, 931–44.

169 In 1876, a few years after: J. A. Allen, "The American Bisons, Living and Extinct," *Memoirs of the Museum of Comparative Zoology, at Harvard College, Cambridge, Massachusetts* 4 (1876).

169 "the close of the next half-century": Allen, "On the Decrease of Birds in the United States," 944.

170 "[I]t is greatly to our disgrace": J. A. Allen, "The North American Bison and Its Extermination," *Penn Monthly*, March 1876, 223.

170 "Though both are noble in their way": Ibid., 215.

170 "After having formed for thousands": Ibid., 222–23.

171 **In March 1874, Representative Greenbury Fort:** "A Century of Lawmaking for a New Nation: U.S. Congressional Documents and Debates, 1774–1875," *Congressional Record,* House of Representatives, 43rd Congress, 1st Session. Library of Congress, 2105, https://memory.loc.gov/.

171 **Fort's was not the first bill:** William Hornaday, "The Extermination of the American Bison," *Annual Report of the Board of Regents of the Smithsonian Institution* (Washington, DC: Government Printing Office, 1889), 514–15.

171 **New York Representative Samuel Cox:** "A Century of Lawmaking for a New Nation: U.S. Congressional Documents and Debates, 1774–1875," *Congressional Record,* House of Representatives, 43rd Congress, 1st Session. Library of Congress, 2106, https://memory.loc.gov/.

171 **Others echoed Interior Secretary:** Ibid., Library of Congress, 2107.

171 **But the real reason to reject the bill:** Ibid., Library of Congress, 2107.

171 **Congressmen on both sides of the debate:** Ibid., Library of Congress, 2105–2109.

171 **Pro-protection delegate Richard McCormick:** Ibid., Library of Congress, 2106.

171 **H.R. 921 passed the House:** Ibid., Library of Congress, 2109.

171 **The bison bill came before:** Ibid., Library of Congress, 5413–14.

172 **President Grant allowed H.R. 921:** "The Extermination of the American Bison," *Annual Report of the Board of Regents of the Smithsonian Institution* (Washington, DC: Government Printing Office, 1889), 517.

Chapter 9: Slippery Slopes

175 **"who cannot be happy":** "The Polypragmonous Bergh," *The World* (New York), February 11, 1875, 4.

176 **Catholic clergy in the state:** "Objections to the Cruelty to Children Bill," *New York Herald,* February 3, 1875, 7.

176 **"poor parents, inexperienced in law":** "Debate on the Bill to Prevent Cruelty to Children," *The World* (New York), February 10, 1875, 8.

176 **"monstrous offence against justice":** "The Polypragmonous Bergh," *The World* (New York).

177 **One infamous defense of incest:** See, for example, Merrilee H. Salmon, *Introduction to Logic and Critical Thinking* (Boston: Wadsworth, 2013), 142.

178 **"I don't know how old I am":** "The Courts," *New York Herald,* April 10, 1874, 5.

178 **"has been in the habit of whipping":** Ibid.

179 **"The child is an animal":** Jacob A. Riis, *The Children of the Poor* (New York: Charles Scribner's Sons, 1892), 143.

179 **"was not within the scope":** "Mr. Bergh Enlarging His Sphere of Usefulness," *New York Times,* April 10, 1874, 8.

180 **"tended streetlamps, maintained sewers":** Susan J. Pearson, *The Rights of the Defenseless: Protecting Animals and Children in Gilded Age America* (Chicago: University of Chicago Press, 2020), 158.

180 **Misconduct charges against New York police:** "New-York Policemen," *New York Times,* October 12, 1874, 4.

181 **"a scandalous stain upon our civilization":** "Another Freak of Bergh," *New York Herald,* February 16, 1875, 8.

181 **Hackett made clear:** "Bergh's Contempt," *New York Herald,* March 2, 1875, 8.

181 The *Herald* compared him: "Prosecuting Poor Bergh," *New York Herald,* February 17, 1875, 6.

182 Four grand hotels: James D. McCabe, *An Illustrated History of the Centennial Exhibition* (Philadelphia: National Publishing Co., 1876), 296–315.

182 "even at this rate": "Financial and Commercial," *The Press* (Philadelphia), March 10, 1876, 3.

182 it had prosecuted just 152 cases: "S.P.C.A.," *The Press* (Philadelphia), January 28, 1876, 6.

182 which had housed more: "Interesting Figures," *Sunday Dispatch* (Philadelphia), January 2, 1876.

182 In April 1876, White convened: "A Work of Mercy," *The Press* (Philadelphia), April 6, 1876, 2.

182 In one particularly dramatic episode: *Second Annual Report of the Woman's Branch* (Philadelphia: Pennsylvania Society for the Prevention of Cruelty to Animals, 1871), 12–17.

183 "I hope your branch": Ibid., 17.

183 "I may remark": Frances Power Cobbe, "The Moral Aspects of Vivisection," *New Quarterly Magazine* 4 (1875): 230–31.

183 which she had laid out: Frances Power Cobbe, *An Essay on Intuitive Morals* (Boston: Crosby, Nichols, and Company, 1859).

184 "the main weapon of the vivisectors": "A Work of Mercy," *The Press* (Philadelphia).

184 "We are well aware": Ibid.

184 "As the main work of civilization": Cobbe, "The Moral Aspects of Vivisection," 234.

185 by the time President Grant: "The Exposition," *New York Herald,* May 11, 1876.

186 "Ten years ago": "Mr. Bergh Expostulates," *New York Herald,* May 11, 1876.

186 George Angell had curated: "Our Centennial Exhibit," *Our Dumb Animals,* July 1876, 12.

186 Bergh had curated an exhibit too: "Mr. Bergh's Museum at the Centennial," *The World* (New York), May 13, 1876, 2.

187 "offense to good taste": *The World* (New York), May 13, 1876, 4.

187 The evidence was right on display: McCabe, *An Illustrated History of the Centennial Exhibition,* 474–75.

Chapter 10: A New Order of Chivalry

191 five thousand Edison lights: "The Exposition As It Is at Present," *The Courier-Journal* (Louisville, KY), August 16, 1884, 8.

191 "My department is now in perfect order": "Letter from Mr. Angell to the 'Massachusetts Ploughman,'" *Our Dumb Animals,* February 1885, 176.

192 he had personally helped start up: George Thorndike Angell, *Autobiographical Sketches and Personal Reflections* (Boston: Franklin Press, 1884), 46, 65–66, 78.

192 Ladies' Moral and Humane Education Society: "The Work of Humanity," *Minneapolis Tribune,* November 21, 1879, 4.

192 Angell had set up shop: Angell, *Autobiographical Sketches,* 71–72.

192   **Two years later, when:** *Our Dumb Animals*, April 1885, 194.

192   **helping to convene a meeting:** "Prevention of Cruelty to Animals," *Daily Pica-yune* (New Orleans), February 6, 1885.

193   **Eliza "E.J." Nicholson:** A colorful biography can be found in B. H. Gilley, "A Woman for Women: Eliza Nicholson, Publisher of the New Orleans *Daily Pica-yune*," *Louisiana History: The Journal of the Louisiana Historical Association* 30, no. 3 (Summer 1989): 233–48.

193   **"There are pictures of beautiful well fed":** "Nature's Dumb Nobility," *Daily Picayune* (New Orleans), January 5, 1885.

193   **The most prominent piece of art:** "Letter from Mr. Angell to the 'Massachusetts Ploughman,'" *Our Dumb Animals*.

193   **"He who serves well and speaks not":** Henry Wadsworth Longfellow, "The Alarm-Bell of Atri," *Atlantic Monthly*, July 1870.

194   **"Some of our friends":** "Sentiment, Sentimental," *Our Dumb Animals*, October 1884, 140.

195   **By the mid-1880s:** David M. Fahey, *Temperance Societies in Late Victorian and Edwardian England* (Newcastle upon Tyne: Cambridge Scholars Publishing, 2020), 30.

195   **when she died:** "Information Respecting Bands of Mercy," *The Sixty-Second Report of the Royal Society for the Prevention of Cruelty to Animals*, July 1886, 165.

195   **his desire to create a "new order of chivalry":** Angell, *Autobiographical Sketches*, 46.

195   **"speak no falsehoods":** "The Work of Humanity," *Minneapolis Tribune*.

195   **By 1882, when he met Thomas Timmins:** Timmins's own account can be found in Rev. Thomas Timmins, *The History of the Founding, Aims, and Growth of the American Bands of Mercy* (Boston: P. H. Foster & Co., 1883).

195   **Angell launched this new crusade:** See *Our Dumb Animals*, September 1882.

196   **"executed under the personal direction":** *The Sixty-Second Report of the Royal Society for the Prevention of Cruelty to Animals*, 166–67.

196   **During his months in New Orleans:** "Nature's Dumb Nobility," *Daily Picayune* (New Orleans), March 16, 1885; see also "Nature's Dumb Nobility," *Daily Pica-yune* (New Orleans), January 19, 1885.

197   **nearly four thousand clubs:** "New Bands of Mercy," *Our Dumb Animals*, March 1885, 183.

197   **Indeed, the rise of public schools:** B. Edward McClellan, *Moral Education in America: Schools and the Shaping of Character from Colonial Times to the Present* (New York: Teachers College Press, 1999), 15–30.

197   **"The germs of morality":** Horace Mann, *The Common School Journal* 1 (November 1838): 14.

197   **"impress on the minds":** *Twenty-First Annual Report of the Board of Educa-tion* (Boston: William White, 1858), 19.

198   **a story about a "big young man":** Timmins, *The History of the Founding, Aims, and Growth of the American Bands of Mercy*, 14.

198   **"marching along, we are marching along":** "Band of Mercy Melodies, No. 1, Supplement to *Our Dumb Animals*," MSPCA scrapbook.

198   **"report of each member":** "Answers to Band of Mercy Questions," *Our Dumb Animals*, May 1883, 190.

198 **"Remember, children, whenever":** "Band of Mercy, or School Exercise, on Kindness for Animals," *Our Dumb Animals,* December 1883, 51.

198 **"not think lightly of it":** "Our Band of Mercy Badge," *Our Dumb Animals,* June 1884, 107.

199 WHAT A CHICAGO "BAND OF MERCY" SCHOOL GIRL DID: *Our Dumb Animals,* June 1884, 105.

199 **"It is a charming style of whipping":** "Henry Bergh's Vigorous Call for the Whipping Post," *St. Louis Post-Dispatch,* January 4, 1881, 2.

200 **"There is something melancholy":** *Brooklyn Union,* January 19, 1881, 2.

200 **made a serious strategic error in 1875:** Ernest Freeberg, *A Traitor to His Species* (New York: Basic Books, 2020), 174–75.

200 **"So-Called Sport and Its Victims":** "Mr. Bergh and the Sportsmen," *New-York Tribune,* June 22, 1881, 8.

200 **"The feathers of the slain pigeons":** "Flight of the Feathers," *New York Herald,* June 26, 1881, 8.

200 **"dying by slow degrees in awful agony":** Quoted in "No Taste for Cruelty," *Brooklyn Union,* June 28, 1881, 2.

201 **a rat-killing ferret exhibition:** "The Ferrets' Fun Stopped," *New York Times,* February 7, 1885, 2.

201 **the practice of applying red-hot shoes:** "Current Events," *Brooklyn Daily Eagle,* October 10, 1885, 4.

201 **and of clipping their coats:** "Mr. Bonner on the Horse," *The Enquirer* (Cincinnati), September 20, 1884, 12.

201 **his fight against cruelty:** "Disorder at Jerome Park," *New-York Tribune,* October 8, 1884, 2.

201 **"the best thing one can do":** Richard T. Ely, "Recent American Socialism," *The Johns Hopkins University Studies in Historical and Political Science,* vol. 4 (Baltimore: N. Murray, 1885), 42–43.

202 **the urban crime rate:** Barry Latzer, *The Roots of Violent Crime in America* (Baton Rouge: Louisiana State University Press, 2020), 102–3.

202 **a sociologist of the period estimated:** Ibid., 106.

202 **New York tenements would often pack:** Ibid., 105.

202 **In 1880, Bergh had successfully appealed:** Zulma Steele, *Angel in Top Hat* (New York: Harper & Brothers, 1942), 157–58.

202 **"unblushingly announces to the world":** "Mr. Bergh to Gov. Glick," *Dodge City Globe,* July 29, 1884, 7.

202 **he prevailed on Louisiana's governor:** "A Disgrace Averted," *Our Dumb Animals,* February 1885, 176.

202 **In March 1883, he wrote:** Bergh to George L. Clarke, March 3, 1883, ASPCA Papers, Museum of the City of New York. Thanks to Leela Outcalt and Christina Chavez for digitizing this letter during a lengthy research shutdown at the museum.

203 **"I wish to submit to intelligent readers":** "Dynamite or Humane Education,—Which Shall It Be?," reprinted in *Our Dumb Animals,* October 1883, 33.

204 **delivering a speech on the subject:** George T. Angell, "The New Order of Mercy; or, Crime and Its Prevention," reprinted in the appendix of the 1892 edition of his memoirs, *Autobiographical Sketches and Personal Recollections* (Boston: American Humane Education Society, 1892), 23–33.

204 **Angell marshaled some dubious statistics:** Ibid., 31.

204 **"There are hundreds of thousands of parents":** Ibid., 33.

205 **He helped to found a new state SPCA:** "Significant Extracts from Southern Papers" and "Extracts from Mr. Angell's Florida Letters," *Our Dumb Animals,* May 1885, 202; "Four Weeks in Florida," *Our Dumb Animals,* June 1885, 214.

205 **As early as the 1830s:** John James Audubon, *Ornithological Biography, or an Account of the Habits of the Birds of the United States of America* (Philadelphia: E. L. Carey and A. Hart, 1832), 603–4.

206 **the naturalist W. E. D. Scott made a trip:** W. E. D. Scott, "The Present Condition of Some of the Bird Rookeries of the Gulf Coast of Florida," *The Auk,* April 1887, 135–44.

Chapter 11: Here Come the Elephants!

209 **The blaring of bugles:** "The Circus in Town—A Bright Day and a Great Crowd on the Streets," *Lancaster Daily Intelligencer,* May 6, 1885, 1. See also Charles Philip Fox, *Circus Parades: A Pictorial History of America's Greatest Pageant* (Watkins Glen, NY: Century House, 1953), 8.

209 **Lancaster was the sixth stop:** Alvaro Betancourt, ed., *Route Book of P.T. Barnum's Greatest Show on Earth and the Great London Circus—Since the Consolidation Seasons of 1881, 1882, 1883, 1884, 1885—P.T. Barnum, J.A. Bailey, J.L. Hutchinson, Sole Proprietors* (no publication info.), 28.

210 **By the time the special train:** "The Circus in Town," *Lancaster Daily Intelligencer,* May 6, 1885, 1. See also Fox, *Circus Parades,* 8.

210 **During decades past:** Fox, *Circus Parades,* 12–14.

210 **After American circuses adapted:** Ibid., 14. See also Fred Dahlinger Jr., "The Development of the Railroad Circus, Part Two," *Bandwagon* 28 (January–February 1984): 19.

210 **Barnum's circus procession rolled:** "'The Greatest Show on Earth,'" *Lancaster New Era,* May 6, 1885, 4. See also "The Circus in Town," *Lancaster Daily Intelligencer,* May 6, 1885, 1; Fox, *Circus Parades,* 156–60; and "Barnum's Street Parade," *Boston Evening Journal,* June 8, 1885, 1.

211 **Before the day was out:** "The Circus in Town," *Lancaster Daily Intelligencer,* May 6, 1885, 1.

212 **Sipping lemonade and snacking on peanuts:** Betancourt, *Route Book,* 4–26. See also "The Circus in Town," 1; and "Barnum's Big Show," *Lancaster Daily Intelligencer,* May 6, 1885, 1.

212 **Punctuating the show:** "Barnum's Big Show," *Lancaster Daily Intelligencer,* May 6, 1885, 1. See also "Barnum's," *The Morning News* (Belfast, Ireland), June 2, 1885, 7.

213 **"Tom Thumb," the world's only "dwarf clown elephant":** Betancourt, *Route Book,* 24–25. See also "Barnum's Baby Elephant. Great Rejoicings Over Its Birth at Bridgeport," *New York Times,* February 4, 1882, 8; and "Barnum's Big Show," *Lancaster Daily Intelligencer,* May 6, 1885, 1.

213 **The little female was only the second:** A. H. Saxon, *P. T. Barnum: The Legend and the Man* (New York: Columbia University Press, 1989), 283–86. See also William Lawrence Slout, *A Royal Coupling: The Historic Marriage of Barnum and Bailey* (San Bernardino, CA: Emeritus Enterprise Books, 2000), 98–101;

and Eric Scigliano, *Love, War, and Circuses: The Age-Old Relationship Between Elephants and Humans* (Boston: Houghton Mifflin, 2002), 186–87.

213 **Jumbo was the undisputed star:** "Jumbo & Co.—The First Day of the Great Show in Brooklyn," *Brooklyn Daily Times,* May 23, 1882, 4.

213 **on posters and handbills:** P.T. Barnum's Greatest Show on Earth, the Great London Circus, Sanger's Royal British Menagerie, and Great [*sic*] International Allied Shows, "Barnum's Shows," *Lancaster Daily Intelligencer,* May 4, 1885, 4. See also Betancourt, *Route Book,* 4–26.

213 **Today, scientists and veterinarians:** Jeffrey P. Cohn, "Do Elephants Belong in Zoos?," *BioScience* 56 (September 2006): 714–17.

214 **Jumbo and other elephants:** Susan Nance, *Entertaining Elephants: Animal Agency and the Business of the American Circus* (Baltimore: Johns Hopkins University Press, 2013).

214 **Jumbo entered captivity early:** Les Harding, *Elephant Story: Jumbo and P.T. Barnum Under the Big Top* (Jefferson, NC: McFarland & Company, 2000), 12–24. See also Sandra Lash Shoshani, Jeheskel Shoshani, and Fred Dahlinger Jr., "Jumbo: Origin of the Word and History of the Elephant," *Elephant* 2 (September 6, 1986): 87–88.

214 **Over the next seventeen years:** Matthew Scott, *Autobiography of Matthew Scott, Jumbo's Keeper, Formerly of the Zoological Society's Gardens, London, and Receiver of Sir Edwin Landseer Medal in 1866; also Jumbo's Biography, by the Same Author* (Bridgeport, CT: Trow's Printing and Bookbinding Company, 1885).

214 **Offerings of oranges:** Paul Chambers, *Jumbo: This Being the True Story of the Greatest Elephant in the World* (Hanover, NH: Steerforth Press, 2008), 90. See also W. P. Jolly, *Jumbo* (London: Constable and Company, 1976), 26.

215 **With adolescence came changes:** Jolly, *Jumbo,* 37–45. See also Chambers, *Jumbo,* 109–26.

215 **For the modest price of two thousand:** Harding, *Elephant Story,* 40–66. See also Jolly, *Jumbo,* 45–114.

216 **He was heartily greeted:** "Jumbo Landed in Safety," *New York Times,* April 10, 1882, 1.

216 **When one reporter asked:** Ronald B. Tobias, *Behemoth: The History of the Elephant in America* (New York: Harper Perennial, 2013), 168.

216 **Jumbo's footprints were so large:** Christabelle Sethna, "The Memory of an Elephant: Savagery, Civilization, and Spectacle," in *Animal Metropolis: Histories of Human-Animal Relations in Urban Canada,* ed. Joanna Dean, Darcy Ingram, and Christabelle Sethna (Calgary: University of Calgary Press, 2017), 35–36.

217 **Jumbo crisscrossed the country:** "Jumbo on His Travels," *New York Times,* April 23, 1882, 9.

218 **"Mr. Arstingstall has very fixed":** "Jumbo Landed in Safety—He Celebrates His Arrival in a Bottle of Whisky," *New York Times,* April 10, 1882, 1.

218 **As a teenager, not long after:** Slout, *A Royal Coupling,* 101–2.

218 **A long fall brought his short stint:** William Lawrence Slout, "Arstingstall, George," *Olympians of the Sawdust Circle: A Biographical Dictionary of the Nineteenth Century American Circus* (San Bernardino, CA: Borgo Press, 1998), 7–8.

218 His supervisor there, Stuart Craven: Michael Daly, *Topsy: The Startling Story of the Crooked-Tailed Elephant, P.T. Barnum, and the American Wizard, Thomas Edison* (New York: Grove Press, 2014), 99–101.

218 "I will tell you something": "Training Elephants—The Methods Used and the Curious Results Obtained," *St. Louis Daily Globe-Democrat*, August 11, 1879, 1.

219 It began in March 1879: "Punishing Old Emperor—Why It Was Thought Necessary to Apply the Red-Hot Iron," *The Sun* (New York), March 23, 1879, 1. See also *The Daily Gazette* (Kalamazoo, MI), April 5, 1879, 2; *New Haven Evening Register*, March 28, 1879, 2; and *Washington Standard* (Olympia, WA), June 6, 1879, 9.

219 "Why, it requires but one sober thought": Quoted in "About That Elephant—Mr. Bergh and the 'Emperor,'" *Harrisburg Independent*, March 25, 1879, 1.

219 Bailey himself described its use: "Elephants and Hot Irons," *The Sun* (New York), March 28, 1879, 3.

219 The ASPCA would later make an arrest: "Buckshot and Pokers," *New York Herald*, March 28, 1879, 5.

220 Several months later, Bergh: Saxon, *P. T. Barnum*, 238.

220 Historians disagree about what caused: Andrew A. Robichaud, *Animal City: The Domestication of America* (Cambridge, MA: Harvard University Press, 2019), 236–37. See also Saxon, *P. T. Barnum*, 238; and Zulma Steele, *Angel in Top Hat* (New York: Harper & Brothers, 1942), 244–46.

220 Barnum enthusiastically accepted: Robichaud, *Animal City*, 226–27.

220 "If I had my way": "About That Elephant," *Harrisburg Independent*, March 25, 1879.

220 In another of Barnum's favorite anecdotes: P. T. Barnum, *Struggles and Triumphs: Or, Sixty Years' Recollections of P. T. Barnum, Including His Golden Rules for Money-making* (Buffalo: The Courier Company, 1889), 322.

221 After hearing a report: Saxon, *P. T. Barnum*, 236.

221 "I know more about animals": Barnum, *Struggles and Triumphs*, 322.

222 in a letter to the *Evening Post*: Quoted in Saxon, *P. T. Barnum*, 237–38.

222 On April 1, 1883, the following item: "Bergh and the Elephant," *New York Herald*, April 1, 1883, 11.

222 Its sturdy handle: Nance, *Entertaining Elephants*, 88–91.

223 "They want to know": Horace Townsend, "Animals and Their Trainers," *Frank Leslie's Popular Monthly* 26 (December 1888): 730.

223 He had provided a close-up demonstration: "Jumbo on His Travels," *New York Times*, April 23, 1882, 9.

224 Bergh ordered Arstingstall: *New Haven Evening Register*, April 18, 1883, 2.

224 Even then, no real harm: "Letter from New York," *Evening Star* (Washington, DC), April 21, 1883, 5.

224 Arstingstall predicted that the elephants: *New Haven Evening Register*, April 18, 1883, 2.

224 Even these precautions failed: "Letter from New York," *Evening Star* (Washington, DC), April 21, 1883, 5.

224 On the morning of April 4: "Battle Between Elephants. Barnum's Pilot Attacks His Stall-Mate and Demolishes Everything near Him," *New-York Tribune*,

April 5, 1883, 8. See also "The Elephants' Fight," *New Haven Evening Register,* April 5, 1883, 3.

224 **Pilot was tied down:** "The Elephant Pilot Put to Death," *New-York Tribune,* April 6, 1883, 5.

225 **After briefly describing:** "Subdued Only by Death," *New York Times,* April 6, 1883, 5

225 **This was akin to satirizing:** Amy Louise Wood, " 'Killing the Elephant': Murderous Beasts and the Thrill of Retribution, 1885–1930," *Journal of the Gilded Age and Progressive Era* 11 (July 2012): 410.

225 **In a letter to Barnum:** "A Pert Communication from Bergh," *The Sun* (Baltimore), April 9, 1883, 1.

225 **According to a paraphrase:** "Mr. Bergh and Barnum," *New-York Tribune,* April 8, 1883, 7.

226 **In a telephone interview:** "Through the Telephone," *Truth* (New York), April 8, 1883, 5.

226 **"It is much to be regretted":** *Brooklyn Union,* April 9, 1883, 2.

226 **"Mr. Bergh yesterday came":** *New Haven Evening Register,* April 18, 1883, 2.

227 **When, in the spring of 1885:** "Bergh and Barnum," *Rochester Democrat and Chronicle,* April 27, 1885, 4.

227 **On July 18, while waiting:** P. T. Barnum, "Clipper Letter," in Betancourt, ed., *Route Book,* 42–43.

227 **There, Barnum and his partners:** Wood, " 'Killing the Elephant,' " 413–19.

228 **Although the event was widely discussed:** "Driving Elephants Mad by False Education," *Brooklyn Daily Eagle,* July 27, 1885, 2

228 **On the evening of September 16:** "The Great Jumbo Killed," *New York Times,* September 17, 1885, 5.

228 **A reporter on the scene:** "Jumbo's Tragic Death. Barnum's Monster Elephant Killed by a Train in Canada. Dying Like a Hero," *New York Herald,* September 17, 1885, 5.

229 **A day later, Barnum's agents:** "How Jumbo Was Killed. He Lost His Own Life in Trying to Save That of the Baby Elephant," *The Sun* (New York), September 18, 1885, 1.

229 **In the following week's version:** *New York Times,* September 20, 1885, 8. See also Harding, *Elephant Story,* 99.

229 **Barnum, as usual, took:** Quoted in Barnum, *Struggles and Triumphs,* 344.

229 **Henry Augustus Ward, a well-respected:** "Jumbo Double in Death. His Stuffed Skin Gazes at His Bones. Are Two Dead Elephants Better Than a Live One?," *New-York Tribune,* February 28, 1886, 2.

229 **Jumbo's remains rejoined:** Tobias, *Behemoth,* 203.

230 **When Bergh himself died, in 1888:** "Henry Bergh's Funeral," *New York Times,* March 16, 1888, 8. See also "Henry Bergh's Funeral," *New York Times,* March 17, 1888, 8.

Chapter 12: An Eye on Your Dog

233 **On April 15, 1886:** "Mistaken for Finette," *New York Times,* April 16, 1886, 2. See also "A Dog Bites Miss Morosini," *New York Herald,* April 16, 1886, 9;

"Miss Morosini Bitten," *New-York Daily Tribune,* April 16, 1886, 4; "Bitten by a Dog," *Buffalo Evening News,* April 20, 1886, 2; and John D. Blaisdell, "Louis Pasteur, Alexandre Liautard, and the Riverdale Dog Case," *Veterinary Heritage* 15 (March 1992): 2–3.

233 **Amalia was the youngest daughter:** "G. P. Morosini Dies at His Country Home," *New York Times,* September 16, 1908, 1.

234 **Along with their grand home:** "Mistaken for Finette," *New York Times,* April 16, 1886, 2.

234 **Amalia's mother hurriedly transported:** Ibid., 2.

234 **The swift application:** "Prophylactic Cauterisation in Rabies," *The Hospital* 26 (April 8, 1899): 23. See also Bill Wasik and Monica Murphy, *Rabid: A Cultural History of the World's Most Diabolical Virus* (New York: Viking, 2012), 53.

234 **Science was still struggling to explain:** John D. Blaisdell, "Louis Pasteur, Alexandre Liautard, and the Riverdale Dog Case," *Veterinary Heritage* 15 (March 1992): 3–4. See also Wasik and Murphy, *Rabid,* 110.

234 **Determined to receive:** Blaisdell, "Louis Pasteur, Alexandre Liautard, and the Riverdale Dog Case," 5. See also "A Dog Bites Miss Morosini," *New York Herald,* April 16, 1886, 9; and "Miss Morosini's Peril," *New York Herald,* May 19, 1886, 9.

235 **The New York College of Veterinary Surgeons:** American Veterinary Medical Association, "Former Veterinary Medical Institutions in the United States," *AVMA Membership Directory and Resource Manual,* 2008, https://www.avma .org/.

235 **Under Liautard's leadership:** American Veterinary College, *Annual Announcement, Session 1881–1882. Catalogue 1880–1881* (New York: Holt Brothers Printers, 1881), 4. See also Everett B. Miller, VMD, "Private Veterinary Colleges in the United States, 1852–1927," *Journal of the American Veterinary Medical Association* 178 (March 15, 1981): 585–86; Jeanette Mitchell-Vigneron, "Alexandre Liautard (1835–1918), Sa Vie—Son Oeuvre," PhD diss. (Ecole Nationale Vétérinaire D'Alfort, 1982), 39–46.

235 **At the 1883 commencement ceremony:** "Mr. Beecher on the Horse—An Address at the American Veterinary College," *New York Times,* March 1, 1883, 2.

235 **"knows more through instinct":** "Mr. Beecher's Scientific Suggestions—He Says a Good Word for the Horse and the Ass, and Their Mutual Friend Mr. Henry Bergh," *Brooklyn Daily Eagle,* March 1, 1883, 2.

235 **Beecher concluded his remarks:** Ibid., 2.

236 **After the speeches:** "American Veterinary College—Commencement Exercises for the Sessions 1882–3," *American Veterinary Review* 6 (March 1883): 556.

236 **"keep from the eyes of all visitors":** Reprinted as "A Horse and Dog Hospital," *Wallace's Monthly,* November 1884, 738.

236 **Photographs taken some years later:** S. K. Johnson, *The Dog: Management in Health, Treatment in Disease* (New York: New York Veterinary Hospital, 1900), 17, 21, 29, 37.

236 **A long, narrow room was set aside:** "New York's Danger from Dogs," *New York Herald,* December 18, 1885, 2.

236 **On Wednesday afternoons:** "A Horse and Dog Hospital," *Wallace's Monthly,* November 1884.

236 **In 1887, a reporter from the local paper:** "A Want Supplied," *Leavenworth Times* (Leavenworth, KS), April 3, 1887, 8.

237 **The one at the University of Pennsylvania:** "A Hospital for Animals," *Record of the Times* (Wilkes-Barre, PA), September 5, 1885, 3.

237 **That same year, the hospital:** "Surgery for Brutes," *Boston Globe,* May 3, 1885, 2.

237 **In 1888, a *Brooklyn Daily Eagle*:** "The Ills of Horse Flesh," *Brooklyn Daily Eagle,* November 4, 1888, 15.

237 **In 1886, a court in Cambridge:** "Against Harvard College," *Boston Herald,* January 21, 1886, 6.

238 **"Fifth Avenue is given over":** *Brooklyn Daily Eagle,* December 13, 1885, 2.

238 **A few years later, a *Sun* story:** "Very Fashionable Dogs," *The Sun* (New York), May 13, 1888, 6.

238 ***Harper's Bazaar* noted in 1887:** Quoted in "Fashionable Dogs," *The Evening News* (Emporia, KS), July 27, 1887, 3.

238 **The following year, the *Sun*:** "Very Fashionable Dogs," *The Sun,* May 13, 1888.

238 **Selective breeding for traits:** Heidi G. Parker et al., "Genomic Analyses Reveal the Influence of Geographic Origin, Migration, and Hybridization on Modern Dog Breed Development," *Cell Reports* 19 (April 25, 1997): 697–708. See also Emily V. Dutrow, James A. Serpell, and Elaine A. Ostrander, "Domestic Dog Lineages Reveal Genetic Drivers of Behavioral Diversification," *Cell* 185 (December 8, 2022): 4737–55.

239 **Cats entered into the domestication relationship:** Michael J. Montague et al., "Comparative Analysis of the Domestic Cat Genome Reveals Genetic Signatures Underlying Feline Biology and Domestication," *Proceedings of the National Academy of Sciences* 111 (November 10, 2014): 17230–5. See also Monika J. Lipinski et al., "The Ascent of Cat Breeds: Genetic Evaluations of Breeds and Worldwide Random-Bred Populations," *Genomics* 91 (January 2008): 12–21.

239 **By 1886, the American Kennel Club:** *The American Kennel Stud Book,* vol. 3 (Chicago: N. Rowe, 1886).

239 **For that year's Westminster dog show:** Westminster Kennel Club, *Tenth Annual New York Bench Show Catalogue* (New York: Rogers & Sherwood, 1886).

239 **Of the many "famous dogs" expected:** "Many Famous Dogs Entered," *New York Times,* April 25, 1886, 14.

239 **a rapturous local reporter in Memphis:** "Field and Kennel," *Memphis Avalanche,* January 21, 1886, 2.

239 **"Luxurious self-gratification":** Gaston Fay, "Typical Dogs," *Century Magazine* 30 (May 1885): 29.

239 **A reporter in 1887 claimed:** "Coddled like Babies," *Saint Paul Globe* (Saint Paul, MN), January 23, 1887, 15.

240 **Similarly, in 1888, the *Sun*'s report:** "Very Fashionable Dogs," *The Sun.*

240 **A reporter for New York's *Sunday Star*:** Reprinted as "Dogs in Gold and Silver," *Kansas City Times* (Kansas City, MO), May 17, 1885, 10.

240 **New York society denizen Harry Lehr:** Elizabeth Drexel Lehr, *"King Lehr" and the Gilded Age* (New York: J. B. Lippincott, 1935), 211.

240 **"The reporter was shown little smoking caps":** "Coddled like Babies," *Saint Paul Globe.*

241 **It was popularly believed:** John D. Blaisdell, "With Certain Reservations: The American Veterinary Community's Reception of Pasteur's Work on Rabies," *Agricultural History* 70 (Summer 1996): 510.

241 **Veterinarians endeavored:** Henri Bouley, *Hydrophobia: Means of Avoiding Its Perils and Preventing Its Spread,* trans. Alexander Liautard (New York: Harper and Brothers, 1874), 9–32. See also George Fleming, *Rabies and Hydrophobia: Their History, Nature, Causes, Symptoms, and Prevention* (London: Chapman and Hall, 1872), 189–248; and "Editorial—Cerebral Inoculation in Doubtful Cases of Rabies," *American Veterinary Review* 10 (August 1886): 201–2.

241 **In 1885, several months prior:** Louis Pasteur, "Inoculation Against Hydrophobia" (a translation of the paper read before the French Academy of Sciences on October 26, 1885), *Popular Science Monthly* 28 (January 1866): 292.

241 **Pasteur had developed:** Wasik and Murphy, *Rabid,* 128–40.

241 **The medical community outside:** Bert Hansen, "America's First Medical Breakthrough: How Popular Excitement About a French Rabies Cure in 1885 Raised New Expectations for Medical Progress," *American Historical Review* 103 (April 1998): 409. See also Blaisdell, "With Certain Reservations," 508–9; and Blaisdell, "Louis Pasteur, Alexandre Liautard, and the Riverdale Dog Case," 2–3.

242 **Of all the contributions:** J. F. Smithcors, *The American Veterinary Profession: Its Background and Development* (Ames: Iowa State University Press, 1963), 341–47.

242 **The seventh issue of the *Review*:** M. H. Bouley, "On the Identity of Anthrax in All the Species of Domestic Animals," translated by A. Liautard, *American Veterinary Review* 1 (September 1877): 214.

243 **The scientific debate between:** Phyllis Allen Richmond, "American Attitudes Toward the Germ Theory of Disease (1860–1880)," *Journal of the History of Medicine and Allied Sciences* 9 (October 1954): 430–31.

243 **Many (but not all):** Nancy J. Tomes, "American Attitudes Toward the Germ Theory of Disease: Phyllis Allen Richmond Revisited," *Journal of the History of Medicine and Allied Sciences* 52 (January 1997): 29–50.

243 **Largely due to the editorial influence:** Smithcors, *The American Veterinary Profession,* 389–96.

243 **According to the calculations of historian:** Blaisdell, "With Certain Reservations," 505–6.

244 **In an 1880 editorial:** "Editorial—Chicken Cholera," *American Veterinary Review* 4 (May 1880): 52.

245 **To ensure the passage:** Messrs. Pasteur, Chamberland, and Roux, "Physiological Pathology: New Experiments on Rabies," *American Veterinary Review* 8 (May 1884): 79–83.

245 **At a USVMA meeting in 1884:** A. Liautard, "New Discoveries in Certain Contagious Diseases, Tuberculosis, Anthrax, Rabies," *American Veterinary Review* 8 (December 1884): 396–408.

247 **The meticulous examination:** James A. Walrath, "Cerebral Inoculation as a Means of Diagnosis in the Post Mortem of Rabid Animals," *American Veterinary Review* 10 (June 1886): 120–21.

247 **The feather, in particular:** Bouley, *Hydrophobia,* 9–32.

247 **Liautard urged Amalia's parents:** Walrath, "Cerebral Inoculation as a Means of Diagnosis in the Post Mortem of Rabid Animals," 121.

247 **The Morosinis accepted:** "Miss Morosini Going to Pasteur," *New-York Tribune,* April 21, 1886, 5.

247 **While the American medical community:** Bert Hansen, "America's First Medical Breakthrough: How Popular Excitement About a French Rabies Cure in 1885 Raised New Expectations for Medical Progress," *American Historical Review* 103 (April 1998): 373–409.

248 **Enthusiasm for scientific:** "The Dog Was Not Mad," *New York Times,* March 2, 1886, 4. See also Blaisdell, "With Certain Reservations," 3.

249 **Meanwhile, from Europe:** "Current Foreign Topics," *New York Times,* April 8, 1886, 1.

249 **Experts who doubted:** F. S. Billings, "Rabies in the Dog in Relation to Rabies in Man," *Journal of Comparative Medicine and Surgery* 7 (April 1886): 172–73.

249 **The popular perception:** Hansen, "America's First Medical Breakthrough," 402–6.

249 **And so, on the morning:** "To See Pasteur and Paris. Miss Morosini Sails in the Germanic, and So Do All the Family," *New York Herald,* April 23, 1886, 9

249 **Alexandre Liautard and his colleagues:** Walrath, "Cerebral Inoculation as a Means of Diagnosis in the Post Mortem of Rabid Animals," 120–21.

249 **The resulting paper:** Ibid., 120–22.

250 **"We may therefore conclude":** "Miss Morosini's Peril," *New York Herald,* May 19, 1886, 9.

250 **Liautard considered Miss Morosini's escape:** "The Dog That Bit Miss Morosini. Was It Mad?," *New-York Tribune,* May 20, 1886, 1.

250 **Liautard was enthusiastic:** "Rabies," *American Veterinary Review* 10 (June 1886): 97.

251 **When Liautard was announcing:** "Miss Morosini's Peril, "*New York Herald,* May 19, 1886, 9. See also "Editorial. Preventive Vaccination in Domestic Animals—Ought It Be Made Obligatory?," *American Veterinary Review* 9 (December 1885): 337–39.

252 **"[E]xperiment on animals":** Robert Meade Smith, "Experiments on Animals," *American Veterinary Review* (June 1885), 103–4.

252 **Charles Darwin, who cited Pasteur:** "Mr. Darwin on Vivisection," *The Times* (London), April 18, 1881, 10.

252 **Rather than celebrating:** Henry Bergh, "The Lancet and the Law," *North American Review* 134 (February 1882): 161–69.

253 **In October 1885:** "Fighting Against Vaccination," *New York Times,* October 27, 1885, 2.

253 **Beginning in May 1886:** "Disagreeing with Dr. Liautard," *New-York Tribune,* May 31, 1886, 5.

253 **A few months later:** E. C. Spitzka, "How Can We Prevent False Hydrophobia?," *Journal of Comparative Medicine and Surgery* 7 (July 1886): 260–64. See also "Mad Dogs. A New York Doctor Contests M. Pasteur's Theories," *Abbeville Press and Banner,* June 30, 1886, 7.

254 **Bergh sided with Spitzka:** "Dr. Spitzka's Experiments. Mr. Bergh Has No Intention of Interfering with Them," *New York Times,* June 12, 1866, 8.

254 **That same summer:** "No Inoculation for Bergh. The Noted Friend of Animals Does Not Believe in Pasteur's System," *Kansas City Times* (Kansas City, MO), July 23, 1886, 1.

255 **Liautard's cerebral inoculation test:** Blaisdell, "Louis Pasteur, Alexandre Liautard, and the Riverdale Dog Case," 9–11.

256 **On the evening of June 13:** "Miss Morosini's Return," *New York Herald,* June 13, 1886, 9.

Chapter 13: For the Birds

259 **Chilled by choppy, gray-blue waves:** William Brewster, "The Terns of the New England Coast," *Bulletin of the Nuttall Ornithological Club* 4 (January 1879): 15–17.

259 **Tern pairs form, or re-form:** Jennifer M. Arnold et al., "Common Tern *Sterna hirundo*," in *Birds of the World,* ed. S. M. Billerman (Cornell Lab of Ornithology, 2020), https://birdsoftheworld.org/.

260 **Doting tern parents:** Joanna Burger and Michael Gochfeld, *The Common Tern: Its Breeding Biology and Social Behavior* (New York: Columbia University Press, 1991), 12.

260 **Ferrying small silvery fish:** Brian G. Palestis, "Nesting Stage and Nest Defense by Common Terns," *Waterbirds: The International Journal of Waterbird Biology* 28 (March 2005): 87–94.

260 **Although a variety of animals:** Arnold et al., "Common Tern *Sterna hirundo*."

260 **the species that most imperiled:** Brewster, "The Terns of the New England Coast," 17.

260 **As urban populations swelled:** Phillipe Perrot, *Fashioning the Bourgeoisie: A History of Clothing in the Nineteenth Century,* trans. Richard Bienvenu (Princeton, NJ: Princeton University Press, 1994), 26–79.

261 **Feathers frequently festooned:** Robin W. Doughty, *Feather Fashions and Bird Preservation: A Study in Nature Protection* (Berkeley: University of California Press, 1975), 14–23.

261 **In a letter to *Forest and Stream*:** Frank M. Chapman, "Letter: Birds and Bonnets," *Forest and Stream* 26 (February 25, 1886): 84.

261 **In 1873, he had co-founded:** Mark V. Barrow Jr., *A Passion for Birds: American Ornithology After Audubon* (Princeton, NJ: Princeton University Press, 1998), 47–50. See also John R. Nelson, "Thomas Nuttall: Pioneering Naturalist (1786–1859)," *Bird Observer* 43 (December 2015): 360–69.

262 **He discusses, chillingly:** Brewster, "The Terns of the New England Coast," 17.

262 **"[a] graceful pearl-tinted wing":** Ibid., 17.

262 **His pilgrimages to the island:** Ibid., 18–20.

263 ***Forest and Stream* put a historic notice:** "The Audubon Society," *Forest and Stream,* February 11, 1886, 1.

264 **an editorial called "Spare the Swallows":** "Spare the Swallows," *Forest and Stream,* September 3, 1883, 1.

264 **A *Forest and Stream* issue in August 1884:** "The Sacrifice of Song Birds," *Forest and Stream,* August 7, 1884, 1.

265 **a "Natural History" column that put numbers:** "The Destruction of Small Birds," *Forest and Stream,* August 7, 1884, 24.

265 **in June, he proudly reported:** *Forest and Stream,* June 24, 1886, 1.

265 **By the summer of 1886, when Grinnell:** "New Bands of Mercy Formed by Mass. S.P.C.A.," *Our Dumb Animals,* July 1886, 13.

266 **"that every one who joins them"**: "Audubon Societies," *Our Dumb Animals,* June 1886, 6.

266 **By the 1880s, there were Sorosis chapters:** J. C. Croly, *The History of the Woman's Club Movement in America* (New York: H. G. Allen & Company, 1898), 15–34.

266 **other groups focused on female success:** See *Transactions of the National Council of Women of the United States* (Philadelphia: J. B. Lippincott Company, 1891), 23.

266 **"representative women, superior women":** "A Famous Fraternity," *Chattanooga Daily Times,* April 12, 1885, 7.

266 **the Chicago writer Rose Elizabeth Cleveland:** Quoted in "The Audubon Societies," *Cherryvale Globe and Torch* (Cherryvale, KS), February 11, 1887, 8.

268 **"was got up by a lot of cranks":** *New-York Tribune,* quoted in *The Millbrook Herald* (Millbrook, KS), November 24, 1886, 8.

268 **20,000 members in 400 different towns:** *The Audubon Magazine,* February 1887, 5.

268 **George Angell, Henry Bergh, and Caroline Earle White:** Ibid., 20.

268 **White's personal efforts to rescue the terns:** *The Audubon Magazine,* March 1887, 43–44.

268 **"will aim to be practical, instructive and helpful":** "The Audubon Magazine," *The Audubon Magazine,* February 1887, 5.

268 **fables like "The Two Princesses":** "The Two Princesses," in ibid., 17–18.

268 **"Charley's Wonderful Journey," a Lewis Carroll–like tale:** *The Audubon Magazine,* March 1887, 40–42.

268 **A bracing essay:** "Woman's Heartlessness," *The Audubon Magazine,* February 1887, 13–14.

269 **On a less strident note:** "Princess Ruby-Throat," *The Audubon Magazine,* December 1887, 249–54.

269 **Seventy students joined:** "Our Smith College Audubon," *The Audubon Magazine,* September 1887, 175–78.

270 **"When you have saved a man's life":** Florence A. Merriam, "Fifty Common Birds, and How to Know Them," *The Audubon Magazine,* June 1887, 108.

270 **The robin:** Ibid., 109.

270 **The chickadee:** Florence A. Merriam, "Hints to Audubon Workers: Fifty Common Birds and How to Know Them," *The Audubon Magazine,* July 1887, 135.

271 **The meadowlark:** Ibid., 133.

271 **While sightseeing in Kentucky and Ohio:** Albert Hazen Wright, "Early Records of the Carolina Paroquet," *The Auk* 29 (July 1912): 352–53.

271 **Twelve inches from hooked beak:** Edwin M. Hasbrouck, "The Carolina Paroquet *Conurus carolinensis*," *The Auk* 8 (October 1891): 368–73. See also John James Audubon, "The Carolina Parrot," in *Ornithological Biography, or an Account of the Habits of the Birds of the United States of America,* vol. 1 (Philadelphia: E. L. Carey and A. Hart, 1832): 135–40.

271 **Able to eke out a living:** Mikko Saikku, "The Extinction of the Carolina Parakeet," *Environmental History Review* 14 (Autumn 1990): 7–8.

272 **Not all observers:** Audubon, "The Carolina Parrot," 138–39.

272 **parakeets had disappeared:** Amos W. Butler, "Notes on the Range and Habits of the Carolina Parakeet," *The Auk* 9 (January 1892): 52–53.

272 While commercial hunters: Saikku, "The Extinction of the Carolina Parakeet," 9–10.

273 "call attention to the wholesale slaughter": "Second Meeting of the American Ornithologists' Union," *The Auk* 1 (October 1884): 374.

273 A sixteen-page supplement: *Science* 7 (February 26, 1886): 191–205.

273 Allen, in his own urgent essay: J. A. Allen, "The Present Wholesale Destruction of Bird-Life in the United States," *Science* 7 (February 26, 1886): 191–95.

274 W. E. D. Scott's dire April 1887 account: "The Present Condition of Some of the Bird Rookeries of the Gulf Coast of Florida," *The Auk*, April 1887, 135–44; continued in *The Auk*, July 1887, 213–22, and in *The Auk*, October 1887, 273–84.

274 "relatively few in comparison": "Bird-Laws," *Science* 7 (February 26, 1886): 203.

274 Heated letters to *Ornithologist and Oölogist:* "Correspondence," *Ornithologist and Oölogist,* November 1886, 176; "The A.O.U. and the Amateurs," *Ornithologist and Oölogist,* December 1886, 192.

274 a passionate riposte noting: "The A.O.U. and the Amateurs," *Ornithologist and Oölogist,* March 1887, 47–48.

274 confined his own articles: J. A. Allen, "Descriptions of Two New Subspecies of the Seaside Sparrow (*Ammodramus Maritimus*)," *The Auk,* July 1888, 284–87; J. A. Allen, "Description of a New Species of the Genus *Tityra,* from Ecuador," *The Auk,* July 1888, 287–88.

275 By the beginning of 1889: "Discontinuance of 'The Audubon Magazine,'" *The Audubon Magazine,* January 1889, 262.

275 "We learn from sources": "Reintroduction of Feather Millinery," *The Audubon Magazine,* November 1888, 207–8.

276 "have killed one or more varieties": "Snap Shots," *Forest and Stream,* February 16, 1888, 61.

277 By their second meeting: "The Boone and Crockett Club," *Forest and Stream,* March 8, 1888, 124.

277 But at Grinnell's urging: *Forest and Stream,* April 11, 1889, 235.

278 "a decrease in the number of parakeets": Barrow, *A Passion for Birds,* 102.

278 "I shall make no further attempts": Quoted in ibid., 105.

278 Two days later, encountering: Ibid., 106.

Chapter 14: A Great Preacher

281 "For more than twenty years": "The 'Uncle Tom's Cabin' of the Horse," *Our Dumb Animals,* March 1890, 114.

281 whose monthly circulation: "75,000 Copies of This Paper," *Our Dumb Animals,* February 1890, 102.

281 The group regularly awarded prizes: "Our Work," *Our Dumb Animals,* June 1876, 8.

282 by 1890, six years in: *Our Dumb Animals,* January 1890, 95.

282 news of which, owing: "Henry Bergh," *Our Dumb Animals,* April 1888, 124.

282 "nothing could have better suited": Frederick Douglass, *Life and Times of Frederick Douglass* (Hartford, CT: Park Publishing Company, 1882), 351.

282 This story first surfaced in 1896: Daniel R. Vollaro, "Lincoln, Stowe, and the 'Little Woman/Great War' Story," *Journal of the Abraham Lincoln Association* 30, no. 1 (Winter 2009): 20.

283 **one of Angell's humane correspondents:** George Angell, *Autobiographical Sketches and Personal Recollections* (Boston: American Humane Education Society, 1892), 94.

283 **what contemporary biographers suspect:** See, for example, Adrienne E. Gavin, *Dark Horse: A Life of Anna Sewell* (Gloucestershire, UK: Sutton Publishing, 2004), 165.

283 **"Years went on, and no progress was made":** "A Biographical Sketch," *Black Beauty: The Autobiography of a Horse* (New York: Rand McNally, 1904), 282.

284 **"Through the kind gifts of friends":** Angell, *Autobiographical Sketches,* 95.

284 **a lineage of first-person animal tales:** Tess Cosslett, *Talking Animals in British Children's Fiction, 1786–1914* (New York: Routledge, 2006), 63–92.

284 **In 1871, the publication gave space:** "The Old Horse's Story," *Our Dumb Animals,* November 1871, 151.

285 **"pride of his family":** Anna Sewell, *Black Beauty: The Autobiography of a Horse* (London: Jarrold & Sons, 1885), 16.

285 **"good bold horse":** Ibid., 17.

285 **"Not many days after":** Ibid.

286 **"instead of starting at an easy pace":** Ibid., 138.

286 **"black eyes and a hooked nose":** Ibid., 226.

286 **"Fancy now yourself":** Ibid., 39.

286 **"I was tied up, and made fast":** Ibid., 50.

286 **"There was not a well-bred horse":** Ibid., 51.

286 **"I was struggling to keep on":** Ibid., 227–28.

287 **In a 1997 paper, the academic:** Robert Dingley, "A Horse of a Different Color: 'Black Beauty' and the Pressures of Indebtedness," *Victorian Literature and Culture* 25, no. 2 (1997): 241–51.

287 **"this period of relative":** Ibid., 242.

287 **"speaks to her audience directly":** Jane Tompkins, *Sensational Designs: The Cultural Work of American Fiction, 1790–1860* (New York: Oxford University Press, 1985), 139.

288 **"The implantation of virtue":** Ibid., 157.

288 **Two months in, Angell himself:** *Our Dumb Animals,* June 1890, 4.

288 **was launching a new, even cheaper:** " 'Black Beauty.' Important Notice," *Our Dumb Animals,* July 1890, 3.

288 **By July, the total:** *Our Dumb Animals,* September 1890, 41.

288 **and by October 156,000:** *Our Dumb Animals,* October 1890, 53.

288 **A rave appeared in *The Critic*:** *The Critic,* June 21, 1890, 305.

288 **"I sat down to read it last night":** "Captain John Codman on 'Black Beauty,' " *Our Dumb Animals,* June 1890, 2.

289 **"We do not often speak of preachers by name":** "A Great Preacher," *The New York Parish Visitor,* quoted in *Our Dumb Animals,* September 1890, 41.

289 **in the fall he announced:** "Addresses," *Our Dumb Animals,* October 1890, 54.

289 **He began to arrange for translations:** "Over 150,000," *Our Dumb Animals,* October 1890, 50.

289 **Some correspondents offered money:** "A Monument to Anna Sewell," *Our Dumb Animals,* November 1890, 63; "A Monument to Anna Sewell," *Our Dumb Animals,* February 1891, 105.

289 **"I stopped an expressman":** "Chicago," *Our Dumb Animals,* October 1890, 54.

290 **Henry Ward Beecher's widow, Eunice:** "Mrs. Henry Ward Beecher," *Our Dumb Animals,* September 1890, 39.

290 **"most earnestly wish the book":** "Bishop Mallalieu," *Our Dumb Animals,* September 1890, 39.

290 **"hope that its kind teachings":** "What Some of Our College Presidents, Educators, and Eminent Clergy Think of 'Black Beauty,'" *Our Dumb Animals,* April 1891, 125.

290 **Scores of university presidents wrote in:** Ibid., 126.

290 **Angell's longtime benefactor:** *Our Dumb Animals,* June 1890, 2.

290 **"every driver of a grocer's delivery wagon":** *Our Dumb Animals,* September 1890, 41.

290 **"leave out all the humane pictures":** "Be Sure You Pick the Right Book," *Our Dumb Animals,* September 1890, 39.

290 **Angell's response was to harp:** "'Go Ye into All the World and Preach the Gospel to Every Creature,'" *Our Dumb Animals,* March 1891, 113.

291 **"The Gospel of Dumb Animals":** "'American Humane Education Society,' and 'Massachusetts Society for the Prevention of Cruelty to Animals,' President's Annual Report, March, 1891," *Our Dumb Animals,* April 1891, 129.

291 **he happily reprinted speculation:** "Except the Bible," *Our Dumb Animals,* March 1891, 114.

291 **at times he allowed himself to lump:** "Possibly 500,000," *Our Dumb Animals,* April 1891, 128.

291 **the December 1891 issue:** *Our Dumb Animals,* December 1891, 82–83.

291 **In the summer of 1890:** "A Most Important Meeting," *Our Dumb Animals,* July 1890, 16.

292 **an address he prepared:** George T. Angell, "Address to the Boston Public Schools," American Humane Education Society pamphlet.

292 **"I didn't care half so much":** Ibid., 3.

292 **"These lower creatures know the tones":** Ibid., 18.

292 **"I hope you will always do":** Ibid., 15.

293 **"I tell all the boys and girls":** Ibid., 16–17.

293 **"It may be worth a thousand dollars":** Ibid., 12.

293 **"Please think and tell me":** "Thoughts for Teachers and Clergymen," *Our Dumb Animals,* December 1891, 80.

294 **The February 1892 edition of *Our Dumb Animals:*** "The Carriage of the Future," *Our Dumb Animals,* February 1892, 105.

294 **"I'm the happiest horse in town to-night!":** "The Boston Horse and the Electric Car," *Our Dumb Animals,* March 1892, 114.

295 **"My troubles are all over, and I am at home":** Sewell, *Black Beauty,* 238.

Chapter 15: The Slaughter Factories

297 **A two-year-old Hereford:** "The American Stock Show," *Kansas Farmer,* October 25, 1891, 9.

298 **Two separate domestication events:** Daniel Pitt et al., "Domestication of Cattle: Two or Three Events?," *Evolutionary Applications* 12, no. 1 (January 2019): 123–36.

298 **The early American cattle herd:** Charles T. Leavitt, "Attempts to Improve Cattle Breeds in the United States, 1790–1860," *Agricultural History* 7, no. 2 (April 1933): 51–67.

298 **Over the course of the 1870s:** James W. Whitaker, *Feedlot Empire: Beef Cattle Feeding in Illinois and Iowa, 1840–1900* (Ames: Iowa State University Press, 1975), 68–69.

299 **Hickory Nut, however, saw his end:** "The Fat Stock Show," *The Daily Inter Ocean* (Chicago), November 19, 1891, 8.

299 **"What will Chicago do with an undertaking":** "What Will Chicago Do with It?," *The Sunday Herald* (Boston), March 2, 1890, 20.

300 **The city's total livestock trade:** "Chicago," *The Live Stock Report*, January 6, 1893, 4.

300 **Specially for the fair, Armour:** "Trip to the Stock Yards," *The Inter Ocean* (Chicago), May 28, 1893, 7.

300 **His firm by then employed:** Arthur Warren, "Philip D. Armour," *McClure's*, February 1894, 262.

300 **the roughly four million animals:** Ibid., 265.

300 **Phil Armour's own work ethic:** "Busy Life of Mr. Armour," *Chicago Tribune*, January 7, 1901, 2; Warren, "Philip D. Armour," 278.

301 **"If you showed me a piece of meat":** *Testimony Taken by the Select Committee of the United States Senate on the Transportation and Sale of Meat Products* (Washington, DC: Government Printing Office, 1889), 457.

301 **He famously led the industry:** Mary Yeager, *Competition and Regulation: The Development of Oligopoly in the Meat Industry* (Greenwich, CT: Jai Press, 1981), 87–109.

301 **the foresight to stash away eight million:** Cora Lillian Davenport, "The Rise of the Armours, an American Industrial Family," master's thesis (University of Chicago, 1930), 63.

302 **the business historian Alfred D. Chandler:** Alfred D. Chandler Jr., *The Visible Hand: The Managerial Revolution in American Business* (Cambridge, MA: Belknap Press of Harvard University Press, 1977), 394–95.

302 **the elaborate system of regional offices:** Davenport, "The Rise of the Armours," 49–50.

302 **to reduce to fourteen days:** Ibid., 67.

302 **how many different products:** Ibid., 41–46.

303 **an estimated 10,000 fairgoers came to Packingtown:** Louise Carroll Wade, *Chicago's Pride: The Stockyards, Packingtown, and Environs in the Nineteenth Century* (Urbana: University of Illinois Press, 1987), 370.

303 **these structures bore no resemblance:** "Chicago," *The Lancet*, January 7, 1905, 50; "Chicago," *The Lancet*, January 14, 1905, 121.

303 **These were grim, poorly ventilated buildings:** "Chicago," *The Lancet*, January 7, 1905, 50.

303 **The killing tended to take place:** F. W. Wilder, *The Modern Packing House* (Chicago: Nickerson & Collins, 1905), 17–48. Thanks to Dominic Pacyga for pointing us to this fascinating sourcebook.

304 **The killing process for pigs:** Ibid., 247–72.

304 **One federal survey:** *The Report of the U.S. Commissioner of Corporations on the Beef Industry* (Washington, DC: Government Printing Office, 1905), 17–18.

304 **At that, the various disassemblers:** Ibid.; Wilder, *The Modern Packing House,* 72–89.

304 **Sometimes a cow:** "Chicago," *The Lancet,* January 14, 1905, 121–22.

305 **"[N]ot infrequently":** "Horrible—Cruelties Worse Than the Tortures of the Inquisition," *Chicago Tribune,* March 6, 1880, 7.

305 **"The uproar was appalling":** Upton Sinclair, *The Jungle* (New York: Grosset & Dunlap, 1906), 40.

306 **The Humane Society heralded the news:** *Ninth Annual Report* (Chicago: Illinois Humane Society, 1880), 5–8.

306 **Born in Dublin in 1838:** *Encyclopaedia of Biography of Illinois,* vol. 1 (Chicago: Century Publishing and Engraving Company, 1892), 342.

306 **Shortall and a friend forced a wagon driver:** Joseph Kirkland, *The Story of Chicago* (Chicago: Dibble Publishing Company, 1892), 310–15.

306 **Shortall made his residence:** "The Madding Crowd," *The Inter Ocean* (Chicago), April 15, 1888, 1.

307 **In 1893, when Shortall wanted:** *Twenty-Fourth Annual Report* (Chicago: Illinois Humane Society, 1893), 16–18.

307 **the society published an encomium:** *Thirty-Second Annual Report* (Chicago: Illinois Humane Society, 1901), 27.

308 **a red-headed, freckle-faced Irishman:** "Wants a Building—The Great Need of the Illinois Humane Society," *The Inter Ocean* (Chicago), February 4, 1892, 1.

308 **Multiple drovers at the yards:** Group letter to Shortall, September 18, 1885, Abraham Lincoln Presidential Library and Museum (henceforth ALPLM); E. E. Brown to Shortall, October 15, 1885, ALPLM.

308 **the governor, Richard J. Oglesby, expressed alarm:** Oglesby to Shortall, February 16, 1886, ALPLM.

308 **a petition supporting him:** Petition to Governor-Elect Fifer, November 10, 1896, ALPLM.

308 **sent Shortall a letter:** "Henry Bergh per E.B." to Shortall, January 26, 1888, ALPLM.

308 **"I beg leave to state":** William Mitchell to Shortall, February 10, 1888, ALPLM.

309 **By 1908, when there were 354 anti-cruelty organizations:** Susan J. Pearson, *The Rights of the Defenseless: Protecting Animals and Children in Gilded Age America* (Chicago: University of Chicago Press, 2020), 2.

310 **one agent's files in 1883 and 1884:** "Case Records—Children," 1883–84, Illinois Humane Society Records, University of Illinois at Chicago (henceforth UIC).

310 **campaign against public performances:** "There Must Be an End to the Juvenile Opera," *The Inter Ocean* (Chicago), June 21, 1892; Illinois Humane Society scrapbook, ALPLM; Shortall to "Signor Romeo," January 7, 1888, ALPLM.

310 **sending agents to shut down:** "After Stage Children," *The Inter Ocean* (Chicago), July 27, 1892, 4.

310 **"It is not alone the possibility":** "Bike Papas Angry," *The Inter Ocean* (Chicago), May 17, 1896, 1.

311 **"It was feared that with a horse":** John G. Shortall, "Child-Saving Work of the Humane Societies," unpublished speech, 1897, 2, UIC.

311 **so much sentimental art of the period:** See J. Keri Cronin's splendid *Art for Animals: Visual Culture and Animal Advocacy, 1870–1914* (University Park: Pennsylvania State University Press, 2018).

312 **The most vivid and vexing description:** Collected in Rudyard Kipling, *From Sea to Sea: Letters of Travel, Part 2* (New York: Charles Scribner's Sons, 1900), 230–48.

312 **"the other places do not count":** Ibid., 230.

312 **"interminable vistas flanked":** Ibid., 231.

312 **"still kicking":** Ibid., 244.

312 **"were slain at the rate of five a minute":** Ibid., 247.

312 **"a young woman of large mould":** Ibid., 247–48.

313 **"the presentation of the modern":** Anne Bramley, "How Chicago's Slaughterhouse Spectacles Paved the Way for Big Meat," NPR News, WBUR.org, December 3, 2015.

314 **"awarded honorable mention":** *Twenty-Fifth Annual Report* (Chicago: Illinois Humane Society, 1894), 11.

314 **Shortall's correspondence from 1892 and 1893:** "Humane Congress at the World's Fair," subject file, ALPLM.

314 **the naturalist William Hosea Ballou noted:** "To Protect Animals," *Chicago Tribune,* October 12, 1893, 10.

314 **A Hindu priest, B. B. Nagarkar:** Ibid.

315 **all the relevant economic indicators:** "Stocks and Bonds," *The Inter Ocean* (Chicago), October 10, 1893; "The World of Trade," *The Inter Ocean* (Chicago), October 11, 1893; "The World of Trade," *The Inter Ocean* (Chicago), October 12, 1893.

Chapter 16: The Zoophilists

317 **a *Philadelphia Inquirer* piece described:** "Philadelphia Medical Students," *Philadelphia Inquirer,* February 23, 1896, 33.

317 **Keen devised a radical operation:** W. W. Keen to C. E. White, March 6, 1895, from "Vivisection Correspondence, 1883–1919," a collection of the Historical Medical Library of the College of Physicians of Philadelphia (HMLCPP). Many thanks to archivist Christina Perella for digitizing the Keen-White correspondence for us during the COVID-19 shutdown.

317 **pathbreaking methods of treating:** S. Weir Mitchell et al., *Gunshot Wounds and Other Injuries of Nerves* (Philadelphia: J. B. Lippincott & Co., 1864).

317 **In 1893, it was Keen:** William W. Keen, *The Surgical Operations on President Cleveland in 1893* (Philadelphia: George W. Jacobs & Co., 1917).

318 **"I regard it as a scientific":** *Keen of Philadelphia: The Collected Memoirs of William Williams Keen Jr.* (Dublin, NH: William L. Bauhan, 2002), 206.

318 **dueling addresses on the subject:** William W. Keen, *Our Recent Debts to Vivisection* (Philadelphia: Porter and Coates, 1885); Caroline Earle White, *An Answer to Dr. Keen's Address Entitled "Our Recent Debts to Vivisection"* (Philadelphia: American Society for the Restriction of Vivisection, 1886).

318 **He wrote to White:** Keen to White, March 6, 1895.

320 **White confided to her fellow founders:** "Reasons Given by Mrs. Caroline Earle White in Offering the Following Resolution to the Society for the 'Restriction of Vivisection,'" *Fifth Annual Report of the American Anti-Vivisection Society,* 8.

320 **"public institutions where woman's work":** "President Hayes' Visit," *Philadelphia Inquirer,* April 25, 1878, 2.

320   requiring that anyone engaging in vivisection: "Facts in Regard to the Failure of
        the Bills Presented to the Legislature for the Restriction of Vivisection," *Third
        Annual Report of the American Society for the Restriction of Vivisection*, 8–11.
321   Wood proposed instead that: Ibid., 12.
321   "had accomplished marvels in aiding": Ibid., 14.
322   "Have we not within a few months": White to Keen, October 25, 1885,
        HMLCPP.
322   she sketched out a lineage: White, *An Answer to Dr. Keen's Address*, 4.
322   "almost indescribable barbarities": Ibid., 21.
322   "With some few noble exceptions": "Reasons Given by Mrs. Caroline Earle
        White," *Fifth Annual Report*, 9.
322   "Our opponents can say to us": Ibid., 10.
323   "Is it probable that a scientist": Ibid., 10–11.
323   "It is true that the prospect": Ibid., 11.
323   "As an Association having for its object": *Sixth Annual Report of the American
        Anti-Vivisection Society*, 3.
324   a series of essays on the subject: These were later collected as Albert Leffing-
        well, *The Vivisection Question* (New Haven, CT: Tuttle, Morehouse and Taylor
        Company, 1901).
324   Another bill went before: *Eleventh Annual Report of the American Anti-
        Vivisection Society*, 8.
324   Washington State activists fared similarly: "The Governor's Veto," *Seattle Post-
        Intelligencer*, February 22, 1895, 2.
324   The modest success was Massachusetts: "Our Law Against Vivisection," *Our
        Dumb Animals*, May 1894, 136.
324   Still, by 1895, a project: *Report of the American Humane Association on Vivi-
        section in America, Adopted at Minneapolis, Minn., September 26, 1895* (Chi-
        cago: American Humane Association, 1896).
324   the group polled physicians: Ibid., 8.
324   "Should the law restrict": Ibid., 8.
325   "serves no purpose": Ibid., 13.
325   "the progress of medicine is *retarded*": *Ninth Annual Report of the American
        Anti-Vivisection Society*, 5.
325   "Who would think it right": William W. Keen, *Our Recent Debts to Vivisection*
        (Philadelphia: Porter and Coates, 1885), 5.
325   "The spleen has been removed": Ibid., 8.
326   treatment of heat stroke: Ibid., 9–12.
326   the remarkable research being done: Ibid., 13–14.
326   a textual reliquary of sorts: Many of these tidbits found their way into Mat-
        thew Woods's address upon assuming the AAVS presidency, reprinted in *Ninth
        Annual Report of the American Anti-Vivisection Society*, 3–9.
327   That heat-stroke research on rabbits: White, *An Answer to Dr. Keen's Address*,
        9–10.
327   That research on the effects: Ibid., 11–12.
327   "is often so different in men and animals": Ibid., 6.
328   "sacrifice their better feelings to plow": *Ninth Annual Report of the American
        Anti-Vivisection Society*, 5.
328   "Divine Providence has, we believe": White, *An Answer to Dr. Keen's Address*, 7.

329 **Keen could crow about multiple new treatments:** Keen to White, March 12, 1895, HMLCPP.

329 **"In your misguided zeal for dogs":** Ibid.

330 **The item was picked up:** "Dog or Man?," *The State* (Columbia, SC), March 17, 1895, 12.

330 **Later in life, Keen assembled:** W. W. Keen, "The Influence of Antivivisection on Character," *Boston Medical and Surgical Journal* 166, no. 18 (May 2, 1912): 651–58.

330 **"Can a cause which so seriously injures":** Ibid., 653.

331 **a master class in passive aggression:** *Journal of Zoophily*, January 1892, 13.

331 **The first item in the first section:** "The Golden-Crested Wren," *Journal of Zoophily*, January 1892, 6.

332 **"As the winter grew intensely cold":** "Its Winter Nap," *Journal of Zoophily*, June 1892, 86.

332 **"matter of common observation":** "How Fishes Breathe," *Journal of Zoophily*, November 1892, 167.

332 **an essay by Minnie Ward Patterson:** "The Story of a Beetle," *Journal of Zoophily*, October 1892, 151.

333 **by 1895, the group's:** *Thirteenth Annual Report of the American Antivivisection Society*. See also Craig Buettinger, "Women and Antivivisection in Late Nineteenth-Century America," *Journal of Social History* 30, no. 4 (Summer 1997): 859.

333 **"Will you, with the chivalry":** Lovell's speech was reprinted as "The Worst Thing in the World," in *Journal of Zoophily*, April 1895, 47.

333 **White upped the spiritual ante:** Reprinted as "Is Vivisection Morally Justifiable?," in *Journal of Zoophily*, April 1895, 55–57.

333 **A *Popular Science* review:** David Starr Jordan, "Scientific Temperance," *Appletons' Popular Science Monthly*, January 1896, 348.

334 **"It is the testimony of sagacious physicians":** Ibid., 348–49.

334 **"Alcohol and tobacco act as poison":** Ibid., 349.

334 **the German bacteriologist Robert Koch:** See Thomas Goetz's *The Remedy: Robert Koch, Arthur Conan Doyle, and the Quest to Cure Tuberculosis* (New York: Avery, 2015).

334 **a pamphlet with that title:** Frances Hoggan, *The Scientist at the Bedside* (London: Victoria Street Society, 1883), reprinted from *The Zoophilist*, April 12, 1882, 3–4.

334 **the rise of the speculum:** See Rose Eveleth, "Why No One Can Design a Better Speculum," *The Atlantic*, November 17, 2014.

335 **the effects of alcohol (especially in women):** See, for example, Ann Goding Sauer et al., "Proportion of Cancer Cases and Deaths Attributable to Alcohol Consumption by US State, 2013–2016," *Cancer Epidemiology*, January 19, 2021.

335 **"In view of the fact":** White to Keen, March 4, 1895, HMLCPP.

336 **the disappointing history of those attempts:** David K. C. Cooper et al., "A Brief History of Clinical Xenotransplantation," *International Journal of Surgery*, November 2015, 205–10.

336 **In 2022, a team from the University of Maryland:** "Patient in Groundbreaking Heart Transplant Dies," *New York Times*, March 9, 2022.

336 helping to block the cause: *Keen of Philadelphia*, 208.
336 "In season and out of season": Ibid., 206.

Chapter 17: Died Beloved

339 fifty-ton mausoleum: "Final Resting Place for Beloved Pets," *New York Times*, December 17, 1995.
339 Annie De Voe, a Manhattan boardinghouse owner: Peggy Gavan excavated Annie's story in a post entitled "Sydney De Voe, the Chelsea Collie That Lived Like a Gentleman and Died Beloved," on her Hatching Cat blog (hatchingcatnyc .com).
340 "the late lamented gazing soulfully": "Cemetery for Dogs and Cats," *Pittsburgh Daily Post*, May 20, 1906, 30.
340 complete with his own line: See "Dr. Johnson's Dog Remedies," *The Dog: Management in Health, Treatment in Disease* (New York: New York Veterinary Hospital, 1900), 4.
340 Bereaved owners would bring: "Where Dogs and Cats Are Buried," *The News and Courier* (Charleston, SC), May 29, 1906, 6.
340 In the earliest days, prices ranged: "A Cat and Dog Cemetery," *The Sun* (New York), October 16, 1898, 7.
340 who made her primary residence: "Recorded Real Estate Transfers," *New York Times*, March 16, 1895, 12; "Mrs. Emily C. Berthet," *Asbury Park Press*, May 1, 1913, 2.
340 an 1896 newspaper interview: "Cemetery for Dogs," *The Columbus Journal* (Nebraska), April 1, 1896, 1.
341 brand-new shelters in Manhattan and Brooklyn: "Home for Strayed Dogs," *New York Times*, January 18, 1895, 8; "Dogs and Cats in Pound," *New York Times*, September 14, 1895, 14.
341 when the nation had grown: "Societies of North America," in *Thirty-First Annual Report*, American Society for the Prevention of Cruelty to Animals (New York: J. J. Little, 1897), 55–79.
341 "Children relieved from distress": *Report of the Proceedings of the Twentieth Annual Convention of the American Humane Association, Held at Cleveland, Ohio* (Chicago: American Humane Association, 1896), 13.
342 The AHA also printed: Ibid., 50–52.
342 In 1896, the modern answer: James Andrew Dolph, "Bringing Wildlife to Millions: William Temple Hornaday, the Early Years, 1854–1896," PhD diss. (University of Massachusetts, Amherst, 1975), 668–69.
343 Embittered by a previous experience: Gregory J. Dehler, *The Most Defiant Devil: William Temple Hornaday and His Controversial Crusade to Save American Wildlife* (Charlottesville: University of Virginia Press, 2013), 69–71.
343 Hornaday replied to Osborn's letter: Dolph, "Bringing Wildlife to Millions," 670.
343 "Fight in the Treetops": Dehler, *The Most Defiant Devil*, 52–53.
344 Appointed chief taxidermist: Ibid., 58–63.
344 noting on his return trip: "Buffalo Specimens," *Evansville Daily Courier* (Indiana), December 30, 1886, 1.
344 The monumental diorama: Dehler, *The Most Defiant Devil*, 64–66.

344 **This moment marked:** Dolph, "Bringing Wildlife to Millions," 567.

345 **One month after:** Ibid., 675.

345 **The zoo Hornaday imagined:** "Statement of Plans and Purposes," *First Annual Report of the New York Zoological Society* (New York: New York Zoological Society, 1897), 14.

345 **He wished, wherever possible:** Ibid., 17.

346 **"As the vertebrate fauna":** Ibid., 19.

346 **"Throughout the entire continent":** Ibid., 19.

346 **"Unless we can create":** Ibid., 21.

346 **"checked by the spread":** Ibid., 21.

346 **Through explanatory scientific labeling:** Ibid., 17–21.

347 **"a great institution":** "New York's Splendid Zoo," *New York Times*, May 3, 1896, 28.

347 **"Wild animal performances":** William Temple Hornaday, *The Minds and Manners of Wild Animals: A Book of Personal Observations* (New York: Charles Scribner's Sons, 1927), 53.

347 **In an especially reprehensible:** Mitch Keller, "The Scandal at the Zoo," *New York Times*, August 6, 2006, https://www.nytimes.com/.

347 **In 1905, with Ernest Baynes:** Ernest Harold Baynes, "History and Proceedings of the Society," *[First] Annual Report of the American Bison Society, 1905–1907* (n.p.: American Bison Society, 1908), 1–7.

347 **Two years later, fifteen captively bred:** William Temple Hornaday, "The Founding of the Wichita National Bison Herd," *[First] Annual Report of the American Bison Society, 1905–1907* (n.p.: American Bison Society, 1908), 55–69.

348 **In this case, the spark:** John H. Mitchell, "The Mothers of Conservation," *Sanctuary* (January/February 1996): 3.

349 **"Perfectly delicate in form":** John Ruskin, "The Story of the Halcyon," *The Eagle's Nest* (London: Smith, Elder, & Co., 1872), 170.

349 **In the midst of the economic depression:** "Better Than Gold Mining," *Orange County Observer*, December 24, 1896, 5.

349 **Middlemen shipped the precious plumes:** Robin W. Doughty, *Feather Fashions and Bird Preservation: A Study in Nature Protection* (Berkeley: University of California Press, 1975), 23–31.

349 **During the winter of 1895–96:** "The Latest Fashions Seen in the Boxes," *Philadelphia Inquirer*, January 19, 1896, 20. See also Ellen Osborn, "Ellen Osborn's Talk—Hats, Toques and Bonnets in the Latest Parisian Styles," *Times Union*, February 8, 1896, 12.

350 **"Gladly would I write":** Ellen Osborn, "Ellen Osborn's Letter—The Importance of the Frolic Feather in This Season's Fashionable Frippery," *Boston Post*, December 15, 1895, 20.

350 **Hemenway and Hall:** Mitchell, "The Mothers of Conservation," 4.

350 **A few weeks later:** Winthrop Packard, *The Story of the Audubon Society: Twenty-five Years of Active and Effective Work for the Preservation of Wild Birdlife* (Boston: Massachusetts Audubon Society, 1921), 2–5.

351 **The mania for egret plumes:** "Cruelty Encouraged by Fashion," *Boston Globe*, March 6, 1886, 3.

351 **"To the Editor":** "Facts About Feathers," *Boston Evening Transcript*, October 24, 1896, 17.

351 One year after its founding: Mitchell, "The Mothers of Conservation," 5.

351 In 1897, the club persuaded: "Table Gossip," *Boston Globe,* April 18, 1897, 21.

351 By the end of 1897: Packard, *The Story of the Audubon Society,* 3.

352 In a 1909 letter: Mitchell, "The Mothers of Conservation," 6.

352 *"If we could have our way":* "War," *Our Dumb Animals,* February 1896, 98.

353 "If we had the power": "Army and Navy Officers," *Our Dumb Animals,* January 1896, 86.

353 "We notice in the newspapers": "A Very Different Individual," *Our Dumb Animals,* February 1896, 98.

353 "perfect nonsense": "The Monroe Doctrine," *Our Dumb Animals,* January 1896, 86.

353 "Ranchman Roosevelt": "Ranchman Roosevelt," *Our Dumb Animals,* February 1896, 100; "Ranchman Roosevelt," *Our Dumb Animals,* March 1896, 115.

353 the *Chicago Tribune* called him: *Chicago Tribune,* January 14, 1896, 6.

353 The San Francisco *Examiner* described: *The Examiner* (San Francisco), March 5, 1896, 6.

353 *The Sacramento Bee* reported: "Shut Out Here," *The Evening Bee* (Sacramento), March 13, 1896, 4.

354 offering a bounty of $100: "Prizes $675," *Our Dumb Animals,* February 1896, 103.

354 "perfectly reliable authority": "Boston University Medical School," *Our Dumb Animals,* May 1896, 145.

354 One of the twenty-one entries: "American Humane Education Society's Prizes for Stories," *Our Dumb Animals,* July 1893, 18.

354 inspired by Sewell's novel: "How 'Beautiful Joe' Came to Be Written," *Our Dumb Animals,* March 1896, 113.

355 "I am an old dog now": Marshall Saunders, *Beautiful Joe* (Philadelphia: Charles H. Banes, 1894), 14.

355 By the end of 1896: *Our Dumb Animals,* January 1897, 88.

355 "We think a peaceful way out": "The Remedy for Present Hard Times," *Our Dumb Animals,* September 1896, 37–38.

355 "little states of some 50,000": "The United States Senate," *Our Dumb Animals,* September 1896, 38.

355 "A million men could": "Plenty of Work," *Our Dumb Animals,* September 1896, 38.

356 He pleaded for the restriction: "Vivisection at Our State House," *Our Dumb Animals,* April 1896, 131; "Our Battle at the State House," *Our Dumb Animals,* May 1896, 138.

356 "One thing we must never forget": *Our Dumb Animals,* January 1896, 89; *Our Dumb Animals,* February 1896, 103; *Our Dumb Animals,* March 1896, 115; etc.

Afterword: The Exploded Circle

359 "in the harness": "Death Takes Geo. T. Angell," *Boston Globe,* March 16, 1909, 1.

359 In his funeral procession: "Horses and Men in Last Tribute," *Boston Globe,* March 21, 1909, 24.

359 **"As a pleasure vehicle":** "The Future of the Horse," *American Veterinary Review,* August 1899, 319.

359 **the last horsecar was retired:** "New York Loses Its Last Horsecar," *New York Times,* July 27, 1917, 18.

360 **remains a controversial subject:** See Louise Carroll Wade, "The Problem with Classroom Use of Upton Sinclair's *The Jungle,*" *American Studies* 32, no. 2 (Fall 1991): 79–101.

360 **"I aimed at the public's heart":** Upton Sinclair, "What Life Means to Me," *Cosmopolitan Magazine,* October 31, 1906, 594.

360 **ten different "stocks":** Karen Rader, *Making Mice: Standardizing Animals for American Biomedical Research, 1900–1955* (Princeton, NJ: Princeton University Press, 2004); see also Daniel Engber, "The Trouble with Black-6," *Slate,* November 17, 2011.

361 **Today, well over 90 percent:** David Grimm, "How Many Mice and Rats Are Used in U.S. Labs? Controversial Study Says More Than 100 Million," *Science,* January 12, 2021.

361 **Edward Lowe:** Daniel A. Gross, "How Kitty Litter Went from Happy Accident to $2 Billion Industry," *Washington Post,* February 2, 2015.

362 **per capita consumption of pork:** "Per Capita Consumption of Poultry and Livestock, 1965 to Forecast 2022, in Pounds," National Chicken Council website.

362 **With pigs, this is generally done:** "An Inside Look at Pork Processing," Michigan State University website.

362 **Per capita beef consumption:** "Per Capita Consumption of Poultry and Livestock, 1965 to Forecast 2022, in Pounds."

362 **Dairy cows, which naturally live:** A. De Vries and M. I. Marcondes, "Review: Overview of Factors Affecting Productive Lifespan of Dairy Cows," *Animal* 14 (February 6, 2020).

363 **As of this writing, America is home:** "Cattle," released July 22, 2022, by the National Agricultural Statistics Service (NASS), United States Department of Agriculture; "Quarterly Hogs and Pigs," released September 29, 2022.

363 **those of dogs and cats:** "Pet Population Still on the Rise, with Fewer Pets per Household," *JAVMA News,* December 1, 2021.

363 **The psychologist Jonathan Haidt:** Jonathan Haidt, *The Righteous Mind: Why Good People Are Divided by Politics and Religion* (New York: Pantheon, 2012).

363 **thirty-point swing in just twelve years:** "Record-High 70% in U.S. Support Same-Sex Marriage," Gallup, June 8, 2021.

364 **"our Love and Mercy are not to be confined":** Humphry Primatt, *A Dissertation on the Duty of Mercy and Sin of Cruelty to Brute Animals* (London: R. Hett, 1776), iii.

364 **"the benevolent affections embrace":** William Edward Hartpole Lecky, *A History of European Morals from Augustus to Charlemagne,* vol. 1 (London: Longmans, Green, and Co., 1869), 103.

365 **"The only justifiable stopping place":** Peter Singer, *The Expanding Circle* (Princeton, NJ: Princeton University Press, 2011), 120.

365 **British psychologists recently taught:** "Pigs Can Play Video Games with Their Snouts, Scientists Find," *BBC News,* February 11, 2021.

367 **roughly one-seventh of all carbon emissions:** *Tackling Climate Change Through*

Livestock, Food and Agriculture Organization (FAO) of the United Nations, 2013.

367 **a recent University of Arizona study:** "One-Third of Plant and Animal Species Could Be Gone in 50 Years," *University of Arizona News,* February 12, 2020.

367 **A 2019 research effort found:** Kenneth V. Rosenberg et al., "Decline of the North American Avifauna," *Science,* September 19, 2019, 120–24.

367 **a 90 percent drop in U.S. butterflies:** "Monarch Butterflies Have Declined 90%; Conservationists Seek Extra Protection," *Newsweek,* August 27, 2014.

367 **an 87 percent decline in one formerly common:** "U.S. Fish and Wildlife Service Announces Final Plan to Recover the Endangered Rusty Patched Bumble Bee," U.S. Fish and Wildlife Service, August 27, 2021.

368 **whose book *Reason in a Dark Time:*** Dale Jamieson, *Reason in a Dark Time: Why the Struggle Against Climate Change Failed—and What It Means for Our Future* (New York: Oxford University Press, 2014).

368 **As the historian Peter Bernstein:** Peter L. Bernstein, *Against the Gods: The Remarkable Story of Risk* (New York: Wiley, 1998).

369 **A notable exception, which Jamieson:** Dale Jamieson, "Slavery, Carbon, and Moral Progress," *Ethical Theory and Moral Practice* 20, no. 1 (February 2017): 169–83.

370 **In January 1919, a San Francisco alderman:** "San Franciscans Will Again Don Influenza Masks Next Friday," *San Francisco Chronicle,* January 11, 1919, 1.

371 **exceeds what the poorest 20 percent:** U.S. Bureau of Labor Statistics, "Table 1101. Quintiles of Income Before Taxes: Annual Expenditure Means, Shares, Standard Errors, and Coefficients of Variation," Consumer Expenditure Surveys, 2021.

SELECTED BIBLIOGRAPHY

Angell, George Thorndike. *Autobiographical Sketches and Personal Reflections*. Boston: Franklin Press, 1884.

Audubon, John James. *John J. Audubon's Birds of America*. Online resource: audubon.org/birds-of-america.

Audubon, John James. *Ornithological Biography, or an Account of the Habits of the Birds of the United States of America*. Philadelphia: E. L. Carey and A. Hart, 1832.

Barbeau, Jeffrey W., ed. *Religion in Romantic England*. Waco, TX: Baylor University Press, 2018.

Barnum, P. T. *Struggles and Triumphs; or, Forty Years' Recollections of P. T. Barnum*. Buffalo: The Courier Company, 1875.

Barnum, P. T. *Struggles and Triumphs: Or, Sixty Years' Recollections of P. T. Barnum, Including His Golden Rules for Money-making*. Buffalo: The Courier Company, 1889.

Barrow, Mark V., Jr. *Nature's Ghosts: Confronting Extinction from the Age of Jefferson to the Age of Ecology*. Chicago: University of Chicago Press, 2009.

Barrow, Mark V., Jr. *A Passion for Birds: American Ornithology After Audubon*. Princeton, NJ: Princeton University Press, 1998.

Blaisdell, John D. "Louis Pasteur, Alexandre Liautard, and the Riverdale Dog Case." *Veterinary Heritage* 15 (March 1992).

Blaisdell, John D. "With Certain Reservations: The American Veterinary Community's Reception of Pasteur's Work on Rabies." *Agricultural History* 70 (Summer 1996): 2–15.

Brinkley, Catherine, and Dominic Vitiello. "From Farm to Nuisance: Animal Agriculture and the Rise of Planning Regulation." *Journal of Planning History* 13 (May 2014): 113–35.

Buel, Clarence C. "Henry Bergh and His Work." *Scribner's*, April 1879, 872–84.

Buffet, Edward P. "Bergh's War on Vested Cruelty" and "A General History of the Society." American Society for the Prevention of Cruelty to Animals Archive, North Carolina State University Libraries' Digital Collections: Rare and Unique Materials, https://d.lib.ncsu.edu/.

Campbell, Jane. "Mrs. Caroline Earle White, Reformer." *Records of the American Catholic Historical Society of Philadelphia* 33, no. 1 (March 1922).

Chandler, Alfred D., Jr. *The Visible Hand: The Managerial Revolution in American Business.* Cambridge, MA: Belknap, 1977.

Cronin, J. Keri. *Art for Animals: Visual Culture and Animal Advocacy, 1870–1914.* University Park: Pennsylvania State University Press, 2018.

Davenport, Cora Lillian. "The Rise of the Armours, an American Industrial Family." Master's thesis, University of Chicago, 1930.

Dehler, Gregory J. *The Most Defiant Devil: William Temple Hornaday and His Controversial Crusade to Save American Wildlife.* Charlottesville: University of Virginia Press, 2013.

Dickey, Bronwen. *Pit Bull: The Battle Over an American Icon.* New York: Alfred A. Knopf, 2016.

Dolph, James Andrew. "Bringing Wildlife to Millions: William Temple Hornaday, the Early Years, 1854–1896." PhD diss., University of Massachusetts, Amherst, 1975.

Doughty, Robin W. *Feather Fashions and Bird Preservation: A Study in Nature Protection.* Berkeley: University of California Press, 1975.

Freeberg, Ernest. *A Traitor to His Species: Henry Bergh and the Birth of the Animal Rights Movement.* New York: Basic Books, 2020.

Gavan, Peggy. The Hatching Cat blog, hatchingcatnyc.com.

Greene, Ann Norton. *Horses at Work: Harnessing Power in Industrial America.* Cambridge, MA: Harvard University Press, 2008.

Grier, Katherine C. *Pets in America: A History.* Orlando, FL: Harcourt, 2006.

Guerrini, Anita. *Experimenting with Humans and Animals.* Baltimore: Johns Hopkins University Press, 2003.

Hansen, Bert. "America's First Medical Breakthrough: How Popular Excitement About a French Rabies Cure in 1885 Raised New Expectations for Medical Progress." *American Historical Review* 103 (April 1998): 373–418.

Harding, Les. *Elephant Story: Jumbo and P.T. Barnum Under the Big Top.* Jefferson, NC: McFarland & Company, 2000.

Harris, Neil. *Humbug: The Art of P. T. Barnum.* Chicago: University of Chicago Press, 1973.

Huhndorf, Shari M., *Going Native: Indians in the American Cultural Imagination.* Ithaca, NY: Cornell University Press, 2001.

Jamieson, Dale. *Reason in a Dark Time: Why the Struggle Against Climate Change Failed—and What It Means for Our Future.* New York: Oxford University Press, 2014.

Jolly, W. P. *Jumbo.* London: Constable and Company, 1976.

"The Lost Museum." City University of New York online project, https://lostmuseum.cuny.edu/.

MacDonald, Douglas H. *Before Yellowstone.* Seattle: University of Washington Press, 2018.

McShane, Clay, and Joel A. Tarr. *The Horse in the City.* Baltimore: Johns Hopkins University Press, 2007.

Miltenberger, Scott. "Promiscuously Mixed Together: New Yorkers and Domestic Animals in the Nineteenth-Century Anthrozootic City." PhD diss., University of California, Davis, 2006.

Mitchell, John H. "The Mothers of Conservation." *Sanctuary* (January/February 1996): 1–20.

Mitchell-Vigneron, Jeanette. "Alexandre Liautard (1835–1918), Sa Vie—Son Oeuvre." PhD diss., Ecole Nationale Vétérinaire D'Alfort, 1982.

Nance, Susan. *Entertaining Elephants: Animal Agency and the Business of the American Circus.* Baltimore: Johns Hopkins University Press, 2013.

Pacyga, Dominic A. *Slaughterhouse: Chicago's Union Stock Yard and the World It Made.* Chicago: University of Chicago Press, 2015.

Pearson, Susan J. *The Rights of the Defenseless: Protecting Animals and Children in Gilded Age America.* Chicago: University of Chicago Press, 2020.

Preece, Rod. *Awe for the Tiger, Love for the Lamb: A Chronicle of Sensibility to Animals.* London: Routledge, 2003.

Robichaud, Andrew A. *Animal City: The Domestication of America.* Cambridge, MA: Harvard University Press, 2019.

Rupke, Nicolaas A., ed. *Vivisection in Historical Perspective.* New York: Routledge, 1987.

Saxon, A. H. P. T. *Barnum: The Legend and the Man.* New York: Columbia University Press, 1989.

Schorger, A. W. *The Passenger Pigeon: Its Natural History and Extinction.* Madison: University of Wisconsin Press, 1955.

Smithcors, J. F. *The American Veterinary Profession: Its Background and Development.* Ames: Iowa State University Press, 1963.

Speicher, Anna M. *The Religious World of Antislavery Women.* Syracuse, NY: Syracuse University Press, 2000.

Steele, Zulma. *Angel in Top Hat.* New York: Harper & Brothers, 1942.

Taliaferro, John. *Grinnell: America's Environmental Pioneer and His Restless Drive to Save the West.* New York: Liveright, 2019.

Tompkins, Jane. *Sensational Designs: The Cultural Work of American Fiction, 1790–1860.* New York: Oxford University Press, 1985.

Turner, James. *Reckoning with the Beast.* Baltimore: Johns Hopkins University Press, 1980.

Unti, Bernard. "The Quality of Mercy: Organized Animal Protection in the United States, 1866–1930." PhD diss., American University, 2002.

Wade, Louise Carroll. *Chicago's Pride: The Stockyards, Packingtown, and Environs in the Nineteenth Century.* Urbana: University of Illinois Press, 1987.

Walrath, James A. "American Veterinary College, Hospital Records—Cerebral Inoculation as a Means of Diagnosis in the Post Mortem of Rabid Animals." *American Veterinary Review* 10 (June 1886): 120–2.

Whitaker, W. *Feedlot Empire: Beef Cattle Feeding in Illinois and Iowa, 1840–1900.* Ames: Iowa State University Press, 1975.

Wilson, Robert. *Barnum: An American Life.* New York: Simon & Schuster, 2019.

Wing, Jack. *The Great Union Stock Yards of Chicago.* Chicago: Religio-Philosophical Publishing Association, 1865.

Wood, Amy Louise. "'Killing the Elephant': Murderous Beasts and the Thrill of Retribution, 1885–1930." *Journal of the Gilded Age and Progressive Era* 11 (July 2012).

INDEX

Page numbers in *italics* refer to illustrations.

ILLUSTRATION CREDITS

of New York," *Harper's Weekly,* January 14, 1888. Images from the History of Medicine collection, National Library of Medicine, NIH.

139 Wikimedia Commons

156 "Slaughtered for the Hide," *Harper's Weekly,* December 12, 1874, 1

164 National Portrait Gallery

169 *Autobiographical Notes and a Bibliography of the Scientific Publications of Joel Asaph Allen* (New York: American Museum of Natural History, 1916)

174 Caricature of Henry Bergh from *Puck.* Wallach Division Picture Collection, The New York Public Library

190 "The Alarm-Bell of Atri," *Our Dumb Animals,* April 1885, 196

196 MSPCA Archive

208 Hatch Lithographic Company, *Barnum & London: Jumbo the Children's Giant Pet,* 1882. Ink on paper, 49⅛ × 31⅝ in. (124.8 × 80.3 cm.), ht2004500. Collection of the John and Mable Ringling Museum of Art Tibbals Circus Collection

217 Tufts University Digital Collections and Archives

232 "A Summer Scene in New York City—a Persecuted Dog on a Leading Avenue," *Frank Leslie's Illustrated Newspaper,* June 27, 1874, 1

245 Images from the History of Medicine collection, National Library of Medicine, NIH

249 Wikimedia Commons

258 Women in bird hats, collection of the authors

267 Library of Congress

269 Smith College Special Collections

280 American Humane Education Society edition of *Black Beauty,* circa 1890. MSPCA Archive

296 Image from stereocard by B. L. Singley, "Hanging Room, Armour's Packing House," 1896. Library of Congress

301 National Portrait Gallery

302 *System: The Magazine of Business,* September 1907, 220

307 Chicago History Museum

316 William W. Keen's clinic, Jefferson Medical College. Library of Congress

320 American Anti-Vivisection Society

329 Images from the History of Medicine collection, National Library of Medicine, NIH

338 Headstone at Hartsdale Pet Cemetery, photograph by the authors

350 Mass Audubon

354 MSPCA Archive

358 Illustration by Walter Crane, from *Rumbo Rhymes, or, The Great Combine: A Satire* (London: Harper Brothers, 1911), 19

A NOTE ABOUT THE AUTHORS

BILL WASIK is the editorial director of *The New York Times Magazine*. MONICA MURPHY is a veterinarian and writer. Their previous book, *Rabid: A Cultural History of the World's Most Diabolical Virus*, was a *Los Angeles Times* bestseller and a finalist for the PEN/E.O. Wilson Literary Science Writing Award. They live in Brooklyn with a teenager and a poodle-ish dog.

A NOTE ON THE TYPE

The text of this book was set in Sabon, a typeface designed by Jan Tschichold (1902–1974), the well-known German typographer. Designed in 1966 and based on the original designs by Claude Garamond (ca. 1480–1561), Sabon was named for the punch cutter Jacques Sabon, who brought Garamond's matrices to Frankfurt.

Composed by North Market Street Graphics
Lancaster, Pennsylvania

Printed and bound by Berryville Graphics
Berryville, Virginia

Designed by Michael Collica